Asian Geopolitics and the US-China Rivalry

This book analyses the ways in which foreign policy actors in Asia have responded to the emerging great power conflict between the US and the People's Republic of China focusing on medium and small states across the Indo-Pacific.

This book offers a much-needed counterpoint to existing analyses on the Indo-Pacific and China's Belt and Road Initiative (BRI) and presents a new perspective by examining how great power politics are locally reinterpreted, conditioned or, at times, even contested. It illustrates the policy-level challenges which the US-China rivalry poses for established political and economic practices and outlines how these challenges can be best addressed by smaller states and their societies.

A timely assessment of the power play in the Indo-Pacific with the angle of Sino-American rivalry, this book makes an important contribution to the study of Political Science, International Relations, Asian Studies and Security Studies.

Felix Heiduk is Senior Associate at the German Institute for International and Security Affairs, Germany.

Routledge Studies on Think Asia
Edited by Jagannath P. Panda, Institute for Defence Studies and Analyses, India

This series addresses the current strategic complexities of Asia and forecasts how these current complexities will shape Asia's future. Bringing together empirical and conceptual analysis, the series examines critical aspects of Asian politics, with a particular focus on the current security and strategic complexities. The series includes academic studies from universities, research institutes and think-tanks and policy-oriented studies. Focusing on security and strategic analysis on Asia's current and future trajectory, this series welcomes submissions on relationship patterns (bilateral, trilateral and multilateral) in Indo-Pacific, regional and sub-regional institutions and mechanisms, corridors and connectivity, maritime security, infrastructure politics, trade and economic models and critical frontiers (boundaries, borders, bordering provinces) that are crucial to Asia's future.

6. Identity, Culture, and Chinese Foreign Policy
THAAD and China's South Korea Policy
Kangkyu Lee

7. Japan's Evolving Security Policy
Militarisation within a Pacifist Tradition
Kyoko Hatakeyama

8. India and the Arab Unrest
Challenges, Dilemmas and Engagements
Prashanta Kumar Pradhan

9. The Future of the Korean Peninsula
Korea 2032 and Beyond
Edited by Mason Richey, Jagannath P. Panda and David A. Tizzard

10. Mongolia and Northeast Asian Security
Nuclear Proliferation, Environment, and Civilisational Confrontations
Edited by Alicia J. Campi and Jagannath P. Panda

11. Asian Geopolitics and the US-China Rivalry
Edited by Felix Heiduk

Asian Geopolitics and the US-China Rivalry

Edited by Felix Heiduk

LONDON AND NEW YORK

First published 2022
by Routledge
2 Park Square, Milton Park, Abingdon, Oxon OX14 4RN

and by Routledge
605 Third Avenue, New York, NY 10158

Routledge is an imprint of the Taylor & Francis Group, an informa business

© 2022 selection and editorial matter, Felix Heiduk; individual chapters, the contributors

The right of Felix Heiduk to be identified as the author of the editorial material, and of the authors for their individual chapters, has been asserted in accordance with sections 77 and 78 of the Copyright, Designs and Patents Act 1988.

With the exception of Chapter 10, no part of this book may be reprinted or reproduced or utilised in any form or by any electronic, mechanical, or other means, now known or hereafter invented, including photocopying and recording, or in any information storage or retrieval system, without permission in writing from the publishers.

Chapter 10 of this book is available for free in PDF format as Open Access from the individual product page at www.routledge.com. It has been made available under a Creative Commons Attribution-Non Commercial-No Derivatives 4.0 license.

Trademark notice: Product or corporate names may be trademarks or registered trademarks, and are used only for identification and explanation without intent to infringe.

British Library Cataloguing-in-Publication Data
A catalogue record for this book is available from the British Library

Library of Congress Cataloging-in-Publication Data
A catalog record has been requested for this book

ISBN: 978-0-367-60816-3 (hbk)
ISBN: 978-0-367-61846-9 (pbk)
ISBN: 978-1-003-10681-4 (ebk)

DOI: 10.4324/9781003106814

Typeset in Times New Roman
by Apex CoVantage, LLC

Contents

List of illustrations vii
Acknowledgements viii
Notes on contributors ix
List of abbreviations xii

1 **Dancing with elephants: Asia and the Sino-American rivalry** 1
   FELIX HEIDUK

2 **From globalisation to fragmentation? The erosion of confidence in the Asia-Pacific** 17
   ROSEMARY FOOT

3 **Many players, many layers: the Indo-Pacific long game** 32
   RORY MEDCALF

4 **"Making Multilateralism Matter": middle powers in the era of the US-China competition** 47
   JOO HEE KIM

5 **Security order and state transformation in Asia: beyond geopolitics and grand strategy** 65
   LEE JONES

6 **Reflecting on US-China rivalries in post-conflict Sri Lanka** 81
   GANESHAN WIGNARAJA

7 **India, Indo-Pacific coalitions and China: from alignment to alliance?** 103
   JAGANNATH P. PANDA

Contents

8 Major power competition and Southeast Asia: institutional
   strategies and resources   127
   ALICE D. BA

9 From appeasement to soft balancing: the Duterte
   administration's shifting policy on the South China
   Sea *imbroglio*   142
   RENATO CRUZ DE CASTRO

10 Beyond strategic hedging: Mahathir's China policy and the
   changing political economy of Malaysia, 2018–2020   159
   HONG LIU

11 Midfield or margin? Myanmar and neighbours in the game   177
   THI THI SOE SAN

12 The role of domestic political constraints in navigating great
   power relations: the case of South Korea   193
   SEO-HYUN PARK

   Index   211

Illustrations

Tables

6.1	Indicators of US and China Ties with Sri Lanka (US$ Millions)	86
7.1	Quad's Official Consultations (2017–2019)	106
11.1	Burma Communist Party	181
11.2	Attitudes towards the Belt and Road Initiative among Domestic Stakeholders	183
11.3	Three Sectors or Regions with Projects in Competition with One Another	187

Map

6.1	Sri Lanka at a Glance	84

Acknowledgements

I would like thank all participants of the 13th Berlin Conference on Asian Security (BCAS) that took place in November 2019. Taking place annually in Berlin at the German Institute for International and Security Affairs (*Stiftung Wissenschaft und Politik*, SWP), the BCAS aims to facilitate an exchange of information and views among European, American and Asian scholars and officials on regional security issues in Asia. This book is based on the excellent presentations as well as discussions during the conference, as well as the numerous intellectual exchanges between conference participants that followed suit.

I am extremely thankful to the staff of the German Institute for International and Security Affairs for working tirelessly behind the scenes to ensure a successful conference and to help prepare the papers which were eventually submitted for publication.

Last but not least, I would like to take this opportunity to sincerely thank all contributors for their hard work, diligence and patience during the editorial process. Especially as most of the work took place during the COVID-19 pandemic.

Felix Heiduk

Berlin, December 2020

Notes on contributors

Alice D. Ba is Professor of Political Science & International Relations at the University of Delaware. Her research interests include Southeast Asia's relations with China and the US, ASEAN; comparative regionalisms and the politics of cooperative regime building and institutional change. A recipient of US Fulbright awards for work in Beijing and Singapore, she has also published on multilateralism and system change, the role of strategic narratives in China-Southeast Asia relations and institutional legitimacy.

Renato Cruz De Castro is Professor in the International Studies Department, De La Salle University, Manila. He is the Chair-holder of the Dr. Aurelio Calderon Chair in Philippine-American Relations. As a member of the Board of Trustees of the Albert Del Rosario Institute of Strategic and International Studies (ADRI), he contributes his two monthly opinion columns to the Business World and Philippine Star. He has written over 100 articles on international relations and security that have been published in a number of scholarly journals, monographs and edited works in the several countries.

Rosemary Foot (Professor Emeritus) is currently Senior Research Fellow at the University of Oxford's Department of Politics and International Relations, a Research Associate at the Oxford China Centre and an Emeritus Fellow of St Antony's College, Oxford. She is also an elected Fellow of the British Academy. Her research interests and publications mainly focus on security issues in the Asia-Pacific, human rights, China and world order, and China-US relations. In 2020, she published *China, the UN, and Human Protection: Beliefs, Power, Image*.

Felix Heiduk is Senior Associate in the Asia Research Division at the *Stiftung Wissenschaft und Politik* (German Institute for Foreign and Security Affairs) in Berlin. His main research focus is on international politics and security affairs in Southeast Asia, specifically on interstate and civil conflicts, arms dynamics, civil-military relations and regional integration processes. Dr. Heiduk received his PhD in Political Science from Free University Berlin. He has published books, book chapters, policy papers as well as articles in peer-reviewed journals such as *The Pacific Review*, *Third World Quarterly*, *Cooperation and Conflict*, *East Asia* or *The Journal of European Integration*.

Notes on contributors

Lee Jones is Reader in International Politics at Queen Mary University of London. His research focuses on political economy, security, governance and state transformation, particularly with respect to Southeast Asia and China. His most recent book, with Shahar Hameiri, is *Fractured China: How State Transformation is Shaping China's Rise* (Cambridge University Press, 2021). His website is www.leejones.tk.

Joo Hee Kim, Assistant Professor of Political Science and International Relations at Pukyong National University in Busan and a Centre Director of the Centre for Global Multilevel Governance, focuses on international/regional cooperation and multilateralism. Her publications include *A Critical Analysis of Multilateral Aid of Middle Power States* (2017) and *How Ideas of European Integration Matter?: Explaining the Different Approaches of South Korea and Japan Toward East Asian Regionalism During 1998–2007* (2014).

Hong Liu is Tan Lark Sye Chair Professor of Public Policy and Global Affairs at the School of Social Sciences, Nanyang Technological University (NTU), Singapore.

Professor Rory Medcalf is Head of the National Security College at the Australian National University. His has three decades of experience across diplomacy, intelligence analysis, think-tanks, academia and journalism. He has been recognised as a thought leader internationally for his work on the Indo-Pacific strategic concept, as articulated in his acclaimed 2020 book *Indo-Pacific Empire*. He is an informal adviser to the Australian Government and a regular voice in international media.

Dr. Jagannath P. Panda is Research Fellow and Centre Coordinator for East Asia at the Manohar Parrikar Institute for Defence Studies and Analyses (MP-IDSA), New Delhi, India. He is the Series Editor for *Routledge Studies on Think Asia*. Dr. Panda is the author of *India-China Relations: Politics of Resources, Identity and Authority in a Multipolar World Order* (Routledge: 2017). He is also the author of *China's Path to Power: Party, Military and the Politics of State Transition* (Pentagon Press: 2010). Dr. Panda has also edited a number of books to his credit. Most recently, he has published an edited volume *Scaling India-Japan Cooperation in Indo-Pacific and Beyond 2025: Connectivity, Corridors and Contours* (KW Publishing Ltd. 2019) and *The Korean Peninsula and Indo-Pacific Power Politics: Status Security at Stake* (Routledge, 2020).

Seo-Hyun Park is Associate Professor in the Department of Government and Law at Lafayette College. Her primary areas of research are international relations and East Asian security, focusing on issues of national identity politics, state sovereignty and state-building, alliance politics, regionalism and historical influences on contemporary international relations. She is the author of *Sovereignty and Status in East Asian International Relations* (Cambridge University Press, 2017) and several articles in peer-reviewed journals, such as the *Review of International Studies*, *International Relations*, *Journal of East Asian*

Studies and *Chinese Journal of International Politics*. Her current research project is on the diffusion of different forms of political violence and military competition in late nineteenth-century East Asian international relations.

Dr. Thi Thi Soe San is Associate Professor at the Department of International Relations, University of Mandalay, Myanmar. She received a bachelor's degree from the University of Mandalay in 1995 and in 1998 she was appointed a tutor at the Department of International Relations. In 2000, she submitted her master's thesis on *The Role of Bureaucracy in Myanmar Politics (1923–1961)* and received a Master of Research degree in 2001 for her thesis on *Bribery and Corruption in Bureaucracy (1923–1961)*. Her PhD, accomplished in 2007, analysed *Civil Service Reforms in Myanmar (1923–1987)*. Her area of specialisation is Public Administration and Geopolitics.

Ganeshan Wignaraja is Senior Research Associate at the Overseas Development Institute in London and Non-Resident Senior Fellow at the Institute of South Asian Studies at the National University of Singapore. Previously, he was the Executive Director of the Lakshman Kadirgamar Institute of International Relations and Strategies Studies in Colombo and the Director of Research at the Asian Development Bank Institute in Tokyo. He holds a DPhil in Economics from Oxford University and has authored or edited 20 books including *Connecting Asia* and *Asia's Free Trade Agreements*.

Abbreviations

ACSA	Acquisition and Cross Servicing Agreement
ADMM+	ASEAN Defence Ministers Meeting Plus
AI	Artificial Intelligence
AIIB	Asian Investment and Infrastructure Bank
AFP	Armed Forces of the Philippines
AJI	Australia-Japan-India Trilateral Meeting
APEC	Asia-Pacific Economic Cooperation
APT	ASEAN Plus Three
ARF	ASEAN Regional Forum
ASEAN	Association of Southeast Asian Nations
BBC	British Broadcasting Corporation
BDN	Blue Dot Network
BRI	Belt and Road Initiative
CARAT	Cooperation Afloat Readiness and Training Exercise
CCCC	China Communications Construction Company
CCP	Chinese Communist Party
CDC	Centers for Disease Control and Prevention
CECA	Australia-India Comprehensive Economic Cooperation Agreement
CHEC	China Harbour Engineering Company
CICA	Conference on Interaction and Confidence-Building Measures in Asia
CMEC	China Myanmar Economic Corridor
CMP	China Merchant Ports
COC	Code of Conduct
COMCASA	Communications Compatibility and Security Agreement
CPTPP	Comprehensive and Progressive Agreement for Trans-Pacific Partnership
CSP	Comprehensive Strategic Partnership
DFA	Department of Foreign Affairs
DOC	Declaration on a Code of Conduct
DPRK	Democratic People's Republic of Korea
EAM	External Affairs Minister

EAS	East Asia Summit
ECRL	East Coast Rail Link
ECS	East China Sea
EDCA	Enhanced Defence Cooperation Agreement
EEZ	Exclusive Economic Zone
EU	European Union
FAO	Food and Agriculture Organization
FATF	Financial Action Task Force
FDI	Foreign direct investment
FOIP	Free and Open Indo-Pacific
FONOP	Freedom of Navigation Operation
FTA	Free Trade Agreement
G-7	Group of 7
G-20	Group of Twenty
GDP	Gross Domestic Product
GNP	Grand National Party
GSOMIA	General Security of Military Information Agreement
GSP+	Generalised System of Preferences Plus
HADR	humanitarian Assistance and Disaster Relief
IMF	International Monetary Fund
IMO-ISPFS	International Maritime Organisation's International Ship and Port Facility Security Code Programme
IMSC	International Maritime Security Construct
IOR	Indian Ocean Region
IPOI	Indo-Pacific Oceans Initiative
IPSP	International Port Security Program
IR	International Relations
ISIS	Islamic State of Iraq and Syria
JCPOA	Joint Comprehensive Plan of Action
JSDF	Japan Self-Defence Forces
LAC	Line of Actual Control
LEMOA	Logistics Exchange Memorandum of Agreement
LM-LESC	Lancang-Mekong Integrated Law Enforcement and Security Cooperation Centre
LSA	Logistics Support Agreement
JAEPA	Japan-Australia Economic Partnership Agreement
JAI	Japan-America-India Trilateral Meeting
MBDS	Mekong Basin Disease Surveillance
MCA	Malaysian Chinese Association
MCBC	Malaysia-China Business Council
MCC	Millennium Challenge Corporation
MDP	Major Defence Partner
MDT	Mutual Defence Treaty
MFA	Multi-Fibre Arrangement

MNC	Multinational Corporation
MPS	Ministry of Public Security
MOFCOM	Ministry of Commerce
MOU	Memorandum of Understanding
MRRV	Multi-Role Response Vessels
MSA	Maritime Safety Administration
MSRI	Maritime Silk Road Initiative
NAM	Non-Aligned Movement
NATO	North Atlantic Treaty Organization
NEP	New Economic Policy
NLD	National League for Democracy
NSS	National Security Strategy
NTS	Non-traditional Security
ODA	Official Development Assistance
OSP	Opioid Substitution Programme
PAF	Philippine Air Force
PAS	Malaysian Islamic Party
PCG	Philippine Coast Guard
PESCO	Permanent Structured Cooperation
PLAN	People's Liberation Army Navy
PLANMC	People's Liberation Army Navy Marine Corps
PN	Philippine Navy
PPP	Purchasing Power Parity
PRC	People's Republic of China
PSI	Proliferation Security Initiative
Quad	U.S.-Australia-India-Japan Quadrilateral Security Dialogue
RCEP	Regional Comprehensive Economic Partnership
RIMPAC	Rim of the Pacific Exercise
ROK	Republic of Korea
SARS	Severe Acute Respiratory Syndrome
SCS	South China Sea
SLOC	Sea Lanes of Communication
SMA	Special Measures Agreement
SME	Small and Medium Enterprises
SOE	State-owned Enterprise
SOFA	Status of Forces Agreement
SREB	Silk Road Economic Belt
TCOG	Trilateral Coordination and Oversight Group
TEU	Twenty-foot Equivalent Units
THAAD	Theater High Altitude Area Defense
TIFA	Trade and Investment Framework Agreement
TPP	Trans-Pacific Partnership
UMNO	United Malays National Organisation
UN	United Nations

UNCLOS	United Nations Convention on the Law of the Sea
U.S.	United States of America
USAID	United States Agency for International Development
WHO	World Health Organization
ZOPFAN	Zone of Peace, Freedom and Neutrality

1 Dancing with elephants

Asia and the Sino-American rivalry

Felix Heiduk

'When elephants dance, the grass gets beaten' is a proverb often used to highlight the challenges great power competitions or conflicts pose for other states. With regard to Asia, the current rivalry between Washington and Beijing seems to make the proverb's core message ring ever so loud and clear. Observers have referred to an 'anti-China mood' in Washington across partisan divides,[1] based on the widespread assumption that Beijing essentially poses a threat to U.S. interests across the board. Accordingly, the 2018 U.S. National Defence Strategy called for a new focus on 'great power competition' with China.[2] The long-held belief that continuous U.S. engagement with China would bring about domestic liberalization in China, as well as turn Beijing into a responsible, peaceful stakeholder of the U.S.-led world order, currently appears to be widely rejected. Instead, China is now perceived as openly challenging U.S. dominance in Asia through, amongst other factors, its trade policies, its assertive foreign policy in the South China Sea, its pursuit of cutting-edge technology (often at the expense of others), its illiberal, state-run market economy, its military modernization programmes and its growing authoritarianism. China is referred to in the December 2017 National Security Strategy (NSS) as a 'revisionist power' whose objective is not merely to alter the status quo in Asia and beyond in its favour but to 'shape a world antithetical to U.S. values and interests'[3]. This in turn is widely understood to necessitate not acquiescence but a bold response from the U.S. and its allies.[4] Hence, many in the U.S. appear to subscribe to the view that the Sino-U.S. relationship has fundamentally changed in recent years from engagement to open conflict.[5]

For its part, China has shied away from such strong language in official documents, but state-controlled media outlets and officials have nonetheless also often struck a more assertive tone. Under the presidency of Xi Jinping, China has been openly aspired to challenge the U.S. military presence in Asia. It has made aggressive moves towards Taiwan and towards U.S. warships in the South China Sea. Anti-U.S.-rhetoric has also prevailed when it comes to what are perceived as sensitive issues surrounding Sino-U.S. relations, such as the country's territorial integrity (i.e. with regard to Taiwan),[6] as well as U.S. interference in China's domestic affairs, for example, with regard to the plight of the Uighurs,[7] or its crisis-management with regard to the coronavirus outbreak.[8] President Xi

DOI: 10.4324/9781003106814-1

Jinping has repeatedly blamed 'foreign hostile forces' to aim for the destruction of the entire political and ideological system that he helms. With regard to foreign policy, Xi Jinping has made it clear that he intends to reinstate China to what he perceives to be the country's rightful place as a global power and a hegemon in Asia.[9] Additionally, Foreign Minister Wang Yi, for example, has argued for a

> need to work together for the reform and improvement of the international order and system to make it more fair and equitable, and better serve the aspirations of the international community, especially the large group of developing countries which have grown stronger since the second World War.[10]

Chinese academics, too, have argued that the country is now 'ready and determined to reshape the existing order'.[11]

China's rise and U.S. decline?

All of this has sparked a lively debate on the future of the Sino-American relationship, which often tends to juxtapose 'America's decline' and 'China's rise'. Some scholars have argued that fears over China's dominance are largely unwarranted as its technological and military capabilities are still significantly lower relative to those of the U.S.[12] Others have used parameters such as China's growing economic prowess relative to the U.S., as well as domestic instabilities in the U.S.,[13] as indicators of China's certain ascent to regional hegemony in the Asia-Pacific region.[14] Notwithstanding the competing arguments over the possible outcome of the Sino-American rivalry, worries about the impact of the U.S.-China rivalry on Asia as a region are widespread amongst policy makers and academics alike. At the 2019 Shangri-La Dialogue, one of the key annual defence and security meetings in the region, senior officials from across Asia expressed their worries about the negative implications a spiralling Sino-American rivalry would have for regional security and stability. As part of his opening speech, Singapore's Prime Minister described the 'U.S.-China bilateral relationship' as the 'most important in the world today' and went further to argue 'how the two work out their tensions and frictions will define the international environment for decades to come'. He also reminded the audience of the devastating impact the Soviet-U.S. rivalry, which he referred to as Asia's 'great game', had on the region during the Cold War.[15] Similarly, Defence Minister Lorenza Delfin from the Philippines spoke of a 'seismic geopolitical shift that is changing the very fabric of international relations in the twenty-first century',[16] while his Malaysian counterpart argued that 'the uncertain relationship between the US and China will remain as an implicit factor in shaping the stability of the Asia-Pacific region'.[17] Scholars like David Shambaugh have also described the Sino-American rivalry as major challenges for the region: 'Under these conditions, managing the competition to ensure peaceful coexistence rather than adversarial polarization of the region – or possibly war – will be the principal challenge for both powers and all states in the region in the years to come'.[18]

From the BRI to the FOIP

The U.S.-China rivalry is most visible not simply in assertive speeches or the current trade war, but in sharply different visions for the broader region. Competing ideas of order for the region have emerged in recent years, with the potential to spark multiple conflicts. For almost 70 years, the system of order in the Asia-Pacific region, often referred to as 'Pax Americana' and dominated by the U.S., had not been called into question. This has changed in the second decade of the 21st century. In the context of China's rise to become the world's largest economy, which has also changed the regional balance of power in political and military terms, Beijing developed its own ideas and concepts of regional order and subsequently launched its own initiatives. China's Belt and Road Initiative (BRI), consisting of the Maritime Silk Road Initiative (MSRI) and the Silk Road Economic Belt (SREB), has become the focus of much debate lately. It is hereby widely assumed that BRI will transform not only China itself, but also its immediate neighbourhood in Central and East Asia, its relations with the U.S., Europe, Japan and other powers, and even global politics and the entire international order. The assumption that BRI will have transformative effects rests on the observation that China will soon become the dominant global economy coupled with the fact that 'it will, most remarkably of all, have done this under one party enjoying a monopoly on power and practicing hybrid Chinese socialism'.[19] More so, BRI was launched at a time when Chinese foreign policy was seen as becoming more and more assertive, while its domestic politics have become increasingly authoritarian. In the years following his ascent to power, Xi Jinping has cemented his own power grip on the Chinese Communist Party (CCP), the military and the state apparatus, has repeatedly cracked down on opponents within the party and outside it, as well as successfully abolishing term limits on the presidency, which could enable him to rule indefinitely. With regard to foreign policy, Xi Jinping has made it clear that he aims to restore China to what he considers its rightful place as a global power and a hegemon in Asia. He has pressed China's claims over the South China Sea and East China Sea, fostered closer military ties with numerous Asian countries, tightened bilateral ties with dozens of countries worldwide, forged new multilateral institutions (i.e. Asian Investment and Infrastructure Bank or AIIB, Silk Road Fund, New Development Bank) and forums, as well as introducing new concepts such as his 'new type of international relations'. Also, China increasingly promotes its own developmental path as a model for other nations. China's newfound foreign policy assertiveness, its growing impact on global economic development and its proclaimed return to global power status are often regarded as outright challenging U.S. power and dominance regionally and internationally. To some observers, the national restoration of China is even 'no longer a blueprint for a single nation'; instead 'Beijing appears to have committed itself to remaking the whole world'.[20]

While observers seem to agree on the BRI's general transformative effects in China and outside China, diverging interpretations of the project's objectives, drivers and possible outcomes have emerged. The main controversy in the (still rather young) scholarly debate on the BRI concerns the initiatives' drivers: is BRI driven by geopolitical or geo-economic motives? Or, does BRI even merge geopolitical and geo-economic motives into something akin to a grand strategy to transform the existing (Western, liberal) international order? In addition, a second, albeit interlinked scholarly debate, touches on challenges and pitfalls of BRI, especially regarding its implementation but also in terms of concept. This is not all that surprising given the general impression that for all its often flamboyant rhetoric and symbolism BRI has been a slow starter. Multiple BRI projects have been announced with big fanfare, yet little actual implementation. Various Western analysts have argued that BRI may never come fully to fruition due to numerous obstacles and challenges, including a lack of conceptual clarity, high-risk investments with strong associated uncertainties, implementation problems due to the sheer size if the associated initiatives, political instability in partner countries (i.e. local insurgencies) and a lack of concern for local communities or corruption amongst other factors.[21]

These issues notwithstanding, there is little doubt that China's BRI, first and foremost through the construction of interrelated infrastructure projects including ports, highways, railways and pipelines, is having a transformative effect on the region. Hard infrastructure projects in turn have necessitated the complementary creation of soft infrastructure, such as free trade and investment agreements, the internationalization of Chinese domestic technical standards along the routes, and other accords. At the same time, new regional institutions (i.e. the Silk Road Fund) and new forums (i.e. the Belt and Road Forum) were launched by Beijing. Hence, the BRI has often been perceived as a major challenge to U.S. hegemony in the region.

In response to this, in recent years, a number of states have developed alternative concepts under the label 'Indo-Pacific'. First and foremost, the U.S. under then President Donald Trump has attempted to respond directly to the perceived Chinese challenge by presenting a strategic concept called the 'Free and Open Indo-Pacific' (FOIP) as a counter-narrative to a potential Sino-centric reorganization or restructuring of the region. The FOIP is widely regarded in Washington as a means to rebalance U.S. foreign, security and economic policy towards China. Its main objectives include providing alternatives to China's BRI for Asian countries, securing freedom of navigation throughout the Indian and Pacific Oceans, the maintenance of the (U.S.-dominated) rules-based international order, and free, fair, reciprocal trade between the U.S. and the countries of the region through bilateral trade agreements. In addition, the FOIP-relevant documents emphasize the importance of investments, especially in the area of infrastructure, for the region and strive for a stronger role for the U.S. in the area of infrastructure investment. The U.S. thereby wants to offer an alternative to 'state controlled', i.e. Chinese, investments, which Washington regards has criticized for creating 'debt traps' and overtly benefitting Chinese companies and workers. And past years' revival of the defunct U.S.-Australia-India-Japan quadrilateral security dialogue with Washington (the so-called Quad) at the helm was widely regarded as an indirect rebuke of Beijing's geopolitical ambitions. The FOIP was also seen as instrumental for the U.S. to maintain its relevance as a resident power in Asia. Thus, there is little doubt that the FOIP's main thrust is directed against what the U.S. government perceives as China's increasingly 'aggressive' behaviour and its attempts to 'undermine' the rules-based international order.[22] In addition to the FOIP, Japan, Australia, India and the Association of Southeast Asian Nations (ASEAN) have also presented their own concepts of the Indo-Pacific. France, Germany and the Netherlands are currently the only member-states of the European Union (EU) that have adopted the term and drawn up corresponding strategy papers or guidelines.

As with the BRI, a young scholarly debate on the Indo-Pacific has emerged.[23] And while the majority of contributors seem to interpret it as a response to China's rise and the BRI, observers have pointed out that the Indo-Pacific currently lacks conceptual clarity, too. For the time being, no uniform, homogenous conceptualization of the Indo-Pacific has emerged to date. Rather, the term is used by the U.S., Japan, Australia, India or the ASEAN to refer to very different, in part divergent concepts, which in turn are based on different ideas on regional order. The divergences involve, amongst other things, a) the extension of the Indo-Pacific as a geographical area, b) the objectives associated with each respective concept, c) the focus or weighting of different policy fields within each respective concept, d) the question of China's inclusion or exclusion and e) the significance of bi-, mini- and multilateral approaches to trade and security policy. And while the U.S., in particular, is using the FOIP to openly position itself against China across policy fields, states such as Japan, ASEAN or Germany are not seeking a comprehensive 'decoupling' from China, especially not economically.[24]

The various conceptions or understandings are also reflected in the corresponding priorities and initiatives. While one of Japan's priorities is the conclusion of multilateral free trade agreements, for example, India views such efforts rather ambivalently and withdrew from the RCEP negotiations at the end of 2019. The Trump administration is also opposed to multilateral free trade agreements but is seeking to conclude bilateral agreements. Differences also exist in the weighting of individual policy areas. The strong focus on security and defence policy in Washington is particularly striking here, whereas Japan, Australia and India have so far attached greater importance to areas such as infrastructure development and connectivity. This weighting is also reflected in the approaches chosen: all actors, except ASEAN (which is concerned with maintaining its own centrality), have so far refrained from pursuing multilateral approaches to security policy, though all actors rhetorically stress the importance of existing regional forums such as ARF and EAS. In terms of infrastructure policy, the approaches chosen are mostly bilateral or minilateral. In economic policy, on the other hand, all actors, with the exception of the U.S. and India, prefer predominantly multilateral approaches. In China, however, the Indo-Pacific is viewed, regardless of the different conceptualizations outlined earlier, as part and parcel of an anti-Chinese containment strategy led by Washington.[25]

A binary choice?

Against this background U.S. policy makers have been arguing that the intensifying Sino-American rivalry leaves Asian states little choice but to choose sides. Accordingly, Asian states, and by extension all other states around the globe, now face a stark choice: between a U.S.-centric and a Sino-centric order. Some scholars have concurred with this assessment.[26] The depiction of such choice as one of mutually exclusive types of orders, 'between free and repressive world order visions'[27] as the U.S. Department of Defence put it, seems to create little else but a binary choice for all others. A binary choice between a U.S.-centric order, which 'promotes long-term peace and prosperity' and 'will not accept policies or actions that threaten or undermine the rules-based international order', on the one hand. And a Sino-centric order on the other, in which China is able to 'reorder the region to its advantage by leveraging military modernization, influence operations, and use predatory economics to coerce other nations'.[28]

Based on a quick glance at opinion surveys, one might infer, however, that to many an international audience such binary choice might appear like one between the devil and the deep blue sea. Take, for example, the global country poll commissioned by the BBC in 2017. It asked respondents to rate different countries, including, but not limited to, the U.S. and China and their influence in the world. One key finding alluded to a massive deterioration of the U.S. image amongst respondents, with China's image also suffering a deterioration albeit less strong. The survey also showed the gap between self-image and external image with regard to the U.S. and China. While 71 per cent of respondents from the U.S. believed their country to play a positive role in world politics, only 34 per cent of respondents from other countries believed the same. Similarly, 84 per cent of Chinese respondents also believed their country to exert a positive influence in global affairs, while only 41 per cent of respondents from other countries surveyed believed so.[29]

A recent Pew Research Center survey ran similar issues and questions past respondents. While in a majority of the 33 countries, a majority of them in Europe and Asia overall had a more favourable view of the U.S. than China, respondents lacked confidence in the respective leaders of the two nations. A majority of respondents actually held negative views of both, Donald Trump and Xi Jinping with regard to their respective conduct in global affairs.[30] Interestingly enough, the available surveys do not provide data on how respondents assess other nations' foreign policy role or conduct.

Alignment, bandwagoning, hedging or staying neutral

Mainstream International Relations (IR) scholarship, too, has perpetually and predominantly been focused on the foreign policies of great powers. This predisposition stems from the assumption that great powers, because of their size and their capabilities (militarily, diplomatically and economically), have historically exerted structural power by shaping the international system and the international order. They have subsequently been regarded to be at the helm of international politics. It is this assumption about the preponderance of great powers on international affairs, which in turn has effectively led to a bias in the field of IR in favour of the analytical weight of great powers in international affairs. Despite the fact, that, as Han dutifully noted, 'the vast majority of countries in the world are not great powers'.[31] IR scholarship on and in Asia, including, but not limited to, the dominant strand of Realism, has very often subscribed to the aforementioned core assumptions on the preponderance of great powers.[32] For example, China's foreign relations with its neighbours were imagined historically as a tributary system, in which all other states were obliged to serve as tributes in a Sino-centric order.[33] The impact of this predisposition has been manifold.

For starters, it has led to stark linguistic differentiation between 'strong states' or 'great powers' on the one hand, and 'small states',[34] 'weak states',[35] 'small powers'[36], 'tributaries'[37] or 'secondary'[38] states, on the other. More generally, much of IR literature to this day is based on the study of great power politics and how they affect international affairs. Smaller states and their foreign policies are predominantly viewed as heavily constrained in their behaviour by the interests and actions of their hegemons and their structural powers. Thus, it is widely assumed that the respective structure of the international system heavily constrains the foreign policy choices of smaller states. Realists have argued that under hegemony smaller, weaker states lose influence and autonomy and will align, formally or informally, or even bandwagon, with their respective hegemon. A more competitive, open system, however, creates more room for manoeuvre for smaller states as it can enable them to advance their own interests by playing one great power off against another.[39] Liberalists have argued that small states have greater foreign policy options in highly institutionalized, interdependent, rules-based international systems. However, a lack or a dysfunctionality of international institutions, which is often the result of failure by great powers to comply with their principles, norms, rules and decision-making procedures, reduces the room for manoeuvre for smaller states.[40] Hence, mainstream IR literature conceives of smaller powers as lacking autonomy and thus acting as rule takers rather than rule makers in international affairs. Risking overgeneralization, it seems safe to state that mainstream IR literature, therefore, traditionally has focused overtly on great powers in order to explain structural change and continuity in international politics. This has often reduced, conceptually speaking, other states to a de facto secondary or tributary role with their foreign policy options strongly constrained by structural factors over which they have little agency.

However, critics have argued against what they regard as structural over-determinism and an overt focus on great powers in IR scholarship; not least, because it potentially reduces all other actors to mere pawns on a chessboard played by great powers. Various attempts were made to assess the role of domestic factors in explaining the foreign policy behaviour of smaller states vis-à-vis great powers. For example, scholarly works have highlighted the role of domestic ideational factors such as ideas, norms and role conceptions in explaining the foreign policies of smaller states.[41] Domestic politics, including, but not limited to, the type of political regimes, the impact of transition or reform processes, as well as domestic socio-economic power constellations, have also been identified to be important factors in studying the foreign policy behaviour of states vis-à-vis regional hegemons.[42] In addition, studies have found that small states can exercise disproportionate levels of influence internationally (relative to their size and material power capabilities) in specific policy areas due to factors such as their expertise and knowledge, their aid contributions or their close foreign policy coordination and coalition-building with other, like-minded small states in international negotiations.[43] Thus, as observed by Keohane some 50 years ago, 'If Lilliputians can tie up Gulliver, or make him do their fighting for them, they must be studied as carefully as the giant'.[44]

Whilst the aforementioned Gulliver-Lilliput analogy might be considered a somewhat loose fit for Asia as a whole, the region nonetheless provides multiple interesting case studies on how Asian countries have been impacted, and subsequently made sense of and reacted to, great power competition. Additionally, scholarship on Asia's international politics actually offers a fair amount of analysis on the behaviour of quite a range of Asia's smaller or secondary states, thereby often directly or indirectly questioning assumptions over smaller or secondary states as mere 'spectators' or 'pawns'.

Historically, much of the region has experienced the so-called Cold War as more of a 'hot' one. The wars in the 1970s in the Mekong states of Vietnam, Laos and Cambodia, as well as war on the Korean peninsula in the 1950s, serve as two major historic cases, which illustrate how the conflict between the two superpowers, and their local 'proxies', directly affected Asian states. In response to the 'Communist' threat, numerous states in the region closely aligned themselves with the U.S., some even by entering military alliances (i.e. Japan, South Korea, the Philippines and Thailand), whilst others sought close relations with the Soviet Union (Vietnam) and China (Cambodia), albeit short of entering formal alliances.

A majority of Asian states, however, shied away from formal alignment with any of the two blocs during the Cold War. In fact, the roots of the Non-Aligned Movement (NAM) go back to the *Konferensi Asia-Afrika*, often referred as the Bandung conference, held in the Indonesian city of the same name in 1955. The conference was jointly organized by Indonesia, Burma (Myanmar), Pakistan, Ceylon (Sri Lanka) and India. Although many of the countries of the NAM in reality aligned themselves with one great power or another, the NAM did provide a different outlook on international affairs through its core principles: no alignment with any of the great powers, the peaceful resolution of conflict and multilateral cooperation. Hence, the NAM aimed at providing a middle road between the great powers. To this day, it continues to impact on the foreign policy doctrines of some of their members. For example, Indonesia's *bebas-aktif* (independent and active) foreign policy doctrine has incorporated some of the aforementioned NAM principles. Hence, Indonesia, at least rhetorically, has refused to align itself with any great power for decades.[45] Other Asian countries, such as Burma (Myanmar), pursued an isolationist path with little engagement with their neighbours or great powers altogether.[46]

Current scholarship especially on Southeast Asia has revealed that most states in the region actually aim to engage two or more great powers at the same time without fully committing to any of them.[47] For example, John D. Ciorciari, in his book on the foreign policies of Southeast Asian states, argued that even at the height of the Cold War, Southeast Asian states chose 'limited alignments' with major powers over balancing or bandwagoning. He showed that flexible, contingent engagements of major powers, rather than full alignment, in response to strategic uncertainties have actually been the most common foreign policy pattern in Southeast Asia.[48] Ian Storey has argued while states in the region have benefited from closer political and economic ties to China, most of them try to avoid or forestall any overt Chinese dominance in the region by simultaneously continuing to engage with the U.S. and others.[49]

Conceptually speaking, scholars have closely linked this type of foreign policy behaviour in the post-Cold War era, often labelled as hedging, with the strategic uncertainties that arose from a rising, more assertive China on the one hand, and a perceived decline of U.S. prowess in Asia, on the other.[50] The literature on hedging has steadily grown over the past decade or so and has tried to give answers to many of the core issues related to the practices of manoeuvring great power politics. Hedging is characterized by a deliberate ambiguity of smaller states with regard to their positioning vis-à-vis the U.S. and China. Hedging, as commonly understood, is practised by sending mixed signals – of engagement and disengagement, of closeness and distancing – continuously to all great powers.[51] This is to, from the viewpoint of smaller states, maximise a state's own autonomy by engaging all great powers simultaneously in order to keep strategic options flexible as much as possible. As one scholar put it, 'By long and sometimes bitter experience, we have evolved a strategy for dealing with it: using major power competition to advance our own interests and preserving as much autonomy as possible'.[52]

Although scholarly works on limited alignment and hedging have criticized the traditional Realist concepts of balancing and bandwagoning as unfitting to aptly describe the behaviour of many smaller states in Asia and beyond, the concept hedging is not without its shortcomings either. The latter include the conceptual 'looseness' of the term itself situated somewhere between balancing and bandwagoning, the varying definitions of the term. As a result of such conceptual vagueness, Haacke has pointed out to numerous analyses that have come to produce divergent, at times contradictory, findings regarding which states actually do hedge/do not hedge as well as regarding the factors that lead to hedging behaviour.[53] As such, realpolitik hedging in Asia appears to escape conceptual boundaries by not taking on a coherent shape or form. Thus, hedging by smaller states in response to the dynamism of Asia's great power politics has been at times very diverse in practice, 'with the diversity of strategies a consequence of various factors, including size, alliance relationships, national interests, domestic politics and their capacity for strategic manoeuvring'.[54]

Aims and structure of the book

Regardless of different theoretical approaches, it appears that Asian politics are increasingly dominated by the Sino-American rivalry and the associated competing visions of order for and in Asia. Some scholars have even argued that we are currently witnessing something akin to a 'new Cold War' in Asia. Some have even argued that all states in the region are essentially left with a binary choice between a Sino-centric and a U.S.-centric order and thus would need to (formally or informally) align themselves with one of the two major powers. Fears are abundant that this would marginalize regional states' room for manoeuvre and drastically reduce their agency to shape regional affairs amidst the Sino-U.S. strategic rivalry. More so, fears exist amongst policy makers that Asian states might essentially become pawns in a great power game.

However, how states in the region actually make sense of and behave in the context of said rivalry has so far been little analysed and understood. To fill this gap, this book focuses on the ways different foreign policy actors in Asia have responded to the emerging major power conflict between Washington and Beijing. How are great power politics (and policies) locally perceived, reinterpreted, conditioned or, at times, even contested? What challenges at the policy level does the soaring great power rivalry pose for established political and economic practices? What strategies and new avenues for cooperation are imagined, and perhaps even applied, short of, or even beyond, an alignment with either the U.S. or China in the rest of Asia? Finally, how are these challenges addressed by Asian states and their societies?

The first part of the book gives an overview on the numerous conceptual aspects of the Sino-U.S. rivalry. In the second chapter of the book, Rosemary Foot looks at the absence of major inter-state wars for more than 40 years in the Asia-Pacific region, which she describes as a state of affairs that has significantly contributed to the progress of the region's societies and economies. She then proceeds to review the factors that have been identified as helping to generate a relatively peaceful outcome for the Asia-Pacific over the past four decades before examining the extent to which those mechanisms are still in place or weakening at a time of strategic transition in the context of the Sino-U.S. rivalry. Rory Medcalf takes up where Rosemary Foot left off by turning to the competing geopolitical narrative that has emerged in response to a rising China, which is increasingly perceived as assertive or coercive. In the books' third chapter, he argues that the Indo-Pacific, far from being an obscure account of words and maps or a mere geographical descriptor, *is a narrative which* helps nations face one of the great international dilemmas of the 21st century: how can other countries respond to a strong and often coercive China without resorting to capitulation or conflict? With the term Asia-Pacific becoming increasingly supplanted by the term Indo-Pacific, in his chapter Rory Medcalf illustrates the emergence, key characteristics, drivers and implications of the emergence of this new strategic narrative. He furthermore aims to discern what difference to people's lives – to their peace, autonomy, dignity and material wellbeing – does a new name for their part of the world make anyway?

In chapter 4, Kim, Joo Hee describes the current order in Asia as one transitioning from what she labels a rules-based multilateral order to an era of U.S.-China competition and with it a new bipolarity. She then proceeds to discuss how a stable, prosperous order in Asia could look like as well as the roles middle powers could play hereby. Drawing on insights from the study of South Korea's foreign policy vis-à-vis China and the U.S., Kim, Joo Hee then lists numerous ways through which middle powers such as South Korea can manage the changing regional power constellations. Lee Jones takes issue with numerous core assumptions on state and statehood, which typically revolve around questions of geopolitics, the balance of power, the purported grand strategies of major powers, and the form and contribution of formal regional institutions or the so-called 'regional security architecture', which are underpinning much of the current debate on Asia's changing security order. This essentially realist approach operates with a notion of states as coherent, territorially bounded, strategic actors. In chapter 5, he argues that it misses important developments in regional security order associated with the transformation of states beyond this 'Westphalian' model, such as transnational governance networks to address non-traditional security threats or the fragmentation and internationalisation of Chinese state apparatuses associated with China's BRI. Lee Jones' chapter concludes the first part of the book on different conceptual aspects of the Sino-U.S. rivalry.

The second part of the book introduces regional and country perspectives. It starts with two chapters from the sub-region of South Asia. Chapter 6 sees Ganeshan Wignaraja take on Sri Lanka's engagement with the U.S. and China in the post-conflict period, 2010–2019. He lays out why great powers might be interested in Sri Lanka in the context of a scenario he describes as a second Cold War. Then he analyses important aspects of Sri Lanka's engagement with great powers in areas such as trade and foreign direct investment (FDI), development assistance and security cooperation. The author concludes by pointing out various aspects of Sri Lanka's recent experience, which can provide important insights for managing small power–great power relations beyond South Asia. In chapter 7, Jagannath P. Panda argues that minilateralisms, specifically trilateralisms, seem to have emerged as one of the expedient modes or frameworks of multilateral cooperation in Asia. Yet in his case study of the Japan-America-India (JAI) trilateral meeting, the author remains sceptical to what extent the JAI is able to influence the balance of power in the region due to the different foreign policy traditions and divergent strategic interests of its members. The chapter argues that what, however, makes 'JAI' a distinct trilateral in the making is the scope of forging foreign policy complementarities, primarily commercial interests, that exist in the India-U.S., India-Japan and Japan-U.S. bilateral tracks of cooperation in the Indo-Pacific.

Turning to the sub-region of Southeast Asia, in chapter 8, Alice D. Ba discusses ASEAN's position and role in Asia's large power mix. She outlines some of the different ways that multilateral regional institutions, especially ASEAN, have been conceptualized as a response to Asia's changing great power conditions. Her discussion offers some starting points for thinking about the role of regional institutions in Southeast Asian strategies. It then turns to Asia's changing great power conditions, with an eye to drawing connections between the past and the present, and the different strategic effects associated with past periods. The chapter concludes with some additional observations about changing institutional strategies in the context of Asia's increasingly contested multilateralisms. Strategic change (and continuity) is also the focus of Renato Cruz de Castro's examination of the shift in Philippine policy on China under the Duterte administration in chapter 9. He hereby observes a strategic shift from appeasement to soft balancing. Cruz de Castro argues that President Rodrigo Duterte has adopted an appeasement policy vis-à-vis China's expansive design in the South China Sea early on in his presidency. Duterte is, therefore, widely regarded as having distanced the Philippines from the U.S., its long-standing treaty ally and gravitated towards China. However, the author argues that the Duterte administration's actual objective is to restrain Chinese aggressive behaviour in the South China Sea by maintaining its alliance with the U.S., fostering a security partnership with Japan and pursuing a more active participation in ASEAN.

A somewhat similar research puzzle is undertaken in chapter 10: Hong Liu analyses *how* the American-China rivalries in almost all spheres, ranging from diplomatic, trade, technological to ideological, have affected Malaysia's foreign policy options including its relations with China. His chapter starts by briefly examining the factors leading to the resurgence of Mahathir including the opposition alliance's anti-China rhetoric. The second section discusses complex domestic factors and variables in shaping Malaysia's engagement with China and its stance in the great power politics, under the new foreign policy framework that was announced in June 2019. The third part analyses Malaysia's policies towards the BRI through a case analysis of the East Coast Rail Link project as well as the American-China trade war by examining Mahathir's positions on Huawei, which is at the centre of the trade dispute between the two powers. The concluding section explores the implications of Malaysia's dilemmas in a broader context of international political economy and highlights the important roles of local agency (interests, institutions and players) in engaging great power politics.

Moving from maritime to mainland Southeast Asia, Thi Thi Soe San in chapter 11 points out that manoeuvring great power rivalries (the 'Battle of the Titans') is nothing new to Myanmar as the country had been buffeted by the Cold War for decades. Hence, a strong foreign policy tradition has emerged, which tries to steer Myanmar away from becoming entangled in great power politics. More so, the country's numerous internal disputes and conflicts, rather than inter-state rivalries, have been far more damaging to Myanmar's security. Yet the current administration led by Aung San Suu Kyi in September 2018 signed the Memorandum of Understanding for the China Myanmar Economic Corridor (CMEC). Soe San argues that the CMEC will have implications far beyond infrastructure and economic development as it helps to bypass the strategic vulnerabilities of Beijing's oil supply through the South China Sea by connecting the Indian Ocean oil trade to southern China via Myanmar. This could make Myanmar more susceptible to Chinese influence in the future. From Myanmar, the book turns eastward to the sub-region of East Asia. In the last chapter of the book, Seo-Hyun Park illustrates the domestic political constraints – in addition to the external structural pressures – facing South Korean leaders in formulating their foreign policy strategies vis-à-vis the U.S. and China. She shows that political leaders in South Korea must carefully navigate particular narrative frames on alliance-management issues with regard to the U.S., which in turn are linked to the country's particular historical and cultural context, when discussing foreign policy agendas. This has resulted, she argues, in a polarisation of the foreign policy debate with regard to relations with the U.S. and China in post-Cold War South Korea. Seo-Hyun Park concludes by criticizing these in her view too essentialist discourse in favour of broader debates about South Korea's positioning as a secondary versus middle power, regional versus global power, a system-supporting role or an agent of change.

Notes

1 Joe Renouard, "America's Anti-China Mood Is Here to Stay," *The Diplomat*, August 14, 2019, https://thediplomat.com/2019/08/americas-anti-china-mood-is-here-to-stay/.
2 Department of Defense, "2018 National Defense Strategy" (Washington, D.C., January 19, 2018), https://dod.defense.gov/Portals/1/Documents/pubs/2018-National-Defense-Strategy-Summary.pdf.
3 The White House, "National Security Strategy of the United States of America" (Washington, D.C., December 2017), www.whitehouse.gov/wp-content/uploads/2017/12/NSS-Final-12-18-2017-0905.pdf.
4 Graham Allison, "The Thucydides Trap: Are the U.S. and China Headed for War?," *The Atlantic*, September 24, 2015, www.theatlantic.com/international/archive/2015/09/united-states-china-war-thucydides-trap/406756/.
5 Office of Policy Planning, *The Elements of the China Challenge* (Washington, D.C.: U.S. Department of State, November 2020).
6 Catherine Wong, "Chinese Foreign Minister Wang Yi Says Opponents of Taiwan Reunification 'Will Stink for 10,000 Years,'" *South China Morning Post*, January 14, 2020, www.scmp.com/news/china/diplomacy/article/3045974/chinese-foreign-minister-wang-yi-says-opponents-taiwan.
7 Xie Wenting and Fan Lingzhi, "China's Govt Agencies Condemn US Over Xinjiang Bill," *Global Times*, December 4, 2019, www.globaltimes.cn/content/1172205.shtml.
8 Xu Liang, "US Criticism Toward China Reveals a Country Unwilling to Learn – Global Times," *Global Times*, February 9, 2020, www.globaltimes.cn/content/1178944.shtml.
9 Felix Heiduk and Alexandra Sakaki, "Introduction to the Special Issue – China's Belt and Road Initiative: The View from East Asia," *East Asia* 36, no. 2 (2019): 93–113.
10 Wang Yi, "China's Role in the Global and Regional Order: Participant, Facilitator and Contributor" (Fourth World Peace Forum, Beijing, June 27, 2015), www.fmprc.gov.cn/mfa_eng/wjdt_665385/zyjh_665391/t1276595.shtml.
11 Wu Xinbo, "China in Search of a Liberal Partnership International Order," *International Affairs* 94, no. 5 (September 1, 2018): 995–1018.
12 Stephen Brooks and William Wohlforth, "The Rise and Fall of the Great Powers in the Twenty-First Century: China's Rise and the Fate of America's Global Position," *International Security* 40, no. 3 (January 1, 2016): 7–53.
13 Peter Trubowitz and Peter Harris, "The End of the American Century? Slow Erosion of the Domestic Sources of Usable Power," *International Affairs* 95, no. 3 (May 1, 2019): 619–639.
14 Hugh White, *The China Choice: Why We Should Share Power* (Oxford: Oxford University Press, 2013); Hugh White, "The US Is No Match for China in Asia; Trump Should Have Stayed Away," *South China Morning Post*, November 15, 2017, www.scmp.com/comment/insight-opinion/article/2120010/why-us-no-match-china-asia-and-trump-should-have-stayed-home; Gideon Rachman, *Easternisation: War and Peace in the Asian Century* (London: Bodley Head, 2016).
15 Lee Hsien Loong, "Keynote Address at the 18TH IISS Shangri-La Dialogue" (Singapore, May 31, 2019), www.pmo.gov.sg/Newsroom/PM-Lee-Hsien-Loong-at-the-IISS-Shangri-La-Dialogue-2019.

16 Delfin Lorenzana, "Remarks at the 18th IISS Shangri-La Dialogue" (Singapore, June 2, 2019), www.iiss.org/-/media/files/shangri-la-dialogue/2019/speeches/plenary-5-major-general-retd-delfin-lorenzana-transcript.pdf.
17 Haji Mohamad Sabu, "Remarks at the 18th IISS Shangri-La Dialogue" (Singapore, June 1, 2019), www.iiss.org/-/media/files/shangri-la-dialogue/2019/speeches/plenary-3-haji-mohamad-sabu-minister-of-defence-malaysia.pdf.
18 David Shambaugh, "U.S.-China Rivalry in Southeast Asia: Power Shift or Competitive Coexistence?," *International Security* 42, no. 4 (2018): 86.
19 Kerry Brown, "The Belt and Road: Security Dimensions," *Asia Europe Journal* (April 6, 2018): 1–10.
20 Nicholas Szechenyi et al., *China's Maritime Silk Road: Strategic and Economic Implications for the Indo-Pacific Region* (Washington, D.C.: Center for Strategic and International Studies, March 2018).
21 Felix Heiduk and Alexandra Sakaki, no. 9.
22 Mike Pence, "Vice President Mike Pence's Remarks on the Administration's Policy Towards China" (Washington, D.C., October 4, 2018), www.hudson.org/events/1610-vice-president-mike-pence-s-remarks-on-the-administration-s-policy-towards-china102018.
23 See Seng Tan, "Consigned to Hedge: South-East Asia and America's 'Free and Open Indo-Pacific' Strategy," *International Affairs* 96, no. 1 (January 1, 2020): 131–148; Dewi Fortuna Anwar, "Indonesia and the ASEAN Outlook on the Indo-Pacific," *International Affairs* 96, no. 1 (January 1, 2020): 111–129; Axel Berkofsky and Sergio Miracola, *Geopolitics by Other Means: The Indo-Pacific Reality* (Rome: ISPI, January 29, 2019), www.ispionline.it/en/pubblicazione/geopolitics-other-means-indo-pacific-reality-22122; Kei Koga, "Japan's 'Indo-Pacific' Question: Countering China or Shaping a New Regional Order?," *International Affairs* 96, no. 1 (January 1, 2020): 49–73.
24 Felix Heiduk and Gudrun Wacker, *From Asia-Pacific to Indo-Pacific: Significance, Implementation and Challenges* (Berlin: Stiftung Wissenschaft und Politik, June 2020).
25 Ibid.
26 Yuen Foong Khong, "Power as Prestige in World Politics," *International Affairs* 95, no. 1 (January 1, 2019): 119–142.
27 Department of Defense, "Indo-Pacific Strategy Report" (Washington, D.C., June 2019), 1, https://media.defense.gov/2019/Jul/01/2002152311/-1/-1/1/DEPARTMENT-OF-DEFENSE-INDO-PACIFIC-STRATEGY-REPORT-2019.PDF.
28 Ibid., 1.
29 BBC World Service Poll, "Sharp Drop in World Views of US, UK: Global Poll" (July 4, 2017), https://globescan.com/images/images/pressreleases/bbc2017_country_ratings/BBC2017_Country_Ratings_Poll.pdf
30 Pew Research Center, "Around the World, More See the U.S. Positively than China, but Little Confidence in Trump or Xi" (January 10, 2020), www.pewresearch.org/fact-tank/2020/01/10/around-the-world-more-see-the-u-s-positively-than-china-but-little-confidence-in-trump-or-xi/
31 Enze Han, "Under the Shadow of China-US Competition: Myanmar and Thailand's Alignment Choices," *The Chinese Journal of International Politics* 11, no. 1 (March 1, 2018): 85–104.
32 Amitav Acharya, "Thinking Theoretically About Asian IR," in *International Relations of Asia*, eds. David L. Shambaugh and Michael B. Yahuda, Second edition (Lanham: Rowman & Littlefield, 2014), 59–89.
33 John K. Fairbanks, ed., *The Chinese World Order: Traditional China's Foreign Relations* (Cambridge, MA: Harvard University Press, 1968); Zhang Feng, "Rethinking the 'Tribute System': Broadening the Conceptual Horizon of Historical East Asian Politics," *The Chinese Journal of International Politics* 2, no. 4 (December 1, 2009):

545–574; Brantly Womack, "Asymmetry and China's Tributary System," *The Chinese Journal of International Politics* 5, no. 1 (March 1, 2012): 37–54.
34 Christine Ingebritsen et al., eds., *Small States in International Relations* (Seattle: University of Washington Press, 2006).
35 Hanna Samir Kassab, *Weak States in International Relations Theory: The Cases of Armenia, St. Kitts and Nevis, Lebanon, and Cambodia* (New York: Palgrave Macmillan, 2015).
36 Robert L. Rothstein, *Alliances and Small Powers* (New York: Columbia University Press, 1968).
37 John K. Fairbanks, no. 33.
38 Enze Han, no. 31.
39 Donald E. Milsten, "Small Powers–A Struggle for Survival," *The Journal of Conflict Resolution* 13, no. 3 (1969): 388–393; Robert O. Keohane, "Lilliputians' Dilemmas: Small States in International Politics," *International Organization* 23, no. 2 (1969): 291–310.
40 Sverrir Steinsson and Baldur Thorhallsson, "Small State Foreign Policy," in *The Oxford Research Encyclopedia of Politics*, ed. Cameron Thies (Oxford: Oxford University Press, 2017); Annika Björkdahl, "Ideas and Norms in Swedish Peace Policy," *Swiss Political Science Review* 19, no. 3 (2013): 322–337.
41 Stephen Benedict Dyson, "Alliances, Domestic Politics, and Leader Psychology: Why Did Britain Stay out of Vietnam and Go into Iraq?," *Political Psychology* 28, no. 6 (2007): 647–666; Kai Oppermann, "National Role Conceptions, Domestic Constraints and the New 'Normalcy' in German Foreign Policy: The Eurozone Crisis, Libya and Beyond," *German Politics* 21, no. 4 (2012): 502–519, https://doi.org/10.1080/09644008.2012.748268.
42 Jürgen Rüland, "Constructing Regionalism Domestically: Local Actors and Foreign Policymaking in Newly Democratized Indonesia," *Foreign Policy Analysis* 10, no. 2 (April 1, 2014): 181–201, https://doi.org/10.1111/fpa.12002; Aileen S. P. Baviera, "The Influence of Domestic Politics on Philippine Foreign Policy: The Case of Philippines-China Relations Since 2004," *RSIS Working Papers* (Singapore: S. Rajaratnam School of International Studies, 2012), www.rsis.edu.sg/wp-content/uploads/rsis-pubs/WP241.pdf; Le Hong Hiep, "Vietnam's Domestic – Foreign Policy Nexus: Doi Moi, Foreign Policy Reform, and Sino-Vietnamese Normalization," *Asian Politics & Policy* 5, no. 3 (July 1, 2013): 387–406, https://doi.org/10.1111/aspp.12035.
43 Diana Panke, "Dwarfs in International Negotiations: How Small States Make Their Voices Heard," *Cambridge Review of International Affairs* 25, no. 3 (September 1, 2012): 313–328.
44 Robert O. Keohane, no. 39, 310.
45 Rizal Sukma, "The Evolution of Indonesia's Foreign Policy: An Indonesian View," *Asian Survey* 35, no. 3 (1995): 304–315; Andrew Phillips and Eric Hiariej, "Beyond the 'Bandung Divide'? Assessing the Scope and Limits of Australia – Indonesia Security Cooperation," *Australian Journal of International Affairs* 70, no. 4 (July 3, 2016): 422–440.
46 Michael W. Charney, *A History of Modern Burma* (Cambridge: Cambridge University Press, 2009).
47 Ann Marie Murphy, "Great Power Rivalries, Domestic Politics and Southeast Asian Foreign Policy: Exploring the Linkages," *Asian Security* 13, no. 3 (September 2, 2017): 165–182.
48 John D. Ciorciari, *The Limits of Alignment: Southeast Asia and the Great Powers Since 1975* (Washington, D.C.: Georgetown University Press, 2010).
49 Ian Storey, *Southeast Asia and the Rise of China* (London: Routledge, 2013).
50 Evelyn Goh, "Great Powers and Hierarchical Order in Southeast Asia: Analyzing Regional Security Strategies," *International Security* 32, no. 3 (January 1,

2008): 113–157, https://doi.org/10.1162/isec.2008.32.3.113; Cheng-Chwee Kuik, "How Do Weaker States Hedge? Unpacking ASEAN States' Alignment Behavior Towards China," *Journal of Contemporary China* 25, no. 100 (2016): 500–514; Seng Tan, no 23.
51 John D. Ciorciari and Jürgen Haacke, "Hedging in International Relations: An Introduction," *International Relations of the Asia-Pacific* 19, no. 3 (September 1, 2019): 367–374.
52 Bilahari Kausikan, "Dodging and Hedging in Southeast Asia," *The American Interest* (blog), January 12, 2017, www.the-american-interest.com/2017/01/12/dodging-and-hedging-in-southeast-asia/.
53 Jürgen Haacke, "The Concept of Hedging and Its Application to Southeast Asia: A Critique and a Proposal for a Modified Conceptual and Methodological Framework," *International Relations of the Asia-Pacific* 19, no. 3 (September 1, 2019): 375–417.
54 Rebecca Strating, "Small Power Hedging in an Era of Great-Power Politics: Southeast Asian Responses to China's Pursuit of Energy Security," *Asian Studies Review* 44, no. 1 (January 2, 2020): 98.

2 From globalisation to fragmentation?

The erosion of confidence in the Asia-Pacific

Rosemary Foot

The Asia-Pacific region has been recognised over the past several years as the most dynamic region in the world economy, with many hundreds of millions brought out of absolute poverty. It also stands as a relatively stable and peaceful part of the world with no incidence of inter-state war since 1979.[1] Despite these positive outcomes, governmental abuse of domestic populations has been prevalent, and these sources of violence should never be discounted or ignored.[2] Moreover, levels of economic inequality remain high in a number of the regional states. Nevertheless, compared with other regions of the world, the Asia-Pacific economies have become vital in sustaining global economic growth and the region has not experienced inter-state war for over 40 years. This state of affairs has significantly contributed to the broad progress of the region's societies and economies.

This chapter first reviews factors that have been identified as helping to generate a relatively peaceful outcome for the Asia-Pacific over the past four decades. Next it turns to its main focus, which is to examine the extent to which those mechanisms are still in place or undergoing fundamental change at a time of strategic transition. It concludes that a number of those crucial elements no longer work in ways that mirror their operation in an earlier era. It notes in particular the destabilisation that derives from two factors that to a degree are interrelated: threatened disruption in the global and regional production chains that have helped the region's economies to prosper, alongside a steep deterioration in Sino-American relations. There are great uncertainties about how best to sustain the more positive elements in Asian security order in the coming decades, with an attendant rise in prospects for a darker future for the region.

Processes, decisions, and structures generating stability and prosperity

Several factors have contributed in the recent past to relative peace and socio-economic progress in the Asia-Pacific region. Many of these relate to the processes of globalisation and regionalisation, notably in the areas of economic exchange and institutional development. These factors are interrelated with the prospects that a negative development in one particular factor is likely to have negative consequences for some or even all of the others. Indeed, they bear some of the characteristics of what Amitav Acharya has labelled an 'eco-system' made up of highly interdependent components.[3] However, the relationship between the United States and China is crucial to consider and may well determine whether the region's future is one of intense rivalry, or retains a degree of stability that allows its comparatively impressive performance to continue. Equally as important to consider is the evolution of the global and regional supply chains that have in the past deepened connectedness, contributed to gross domestic product (GDP) growth, and helped to mollify Sino-American tensions.

First, at the macro level and as two major analysts of these questions have concluded, the consolidation of most Asian states over the post-1945 era has contributed to both the globalisation and regionalisation of the state-based international system. A majority of these states, with North Korea and Myanmar the most notable of the exceptions, have increased their capacities to respond to regional shocks and have also strengthened their attachment to the goals of national and regional stability. State consolidation has additionally prompted deeper integration into global society.[4]

This is shown especially in the progress of the sub-regional organisation, the Association of Southeast Asian Nations (ASEAN), first established in 1967. ASEAN introduced an institutional design that helped pacify relations among formerly conflicting member-states. The design also provided domestic elites in the post-Cold War era with a model for the expansion of their sub-regional organisation to the wider Asia-Pacific. In Muthiah Alagappa's view, writing in 2003, at that point most Asian states had moved past the point where they feared for their survival. Expectations were that they operated on the basis of norm or rule-governed interaction, and this gave political elites the confidence to consider ways of turning greater state and sub-regional resilience into Asia-Pacific wide resilience.[5] Regional organisations such as the ASEAN Regional Forum (ARF), the ASEAN Defence Ministers Meeting Plus (ADMM+), and the East Asia Summit (EAS), amongst others, incorporated norms that had supported ASEAN state interaction. Although these regional organisations have been consensus based and have shied away from direct attempts at resolution of hard security questions, they have at least offered venues where these norms and rules can be reaffirmed and where some cooperative security practices in non-traditional security areas can make modest headway. The meetings have also provided opportunities to increase transparency and to build elite connections.[6]

Second, most states in the region have struck what might be termed a state-society bargain: the understanding that the legitimacy of the governing regime is highly dependent on 'performance legitimacy,' or effective governance. This is associated with a governmental role in facilitating reasonably high levels of economic growth, together with a degree of social stability. This bargain implies, in particular, a perceived reciprocal relationship between economic development and regime and state security that is not necessarily typical in other world regions. It also encourages a normative commitment to maintaining levels of stability in domestic and regional relations high enough to facilitate global and regional trade and investment and trust in future prospects for the continuation of such exchanges. Etel Solingen's important comparative study of the Middle East and post-colonial East Asia demonstrated how the latter's privileging of the civilian state-led economy over the pursuit of military power contributed to a steady decline in inter-state tension in East Asia. This compares favourably with a persistent resort to armed conflict in the former region.[7]

Third, many of these Asia-Pacific states are also trading or developmental states that have become firmly integrated into the global and regional economies. They are outward looking and have adopted export-led policies. Much of that export trade has been in the form of networked trade, which makes use of the revolution in communications and transportation to break the value chain into various components. It is understood that were this networked production chain to be damaged through actual conflict, through active or deliberate 'decoupling,' or a major unanticipated disaster, there would be several negative effects. One major consequence would be that the economies would contract, the bargain struck between state and society come under strain, and regional resilience be tested. Though possibilities for some adjustment over time to such shocks are available, there would be a short- to medium-term loss of access to export markets as well as loss of access to inputs that are crucial to global competitiveness. As John Ravenhill has argued in contemplating the wider security consequences of such interrelatedness, countries depend on these interlinkages for 'critical inputs into their products,' as well as for 'access to distribution and marketing channels and to brand names.' He goes on: 'Not only is this a world in which the costs of territorial conquest far outweigh any conceivable gains, but the potential costs of severing links with the global economy have also never been greater.'[8]

Fourth, the People's Republic of China (PRC) has itself become deeply embedded in these production chains. From 1978 and the start of 'Reform and Opening,' China became supportive of a 'development first agenda,' and at least while paramount leader Deng Xiaoping's associated maxim of *taoguang yanghui* was dominant in the country's vision of regional order,[9] this started to suggest to Beijing's neighbours that it was becoming more closely aligned with their normative perspectives. It was becoming a part of the region and not an object of suspicion largely isolated from the region. Other states that also previously were distanced from regional and sub-regional neighbours matched China's turn towards an integrated development model. This was most notable in the case of Vietnam, which introduced its own reform movement, labelled *Doi Moi*. The Vietnamese leadership accompanied this move in the early 1990s with the withdrawal of its troops from Cambodia, the decision to join ASEAN in 1995, and the normalisation of relations with both the United States and China.

China's successful turn towards 'Reform and Opening' under Deng was later coupled with a diplomatic strategy of reassurance, prominent between 1997 and 2007. It was designed to show that, even as China's material power grew, the PRC would continue to support the regional norm of non-interference in internal affairs and the non-use of force for settling issues in dispute (for example, in 2003, it became the first external state to sign ASEAN's Treaty of Amity and Cooperation that contains a non-use of force clause). Once Beijing had started to participate in the region's multilateral institutions, it became a supporter of their design structure, especially consensus decision-making, and the emphasis on cooperative security embodied in these process-driven regional institutions.

These predominantly rhetorical steps were markedly helpful in defusing (though not removing) the uncertainty that China's growing material power was beginning to generate. Beijing's argument that its material advancement represented a threat neither to neighbouring states nor to regional order was broadly acknowledged as helpful, if not everywhere accepted. And while Beijing was less able to convince Japan of its benign intentions, nevertheless, Tokyo, plus other US alliance partners as well as those states in close alignment with the United States, could remain watchful, but not alarmed. Moreover, were matters to become more disturbing, they believed that they could rely on the American military presence and its continuing commitment to the bilateral alliance structure that Washington had first put in place in the 1950s.

Fifth, apart from that bilateral US-led 'hub and spokes' security architecture, as noted earlier, regional states were willing to embrace and add other mechanisms that aimed to reflect the transitions in regional order that were taking place. In particular, these mechanisms promoted the norm of inclusiveness. The PRC was encouraged to enter multilateral bodies such as the ARF, Asia-Pacific Economic Cooperation (APEC), and ADMM+, amongst other such institutions. This openness helped to induce Beijing's own reassurance strategy and additionally encouraged the United States to move beyond bilateralism and engage multilaterally with regional states. The US administration did not want to be the one major state rejecting Asia-Pacific regionalism by refusing to participate in the new institutions.

Finally, Beijing's 'Reform and Opening' policy also largely depended for its success on the US-China normalisation of ties. Successful normalisation in 1979 sent major signals to other states in the region that gradually aided a sense of optimism about the prospects for maintaining stability despite regional transition. Important in this regard, normalisation showed that despite ideological differences, states could find a basis for coexistence; that Beijing's economy, while remaining state led, could become flexible enough to generate economic interdependence; and that the PRC had accepted there was a singular global economic order. China and the US would move on to be enveloped into global production chains and both sides perceived a benefit to be had from that interlinkage. Sino-American bilateral economic ties also strengthened, though particularly from the 2000s the United States built up a large trading deficit with China. Nevertheless, even as late as 2017, when Sino-American tensions were beginning to increase, a US-China Business Council study suggested a continuing productive future for the US-China economic relationship. The study expected that US services' and goods' exports to China would rise from US$165 billion in 2015 to about US$525 billion in 2030,[10] a pace of increase far higher than with other of America's major trading partners.

Contentious issues did, of course, regularly arise between the United States and China. Beijing, for example, perceived the Obama administration's 'Pivot to Asia,' later renamed as the rebalance, as part of a US effort to contain China's rise and a form of behaviour reminiscent of the Cold War. The US administration's hostility towards the China-initiated Asian Infrastructure Investment Bank (AIIB) and exclusion of China from negotiations designed to lead to the creation of a Trans-Pacific Partnership trading agreement reinforced these sentiments. For America's part, it noted the increased foreign policy ambitions of Beijing under the leadership of Xi Jinping, one important manifestation of which was the resurfacing of territorial conflicts with Japan over ownership of the Senkaku-Diaoyu Islands in the East China Sea, and the build-up of tensions in the South China Sea. Steady increases in China's relative power in the economic and military fields, especially after the global financial crisis of 2008, additionally raised concerns. This was particularly so when China, from 2014, began to station military equipment on the South China Sea reefs and islands that it had built into permanent structures.

However, while noting these areas of competition, both sides also continued to reference areas of cooperation in their relationship. Beijing and Washington regularly drew attention to issues where actions could be viewed as complementary or where they had worked together: for example, over proposals to end conflict in Afghanistan, to counter terrorist violence, to halt the North Korean nuclear programme, and to sign a nuclear agreement with Iran. They also worked together to make progress at the 2015 Paris Climate Change conference and dealt cooperatively with the Ebola crisis of 2014.[11] The two states continued to engage on a regular basis in strategic dialogues where the two parties could discuss 'big picture' issues. Above all, they appeared to accept that they could rely on economic interdependence to help constrain, though not remove, the more troubling areas in the relationship.

In sum, the Asia-Pacific order has been made up of a range of interconnected factors that have moved the region into a more pacific and prosperous state of affairs than has been the case in a number of other regional worlds. State consolidation, though imperfectly realised across the region, has been built on a perceived link between economic prosperity and state and regime security. The formal security architecture has come to comprise more than the US alliance system, with bilateral alliances existing alongside inclusive multilateral organisations that have been designed to dampen major state competition and to enfold the PRC into their workings in order to diffuse and restrain its growing power. The legitimating function for states deriving from positive economic outcomes has provided some basis for a common value system to develop across a region that is highly diversified in most other respects. It has also encouraged a determination to maintain a stable environment that is attractive to outside investors. The development of networked production and trading has deepened forms of economic interdependence and helped to ameliorate tensions amongst states of the region, and in particular between the US and China. China's decision to embark on 'Reform and Opening' together with the normalisation of ties between Beijing and Washington were major signals underlining the nexus between security and economic issues and downplayed ideological difference as a source of division between the two states as well as among other states within the broader region.

Fragmentation?

How, then, to account for the current sense of insecurity and high levels of uncertainty? None of the factors promoting relative peace and economic advancement since the 1980s have operated in a static manner, and the picture outlining elements of Asia-Pacific regional order presented so far is in many respects stylised. It glosses over elements of instability in order to provide a snapshot of major characteristics that have aided security and prosperity. However, global and regional orders are never fully formed, but are always under construction and reconstruction. Transitions in order may be slow or more violent, and especially swift and comprehensive in the case of major state war. Moreover, the ability to adapt may be greater in some orders than in others. There are also tipping points that can be difficult to spot in advance, but which become plain once they have unfolded.[12]

The transition in order since the 1980s has been gradual in the Asia-Pacific to date, with the US largely remaining in a predominant role and with China gradually enhancing its position. However, certain tipping points do seem to have loomed into view, though they are not yet fully formed. These go beyond the redistribution of power in the region and include a reframed perspective on the relationship between economics and security, particularly in the context of the China-US relationship, a Chinese disavowal of some of the past benefits of its diplomatic reassurance strategy, and the impact of a global health pandemic (COVID-19) that, depending on its duration, threatens not just to disrupt but to transform global and regional supply chains.

Returning to the factors considered in the first section of this chapter, the question becomes one less related to levels of state consolidation and more related to transitions in power. Thus, if we recast this factor and focus not on internal cohesion but on the redistribution of power, this places the PRC in a particularly advantageous regional position, particularly from the second decade of the twenty-first century. Though most regional states have advanced economically and militarily over the past 10 years or so, China has outstripped the pace of that advancement with many advances occurring in the past decade. For example, Beijing became the largest exporter in 2009, the second largest economy in the world in 2010, the largest trading nation in 2013, and in 2015 produced about a quarter of the world's manufacturers. China's defence budget is the second largest in the world and the country has become the world's third largest exporter of weaponry.

Eric Heginbotham and Richard J. Samuels, writing in 2018, have explored that defence budget in some detail. They estimate that in real terms, the budget has grown some 724 per cent between 1996 and 2018.[13] Naval modernisation has been a marked feature of recent expenditure and includes programmes for 'anti-ship ballistic missiles, anti-ship cruise missiles, land-attack cruise missiles, surface-to-air missiles, mines, manned aircraft, unmanned aircraft, submarines, and aircraft carriers.'[14] The Navy then had 133 warships over 1,500 tons and is moving away from having a mainly frigate-based navy to one built around destroyers. Beijing now completes an average of two-and-a-half destroyers on an annual basis compared with one destroyer every 2 years between 2005 and 2011. Similarly, rapid increases in production rates have affected China's fighter aircraft inventory, the rate of increase between 2004 and 2010 standing at 40 fighter aircraft per year, accelerating to 60 per year between 2011 and 2017.[15] Paramilitary coastguard vessels have also increased dramatically in size and number and have been brought into play in support of China's sovereignty claims in the South and East China seas. This broadly leaves intact the non-use of force norm for settling issues in dispute, but weakens the focus on negotiated consensus and replaces it with coercive diplomacy.

In these changing circumstances, and though wariness has markedly increased, Asia-Pacific states nevertheless have continued to deepen various forms of interdependence with Beijing. Most of these states count China as their primary trading, aid, and investment partner. Many have signed Memoranda of Understandings indicating interest and often involvement in China's Belt and Road Initiative (BRI). New agreements involving China have been reached, such as the Regional Comprehensive Economic Partnership (RCEP) trade agreement, signed in 2020, with several states (including Beijing and Japan) ratifying it in 2021. China and ASEAN also are engaged in difficult negotiations on the South China Sea sovereignty disputes, having agreed a single text for those negotiations with the aim of reaching a Code of Conduct. Southeast Asian states continue to attempt to maintain a degree of stability in their relations with China and to encourage more cooperative forms of security. They engage with China in regular defence exchanges and joint military exercises at sea and on the ground and have agreed the establishment of communication hot lines. China-Japan relations, though still tense, are being managed, with Tokyo having made positive, if conditional, moves towards involvement in the BRI, and President Xi Jinping agreeing to be hosted for a summit in Tokyo once post-pandemic conditions allow for travel. The key difference is that where once China was being invited to participate in region-wide institutions, and to deepen bilateral ties, Beijing has now moved into a position where it attempts to control and lead the diplomatic process. Its role in the creation of the AIIB and BRI and its dominant position in RCEP negotiations illustrate this.

Much as before, a number of states would prefer to retain a significant role for the United States in the region: for many, the US presence has long represented a valuable insurance policy at times of strategic uncertainty. Washington has acted as a deterrent force and has contributed towards building the material and defence capacity of several Asia-Pacific states. A number of regional states have shown interest in the American-backed Indo-Pacific Strategy. The Strategy introduces a new regional geography that, for the United States and some other states that are involved in its creation, represents an attempt to change the regional distribution of power in ways that favour actors other than China. However, there are now real doubts about the extent to which these states can rely on the United States in the event of conflict with China over competing sovereignty claims, or other issues in dispute with Beijing, as are discussed in more detail in the next section.[16]

Major sources of disquiet

Thus, while some of the major factors that have aided the Asia-Pacific's enviable advancement remain broadly in place, the balance has shifted in certain cases, and China has become more dominant and less of a supplicant. Three factors are worth contemplating in greater detail: the first brought on in the wake of the Trump and Xi presidencies and the approaches and ambitions of these two leaders; the second relates to the deterioration in Sino-American relations such that the soothing effect of economic interdependence no longer operates in the way that it once did; and the third relates to questioning the wisdom of relying on global and regional supply chains – a questioning that has come from both the growing tensions between the United States and China, as well as, more latterly, from the global health pandemic (COVID-19) that erupted in late 2019/early 2020.

The Trump presidency, for example, brought into being a direct attack on dominant norms in the Asia-Pacific such as diplomacy, multilateralism, inclusiveness, and the maintenance of policy-making autonomy. Most states of this region have not wanted to be forced into a stark choice in terms of alignments with respect to Beijing and Washington, but may well be pressed to change that preferred position. This is so even with the advent of a more sympathetic Biden administration.[17] In terms of America's deterrence function, President Trump in particular has damaged over the longer term America's ability to provide reassurance to its partners and allies. Trump could not have put this more starkly when he stated at the UN General Assembly in 2017:

> As President of the United States, I will always put America first, just like you, as the leaders of your countries will always, and should always, put your countries first. All responsible leaders have an obligation to serve their own citizens, and the nation-state remains the best vehicle for elevating the human condition.[18]

On the basis of the continuing support for Trump in America, it is apparent that such sentiment retains a strong hold among the public and in the Republican Party. Trump made little or no distinction between allies and non-allies, and viewed all as potential competitors, mainly in the economic arena. The Trump administration's attacks on the alleged 'free-riding' of Asian allies have damaged ties, and fears of US abandonment still linger despite Trump's electoral losses.

Manila, for example, has regularly reflected on the credibility of US security assurances given the recent prevalence of US governments that are so internally focused. It has noted, too, that China's military acquisitions have served to complicate the Asian strategic environment for the United States. The United States is less able to respond in military terms as straightforwardly as it once did (for example, as it did in the 1995–1996 Taiwan Straits crisis). Manila additionally contemplates the impact of US-China rivalry on its prospects for maintaining close economic and political ties with Beijing at a time when it is benefitting from Chinese economic largesse. One response in February 2020 was to doubt the value of Manila's Visiting Forces Agreement with the US administration, though the agreement has not been terminated.[19]

The Philippines is not alone in questioning the credibility of US security commitments. Similar sentiments are expressed in Japan, with the government constantly testing the degree of US support for a continuing forward presence in the country and willingness to make reference to Article 5 of their mutual defence treaty in the context of the dispute with China over the Senkaku/Diaoyu islands. The South Korean government was similarly disturbed by both Trump's courting of the North Korean leader, Kim Jung-Un, and his administration's calls to alter the financial terms of America's basing arrangements in the Republic of Korea. Against the background of increases in North Korean military provocations, and continuing uncertainty about its intentions, it took a new US administration before agreement on shared defence costs could be reached.[20]

On the China side, President Xi Jinping has been outspoken about China's regional and global ambitions deriving from the material success of China's politico-economic model. The reassurance policies of an earlier period have been overshadowed. Instead, Xi emphasises the country's commitment to the idea of the 'great revival,' 'renewal,' or 'rejuvenation' of the Chinese nation. As Xi told the 19th Party Congress, China 'has stood up, grown rich, and is becoming strong.' Arguing that China's path could serve as a successful model for other developing countries to follow, Xi stated during that speech that China could offer 'Chinese wisdom and a Chinese approach to solving the problems facing mankind.'[21]

Beijing favours the foundational norm of state sovereignty and non-interference in internal affairs as the path to maintaining a pluralist world order. However, where once its projection of a traditional notion of state sovereignty could be perceived as a protective shield for the region's weaker states – as well as for China itself – in some respects, the norm has been made into a weapon or source of threat. Beijing's determination to protect its designated 'core interests,' especially with regard to the sovereignty disputes in which it is engaged on sea and land, has been stated forthrightly on many occasions. As State Councillor Yang Jiechi put it in September 2013, for example: 'President Xi has stressed that while firmly committed to peaceful development, we definitely must not forsake our legitimate interests or compromise our core national interests.' He went on: 'No country should expect us to swallow the bitter fruit that undermines our sovereignty, security and development interests.'[22] It is this formulation that helps to explain China's intense efforts to delegitimise the judgement of the United Nations Convention on the Law of the Sea (UNCLOS) arbitral tribunal ruling given in July 2016 on the Philippines' claims in the South China Sea. There are few signs that the ruling has constrained Beijing's approach. In March 2020, for example, China stepped up action in the South China Sea, including intimidatory naval tactics, and the establishment of two new administrative districts in disputed waters. This raised concerns of a Chinese willingness to use the distractions of COVID-19 to push forward its claims in the area.[23]

Thus, as this sketch of the worldviews associated with both the United States and China suggests, there are sources of significant change leading regional governments to consider the best means of adjusting to transformations in the strategic reality. This sense of unease is compounded by other significant developments of the contemporary era, the first of which relates to the steep deterioration in China-US relations. Although this relationship began to decline before the advent of the Trump presidency, nevertheless it is clear that his administration accelerated the speed of that deterioration. Moreover, it is a condition unlikely to be alleviated anytime soon since there has developed a broad bipartisan consensus in Washington that China's rise needs to be confronted. Economic interdependence between the two economies is no longer working in the ways it once did and that derives mainly from the 'securitisation' of economic issues, especially in the United States.[24] This feature of the relationship has directly pitted a US desire to remain dominant rather than accept a more equal position between the two states, against Xi's more ambitious path for China.

The main issue in this area of China-US tension is development in technologies that have both high commercial and military value. Until approximately 2015, the economic-security nexus favoured greater rather than lesser economic interdependence between these two countries, based on the argument that the United States could remain ahead and US businesses and society would benefit from the two-way trade and investment. A significant change in perspective came with the growing perception that China might actually be moving faster than predicted, and probably through illicit means such as cyber-theft, the Chinese requirement that US firms hand over their intellectual property (IP), and failures of protection for IP in China because of weak IP laws. The result has been a growing sense in the United States that China's strengths in these new technologies, and determination to adopt a more forward role in global governance, will allow China to set global standards in these areas and constrain US strategic choices.

Beijing, on the other hand, is determined to develop a leading role in technological innovation and has put the funding behind it in an attempt to ensure that outcome. There is also the perception that an elevated role for the Party coats this determination to advance technologically with an ideological ambition. Xi is understood to have been changing the path of China's domestic economic reform: for example, disrupting the trend towards greater market reforms, putting the Party above the state, strengthening the role of State-Owned Enterprises in the economy, and pursuing 'Made in China 2025' – an industrial policy designed to enhance China's independent capacity to produce critical advanced technologies. This added prominence given to a Party-led state adds an ideological dimension to US-China rivalry, which had largely eroded in the earlier periods of this relationship after its normalisation. One major outcome has been contemplation by both parties of decoupling the two economies, though it is difficult to bring this into being. Another effect has been to raise the fears among regional states that they will become uncomfortably embroiled in the spillovers that come from these developments in the China-US relationship. These governments have additionally witnessed the extent to which the policies the two sides have adopted are contributing to a slowing of the regional and global economies, already hit by the health pandemic, thus undermining the strength of yet another of the region's foundational norms.

The advent of COVID-19 has further added to this decoupling fear and to the perception that the region is fragmenting. There is a growing perception that the global and regional production chains on which so much of the region's prosperity and relative tranquillity are perceived to have depended will inevitably transform. ASEAN, for example, dependent for its own manufacture on Chinese-made components and raw materials, has experienced disruptions in both demand and supply and is reconsidering its degree of dependence on China as a major source of components.

This health pandemic has also seriously intensified tensions between the United States and China. Washington has swiftly discovered its own over-dependence on China for many supplies vital to the control and mitigation of this highly infectious virus. In the US case, this has reinforced sentiment in favour of returning the manufacturing process onshore, or at least to diversify its supply chains in order to hedge against future supply shocks.[25]

Moreover, the health crisis, even more than the global financial crisis of 2008, has reinforced protectionist sentiment and scepticism of the benefits of globalisation in the United States as well as elsewhere in the region and beyond. Could it be that, in the longer term, investors base their investment decisions on the robustness of a country's public health infrastructure rather than direct manufacturing costs? If so, that will also change the direction of those global and regional supply chains that weather the storm. Instabilities in inter-state relations may soon follow. In particular, the argument that twenty-first-century forms of economic globalisation and regionalisation have been beneficial to ameliorating tensions in state-to-state relations may face far more significant tests as a result of these breakdowns in networked economic relationships. Moreover, the prospect of a global recession for the export-led open economies that exist throughout the Asia-Pacific is also a particular concern for governments that have sustained their legitimacy predominantly through the promise of growing prosperity.

Conclusion

In a number of respects, the Asia-Pacific region, when viewed in relative terms, has enjoyed an enviable period of advancement over the past four decades. Before the health pandemic, at least one billion of the region's citizens had been brought out of absolute poverty, and the region had not experienced major inter-state war. Remarkable, too, is that as China turned towards 'Reform and Opening' its past position in Maoist times as a disruptive, revolutionary force was seemingly forgotten as it took up its place in regional diplomacy and economic exchange.

However, as has been argued here, the conditions that have underpinned this period of relative peace and prosperity have undergone some considerable transformation. Notable among these changes has been that the redistribution of power in China's favour has been tied to the enactment of more ambitious foreign policies on the part of the Chinese leadership. This has come alongside an attendant weakening in US credibility as a dependable ally or partner for a number of the region's states, despite Biden era efforts to rebuild those ties. These developments have exposed the weaknesses inherent in the process-driven regional multilateral organisations that are unable as presently constituted to provide a security framework robust enough to weather the changes. Indeed, ASEAN states in particular are confronted with the requirement to search for highly creative ways in which to maintain enthusiasm for the maintenance of these organisations and for an influential role for ASEAN states within them.

The heightened tensions in the US-China relationship have also raised the prospects that states in the region may have to move away from their preferred, more flexible, hedging strategy with respect to these two powers and be forced to align more closely with one against the other. Intensified Sino-American rivalry has similarly reduced or removed the pacifying effects that economic interdependence has had in the past on that bilateral relationship and is spilling over to promote reconsideration of their joint participation in global production chains. The neat circularity, where ASEAN states once operated as the major suppliers of certain components to China, which then processed them into finished goods for onward sale in the developed West, is transforming. And reinforcing that is the anti-globalisation sentiment that has emerged from the rise of populism in the United States and elsewhere, further assisted from 2020 by the global health pandemic that these and other countries have been facing.

None of these negative developments are likely to decrease in intensity anytime soon. Geopolitical sentiment has cast a shadow over the integrative approaches that, if not unchallenged, at least were more prominent in earlier periods of the post-Cold War Asia-Pacific. Prime Minister Lee Hsien Loong in his speech at the opening of the Shangri-La Dialogue in 2019 summed up his sense of the times as follows:

> Our world is at a turning point. Globalisation is under siege. Tensions between the US and China are growing. Like everyone else, we in Singapore are anxious. We wonder what the future holds, and how countries can collectively find a way forward to maintain peace and prosperity in the world.[26]

Lee put his faith in several factors in order to try and stem 'growing hostility and instability.' However, there was little new in his formulation. Lee referenced the need for state agency and rationality and for the maintenance of multilateral institutions as part of the 'regional cooperative architecture,' including, in support of the inclusiveness norm, pressing China and a future US administration to join the Comprehensive and Progressive Agreement for Trans-Pacific Partnership (CPTPP). ASEAN member-states, he urged, needed to remain united. He expressed his 'hope' that Beijing and Washington would find a 'constructive way forward' that could somehow balance competition with cooperation. More quietly, and in support of the US deterrence function, the Singaporean government some months later renewed a key defence pact with the United States, extending US use of Singapore's air and naval bases for another 15 years.[27]

What is plain from this speech is the 'hope' among regional states that they will see a consistent and credible US effort to return to a role that more closely resembles what it has offered the region in the past. Chinese realisation that effective management of its region requires not dominance but the building of legitimate authority is additionally a strongly desired outcome.[28] As Lee also put it in his speech, if China were to resolve the South China Sea disputes in accordance with the UNCLOS ruling rather than through force or the threat of force, '[t]hen over time it will build its reputation as a benevolent power that need not be feared. Instead, China will be respected as a power that can be relied on to support a stable and peaceful region.'[29]

Both hoped for developments depend for their fruitful realisation on China's and America's willingness to reflect and build on the norms that have stood the region in good stead in the recent past. In the meantime, we should assume that states are anticipating something much less benign than this.

Acknowledgements

I am grateful to Felix Heiduk for very helpful comments on an earlier draft of this chapter, together with the comments and questions raised by participants at the Berlin Conference on Asian Security held in November 2019 at the *Stiftung Wissenschaft und Politik*. My grateful thanks, too, to Dr. Amy King for giving her permission to draw on our joint article published in the *China International Strategy Review* in 2019.

Notes

1 'Relatively' peaceful as Alex J. Bellamy once aptly put it, compared with "both its own history and to other regions of the world." See *East Asia's Other Miracle*, Oxford University Press, Oxford, 2017, p. 1, note 1. The year 1979 is chosen as the benchmark because the Sino-Vietnamese war, involving disputed but high numbers of casualties, probably in their tens of thousands, occurred that year.
2 Serious forms of abuse have occurred in a range of states: for example, the Tiananmen crackdown in China in 1989, and the mass incarceration of Muslim Uighurs in the contemporary era; the bloodshed associated with Indonesia's occupation of East Timor until the territory's move towards full independence in 2002; the formal accusations of genocide perpetrated by the government of Myanmar against the Rohingya minority Muslim population; and the official finding that North Korea's security forces have committed "unparalleled" and "widespread, systematic abuses" of the human rights of its citizens, to name but five among a number of such instances.
3 Amitav Acharya, "Power Shift or Paradigm Shift: China's Rise and Asia's Security Order," *International Studies Quarterly*, 58(1), 2014, pp. 158–173.
4 See in particular, Muthiah Alagappa (ed.), *Asian Security Order: Instrumental and Normative Features*, Stanford University Press, Stanford, CA, 2003; and more recently, Bellamy's *East Asia's Other Miracle*.
5 Alagappa, "Managing Asian Security: Competition, Cooperation, and Evolutionary Change," in Alagappa (ed.), *Asian Security Order*, pp. 571–606.
6 Rosemary Foot, "Social Boundaries in Flux: Secondary Regional Organizations as a Reflection of Regional International Society," in Barry Buzan and Yongjin Zhang (eds.), *Contesting International Society in East Asia*, Cambridge University Press, Cambridge, UK, 2014, pp. 188–206; Jürgen Haacke, "The ASEAN Regional Forum: From Dialogue to Practical Security Cooperation?" *Cambridge Review of International Affairs*, 22(3), 2009, pp. 427–449.

7. Etel Solingen, "Pax Asiatica versus Belli Levantina: The Foundations of War and Peace in East Asia and the Middle East," *American Political Science Review*, 101(4), 2007. See also Rosemary Foot and Evelyn Goh, "The International Relations of East Asia: A New Research Prospectus," *International Studies Review*, 21(3), 2019, pp. 398–423.
8. John Ravenhill, "Production Networks in Asia," in Saadia M. Pekkanen, John Ravenhill, and Rosemary Foot (eds.), *The Oxford Handbook of the International Relations of Asia*, Oxford University Press, New York, 2014, pp. 348–368. See also Ravenhill's "Economics and Security in the Asia-Pacific Region," *The Pacific Review*, 26(1), 2013. For a more general treatment of this argument, see Stephen Brooks, *Producing Security: Multinational Corporations, Globalization, and the Changing Calculus of Combat*, Princeton University Press, Princeton, NJ, 2005.
9. This phrase in its most extended form is usually translated to mean that the Chinese government should "bide its time, hide its brightness, not seek leadership, but accomplish some things."
10. "Understanding the US-China Trade Relationship," The US-China Business Council, January 10, 2017, at www.uschina.org/sites/default/files/OE%20US%20Jobs%20and%20China%20Trade%20Report.pdf. (Accessed April 14, 2020).
11. See for example the Obama-Xi statement in Washington, September 2015, for an outline of areas of agreement, at https://obamawhitehouse.archives.gov/the-press-office/2015/09/25/fact-sheet-president-xi-jinpings-state-visit-united-states. (Accessed April 14, 2020).
12. Ideas such as these are discussed in Rosemary Foot and Evelyn Goh, no. 7.
13. Eric Heginbotham and Richard J. Samuels, "Active Denial: Redesigning Japan's Response to China's Military Challenge," *International Security*, 42(4), 2018, pp. 128–169, at p. 132.
14. Linda Jakobson and Rory Medcalf, "The Perception Gap: Reading China's Maritime Strategic Objectives in Indo-Pacific Asia," Lowy Institute Report, Sydney, 2015, p. 9.
15. Eric Heginbotham and Richard J. Samuels, no. 13, pp. 133–134.
16. The importance of reliability in allied relations is discussed in Iain D. Henry, "What Allies Want: Reconsidering Loyalty, Reliability, and Alliance Interdependence," *International Security*, 44(2), 2020, pp. 45–83.
17. Jonathan Stromseth, "Don't Make Us Choose: Southeast Asia in the Throes of US-China Rivalry," Brookings Institution, Washington, D.C., Report, October 2019.
18. President Donald Trump, Remarks to the 72nd Session of the United Nations General Assembly, September 19, 2017, at www.whitehouse.gov/briefings-statements/remarks-president-trump-72nd-session-united-nations-general-assembly/. (Accessed May 5, 2020).
19. Aileen S. P. Baviera, "Is the Philippines Moving to Active Middle Power Diplomacy?," East Asia Forum, March 27, 2020, at www.eastasiaforum.org/2020/03/27/is-the-philippines-moving-to-active-middle-power-diplomacy/. (Accessed April 13, 2020).
20. Paul Haenle, "Security Concerns in Asia-Pacific Escalate Amid Coronavirus Scramble," Carnegie Endowment for International Peace, April 29, 2020, at https://carnegieendowment.org/2020/04/29/security-concerns-in-asia-pacific-escalate-amid-coronavirus-scramble-pub-81685. (Accessed May 5, 2020).
21. Xi Jinping, "Secure a Decisive Victory in Building a Moderately Prosperous Society in All Respects and Strive for the Great Success of Socialism with Chinese Characteristics for a New Era," Speech delivered at the 19th National Congress of the Communist Party of China, October 18, 2017, at www.xinhuanet.com/english/download/Xi_Jinping's_report_at_19th_CPC_National_Congress.pdf. (Accessed November 17, 2018).
22. Yang Jiechi, "Implementing the Chinese Dream," *The National Interest*, September 10, 2013, at http://nationalinterest.org/commentary/implementing-the-chinese-dream-9026/. (Accessed August 14, 2018).
23. Paul Haenle, no. 20.

24 Rosemary Foot and Amy King, "Assessing the Deterioration in China-US Relations: US Governmental Perspectives on the Economic-Security Nexus," *China International Strategy Review*, 1(1), June 2019, pp. 39–50.
25 A useful commentary on these types of issues is contained in the CIMB ASEAN Research Institute (CARI) report, "How COVID-19 Will Transform Global Supply Chains and How ASEAN Must Respond," April 11, 2020, at www.cariasean.org/news/how-covid-19-will-transform-global-supply-chains-and-how-asean-must-respond/#.XpRRiS-ZO7A. (Accessed April 13, 2020).
26 "PM Lee Hsien Loong's Speech at the 2019 Shangri-La Dialogue," May 31, 2019, at www.channelnewsasia.com/news/singapore/lee-hsien-loong-speech-2019-shangri-la-dialogue-11585954. (Accessed May 6, 2020).
27 "PM Lee, Trump Renew Key Defence Pact on US Use of Singapore Air, Naval Bases," *Straits Times*, September 24, 2019, at www.straitstimes.com/world/pm-lee-trump-renew-key-defence-pact-on-us-use-of-singapore-air-naval-bases. (Accessed September 30, 2019).
28 Rosemary Foot, "China's Rise and US Hegemony: Renegotiating Hegemonic Order in East Asia?," *International Politics*, 57(2), 2020, pp. 150–165. Published online at https://doi.org/10.1057/s41311-019-00189-5.
29 "Lee's speech at the 2019 Shangri-La Dialogue," no. 26.

3 Many players, many layers
The Indo-Pacific long game

Rory Medcalf

Introduction

Any 21st-century analysis of the strategic dynamics of Asia needs to come to terms with the concept of the Indo-Pacific.[1] The deployment of the term Indo-Pacific, increasingly frequent in recent years, is no mere wordplay, ideological shibboleth or passing fashion. It has been taken to have many meanings – reflected, for instance, in the different definitions accorded to it by various nations' diplomacy, a point explored in this chapter. However, there are patterns to its usage that have implications for the vital contemporary challenge of regional and global power relations. Far from being an obscure account of words and maps, the narrative of the Indo-Pacific helps nations face one of the great international dilemmas of the 21st century: how can other countries respond to a strong and often coercive China without resorting to capitulation or conflict?

At a descriptive level, the Indo-Pacific has validity as a neutral name for a new and expansive map centred on maritime Asia. This conveys that the Pacific and Indian Oceans are connecting through trade, infrastructure and diplomacy, in an era when the world's two most populous states, China and India, are both rising powers. Their economies, along with many others, rely on the sea lanes of the Indian Ocean to ship oil from the Middle East and Africa, and myriad other cargoes in both directions, along the world's vital commercial artery.

However, the Indo-Pacific is also about drawing strength from vast space and from solidarity amongst its many and diverse nations. The term recognises that both economic ties and strategic competition now encompass an expansive two-ocean region, due in large part to China's ascent, and that other countries must protect their interests through new partnerships across the blurring of old geographic boundaries. The Indo-Pacific concept recognises that multipolarity is part of the character of this emerging regional order and offers part of the answer to its looming strategic challenges around managing China power.

What's in a name?

Some see the Indo-Pacific as code for geopolitical agendas: America's bid to thwart China, India's play for greatness, Japan's plan to regain influence,

Indonesia's search for leverage, Australia's alliance-building and Europe's excuse to gatecrash the Asian century. Certainly, China feels risk and discomfort in the term. It hears Indo-Pacific as the rationale for, amongst other things, a strategy to contain its power through a 'quadrilateral' alliance of democracies – the United States, Japan, India and Australia. Chinese Foreign Minister Wang Yi has called the Indo-Pacific an 'attention-grabbing idea' that 'will dissipate like ocean foam'.[2] Chinese diplomats continue to attempt to have the term excised from multilateral diplomatic communiqués, for instance, (without success) at the 2020 East Asia Summit.[3] Yet what most makes the Indo-Pacific real is China's own behaviour – its expanding economic, political and military presence in the Indian Ocean, South Asia, the South Pacific, Africa and beyond. This pan-regional assertiveness in Chinese diplomacy, and the coalitions of resistance it engenders, has continued throughout 2020, confirming that even the discontinuity of COVID-19 has not stopped the Indo-Pacific trend of the times.

In statecraft, mental maps matter.[4] Relations between states, competition or cooperation, involve a landscape of the mind. This defines each country's natural 'region' – what is on the map, what is off the map, and why. What a nation imagines on the map is a marker of what that nation considers important. This in turn shapes the decisions of leaders, the destiny of nations and strategy itself. How leaders define regions can affect their allocation of resources and attention; the ranking of friends and foes; who is invited and who is overlooked at the top tables of diplomacy; and what gets talked about, what gets done and what gets forgotten. A sense of shared geography or 'regionalism' can shape international cooperation and institutions, privileging some nations and diminishing others. For instance, the late 20th-century notion of the Asia-Pacific and an East Asian hemisphere excluded India at the very time Asia's second most populous country was opening up and looking east.

Nations choose maps that help them simplify things, make sense of a complex reality and, above all, serve their interests at a given time. For the moment, a Chinese description of much of the world as simply 'the Belt and Road' has become common parlance, though the meaning and purpose of this term is changeable, opaque and entwined with China's interests. For a long time, people have been accustomed to labels such as the Asia-Pacific, East Asia, South Asia and Southeast Asia, Europe, the North Atlantic, Eurasia and so on. Of an earlier set of politically loaded labels for Asia, the Far East and Near East are less recognised today, but the Middle East has endured.

These are all geographic constructs – invented terms that powerful states have at some time consecrated, with a self-centred political purpose.[5] Even Asia is not originally an Asian framework, but a term Europeans concocted and adjusted for their own reasons. Its imagined boundaries keep shifting. Asia began in ancient times as an Athenian label for everything east of Greece. In the 1820s, only half in jest, Austrian imperial statesman Metternich put the Europe-Asia boundary somewhere between Vienna and Budapest. In 2014, China hosted a conference that called for Asians alone to determine Asia's future, but with an interesting catch: its member-states included the likes of Russia and Egypt, friends of China that are not categorically Asian, yet not Indonesia and Japan, unquestionably Asian countries but also powers that could make life difficult for China in the future.[6]

Like previous mental maps, the Indo-Pacific is in some ways artificial and contingent. But it suits the times: a 21st century of maritime connectivity and multipolar geopolitics. Today, we are seeing a contest of ideas in the mental maps of Asia being simplified down to the big two: China's Belt and Road versus the Indo-Pacific, championed in various forms by countries such as Japan, India, Australia, Indonesia, France and the United States. In 2020, additional nations such as Germany, the Netherlands and the Republic of Korea became increasingly comfortable with using Indo-Pacific terminology to define their regional engagement.[7] Many nations are seeking to understand both concepts and identify how they can leverage, adjust, resist or evade them. The term Indo-Pacific has thus become code for certain decisions of consequence. In part, it is a message to a rising China that it cannot expect others to accept its self-image as the centre of the region and the world. It is also a signal that China and America are not the only two nations that count. Indeed, the diplomatic decision of accepting and using the term Indo-Pacific is not so much a signal of automatic resistance to Chinese policy positions as one of agency and solidarity among middle powers, willing to assert their own interests over the long term.

Beyond binary choices

Of course, simple binary choices are a tempting way to make sense of some of the more mind-numbing headline statistics about the sheer size of the Chinese and American economies. It is illuminating to play with some other numbers – statistics that embed the two leading powers in a system of many substantial nations, the Indo-Pacific. This complex reality includes many 'middle players': significant countries that are neither China nor the United States. Working together, the region's middle players can affect the balance of power, even assuming a diminished role for America.

Consider, for instance, the possibility of a different quadrilateral: Japan, India, Indonesia and Australia. All four have serious differences with China and reasonable (and generally growing) convergences with each other when it comes to their national security. They happen to be champions of an emerging Indo-Pacific worldview. And they are hardly passive or lightweight nations. In 2018, the four had a combined population of 1.75 billion, a combined gross domestic product (GDP) (measured by purchasing power parity or PPP terms) of US$21 trillion and combined defence expenditure of US$147 billion. By contrast, the United States has a population of 327.4 million, a GDP of US$20.49 trillion and defence spending of US$649 billion. For its part, China's population is 1.39 billion, its economy US$25 trillion and its defence budget US$250 billion.[8] (This assumes, of course, that official Chinese statistics about economic growth and population size are not inflated, and there is reason for doubt.[9]) Of course, these numbers and relativities will have been affected by the economic shock of COVID-19, from which, at least initially, China is recovering more quickly than other major economies.

Even so, the following long-term projections remain illustrative of the reality that Chinese power will remain relative and not absolute. Project the numbers forward a generation, to mid-century, and the picture of middle players as potent balancers becomes quite stark. In 2050, the four middle players are expected to have a combined population of 2.108 billion and a combined GDP (PPP) of an astounding $63.97 trillion. By then, America is estimated to have 379 million people and a GDP (PPP) of $34 trillion. China will have 1.402 billion people and a GDP of $58.45 trillion. Even just the big three of these Indo-Pacific partners – India, Japan and Indonesia – would together eclipse China in population and exceed it economically. By then, their combined defence budgets could also be larger than those of the mighty People's Liberation Army. Include one or more other rising regional powers with their own China frictions, such as a Vietnam that may have about 120 million people and a top 20 global economy, and the numbers are stronger still. Even the combination of just two or three of these countries would give China pause. And all of this, for the sake of the argument, excludes any strategic role whatsoever for the United States west of Hawaii, even the prospect of complete US withdrawal from the region remains remote. If added to the enduring heft of the United States, the alignment of just a few middle players would outweigh the Chinese giant.

Of course, at one level, this is all mere speculative extrapolation (albeit from existing numbers and assumed trends). But so is the widely propagated assertion that this unfolding century belongs to Beijing, that Chinese dominance is somehow inevitable. It is one thing to say that various coalitions of Indo-Pacific powers could balance China, provided they all stick together. In reality, it would require breakthroughs in leadership, far-sightedness and diplomacy for coalitions to harden into anything like formal alliances: arrangements that require mutual obligation among parties, underpinned by a willingness to take risks for one another. Moreover, it is difficult to see how loosely arrayed democracies can match authoritarian China's ability to mobilise its national resources. Still, the Indo-Pacific is at the early stages of a long game, in which there will be many plausible combinations of nations that, in the right circumstances, could find their own kind of strength in numbers.[10]

There may be subtle differences in what each country means by the Indo-Pacific label, but for nations like Australia, Japan, India and Indonesia, the Indo-Pacific is a way to navigate turbulence in Asian power politics in which Xi Jinping's China is disruptive, Donald Trump's America has been dysfunctional, and other countries are desperate to preserve what they can of peace, prosperity and sovereignty. The Indo-Pacific does this by breaking through the late 20th-century mental boundary that separated the Pacific and Indian Oceans, ossified into the once-useful but now outmoded idea of the Asia-Pacific. Of course, the term Asia-Pacific remains more recognisable and remains valid in some contexts, such as describing trans-Pacific economic relations. To accept the Indo-Pacific as a valid framework is not to completely dismiss the Asia-Pacific, but rather to recognise that any international 'region' is constructed to represent shifting realities and diplomatic priorities.

In recent years, a diplomatic domino effect has taken hold, with many governments suddenly referring to the Indo-Pacific, even while China warned them away from such language. Indian Prime Minister Modi made it the animating theme of his keynote speech at an Asia security summit in Singapore in 2018.[11] In June 2019, the entire ten countries of the Association of Southeast Asian Nations (ASEAN) agreed to an Indo-Pacific outlook on their relations with an enlarged region.[12] This confirms the Indo-Pacific is not an idea alien to Asia: indeed, it gives the middle players of ASEAN more centrality than they had in the past Asia-Pacific era, or than they would have in a world defined only by Beijing's Belt and Road.

Significantly, the Indo-Pacific is not simply an American concept or the preserve of US allies like Australia and Japan, even though those three countries have been early champions of the term. (Indeed, Australia was the first country to formally introduce the Indo-Pacific as a basis for policy, in its 2013 Defence White Paper.) Traditionally non-aligned and unquestionably Asian powers like India and Indonesia have wholeheartedly incorporated the Indo-Pacific into their foreign policy outlooks. It is easy enough to point out that the different national definitions of the Indo-Pacific do not perfectly align (for example, Japan and America, unlike others have insisted on defining their strategy as a 'Free and Open Indo-Pacific'). However, notable commonalities among all the Indo-Pacific visions include their emphasis on rules, non-coercion and respect for the interests of small and middle powers.[13]

For their part, smaller countries tend to have a mixed reaction. While the Indo-Pacific can be useful as a diplomatic rallying call for the sovereignty and solidarity of nations of any size, the smaller players in the region, from Southeast Asia to the island states of the two oceans, tend to shy away from using any one regional term exclusively. This partly reflects their understandable hedging inclinations, as well as their typically localised focus on the issues that matter to them. For instance, Pacific island countries focus on the Pacific, Indian Ocean states on the Indian Ocean, and ASEAN states on Southeast Asia, even if accepting that all of these are now subregions of a greater Indo-Pacific system.

Game of many

In the contemporary Indo-Pacific moment, nations are interacting in a great game with multiple participants and dimensions. China's expanding economic, military and diplomatic activity in the Indian Ocean marks an emerging Indo-Pacific strategic system, where the actions and interests of one powerful state in one part of the region affect the interests and actions of others. The Indo-Pacific power narrative intersects the interests of at least four major countries – China, India, Japan and the United States – as well as many other players, including Australia, Indonesia and the other Southeast Asian nations, South Korea and more distant stakeholders, not least in Europe. Russia, too, is making its presence felt. The Indo-Pacific is a multipolar system, in which the fate of regional order, or disorder, will not be determined by one or even two powers – the United States and China – but by the interests and agency of many.

The power contest in the region has often been likened to the Great Game between imperial Britain and Russia in the 19th century. This time, though, there are more than two players. Academic theories and games of strategy help explain how nations interact when interests differ. But what if each is playing a different game? And if there is cooperation alongside competition? After all, there may be very different drivers – combinations of interests, values and identity – behind each state's actions in the region. Beyond narrow ideas about defence and security, these may involve nationalism, history, political legitimacy and, of course, economics, including the quest for resources and sustainability in a threatened natural environment.

For China, in particular, there is a troubling thread between the domestic and the international. For Xi Jinping and the Communist Party to maintain their grip on total power, they have found it necessary to raise the Chinese people's expectations that their nation will be great abroad and will successfully handle any resistance. Yet China's expansive policies mean that its problems overseas are accumulating, and the chances of a major misstep are thus increasing. In turn, this puts Xi and the Communist Party at particular risk, because China alone, amongst the great powers, has staked much of the legitimacy of its entire political system on success abroad. When things go wrong, the whole Chinese system could suffer grievously – especially if crises of security, politics and economics intersect in ways hard to predict and impossible to manage.

Interaction between states occurs across many dimensions. Compounding the complexity of a multipolar region, a game with many players, is the reality that this is also a puzzle with many layers. Four stand out: economics (perhaps better termed geo-economics), military force, diplomacy and a clash of national narratives. These blend in patterns of comprehensive competition – combined with elements of cooperation – that will shape the future.

Economics, especially demand for energy, propelled the rise of the modern Indo-Pacific. China, Japan, South Korea, Taiwan, Southeast Asia, Australia and India all depend acutely on the Indian Ocean sea lanes for energy and thus prosperity and security. Seaborne commerce is likewise making this maritime highway – carrying at least two-thirds of the world's oil and a third of the world's bulk cargo – the centre of gravity for the global economy. There are uncertainties about whether international supply and manufacturing chains will extend to South Asia, or remain more Asia-Pacific in character, or tangle and snap in new ways with trends in automation and 'on-shoring' and the prospect of a disruptive 'decoupling' of industrial interdependence between America and China.

There is also a race of connectivity. China and others are competing to build ports, road, rail, electricity and communications infrastructure to bind Asia and connect it with Africa, Europe and the Pacific. This extends to small island states. Globally, meanwhile, the contest is on for the commanding heights of technology: artificial intelligence, quantum computing and 5G telecommunications. Contrary to turn-of-the-century dreams of globalisation, economic interdependence is no longer just about breaking down borders and letting all states rise together: it has become a tool of power and influence, captured in the newly popular catch-all of 'geo-economics'.[14] This represents competition by states for power advantages through economics rather than military force.[15] In 2020, the geo-economic competition has blended with the struggle for influence within diplomatic institutions, through the difficult issue of vaccine diplomacy and COVID-19 recovery. It is not surprising that China has focused on reaching a vaccine deal with Indonesia, the geographically and diplomatically pivotal state in the core Indo-Pacific zone of maritime Southeast Asia. Meanwhile, the Quadrilateral dialogue of India, Japan, Australia and the United States has occasionally expanded to include fellow democracies South Korea, Vietnam and New Zealand on issues of pandemic management and economic recovery.

China's Belt and Road spree of loans and infrastructure has become a geo-economic powerplay, a strategy for pre-eminence.[16] The 'Road' is the Indo-Pacific with Chinese characteristics, a bid to extend influence into the Indian Ocean and the South Pacific. The 'Belt' of overland connectivity through Eurasia is of secondary importance, given that transport of bulk goods and energy by sea will remain cheaper and arguably not riskier – albeit slower – than by land. China needs sea transportation for 90 per cent or more of its imported oil, iron ore, copper and coal.[17] The strategic impacts of the Belt and Road warrant close attention, including a new colonialism – accidental or deliberate – in which Chinese coercion, political influence and security presence become a consequence of connectivity. This does not mean that all such activity began as a grand strategy or – faced with complex local politics – that it will necessarily succeed. For instance, geographically pivotal places like Sri Lanka and Malaysia remain in play.[18]

As with the European empires of old, it is clear that the flag follows trade and that security shadows economics, along with risks of conflict. The Indo-Pacific has a starkly military dimension. A pivotal moment has been China's turn to the sea. Its navy is expanding rapidly, in line with a 2015 proclamation by President, Communist Party General Secretary, military chief and core leader Xi Jinping, that the 'traditional mentality that land outweighs sea must be abandoned' when it comes to protecting China's interests. Instead, the new Chinese strategy is about 'offshore waters defence' and 'open-seas protection': euphemisms for deploying force in distant waters.[19] A massive shipbuilding programme has been underway for years. Aircraft carriers are being commissioned, not primarily to patrol China's proximate waters or even the South China Sea, but to show force on the open ocean. The People's Liberation Army Navy (PLAN) showed up in the Indian Ocean with three warships to counter Somali piracy at the start of 2009 and has never left. For the first time since the voyages of Admiral Zheng He in the 1400s, China is an Indian Ocean power. This time, instead of sailing ships, it has destroyers, marines and submarines. These conduct exercises peaceful and warlike, backed by partnerships, port access rights and the Chinese military's first overseas base. This time China plans to stay.

China is not alone. It has far-flung interests to protect and is hardly the only external power to fly the flag in Indian Ocean waters. The United States has long operated there, including at its base on the contentious UK possession of Diego Garcia. Japan opened a base at Djibouti before China did. European powers have been forth and back and forth again since the days of Vasco da Gama. This century, almost every ocean-going navy, from Russia to Singapore, has sent forces to protect commerce from Somali-based pirates, a rationale for China's mission. The world's navies are converging not only west of the Malacca Strait. Indian, American and Japanese warships practise together from the Bay of Bengal to the Western Pacific. Almost every major navy joins Australia to train in waters north of Darwin. As China militarises artificial islands in the South China Sea, fleets both commercial and military from across the globe exercise their international legal rights by traversing this shared highway at the heart of the Indo-Pacific.

Militaries are modernising and deploying across the region. The trend is towards 'power projection': a capacity to fight far away, across the seas. Nearly all the region's powers are arming and making ready, but for what? Is it mainly about cooperation, on shared concerns like terrorism, piracy, illegal fishing, disaster relief in an age of climate change, search and rescue, peacekeeping, stabilisation of fragile states, evacuations of citizens from trouble spots? Is it to police the sea lanes, protect shipments of energy and commerce, and uphold international law? Or, to deter, coerce, resist and, if need be, fight other nations in new wars, cold or hot? Underlying the military build-up is a gathering atmosphere of suspicion. No nation may plan outright aggression, but intentions are opaque. China does not take America at its word – and America, Japan, India, Australia and Vietnam, amongst others, are deeply wary of China's.

All this armed mistrust would seem an urgent call for greater attention to diplomacy, rules and respect in keeping the peace. The architecture of peace in the Indo-Pacific is woefully flimsy and doubles as another arena for nations to compete for influence. The region's multilateral diplomacy sometimes appears to be little more than an acrimony of acronyms, doing little in a practical sense to build cooperation or reduce risks of conflict. The so-called confidence-building measures are in short supply and little honoured.

Much of the real action is behind the scenes, with China, the United States and others competing to shape agendas. The regular diplomacy in the region remains bilateral: nations dealing with others one on one. This favours the strong. But another trend is about safety in numbers. That brings us back to middle players like Australia, India, Japan and Indonesia, building diplomatic ballast by strengthening their bonds with each other. A new diplomacy, minilateralism, is gaining ground, where small groups of three or more countries form flexible coalitions based on shared interests, values, capability and willingness to get things done. The most controversial is the Quadrilateral dialogue of the United States, Japan, India and Australia, which China sees as an embryonic alliance to counter its rise. This is now resuming a tangible military dimension, with the return of Australia to the Indian-led Malabar naval exercise – effectively now a Quad activity – for the first time since 2007. With less fanfare and more impact, a web of three-sided coalitions is arising: US-India-Japan, India-Japan-Australia, Australia-India-Indonesia; even a so-called 'Indo-Pacific axis' of Australia, India and France, which in 2020 convened for the first time at ministerial level, albeit virtually.

Managing mistrust

Critical questions remain. Can some patchwork of diplomatic arrangements truly keep the peace? Will new partners stand by each other if one finds itself in confrontation with China? And how much difference can middle powers really make when vital interests are at stake?

The answer is partly about perception, for there is another level of contestation abroad – a struggle to shape perceptions and, therefore, reality. Between Beijing and Washington, the many players in the middle are watching each other's responses to Chinese strength and assertiveness. The Indo-Pacific power competition includes efforts to shape attitudes and narratives among populations and decision makers: a classic way to win without fighting. There is now a perpetual fight around perceptions and propaganda, a battle of the narratives. Warnings of 'political warfare' are sounded.[20] The reinvention of law or 'lawfare' plays its part. So does the reinvention of history. Just as the world is now fixated on the dangers of 'fake news', there are subtler risks from 'fake olds' – history fabricated to privilege one nation's interests over others.

China is combining the 'soft power' of persuasion with the 'sharp power' of internal political interference, to neutralise opposition and reconfigure the Indo-Pacific game board, from Australia to Sri Lanka, Pakistan to the Pacific island states.[21] The narrative battle is no longer all going China's way. But there are risks in how America and others respond. Too blunt a pushback can be self-defeating, as one American official discovered when she likened competition with China to a 'clash of civilisations' in disturbingly cultural, even racial, terms. The reality is more like a clash of political systems, where Washington needs to maintain a diverse set of friends, not alienate them.[22]

Other countries are joining the 'soft power' race, with some like Japan, the United States and Australia promoting their own versions of the Indo-Pacific as an alternative to the Belt and Road. Universities, think-tanks and media organisations can no longer imagine themselves detached observers and interpreters. Along with digital technologies, they have rapidly become part of the story: both terrain and instruments of strategic competition. Concerns about foreign interference, propaganda and espionage have resurfaced in new forms and no longer sound like warmed-up Cold War paranoia. In recent years, a reality check on Chinese Communist Party influence in Australia, combined with revelations of Russian and Chinese activity in the United States, has set the tone for the wider global and regional debate. Future strategic competition in the Indo-Pacific will not be confined to seas and contested international boundaries, but will play out also on the home front.

What, then, do the past and present tell us about the risks and opportunities ahead? To understand plausible futures for the Indo-Pacific, it is necessary to consider the choices nations can make, revolving around the question of how to manage coercion without it ending in conflict or capitulation. Relations between nations are a continuum from cooperation at one end, through degrees of coexistence, competition and confrontation, all the way to conflict, including outright war. Presently, the Indo-Pacific dynamic is somewhere at the competition point on the spectrum, with rising risks of confrontation or conflict.

China and the United States have entered a state of comprehensive struggle, amounting to full-spectrum rivalry. The situation could deteriorate further still, whether through miscalculation or coercion. There have long been four well-known flashpoints in East Asia: Taiwan, the South China Sea, the East China Sea and the Korean Peninsula.[23] But beyond these, there are now signs that conflict is increasingly conceivable in the wider Indo-Pacific. America is only one of China's potential adversaries: China-India and China-Japan relations will remain fraught and fragile. In 2020, the violent border clash at Galwan in the disputed Himalayan frontier was a reminder that war between China and India is a plausible future for the Indo-Pacific, with potentially global ramifications. The flashpoints may not all be geographic, but could involve interventions in the information realm, such as cyber intrusions or disputes over freedom of expression. A conflict that begins in East Asia could escalate across the region, for instance, through distant naval blockades, cyber-attacks, economic sabotage, the disabling of nations' critical infrastructure and the pre-emptive destruction of communications networks, including in space. Future US-China crises could play out in the Indian Ocean and the South Pacific.

The outcome of even a limited conflict in the Indo-Pacific is impossible to predict. Reasons include new technologies, economic connectedness, mutual vulnerability and random factors of decision and surprise. Ultimately, the catastrophic risks from nuclear weapons – right up to their actual use – cannot be discounted. But even if conflict ceased at a lower threshold, damage could be severe, including to the stability of states and the foundations of global prosperity and order. Fortunately, no state in the Indo-Pacific seeks war, and most tensions can be managed by other means. But fully fledged cooperation and conflict resolution are impossible under conditions of mistrust.

What can be done? It is difficult to imagine the region's powers accepting new diplomatic institutions and treaties or a meaningful role for the United Nations in addressing their differences. Coexistence is the most reasonable expectation and is an essential starting point for any loftier ambitions of cooperation. But it may take an international near-death experience – the 21st-century Indo-Pacific equivalent of the Cuban missile crisis – to compel governments to get serious about the risk-reduction measures needed to keep the peace. Such a crisis could finally spook nations into making proper use of the existing but under-appreciated 'architecture' of rules and communication channels. Such crisis-management hotlines, along with arms control agreements and diplomatic summits, were used better in the Cold War because the gravity of the stakes was so clear. Scope also remains for today's Indo-Pacific governments to get much more serious about leveraging cooperation against common threats – like climate change, natural disasters, resource depletion, transnational crime, piracy and terrorism. This in turn could improve coordination and transparency in managing strategic mistrust.

In all this, where to begin? And in a complex diplomatic impasse, how is it possible to choreograph compromise? Most governments now understand that they are struggling with a new regional security landscape – the Indo-Pacific – but lack a plan joining up the parts of the puzzle: geo-economics, security, diplomacy and the domestic stage. The race is on for each nation to craft a comprehensive strategy. Progress is uneven. China's Belt and Road is the most advanced. Japan and the United States have their versions of a 'Free and Open Indo-Pacific'. India, Australia and Indonesia are working on their own pragmatic Indo-Pacific blueprints. Australia's 2017 foreign policy white paper, in particular, sketches the contours of a strategy for the emerging era, proposing a whole-of-nation response to regional uncertainty.[24]

In this multipolar age, nations will not succeed in securing their interests if they pursue strategies in isolation. This includes the strongest powers, the United States and China. The region is too vast and complex for any country to protect its interests alone. There will be a premium on partnerships. An understanding of the special nature of the Indo-Pacific region – including its scale and diversity – helps identify the elements of a strategy for navigating likely decades of friction. These include a calibrated mix of diplomacy, development and deterrence, including contingency planning.

There is a need for sustained activism and solidarity among middle players like Australia, India, Japan, Indonesia, and their partners in Southeast Asia and Europe, to show the way for an American strategy that is competitive but not confrontational, confident but not complacent. In dealing with Chinese power, old notions of 'accommodation' and 'containment' need to be discarded in favour of 'incorporation' or 'conditional engagement'. This would be about involving China as a legitimate great power based on mutual adjustment and mutual respect. There is nothing intrinsic about the Indo-Pacific idea that it should exclude China or, to use an outdated and misused Cold War term, 'contain' it. China is, by definition, a major player in such a region, and recognising this means acknowledging, for instance, its right to play a security role in the Indian Ocean.

It is true that the Indo-Pacific idea dilutes and absorbs Chinese influence. That is part of the point. Yet, this is not about shutting China out of its own extended region, but rather incorporating it in one that is large and multipolar. Others need to adjust to China, and China needs to adjust to them, especially Asia's large middle players. Of course, China has a major and rightful place, a status that is respected and prominent – just not dominant. A 'sphere of influence' approach, in which China is allowed to control East Asia while India in turn is allowed to dominate the Indian Ocean, will simply not work: China's seaborne oil dependence and the security, economic and diaspora footprint of its Belt and Road make it too late for that. At the same time, given China's great strategic weight and temptations towards hegemony, the Indo-Pacific idea is empowering for other countries, encouraging them to build new and defensive partnerships across outdated geographic boundaries.

However, such moderation of Chinese power will likely fail if middle powers do not seek solidarity but instead are cowed by the observation that there is little each can do to influence China on its own. Much will depend on how nations choose to use the current window of pan-regional awareness. For example, strategic solidarity and alliances have traditionally applied only to situations of armed conflict. What if Indo-Pacific principles such as respect for rules and sovereignty began to translate into new forms of collective and non-military resistance to maritime bullying, economic coercion or misinformation and interference activities through cyber means? Or, if new international standards were developed to limit the misuse of such connectivity for hostile purposes? These new notions of building common cause among middle powers have increasingly informed the agendas of self-selecting 'minilateral' organisations in recent years, not only in the Indo-Pacific but at a global level arrangements such as the 'Anglosphere' intelligence partnership known as the Five Eyes and a proposed 'D-10' of democracies.

Whatever happens, nations need to build their resilience and harness all elements of their power for a long phase of contestation. This requires not only attention to defence and diplomacy but also bridging policy divides between economics and security. Governments will have to become more direct with civil society and business interests about what is at stake: the fact that no nation can hide from the world, that international tensions cannot be wished away and will touch everyday life.

A course can be charted between naivety and fatalism. There is no guarantee this will work. Still, the very nature of the Indo-Pacific – its connected vastness, its multipolarity as a game with many players – is part of the answer. This is a region too big and diverse for hegemony. It is made for multipolarity and creative new partnerships across collapsed boundaries. What remains to be seen is how effectively and substantially those partnerships can develop, for instance, whether they will simply involve dialogue and informal policy coordination or more tangible mechanisms for alignment, such as formal agreements, intelligence sharing, multi-nation military exercises and supporting secretariats. Nonetheless, criticism of arrangements such as the Quadrilateral on the basis that they are much less developed than, say, the European Union (EU) or North Atlantic Treaty Organization (NATO) miss the point that the Indo-Pacific is starting from a very low base in terms of formal strategic partnership and alliance mechanisms and thus even modest steps can be consequential. For instance, in recent years, Australia, Japan, India and France have established a web of military logistics and access arrangements that will allow their forces to project power across the region, especially the Indian Ocean. This will enable these middle players to more effectively wield strategic weight, regardless of the future American role in the region.

Code for solidarity

The very speed with which Indo-Pacific thinking has arisen fuels doubts about its impact and staying power. After all, the countries that champion the term do not seem to agree precisely on what it means. America and Japan talk about 'free and open', with Indonesia and India emphasising inclusiveness and connectivity, and Australia somewhere in between. This may be a sign of deeper differences over how to respond to Chinese power and US-China tensions. For Americans, the Indo-Pacific is a signal that they are not leaving Asia and – even in spite of Trump – still have many friends there. For others, it is a reminder that this region includes many nations – representing billions of people – who are neither Chinese nor American, and that their views matter too.

Yet there is an underlying solidarity. All countries advocating the Indo-Pacific are using it to signpost what they want: economic connectivity that does not translate interdependence into one country's exploitation; rules and respect for sovereignty; the avoidance of force or coercion in resolving international differences. The question is whether this solidarity will translate into collective action and mutual protection if confrontation comes.

The Indo-Pacific is a work in progress. In keeping with the spirit of diplomacy, it makes a virtue of ambiguity: serving as both an objective description of geopolitical circumstances and the basis for a strategy. That is but one of its useful dualities, and Asian statecraft has long been comfortable with duality – a unity composed of differences, like the yin and the yang of Chinese philosophy. Indeed, the Indo-Pacific encompasses multiple dualities, the reconciliation of contrasting aspects within one idea. It is both inclusive and exclusive: it is about incorporating Chinese interests into a regional order where the rights of others are respected; but it is also about counterbalancing Chinese power when those rights are not. It is both economic and strategic: it has economic origins but profoundly strategic consequences.

The Indo-Pacific's boundaries are fluid – it is, after all, a maritime place – and this helps explain why various countries define it differently (and why that is no great problem). For example, is coastal east Africa part of the Indo-Pacific or not? Perhaps the answer depends on how the interests of key Indo-Pacific powers are engaged in African affairs. But the region's core is clear: the sea lanes of maritime Southeast Asia. As for the periphery, it is defined by connections, not borders. This is consonant with the ancient Asian concept of the mandala, originating from Hindu cosmology, which with many variations defined the universe according to circles and a central point. This informed ancient statecraft in India and Southeast Asia: polities were defined by their centre, not their boundaries. In the mandala model, as opposed to the traditional 'middle kingdom' worldview of China, centrality does not automatically bestow superiority. Rather, the model recognises a world of many places, many islands, each with their own qualities. In modern parlance, this equates to multipolarity, equal sovereignty and mutual respect – many belts and many roads.

Notes

1 This chapter draws upon the author's work in *Indo-Pacific Empire: China, America and the Contest for the World's Pivotal Region*, Manchester University Press, Manchester, 2020.
2 Bill Birtles, 'China mocks Australia over "Indo-Pacific" concept it says will "dissipate"', *ABC News*, 8 March 2018. Some analysts suggest China's response to the Indo-Pacific is merely 'nonchalance', although if this were the case then perhaps China's official position would be either to ignore the construct or to accept it as harmless.

Feng Zhang, 'China's curious nonchalance towards the Indo-Pacific', *Survival*, Vol. 61, No. 3, 2019.
3 'East Asia Summit voices concern over South China Sea', *NHK World-Japan*, 20 November 2020.
4 Robert Kaplan, 'Center stage for the 21st century: Power plays in the Indian Ocean', *Foreign Affairs*, March-April 2009.
5 A similar point is made by Amitav Acharya, *The End of American World Order*, Polity Press, London, 2014, p. 82.
6 Mu Chunshan, 'What is CICA (and why does China care about it)?', *The Diplomat*, 17 May 2014.
7 The German government, for instance, released formal foreign policy guidelines for engaging with the Indo-Pacific region in September 2020, following extension debate about the pros and cons of reframing Berlin's regional engagement in this way. Garima Mohan, 'Germany gets on board with the Indo-Pacific', *9DashLine*, 11 September 2020.
8 Data combined from multiple sources, including United Nations, Department of Economic and Social Affairs, Population Division, 'World Population Prospects 2019', Medium fertility variant; PricewaterhouseCoopers, 'The long view: How will the global economic order change by 2050?', February 2017, pp. 23, 68; Stockholm International Peace Research Institute, 'Military expenditure by country, in constant 2017 US$ 1988–2018'.
9 There is much debate over the reliability of official Chinese data. On possible fabrication of economic statistics, see Wei Chen et al., 'A forensic examination of China's national accounts', *Brookings Papers on Economic Activity*, Spring 2019. On population size, see Yi Fuxian, 'China's population numbers are almost certainly inflated to hide the harmful legacy of its family planning policy', *South China Morning Post*, 20 July 2019.
10 This section builds on an analysis originally provided in Rory Medcalf and Raja C. Mohan, 'Responding to Indo-Pacific rivalry: Australia, India and middle power coalitions', *Lowy Institute Analysis*, 2014.
11 Narendra Modi, keynote address at the Shangri-La Dialogue, Singapore, 1 June 2018.
12 'ASEAN outlook on the Indo-Pacific', *Association of Southeast Asian Nations*, 23 June 2019; Melissa Conley Tyler, 'The Indo-Pacific is the new Asia', *The Interpreter (Lowy Institute blog)*, 28 June 2019.
13 This is discussed at length in Rory Medcalf, 'Indo-Pacific visions: Giving solidarity a chance', *Asia Policy*, Vol. 14, No. 3, 2019.
14 Anthea Roberts, Henrique Choer Moraes, and Victor Ferguson, 'The geoeconomic world order', *Lawfare blog*, 19 November 2018.
15 Robert D. Blackwill and Jennifer M. Harris, *War by Other Means: Geoeconomics and Statecraft*, Harvard University Press, Cambridge, MA, 2016, p. 20.
16 As argued also in Bruno Maçães, *Belt and Road: A Chinese World Order*, Hurst and Company, London, 2018.
17 Cuiping Zhu, *India's Ocean: Can China and India Coexist?* Springer/Social Sciences Academic Press, Singapore, 2018, pp. 142–143.
18 Darren J. Lim and Rohan Mukherjee, 'What money can't buy: The security externalities of Chinese economic statecraft in post-war Sri Lanka', *Asian Security*, Vol. 15, No. 2, 2019.
19 State Council, People's Republic of China, *China's Military Strategy*, 2015.
20 General Angus Campbell, Chief of the Australian Defence Force, 'You may not be interested in war, but war is interested in you', Speech to the Australian Strategic Policy Institute 'War in 2025' Conference, Canberra, 13 June 2019.
21 Rory Medcalf, 'China's influence in Australia is not ordinary soft power', *Australian Financial Review*, 7 June 2017. The concept of sharp power was further developed by

the US National Endowment for Democracy in its report 'Sharp power: Rising authoritarian influence' in December 2017.
22 Peter Harris, 'Conflict with China is not about a clash of civilisations', *The National Interest* online, 3 June 2019.
23 Brendan Taylor, *The Four Flashpoints: How Asia Goes to War*, La Trobe University Press, Melbourne, 2018.
24 Commonwealth of Australia, 'Opportunity, security, strength: The 2017 foreign policy white paper', Canberra, 2017.

4 "Making Multilateralism Matter"

Middle powers in the era of the US-China competition

Joo Hee Kim

Introduction

The conflict and competition between the United States and China, which began as a trade dispute in January 2018, tends to proceed in full scale covering all fields including politics, economy, diplomacy, and security, as well as norms and values. In an era of general uncertainty, the future of the Asia-Pacific region is becoming even more uncertain as a result of the intensifying conflict between the United States and China.

The context of technology and politics is changing rapidly, and instability due to globalisation is intensifying, ranging from climate change to technological development and the emergence of new non-state actors. The outbreak of the COVID-19 pandemic further exacerbates possibilities to solve the complex and difficult global problems. The current system is failing to address this global challenge.

As a consequence of President Trump's "America first" doctrine, the global multilateral rules-based order is being disrupted. In addition, aside from the factors related to President Trump, the multilateral order, which has led the post-war world order with the assertion that multilateral solutions are not very effective in solving global problems, seems to be no longer useful. However, this chapter assumes the significance and relevance of multilateralism in that the multilateral method is the only way to solve the global problem at this time, and at least there is no evidence that the multilateral solution is ineffective.

This chapter explores the role of middle powers in Asia as well as in the global arena, especially with regard to the US-China competition, and then considers how middle powers can contribute to a stable, peaceful, rules-based order based on multilateral cooperation.

South Korea (ROK) has relied on the US-ROK alliance to guarantee its security, enable its prosperity, and hoped to achieve Korean unification, given the fact that no viable alternative to the US-ROK alliance exists. However, China's rapid rise, its increasing role in international affairs, and geographic proximity to the Korean Peninsula have facilitated a vigorous debate within South Korea over how it should respond to the altered strategic environment. Koreans are increasingly bearing in mind the need to balance among their fundamental goals.

DOI: 10.4324/9781003106814-4

Making a wrong strategic choice between the United States and China could have high costs and serious consequences for South Korea, since China would likely be an alliance partner with capability and will to act as a security guarantor for South Korea. The parameters of this debate are influenced even more by a variety of factors, including the relative power, influence, and commitment of the United States. Further, these parameters are also influenced by the extent to whether the relationship between the United States and China is cooperative or competitive, and the South Korean public satisfaction with the relative level of autonomy and respect that their country receives from both countries.

How could a middle power manage the changing constellation? I argue that the role of the middle power states is to promote multilateralism and a democratic and rules-based global order.

This chapter proceeds as follows. The intensification of the US-China competition and the seriousness of global problems limit the role of the United States in leading the existing liberal world order. It shows the limits of a new China-led international order that could be a potential successor to the US-led order and presents a democratic, rules-based multilateral order led by middle powers as an alternative international order in the future. To this end, the concepts of middle powers and the multilateralism of middle powers are discussed theoretically. As a new middle power country, Korea is now trying to shift its role from a consumer to a producer of the international order. Hence, in order to determine possible avenues for South Korea to pursue, the chapter analyses the discussion of European strategic autonomy as a response strategy vis-à-vis US-China competition and aim to identify Europe's impetus for a middle power multilateral order in the making. Based on this, I would like to examine Korea's strategy of promoting multilateralism as a middle power and assess its possibilities and limitations.

Changing world order: alternatives to US-led world order

There is no stable world order. There is no eternal world order as the dominant order will eventually end someday. The shape of the newly emerging order relies on the conditions and hopes of all participants. This period of change requires a stable distribution of power and widespread acceptance of rules governing the international order. It also requires elaborated statecraft, since an order is made, not naturally born. In addition, no matter how ripe the starting conditions or strong the initial desire, there needs to be creative diplomacy, functioning institutions, and effective action to adjust it when circumstances change and reinforce it when challenges come.

The liberal world order formed after Second World War was a product of the Cold War, that is, competition between the United States and the Soviet Union, and has guided the direction of foreign policy of democratic countries during the Cold War and countries around the world after the post-Cold War. Many scholars talked about "the end of history"[1] and "New Peace,"[2] emphasising the role of the United States as a hyper-superpower after the post-Cold War and considered that great power conflict was obsolete due to the newly changed norms.[3]

The rise of China and the intensification of the US-China competition raised the question of whether a liberal world order could be maintained. In addition, the election of President Trump has furthered scepticism about the possibility of maintaining multilateralism, which can be regarded as the basis of the liberal world order. The United States and China are diverging in key areas. The United States has been openly showing a departure from the multilateral arena, especially when negotiations are difficult or when there is no room for compromise.

The United States, which has led the multilateral liberal order around the world since 1945, no longer appears to be a reliable leader to promote and defend that order. Scepticism about US reliability has increased under President Donald Trump's "America First", due to its withdrawal from several international agreements. Especially, 2 years and 5 months after President Trump announced his withdrawal from the Paris Climate Change Convention in June 2017, the United States finally entered the formal process of withdrawal. Moreover, the United States has caused long-time US allies, especially those who depend entirely on the provision of security by the United States to question US leadership and credibility. For some of these, predicaments have come up due to the novel conditional approach of the previously unbreakable US alliance commitment in Asia and Europe. This US position is embodied in the issue of United States Forces Korea (USFK) contributions and the case of Huawei.

What about the alternatives to a US-led world order? There are two possible alternatives. One is a world order led by China, and the other is a rules-based multilateral world led by small and middle power countries.[4]

The first alternative could emerge from the rise of China. A China-led order could actually challenge the US-led order and be based on resources rather than values. China is ready to support multilateralism with China's interests, but not with rules-based multilateralism. Although discussions on US-China competition mostly focus on US-China bilateral relations, the United States will eventually have to form its China strategy in a multilateral way in various networks of relations and institutions in Asia. In contrast to the US-led order, the China-led order could not be a liberal one, as its authoritarian domestic political system, coupled with the dire human rights situation and statist economies, stands in stark opposition to liberal values.[5] Therefore, China's Belt and Road Initiative could likely crash with other regional actors.[6] In other words, like-minded countries such as Japan and Australia would eventually form strategic multilateral groups, either separately or following the United States, to prevent the regional rise of China, and for specific purposes, this multilateralism would supplement the existing order. However, this alternative might be unlikely and/or unattractive. Presently, a new world order led by China does not seem to be such an attractive alternative, in that this the new world order does not appear to coincide with the interests of the global community, but also regarding its ability to gain legitimacy, which seems limited at best.

As climate change, cybersecurity threats, and the pandemic show, we need to make clear that no powerful country alone can solve issues with global ramifications. Essentially, the multilateral way might be the only way to confront these issues. However, what is the role of the middle powers in the era of US-China competition? In what ways can middle power countries maintain their security and prosperity and contribute to the stabilisation of a changing world order?

The second alternative could be "a new democratic, rules-based order of multilateralism"[7] created and led by middle powers in Asia and Europe, as well as Canada and Australia. Of course, the concept of a rule-based multilateralism led by the middle powers might be attractive, but not feasible, in terms of capability, namely due to their weak military power and lack of domestic political will, in some instances. Yet, the intensifying conflict between the United States and China has detrimental effects on the ability to reach consensus among countries on important global issues. Recent works of contested multilateralism argue that in the context of the intensifying Sino-US rivalry, multilateral institutions have become both the site of great power contestation and a strategic means for great power contestation. From a negative perspective, a key consequence of contesting regional dynamics in Asia might be to weaken the policy impact of existing institutional efforts and to promote zero-sum approaches to international policy among many Asian states.[8] From a partly positive perspective, the regional order in the Asia-Pacific could well transformed to a more peaceful one if regional security issues such as the North Korea and South China Sea dispute could be managed appropriately.[9]

Consequently, the international community has not been able to solve numerous problems such as climate change and international migration effectively. The two great powers, who should actively lead the way in solving problems, are disrupting the global multilateral order by giving up their participation or attempting to set new rules. However, the actions of these two great powers also serve as new opportunities for a majority of middle powers seeking to strengthen multilateralism.

The definition of middle powers

A middle power is perceived as part of a state-centric conception of the international community. Carsten Holbraad refers to four characteristics of middle powers: balancers of the state system, mediators between two opposing states, bridges between rich and poor states, and promoters of international understanding among culturally different states.[10] Later, he elaborated his definition of middle powers, including geographic location, gross national product, and population.[11] Bernard Wood developed five notions of the role played by middle powers: regional leaders, functional leaders, conflict stabilisers, status seekers, and multilateral moral powers.[12]

To define a middle power, it is useful to classify Cooper's four approaches: positional, geographic, normative, and behavioural.[13] First, a positional approach locates a middle power at the middle point in size in terms of population, economic strength and complexity, and military capability. Second, a geographic approach places a middle power physically and ideologically between the system's great powers. Both approaches are based on traditional definitions of middle powers according to criteria of size, power, and geographic location, which are controversial and difficult to measure. Third, a normative approach considers a middle power as potentially wiser, more virtuous, and more trustworthy in its recourse to diplomatic influence rather than to force, and less selfish when taking responsibility for the creation and maintenance of the global order. Fourth, a behavioural approach defines a middle power by its behavioural tendency to engage in "middlepowermanship", for example, pursuing multilateral solutions to international problems, embracing compromise positions in international disputes, or adopting notions of "good international citizenship" to guide its diplomacy.[14] Overall, the behavioural approach synthesises the three notions of multilateralism, conflict management, and moral power.[15]

In another vein, Ping argues that the statistical definition is more plausible to grasp middle powers, in that the normative and behavioural approach is based on Western values of developed countries, thus excluding non-Western middle powers.[16] Being a middle-sized country does not determine foreign policy behaviour, but having middle-ranking economic, military, and diplomatic capabilities and actively pursuing a middle power strategy to international affairs do offer some insight into what certain states can do. To investigate middle powers' preferences to multilateral engagements in international cooperation, therefore, the concept of middle powers will be qualified by incorporating specific roles with positional and geographical orientation and behavioural patterns normatively based on multilateralism.

In order to conceptualise the multilateralism of the middle powers, Jordaan's definition is particularly useful: "Middle powers are states that are neither great nor small in terms of international power, capacity and influence, and demonstrate a propensity to promote cohesion and stability in the world system."[17]

Despite the quantity of research on the subject and its salience, the term "middle power" remains ambiguous. However, focusing on the middle powers' behavioural approach is more beneficial for understanding middle powers' foreign policy, given the fact that this study deals with the multilateral engagement of middle powers. Based on a synthesis of existing approaches and definitions, certain states are viewed as middle powers if they have less capacity utilising material resources than great powers, and if they employ good global citizenship, work with a multilateral way through international organizations and agencies, promote mediation and peaceful conflict resolution, and participate in peace-keeping operations.

The main proponents of multilateralism have traditionally been middle powers such as Canada, Australia, the Benelux countries, and the Nordic countries.[18] Based on a synthesis of existing approaches and definitions, certain states are viewed as middle powers if they have less capacity utilising material resources than great powers, and if they employ good global citizenship, work with a multilateral way through international organisations and agencies, promote mediation and peaceful conflict resolution, and participate in peacekeeping operations. Based on these criteria, states such as Canada,[19] Australia,[20] Norway,[21] Sweden,[22] the Netherlands[23] are described as middle powers.[24] Therefore, this book groups major countries conducting foreign policy like middle powers, for example, the United Kingdom, Germany, France, and Japan and a group of traditional middle powers such as Canada, Australia, Sweden, Norway, the Netherlands, and South Korea as a new middle power.

Middle power's multilateralism

Global multilateral activity is a main pillar of international relations, since special issue of International Organisation in 1992 research of multilateralism has been elaborated and deepened, dealing with the expansion of actors and various issues. Middle power's multilateralism still does not play a large role in international political theory. Therefore, this book intends to discuss middle power's countermeasure strategies in the era of a changing world order based on the concepts of middle power and international relations theory of multilateralism.

Caporaso distinguishes multilateral institutions and the institution of multilateralism: multilateral institutions refer to the elements of formal organisation characterised by permanent locations with addresses and headquarters with staff and secretariats, while the institution of multilateralism is based on the less formal, less categorised habits, practices, ideas, and norms of international society.[25] As Morse and Keohane[26] indicated, the two strands of multilateralism could be divided into one of an older strand focusing on formal state cooperative activities and the other of a newer strand of multilateralism pointing out informal complex of multilateralism. They suggest a conception of contested multilateralism, which reconciles both strands and emphasises the characterization of "competing coalitions and shifting institutional arrangements, informal as well as formal."[27]

Caporaso also defines the term "multilateral" as an organising principle, an organisation, or an activity. These can be multilateral if they are related to cooperative activity among multiple countries. However, recent discussions on multilateralism have expanded to global governance, including the expansion of the influence of various actors beyond state actors.[28] However, "multilateralism" is "a belief that activities ought to be organized on a universal [. . .] basis" at least for a "relevant" group, namely like-minded countries regarding middle powers.[29] It might be understood as an ideology "designed" to promote multilateral activity and combines normative principles with advocacy and existential beliefs.[30]

Zürn reconciles structural realism and constructivism and suggests a structural approach that world politics is now embedded in a normative and institutional structure. Therefore, the structure of hierarchies and power inequalities fundamentally creates contestation, resistance, and distributional struggles.[31]

A new concept of "contested multilateralism 2.0" has been introduced in order to describe the puzzling regional institution-building efforts after the 2008 global financial crisis in the Asia-Pacific.[32] Kai He differentiates the ASEAN-led "multilateralism 1.0" of the 1990s from the "contested multilateralism 2.0" of the late 2000s non-ASEAN led such as the United States, China, Japan, Australia, and South Korea by advancing institutional balancing argument.[33] States leading the second wave of multilateralism conduct the strategies of either by forming new institutions or by reinvigorating existing ones for the sake of institutional balancing among major states under the conditions of high strategic uncertainty and high economic interdependence.[34]

More recently, the work by Bisley explores regional multilateralism of competitive characteristics reflecting Asia's more contested dynamics with regard to the US-China competition. The United States and its allies are trying to use multilateralism as part of their broader strategy to sustain the prevailing regional order. China is also attempting to use multilateralism as a part of its efforts to change the region to one more in line with its interests and values. Multilateralism has become a sublimated form of contestation over the form and function of Asia's international order.[35]

To discuss the role of middle powers in Asia in terms of multilateralism, it is more beneficial to begin with a discussion of the informal aspects of multilateralism rather than the formal mechanism of multilateralism, given the fact that formal multilateral institutions are rarely found in Asia, and in times of US-China competition, it has become more difficult to reach formal multilateral agreements.

Taking off from this assertion, I argue that multilateralism should be encouraged in various multilateral activities of actors in order to establish a new democratic and rule-based world order of multilateralism. In order to settle such a multilateralism, it is then necessary to conceptualise the multilateral activities of the middle powers.

Middle powers are actors who are skilled at inventing new institutional arrangements and brokering the overlapping interests of parties concerned with a particular issue.[36] However, engaging in middle power diplomacy is no less self-interested than the behaviour of any other state in the international system. That self-interest, though, is filtered through the practical consideration of when and where middle powers can achieve successful diplomatic outcomes in pursuit of national interests. In the absence of influence in the international system, middle powers must look for specific, niche opportunities to exercise their power and influence.[37] For the middle powers to take the lead in the multilateral arena, creativity was emphasised as the most important factor.[38]

Recent research tends to develop approaches based on the technical and entrepreneurial capacities of states to provide complementary or alternative initiative-oriented sources of leadership and enhanced coalition-building in issue-specific contexts to capture a new middle power such as South Korea.[39] It coincides with the awareness that the reshaping of the international system requires a fundamental rethinking of what middle powers need to do. Therefore, this kind of approach examines what middle powers actually do in international politics, rather than examining the empirical question of what characteristics they exhibit or the normative question of what they should be doing.[40] Considering these scholarly observations, I assume in this study that the middle powers are more likely to hold multilateral engagements. In the next section, I briefly refer to strategic autonomy, Europe's strategy for responding to a changing world order, which explicitly favours and pursues multilateral strategies of middle powers, seeking potential implications for this chapter.

European middle power strategy: implications for Asia

Europe's strategic autonomy

Besides having an inherently multilateral approach, Europe not only consists of traditional middle power countries such as the Nordic countries but also major countries such as Germany and France employing middle power diplomatic strategies. Through the development and formulation of the concept of strategic autonomy, Europe is beginning to respond to the US-China competition.

Europe's strategic autonomy, which has been discussed actively in recent years, is not a new concept.[41] In fact, the demand for European autonomy initiated the European Union's (EU's) common security and defence policy. The EU needs the capacity to stabilise and secure a threatened country at its periphery without the United States. In 2016, Europe's global strategy sought to rediscover the value of "strategic autonomy,"[42] and in December 2017, the EU established the Permanent Structured Cooperation (PESCO)[43] and discussion of the European Defence Union has been actively progressing. After Brexit, EU leaders have reinitiated the joint security and defence policy. The assuming of office by President Trump has further shaken the belief in the reliability of the Atlantic alliance and given fresh impetus for the concept of strategic autonomy and a recalibration in the relationship between the EU and North Atlantic Treaty Organization (NATO).[44]

Strategic autonomy is still a fluid concept, but the definition of *Stiftung Wissenschaft und Politik* (SWP) is useful. Lippert et al. define strategic autonomy as "the ability to set one's own priorities and make one's own decisions in matters of foreign policy and security," which includes institutional, political, and material resources that can be carried out alone or in cooperation with others.[45] However, due to the relative limitations of the middle powers, the implementation of strategic autonomy will inevitably emphasize multilateralism.

The discussion of European strategic autonomy focuses extensively on the EU's criticism of the United States. Geopolitically and functionally, EU member-states disagree on the need to pursue strategic autonomy. Further, member-states also do not agree on the underlying concept of strategic autonomy. There is also disagreement regarding the development of more capabilities for the EU.[46] However, to fulfil its true potential, the EU needs to stop strategic dissonance and focus on capacity building. The question should not be whether Europe is strategically autonomous or not. Rather, the question should be what the benefits are of bringing Europe's political, military, and industrial autonomy to a higher level. Europe's strategic autonomy is one of the many concepts that seek to promote a more competent and independent EU in times of growing geopolitical competition, such as European sovereignty and strategic sovereignty.[47]

The shift to strategic autonomy is an urgent issue. The United States, China, Russia, and Europe are witnessing the rearrangement of power relations in the international order. Europe can no longer blindly rely on US security and normative positions. Ultimately, strategic autonomy should lead to strengthening of the EU's security role, but this also has limitations. It is difficult for the EU to pursue strategic autonomy proactively from an institutional perspective. Europe's strategic autonomy and preparedness for crises could be featured prominently in discussions surrounding the introduction of Huawei's 5G equipment. In this process, despite EU recommendations, member countries also have taken different approaches depending on their national security and economic conditions and priorities. Amidst the US pressure to exclude Huawei and China's economic leverage by arguing Europe's exclusion of Huawei is a renunciation of strategic autonomy, the strategic choice of Europe will present critical implications for the multilateral strategy of middle power.

The reactions from Washington, Beijing, and Moscow are vague or negative about Europe's strategic autonomy.[48] The three major powers recognise Europe for its strength in trade and regulation but also recognise that it has weaknesses in the military sector or in preparation and action for conflict. Thus, they are taking advantage of the diversified interests and import dependence and security vulnerabilities among European countries. Major countries do not wait for Europe to act together internally. Since they see each other as strategic rivals, they will try to encourage the division of European countries to achieve their goals and force them to accept the rules they have set. This emphasises the need for Europe to move towards gaining strategic autonomy as quickly as possible to overcome its weaknesses and fill the gaps in capacity.

In the recent US withdrawal of support for the multilateral regime, Europe will need to seek economic and diplomatic balance and, for instance, in the case of climate change policy, differentiate it by exerting leadership by working with partners who share will. Vis-à-vis China, this means that European countries and companies need to coordinate their positions. Moreover, considering the economic dimension of China's Belt and Road Initiative, Europeans are urged to take a careful approach when choosing whether to integrate or not. Although the EU has already recognised China as a systemic rival, each member country has different interests in China. In the end, as the Huawei case shows, in the US-China competition, it will be difficult to reach an agreement on the positions and measures of each member country towards China; overall, China should not be judged simply in terms of economics. Rather, there should be a comprehensive and collective approach to respond to the US-China rivalry.

In the context of NATO's role in relations with Russia, security guarantees can no longer be taken for granted due to changes in the position of the United States. There is also a need to reconcile disagreements between member-states. When it comes to the formation of an international order in relation to the liberal principle, it is clear that neither China nor Russia can be partners for Europe. Economic cooperation can be beneficial, but there are elements of conflict in many other political issues

There are two lessons we can draw from European experience. First, Asian security, which is concentrated on traditional security, needs to be broadly defined, including emerging security areas such as climate change and cybersecurity. Second, strategic autonomy is difficult to achieve alone and can be attained through a multilateral way with like-minded countries. This concept focuses on an autonomous actor deciding on its own, based on its own priorities, with which other actors to seek partnerships and alliances. In the end, the concept of strategic autonomy in Europe can be seen as complementing its military capacity, while also rejuvenating the multilateral approach of its middle powers.

It is a very difficult task to not only discuss middle power strategies in Asia, but specifically Korea's middle power in terms of the changing global order, namely the US-China competition. As the discussion on this topic has now just begun, the next section focuses on the background and limitations of the formation of Korea's middle power strategy, primarily based on the existing discussions, and address the necessity of forming such a strategy.

"Making Multilateralism Matter" South Korea as a middle power

A major feature of South Korea's middle power debate mainly focuses on Korea's geopolitical escape from the turbulences emerging from the great powers and their conflicts of interest.[49] However, in order to escape successfully, it needs to benefit from its distinctive advantages and structural position of middle powers, which is usually defined as networking capability or capacity, to promote to a specific issue using the capabilities.[50] Middle powers are considered as "those . . . that possess the material capabilities to shape outcomes in niche areas in the global governance sphere when acting in concert with like-minded states."[51] According to this definition, middle powers are countries with the capacity and willingness to play the role of catalyst, facilitator, and/or manager in support of peace and conflict management, multipolarity, and rule building within the international system. South Korean scholars have utilised these characteristics as measures by which to judge South Korea.[52]

The Middle Power Diplomacy Initiative set up by the East Asia Institute recognises four primary roles that middle powers such as South Korea should seek to play as part of that diplomacy: "early mover," "bridge," "coalition coordinator," and "norm diffuser." These roles, respectively, involve leading by example with a multilateral way, mediating differences in international negotiating settings, building coalitions of like-minded states, and helping to diffuse international norms and standards.[53]

South Korea's positional role as a "node" in a network, according to Sohn Yul, empowers a "middle power diplomacy," which promotes Korea's connectedness, bridging capabilities, and niche diplomacy as a rule-setter in international institutions.[54]

Diffusion of power with the condition of the liberal international order provides middle powers such as Korea with new prospects to play an important role as an agenda-setter. In addition, a power shift from the developed to the developing world places middle powers in strategic and pivotal positions.[55]

South Korea has drawn its own lessons from its experiences with modernisation, democratisation, or specific issues such as international development cooperation or green growth. South Korea should respond to US-China competition by overcoming geopolitical restrictions and historical limitations by defining middle power relationally as the centre of attraction among like-minded parties or as an actor that is able to use catalytic or networking roles as a means of exerting influence.

South Korea has contributed to the international order by playing a niche role and building on non-traditional security issues such as green growth, international development cooperation, nuclear non-proliferation, and international financial governance.[56] In each of these areas, it has been able to highlight presence through its expression of interests, ideas, and capabilities. However, its contributions in non-traditional security areas did not address the regional constraints associated with the power deficit faced by a middle power in comparison with its larger neighbours.

Those who are sceptical about the multilateral order of the middle powers are critical of the following two multilateral approaches. Andrew Carr stresses the need for middle powers to "have some reasonable capacity to protect their core interests, including through military means," which means they should certainly be capable of raising "the costs such as to provide a significant discouragement of attacks on themselves or their core interests."[57] Andrew Carr also emphasizes the middle powers "ability to alter a specific element of the international order through formalised structures, such as international treaties and institutions, and informal means, such as norms or balances of power." This second approach highlights the role of middle powers in the formation of an international multilateral order, not as norm-followers but as norm-creators.[58]

More than ever, South Korea is at a potential turning point in evaluating the direction and strategic choice of its foreign policy. The long dependence on its alliance with the United States was something that needed to be reconsidered. China would be able to continue its economic growth and might become a reliable supplier of regional security in Asia. However, it is unlikely China will emerge as a regional and global rule maker. Moreover, the gap in relative power between South and North Korea continues to grow, but the path to national unification and its potential impact on South Korea's strategic options remains unclear. Although South Korea's growing capability and willingness as a middle power facilitating international issues could suggest broader flexibility in pursuing strategic choices, South Korea, which has a relative weakness in its relations with major neighbouring countries, might necessarily rely on the United States for security and prosperity. However, South Korea has come to recognise the need to differentiated approaches for sectors with strategic interests, thus considering areas for strategic choice in Europe that are currently firmly positioned in the United States. Lastly, it is also important to identify countries that can cooperate, recognising that these strategic choices may be possible through coalition and cooperation with like-minded countries that share common or strategic interests.

Conclusion

Every order will inevitably come to an end; the ending does not come as unexpected as most researchers assume both consciously and unconsciously, but rather through persistent deterioration. Moreover, it has to be recognised that the old order never comes back and the effort to restore the previous order is in vain.

The disruption of the US-centred multilateral order after the US-China competition and President Trump's election ignited the debate about the demand for a new world order and its emerging possibilities. A potential China-led order refers to the limits of a new international order. This chapter considered a democratic, rules-based multilateral order led by middle powers as an alternative to the US-led order. The term *middle powers* refers to "states that are neither great nor small in terms of international power, capacity and influence, and demonstrate a propensity to promote cohesion and stability in the world system."[59]

New middle powers can be identified by the technical and entrepreneurial capacities of states to provide complementary or alternative initiative-oriented sources of leadership and enhanced coalition building in issue-specific contexts. Considering the perspective of middle power multilateralism, we can hold that middle powers are more likely to hold active multilateral engagements.

In order to identify possible strategic avenues for multilateral cooperation, this chapter analysed European strategic autonomy as Europe's response strategy to the US-China competition. Favouring and pursuing multilateral strategies of middle powers, Europe's strategic autonomy is a particularly worthwhile concept, which has implications beyond the European context. This is particularly the case since Europe favours a multilateral approach and does not only consist of traditional middle power countries such as the Nordic countries but also encompasses major countries such as Germany and France using diplomatic strategies of middle powers. The discussion of European strategic autonomy focuses extensively on the EU's criticism of the United States rejecting multilateralism and undermining long-standing alliances.

The United States, China, Russia, and Europe are witnessing the rearrangement of power relations in the international order. Europe can no longer unconditionally answer all the demands of the United States. In relation to China, European countries and companies are urged to coordinate their positions. Regarding China's Belt and Road Initiative, the need to coordinate extends to the economic realm. Further, relations with China should be considered in the context of US-China competition, not just in terms of economic interests.

For South Korea, two lessons from the European case are paramount. First, Asian security needs to be broadly defined. There should be a shift from traditional security to emerging security issues such as climate change and cybersecurity. Although Korea relies on the United States for its traditional security, the scope of emerging security areas is global; thus, it has to explore possibilities for cooperation with various partners. Second, strategic autonomy highlights issue specific cooperation in a multilateral way and with like-minded countries. This concept focuses on an autonomous actor deciding on its own, based on its own priorities, with which other actors to seek partnerships and alliances.

As a new middle power country, Korea has just started to assume its role as a producer of international norms. This chapter examined Korea's strategy of middle power multilateralism and identified its possibilities and limitations. South

Korea is at a crossroads in deciding the orientation and strategy of its foreign policy. A crucial component is South Korea's future relationship with the United States. In this calculation, we still have to wait for China to become an economic giant and emerge as a reliable partner supplying regional security in Asia. However, it is unlikely that China will embark on the path to become a regional and global norm creator or rule maker. Although South Korea is relatively weak in its relations with its neighbouring countries and necessarily depends on the United States for security, it tries to facilitate its growing capability and willingness as a middle power to produce global standard and norms. South Korea needs to expand the room for diplomatic activities while avoiding conflict with the United States, which competes with China, and find various like-minded cooperative partners who share the same ideas. To this end, a democratic and rules-based global cooperation platform for multilateralism will prove essential.

Notes

1 Francis Fukuyama, "The End of History?" *The National Interest*, 16, 1989, pp. 3–18.
2 Michael Mandelbaum, "Preserving the New Peace: The Case Against NATO Expansion," *Foreign Affairs*, 74 (3), 1995, pp. 9–13.
3 John Mueller, "The Obsolescence of Major War," *Bulletin of Peace Proposals*, 21 (3), 1990, pp. 321–328.
4 Richard Haass, "How a World Order Ends: And What Comes in Its Wake," *Foreign Affairs*, January/February 2019.
5 Ibid.
6 Jessica Chen Weiss, "A World Safe for Autocracy? China's Rise and the Future of Global Politics," *Foreign Affairs*, July/August 2019, pp. 92–102.
7 Richard Haass, no. 4.
8 Nick Bisley, "Contested Asia's 'New' Multilateralism and Regional Order," *The Pacific Review*, 32 (2), 2019, pp. 221–231.
9 Kai He, "Contested Multilateralism 2.0 and Regional Order Transition: Causes and Implications," *The Pacific Review*, 32 (2), 2019, pp. 210–220.
10 Carsten Holbraad, "The Role of Middle Powers," *Cooperation and Conflict*, 7 (2), 1971, p. 80.
11 Carsten Holbraad, *Middle Powers in International Politics*, Macmillan, London, 1984, pp. 80–90.
12 Bernard Wood, *The Middle Powers and the General Interest*, The North – South Institute, Ottawa, 1988, pp. 19–20.
13 Andrew Cooper, "Squeezed or Revitalized? The Middle Power Model, the G20, and the Evolution of Global Governance," *Third World Quarterly*, 34 (6), 1993, pp. 17–19.
14 Robert Cox, "Middlepowermanship, Japan, and the Future World Order," *International Journal*, 44 (4), 1989, pp. 826–827; David Dewitt and John Kirton, *Canada as a Principal Power*, John Wiley & Sons, Toronto, 1983, p. 403; Peyton Lyon and Brian Tomlin, *Canada as an International Actor*, Macmillan Press, Toronto, 1979.
15 Adam Chapnick, "The Canadian Middle Power Myth," *International Journal*, 55 (2), 2000, pp. 188–206.
16 Jonathan Ping, *Middle Power Statecraft: Indonesia, Malaysia and the Asia-Pacific*, Ashgate, Aldershot and Burlington, 2005, pp. 51–53.
17 Eduard Jordaan, "The Concept of a Middle Power in International Relations: Distinguishing Between Emerging and Traditional Middle Powers," *Politikon*, 30 (1), 2003, pp. 165–181.

18 Morten Hansen and Torbjørn Gjefsen, *The End of Nordic Exceptionalism?*, Norwegian Church Aid, Finn Church Aid, DanChurchAid and Church of Sweden, 2015.
19 see Jozef Bátora, "Public Diplomacy Between Home and Abroad: Norway and Canada," *Hague Journal of Diplomacy*, 1 (1), 2006, pp. 53–80; Adam Chapnick, no. 14, pp. 188–206.; Andrew Cooper, no. 13; Mark Neufeld, "Hegemony and Foreign Policy Analysis: The Case of Canada as Middle Power," *Studies in Political Economy*, 48, 1995, pp. 7–29; Evan Potter, "Canada and the New Public Diplomacy," *International Journal*, 63 (1), 2003, pp. 43–64; John Ravenhill, "Cycles of Middle Power Activism: Constraint and Choice in Australian and Canadian Foreign Policies," *Australian Journal of International Affairs*, 52 (3), 1998, pp. 309–327.
20 see Mark Beeson and Richard Higgott, "The Changing Architecture of Politics in the Asia-Pacific: Australia's Middle Power Moment?" *International Relations of the Asia-Pacific*, 14 (2), 2014, pp. 215–237; Andrew Carr, "Australia as a Middle Power: Fighting or Fanning the Flames of Asia?" *FRIDE Policy Brief*, 208, 2015; Andrew Cooper, no. 13; John Ravenhill, "Cycles of Middle Power Activism: Constraint and Choice in Australian and Canadian Foreign Policies," *Australian Journal of International Affairs*, 52 (3), 1998, pp. 309–327; Carl Ungerer, "The 'Middle Power' Concept in Australian Foreign Policy," *Australian Journal of Politics and History*, 53 (4), 2007, pp. 538–551.
21 see Jozef Bátora, no. 18, pp. 53–80; Ronald Behringer, "Middle Power Leadership on the Human Security Agenda," *Cooperation and Conflict*, 40 (3), 2005, pp. 305–342; Mark Leonard and Andrew Small, *Norwegian Public Diplomacy*, The Foreign Policy Centre, London, 2003.
22 see Ronald Behringer, no. 21, pp. 305–342; Cranford Pratt, "Middle Power Internationalism and Global Poverty," in Cranford Pratt (ed.), *Middle Power Internationalism: The North-South Dimension*, McGill-Queen's Press, Montreal, 1990.
23 see Ronald Behringer, no. 21; Norichika Kanie, "Leadership in Multilateral Negotiation and Domestic Policy: The Netherlands at the Kyoto Protocol Negotiation," *International Negotiation*, 8 (2), 2003, pp. 339–365.
24 Andrew Cooper, ed., *Niche Diplomacy: Middle Powers at the Cold War*, Palgrave Macmillan, Basingstoke, 1997; Olav Stokke, *Western Middle Powers and Global Poverty: The Determinants of the Aid Policies of Canada, Denmark, the Netherlands, Norway, and Sweden*, Almqwist and Wiksell International, Stockholm, 1989.
25 James Caporaso, "International Relations Theory and Multilateralism: The Search for Foundations," *International Organization*, 46 (3), 1992, pp. 599–632.
26 Julia Morse and Robert Keohane, "Contested Multilateralism," *The Review of International Organizations*, 9 (4), 2014, pp. 385–412.
27 Ibid., p. 386.
28 Michael Zürn, *A Theory of Global Governance: Authority, Legitimacy, and Contestation*, Oxford University Press, 2018. Oxford Scholarship Online, April 19, 2018; Shepard Forman and Derk Segaar, "New Coalitions for Global Governance: The Changing Dynamics of Multilateralism," *Global Governance: A Review of Multilateralism and International Organizations*, 12 (2), 2006, pp. 205–228; Ngaire Woods, "Global Governance After the Financial Crisis: A New Multilateralism or the Last Gasp of the Great Powers?" *Global Policy*, 1 (1), 2010, pp. 51–63.
29 James Caporaso, no. 25, p. 603; Julia Morse and Robert Keohane, no. 25.
30 James Caporaso, no. 25.
31 Michael Zürn, no. 28.
32 Kai He, no. 9, pp. 210–220.
33 Ibid.
34 Ibid.
35 Nick Bisley, no. 8, pp. 221–231.

36 Oran Young, "Political Leadership and Regime Formation: On the Development of Institutions in International Society," *International Organization*, 45 (3), 1991, pp. 281–308.
37 Andrew Cooper, ed., no. 24; Andrew Cooper, "Soft Power and the Recalibration of Middle Powers: South Korea as an East Asian Leader and Canada as the Exemplar of the Traditional Model," in Jan Melissen and Yul Sohn (eds.), *Understanding Public Diplomacy in East Asia*, Palgrave Macmillan, Basingstoke, 2015, pp. 31–50.
38 Gareth Evans and Bruce Grant, *Australia's Foreign Relations: In the World of the 1990s*, Melbourne University Press, Melbourne, 1991.
39 Andrew Cooper, ed., no. 24; Andrew Cooper, no. 37; Andrew Cooper, Richard Higgott, and Kim Nossal, *Relocating Middle Powers: Australia and Canada in a Changing World*, University of British Columbia Press, Vancouver, 1993.
40 John Ikenberry and Jongryn Mo, *The Rise of Korean Leadership: Emerging Powers and Liberal International Order*, Palgrave, New York, 2013; Euikon Kim, "Korea's Middle-Power Diplomacy in the 21st Century," *Pacific Focus*, 30 (1), 2015, pp. 1–9; Sook-Jong Lee, "South Korea as New Middle Power Seeking Complex Diplomacy," *EAI Middle Power Diplomacy Initiative Working Paper*, 25, September, 2012; Seungjoo Lee, "Multilayered World Order and South Korea's Middle Power Diplomacy," *Korean Political Science Review*, 48 (6), 2014, pp. 77–101.
41 Alice Billon-Galland and Adam Thomson, "European Strategic Autonomy: Stop Talking, Start Planning," *European Leadership Network*, Policy Brief, 2018; Hans-Peter Bartels, Anna Maria Kellner, and Uwe Optenhogel, *Strategic Autonomy and the Defence of Europe: On the Road to a European Army*, Dietz, Bonn, 2017; François Heisbourg, "Europe's Strategic Ambitions: The Limits of Ambiguity," *Survival*, 42 (2), 2000, pp. 5–15.
42 Council of the European Union, "Council Conclusions on the Global Strategy on the European Union's Foreign and Security Policy", 3492nd Council Meeting, 17 October 2016, Luxembourg.
43 Council of the European Union, "Defence Cooperation: Council Establishes Permanent Structured Cooperation (PESCO), with 25 Member States Participating," www.consilium.europa.eu/en/press/press-releases/2017/12/11/defence-cooperation-pesco-25-member-states-participating/ (Accessed December 2, 2020).
44 Jolyon Howorth, "EU Defence Cooperation After Brexit: What Role for the UK in the Future EU Defence Arrangements?" *European View*, 16 (2), 2017, pp. 191–200.
45 Barbara Lippert, Nicolai von Ondarza, and Volker Perthes (eds.), *Strategische Autonomie Europas: Akteure, Handlungsfelder, Zielkonflikte*, SWP-Studie 2019/S 02, Februar 2019, p. 5.
46 Ibid.
47 Ulrike Franke and Tara Varma, "Independence Play: Europe's Pursuit of Strategic Autonomy," *Security Scorecard*, 2019, at https://ecfr.eu/special/independence_play_europes_pursuit_of_strategic_autonomy/ (Accessed December 2, 2019).
48 Barbara Lippert, Nicolai von Ondarza, and Volker Perthes, no. 45, pp. 1–39.
49 Brad Glosserman and Scott Snyder, "Confidence and Confusion: National Identity and Security Alliance in Northeast Asia," *Pacific Forum CSIS Issues & Insights*, 8 (16), 2008, pp. 1–42; Zhiqun Zhu, "Small Power, Big Ambition: South Korea's Role in Northeast Asia Security Under President Roh Moo-hyun," *Asian Affairs*, 34 (2), 2007, pp. 67–86; Hyeong Jung Park, "Looking Back and Looking Forward: North Korea, Northeast Asia, and the ROK-U.S. Alliance," *The Brookings Institution for Northeast Asian Policy Studies*, 2007, pp. 1–64.
50 Sangbae Kim, "Middle Power's Diplomatic Strategies in the Perspective of Networks: Applying Theories of Structural Holes and Positional Power," *gug-je-jeong-chi-non-chong*, 51 (3), 2011, pp. 51–77.

51 Scott Snyder, "8: The Paradox of South Korea's Middle-Power Status," in *South Korea at the Crossroads*, Columbia University Press, New York, 2018; Andrew Cooper, no. 37; *see* Antony Dolman, "The Like-Minded Countries and the New International Order: Past, Present and Future Prospects," *Cooperation and Conflict*, 14 (2), 1979, pp. 57–85.
52 Euikon Kim, "Korea's Middle-Power Diplomacy in the 21st Century," *Pacific Focus*, 30 (1), 2015, pp. 1–9.
53 Sook-Jong Lee, no. 40; Seungjoo Lee, no. 40.
54 Yul Sohn, "Regionalization, Regionalism, and Double-Edged Public Diplomacy in East Asia," in Jan Melissen and Yul Sohn (eds.), *Understanding Public Diplomacy in East Asia*, Palgrave Macmillan US, New York, 2015, pp. 31–50; Sangbae Kim, no. 50.
55 Sook-Jong Lee, no. 40.
56 John Ikenberry and Jongryn Mo, no. 40; Scott Snyder, no. 51.
57 Andrew Carr, "Is Australia a Middle Power? A Systemic Impact Approach," *Australian Journal of International Affairs*, 68 (1), 2014, pp. 79–80.
58 Ibid., p. 80.
59 Eduard Jordaan, no. 17.

Bibliography

Adam Chapnick, "The Canadian Middle Power Myth," *International Journal*, 55 (2), 2000, pp. 188–206.
Alice Billon-Galland and Adam Thomson, "European Strategic Autonomy: Stop Talking, Start Planning," *European Leadership Network*, Policy Brief, 2018.
Andrew Carr, "Is Australia a Middle Power? A Systemic Impact Approach," *Australian Journal of International Affairs*, 68 (1), 2014, pp. 70–84.
Andrew Carr, "Australia as a Middle Power: Fighting or Fanning the Flames of Asia?" *FRIDE Policy Brief*, 208, 2015.
Andrew Cooper, "Soft Power and the Recalibration of Middle Powers: South Korea as an East Asian Leader and Canada as the Exemplar of the Traditional Model," in Jan Melissen and Yul Sohn (eds.), *Understanding Public Diplomacy in East Asia*, Palgrave Macmillan, Basingstoke, 2015, pp. 31–50.
Andrew Cooper, "Squeezed or Revitalized? The Middle Power Model, the G20, and the Evolution of Global Governance," *Third World Quarterly*, 34 (6), 1993, pp. 963–984.
Andrew Cooper (ed.), *Niche Diplomacy: Middle Powers at the Cold War*, Palgrave Macmillan, Basingstoke, 1997.
Andrew Cooper, Richard Higgott, and Kim Nossal, *Relocating Middle Powers: Australia and Canada in a Changing World*, University of British Columbia Press, Vancouver, 1993.
Antony Dolman, "The Like-Minded Countries and the New International Order: Past, Present and Future Prospects," *Cooperation and Conflict*, 14 (2), 1979, pp. 57–85.
Barbara Lippert, Nicolai von Ondarza, and Volker Perthes (Hg.), *Strategische Autonomie Europas: Akteure, Handlungsfelder, Zielkonflikte*, SWP-Studie 2019/S 02, February 2019.
Bernard Wood, *The Middle Powers and the General Interest*, The North – South Institute, Ottawa, 1988.
Brad Glosserman and Scott Snyder, "Confidence and Confusion: National Identity and Security Alliance in Northeast Asia," *Pacific Forum CSIS Issues & Insights*, 8 (16), 2008, pp. 1–42.
Carsten Holbraad, *Middle Powers in International Politics*, Macmillan, London, 1984.

Carsten Holbraad, "The Role of Middle Powers," *Cooperation and Conflict*, 7 (2), 1971, pp. 77–90.

Council of the European Union, "Council Conclusions on the Global Strategy on the European Union's Foreign and Security Policy," 3492nd Council Meeting, 17 October 2016, Luxembourg.

Council of the European Union, "Defence Cooperation: Council Establishes Permanent Structured Cooperation (PESCO), with 25 Member States Participating," www.consilium.europa.eu/en/press/press-releases/2017/12/11/defence-cooperation-pesco-25-member-states-participating/ (Accessed December 2, 2020).

Cranford Pratt, "Middle Power Internationalism and Global Poverty," in Cranford Pratt (ed.), *Middle Power Internationalism: The North-South Dimension*, McGill-Queen's Press, Montreal, 1990.

David Dewitt and John Kirton, *Canada as a Principal Power*, John Wiley & Sons, Toronto, 1983.

Euikon Kim, "Korea's Middle-Power Diplomacy in the 21st Century," *Pacific Focus*, 30 (1), 2015, pp. 1–9.

Evan Potter, "Canada and the New Public Diplomacy," *International Journal*, 63 (1), 2002/2003, pp. 43–64.

Francis Fukuyama, "The End of History?" *The National Interest*, 16, 1989, pp. 3–18.

François Heisbourg, "Europe's Strategic Ambitions: The Limits of Ambiguity," *Survival*, 42 (2), 2000, pp. 5–15.

Hans-Peter Bartels, Anna Maria Kellner, and Uwe Optenhogel, *Strategic Autonomy and the Defence of Europe: On the Road to a European Army*, Dietz, Bonn, 2017.

Hyeong Jung Park, "Looking Back and Looking Forward: North Korea, Northeast Asia, and the ROK-U.S. Alliance," *The Brookings Institution for Northeast Asian Policy Studies*, 2007, pp. 1–64.

James Caporaso, "International Relations Theory and Multilateralism: The Search for Foundations," *International Organization*, 46 (3), 1992, pp. 599–632.

Jessica Chen Weiss, "A World Safe for Autocracy? China's Rise and the Future of Global Politics," *Foreign Affairs*, July/August 2019, pp. 92–102.

John Ikenberry and Jongryn Mo, *The Rise of Korean Leadership: Emerging Powers and Liberal International Order*, Palgrave, New York, 2013.

John Mueller, "The Obsolescence of Major War," *Bulletin of Peace Proposals*, 21 (3), 1990, pp. 321–328.

John Ravenhill, "Cycles of Middle Power Activism: Constraint and Choice in Australian and Canadian Foreign Policies," *Australian Journal of International Affairs*, 52 (3), 1998, pp. 309–327.

Jolyon Howorth, "EU Defence Cooperation After Brexit: What Role for the UK in the Future EU Defence Arrangements?" *European View*, 16 (2), 2017, pp. 191–200.

Jonathan Ping, *Middle Power Statecraft: Indonesia, Malaysia and the Asia-Pacific*, Ashgate, Aldershot and Burlington, 2005.

Jozef Bátora, "Public Diplomacy Between Home and Abroad: Norway and Canada," *Hague Journal of Diplomacy*, 1 (1), 2006, pp. 53–80.

Julia Morse and Robert Keohane, "Contested Multilateralism," *The Review of International Organizations*, 9 (4), 2014, pp. 385–412.

Mark Beeson and Richard Higgott, "The Changing Architecture of Politics in the Asia-Pacific: Australia's Middle Power Moment?" *International Relations of the Asia-Pacific*, 14 (2), 2014, pp. 215–237.

Mark Neufeld, "Hegemony and Foreign Policy Analysis: The Case of Canada as Middle Power," *Studies in Political Economy*, 48, 1995, pp. 7–29.

Michael Mandelbaum, "Preserving the New Peace: The Case Against NATO Expansion," *Foreign Affairs*, 74 (3), 1995, pp. 9–13.

Michael Zürn, *A Theory of Global Governance: Authority, Legitimacy, and Contestation*, Oxford University Press, Oxford, 2018. Oxford Scholarship Online, April 19, 2018.

Morten Hansen and Torbjørn Gjefsen, *The End of Nordic Exceptionalism?*, Norwegian Church Aid, Finn Church Aid, DanChurchAid and Church of Sweden, 2015.

Ngaire Woods, "Global Governance After the Financial Crisis: A New Multilateralism or the Last Gasp of the Great Powers?" *Global Policy*, 1 (1), 2010, pp. 51–63.

Norichika Kanie, "Leadership in Multilateral Negotiation and Domestic Policy: The Netherlands at the Kyoto Protocol Negotiation," *International Negotiation*, 8 (2), 2003, pp. 339–365.

Olav Stokke, *Western Middle Powers and Global Poverty: The Determinants of the Aid Policies of Canada, Denmark, the Netherlands, Norway, and Sweden*, Almqvist & Wiksell International, Stockholm, 1989.

Oran Young, "Political Leadership and Regime Formation: On the Development of Institutions in International Society," *International Organization*, 45 (3), 1991, pp. 281–308.

Peyton Lyon and Brian Tomlin, *Canada as an International Actor*, Macmillan Press, Toronto, 1979.

Richard Haass, "How a World Order Ends: And What Comes in Its Wake," *Foreign Affairs*, January/February 2019.

Ronald Behringer, "Middle Power Leadership on the Human Security Agenda," *Cooperation and Conflict*, 40 (3), 2005, pp. 305–342.

Seungjoo Lee, "Multilayered World Order and South Korea's Middle Power Diplomacy," *Korean Political Science Review*, 48 (6), 2014, pp. 77–101.

Shepard Forman and Derk Segaar, "New Coalitions for Global Governance: The Changing Dynamics of Multilateralism," *Global Governance: A Review of Multilateralism and International Organizations*, 12 (2), 2006, pp. 205–228.

Sohn Yul, "Regionalization, Regionalism, and Double-Edged Public Diplomacy in East Asia," in Jan Melissen and Yul Sohn (eds.), *Understanding Public Diplomacy in East Asia*, Palgrave Macmillan US, New York, 2015, pp. 31–50.

Sook-Jong Lee, "South Korea as New Middle Power Seeking Complex Diplomacy," *EAI Middle Power Diplomacy Initiative Working Paper*, 25, September 2012.

Stephan Klingebiel, "Stellungnahme zur Öffentlichen Anhörung des Deutschen Bundestages: Ausschuss für wirtschaftliche Zusammenarbeit und Entwicklung (AwZ) zum Thema," *Bilaterale und multilaterale Entwicklungszusammenarbeit*, Bonn, am March 23, 2012.

Ulrike Franke and Tara Varma, "Independence Play: Europe's Pursuit of Strategic Autonomy," *Security Scorecard*, 2019, at https://ecfr.eu/special/independence_play_europes_pursuit_of_strategic_autonomy/ (Accessed December 2, 2019).

Zhiqun Zhu, "Small Power, Big Ambition: South Korea's Role in Northeast Asia Security Under President Roh Moo-hyun," *Asian Affairs*, 34 (2), 2007, pp. 67–86.

5 Security order and state transformation in Asia

Beyond geopolitics and grand strategy

Lee Jones

Asian security: the statist debate

International Relations' (IR's) subfield of security studies has undeniably broadened in the post–Cold War era. Despite "realist" resistance, the concept of "security" has expanded well beyond a traditional focus on interstate military relations to include diverse "non-traditional" threats, while "human security" scholarship shifted attention from states to communities and individuals. New critical approaches from Marxism, feminism, post-colonialism and post-structuralism have pluralised the subfield, albeit at the cost of growing incoherence, as realists foretold.

However, this intellectual broadening has always been limited within Asian security studies and is arguably dwindling even further amidst intensifying great power competition. Nonetheless, Asian security scholarship has broadened somewhat, with considerable discussion of non-traditional security (NTS), and some attention to human security. However, the mainstream debate remained resolutely "traditional". The vast bulk of scholarship – and certainly discussions at international conferences – remained concerned with either interstate military dynamics or interstate cooperation through formal regional institutions, overwhelmingly those centred on the Association of Southeast Asian Nations (ASEAN).

The main problems (*problematiques*) in this approach concern great power rivalry and how/whether it can be institutionally contained. This focus has generated voluminous yet inconclusive (and highly repetitive) debates on ASEAN-centred institutions and their shortcomings or alternatives – the so-called "regional security architecture". Even NTS and human security are overwhelmingly addressed through this prism, as scholars predominantly assess regional organisations' performance in managing these issues. Shortcomings identified are typically blamed on Asian states' attachment to sovereignty and non-interference, which precludes the emergence of more robust regional governance.

Growing Chinese power has only intensified this traditional focus and increasingly gloomy assessments of security dynamics. Optimistic 1990s/early 2000s scholarship suggesting the emergence of a "regional identity" that could dampen Hobbesian dynamics has given way to dark warnings about ASEAN's divisions when confronted with Chinese assertiveness in the South China Sea; China's

DOI: 10.4324/9781003106814-5

supposed geopolitical gambit, the Belt and Road Initiative (BRI); and endless discussion of mounting Sino-US rivalry.

In short, East Asia is generally seen as a region of "Westphalian" states whose security relationships have progressed very little from the balance-of-power models developed in realist IR. Even when scholars are not explicitly realist, they implicitly use realist ontologies, particularly concerning the state: they portray states as unitary actors, possessing a singular worldview and security outlook, and pursuing a single, coherent foreign and security policy, guided by calculations of national interest or identity. It is entirely normal for scholars to make pronouncements about "China's" foreign policy, or what "the Philippines" is doing, for example, and this approach – ostensibly a linguistic shorthand, but actually expressing deep ontological assumptions – is rarely challenged.

Bringing state transformation in

Notwithstanding relevant insights provided by this statist approach, I argue that this overlooks how states are transforming in an era of globalisation and the attendant impact on Asian security.

Much of my research has challenged the realist conception of the state in IR, promoting a richer, more complex understanding, closer to empirical reality, which allows us to understand and explain security dynamics that are often invisible through realist lenses. Doing so has involved using Gramscian state theory, as developed by Nicos Poulantzas and Bob Jessop.[1] This approach sees states not as "things" – and, therefore, certainly not unitary "actors" – but rather as condensations of social relationships. Because state apparatuses distribute power and resources, they are fought over between socio-political groups – most importantly social classes and class fractions but also state-based forces (e.g. bureaucratic and military groupings) and ethnic, religious and gendered groups – as part of their wider struggle for power and resources. Which institutions emerge, and how they operate in practice, is traceable to these conflicts.

This approach differs from other IR frameworks that attend to domestic politics – e.g. Liberalism, Neoclassical Realism or Foreign Policy Analysis – in two ways. First, it situates socio-political conflict within the broader context of continually evolving capitalist dynamics. The nature, composition and strength of forces contesting state power are intimately related to the development of productive forces in particular societies, which occurs within the wider development of global capitalism. This approach is grounded in political economy analysis.[2] Second, the approach does not assume that domestic struggles are always resolved into a singular policy "decision", which then directs the entire state's behaviour. Instead, it is open to the possibility that different state apparatuses, reflecting their links to, or even capture by, different socio-political forces, may pursue quite distinct, or even contradictory, objectives. As Migdal states,

> The sheer unwieldy character of states' far-flung parts, the many fronts on which they fight battles with groupings with conflicting standards of behavior,

and the lure for their officials of alternative sets of rules that might, for example, empower or enrich them personally or privilege the group to which they are most loyal, all have led to diverse practices by states' parts or fragments. . . . [These] have allied with one another, as well as with groups outside, to further their goals. . . [producing outcomes] often quite distinct from those set out in the state's own official laws and regulations. These alliances, coalitions or networks have neutralized the sharp territorial and social boundary that [Weberian state theory] has acted to establish, as well as the sharp demarcation between the state as preeminent rule maker and society as the recipient of those rules . . . the state is a contradictory entity that acts against itself.[3]

It is theoretically *possible* that political leaders may strive to impose a single strategic vision, reining in wayward state apparatuses, but this is always a political struggle, and success cannot be *taken for granted* as an analytical starting point. Thus, we must remain open to the possibility of different state-society compacts behaving in different ways internationally and actively study state managers' efforts to "impose a measure of coherence" on their conduct,[4] rather than merely assuming that states are either unitary actors or ultimately behave as such after domestic politics have "finished" with the production of a singular foreign policy.

My work with Shahar Hameiri has further complicated the picture by drawing attention to the dynamics of *state transformation*. Building on extensive scholarship in state theory, political geography, public policy, global governance and other subfields, we have foregrounded the transformation of state apparatuses and power by socio-political struggles under globalisation. Despite the Weberian/Westphalian state's frequent depiction in IR as a natural or transhistorical unit,[5] it is actually a recent historical achievement. It consolidated in Europe following the industrial revolution, after centuries of princely struggles to unify disparate territories into national formations, and in the global South only after decolonisation. The Bretton Woods settlement bolstered this form of statehood by supporting Keynesian compacts between capital and labour, which underpinned "the primacy of national economies, national welfare states, and national societies managed by national states concerned to unify national territories and reduce uneven development".[6] However, the Weberian-Westphalian state form has been substantially transformed since the capitalist crises of the 1970s. Led initially by new-right forces in the US and Britain, trade unions were defeated, wage growth was curbed, state assets were privatised and international trade and finance were deregulated.[7] Corporatist and developmentalist apparatuses were dismantled and replaced by new institutions focused on promoting global competitiveness.[8] Ruling elites adapted governance structures to promote and then respond to globalisation, fundamentally reworking the Weberian-Westphalian state in most jurisdictions worldwide.

We summarise the key dynamics under three headings: fragmentation, decentralisation and internationalisation.[9]

1. The *fragmentation* of state authority stems from decades of piecemeal state reform and moves towards regulatory governance. The top-down,

command-and-control systems of Weberian-Westphalian states have given way to regulatory states, where executives use guidelines to loosely "steer" diverse public and private actors towards preferred outcomes.[10] This model has spread to developing countries through decades of Western development programmes and domestic efforts to increase global competitiveness.[11]

2 *Decentralisation* has arisen through the devolution of policymaking and control over resources and the rise of global cities and city-regions.[12] Decentralisation has also spread to developing countries through post-conflict state-building interventions and development projects.[13]

3 Many formerly domestic institutions and agencies have become *internationalised*. To support and govern increasing cross-border economic flows, and threats to these, regulatory and judicial bodies have formed "transgovernmental networks" to harmonise policies and standards.[14] Functional agencies have networked with their foreign counterparts to manage economic and security issues.[15] Rosenau dubs this "fragmegration": state fragmentation enabling new forms of transnational integration.[16] Many subnational governments now engage in quasi-autonomous "paradiplomacy".[17]

These developments render unitary actor models even less plausible. Moreover, they make it even more necessary for us to study how (and how successfully) state managers try to achieve coherence at a time when many more state-society blocs are internationally active than mainstream IR typically imagines.

Implications for Asian security (1): the emergence of transnational governance

The first major implication of this understanding of statehood for the study of Asian security dynamics is that security governance is now emerging beyond the intergovernmental institutions that mainstream, statist scholarship focuses on.

Mainstream approaches identify security problems, survey the main regional institutions supposed to address them, find them deficient and thus declare security governance to be "weak" or even absent in the Asia-Pacific.[18] Asian states' attachment to sovereignty is ostensibly the major obstacle, causing regional security order to stagnate or even regress. A typical judgement is Odgaard's claim that China offers "no viable alternative to the Cold War structure of international relations based on absolute sovereignty, non-interference and traditional power balancing".[19] This contributes to the broader sense that the international system is being dragged "back to Westphalia" by rising powers like China.[20]

Conversely, Hameiri and I show that transnational security governance *is* emerging in Asia – just not where, or in the form, that statists expect.[21] Functional agencies are increasingly networking across state borders to manage shared problems and create new governance systems that better "map onto" these. Such cooperation does not involve states ceding sovereignty to supranational institutions, which intervene directly to solve security problems. Instead, it involves efforts to transform how domestic institutions address particular issues according to internationally agreed standards, processes and rules. These processes are often promoted and supported by international organisations and/or powerful states' agencies, along with like-minded actors within societies targeted by these initiatives. However, because governance transformations involve altering the distribution and use of power and resources, actors who would stand to lose out resist such changes. The practical form and operation of security governance is thus determined by struggles between rival coalitions, rooted in the specific political economy dynamics of particular issue areas.[22]

Because these arrangements often do not map onto established regional organisations, mainstream statists may not even notice their existence. Our book, *Governing Borderless Threats*, considered how three NTS issues were governed in Southeast Asia. One of these, the haze (life-threatening environmental degradation originating in Indonesia), is indeed partly governed through ASEAN structures. However, rather than seeking to empower ASEAN to intervene in Indonesia, the anti-haze regime operates primarily through trying to change how Indonesia is governed internally. Our other issue areas – pandemic disease (avian influenza) and transnational crime/terrorism (money laundering) – were not governed through ASEAN at all. The bird flu case involved interventions led by the World Health Organization (WHO) and Food and Agriculture Organisation designed to transform domestic and animal and human health systems. Money laundering was addressed through the transformation of domestic governance according to the Financial Action Task Force's (FATF's) 40 Recommendations, supervised by the FATF-sponsored Asia Pacific Group, which includes over 50 different territories, cutting right across several traditional international organisations. The efficacy of these security governance regimes did not depend on whether states surrendered sovereignty to supranational enforcement agencies (which were rarely if ever envisaged or established), but rather on struggles between the forces promoting and opposing governance transformation, which also cut across the domestic/international divide.

Contrary to the "Westphalian" images of China repeated ad infinitum in statist scholarship, Hameiri and I have also shown that, reflecting state transformation dynamics, Chinese agencies are increasingly involved in transnational security governance designed to contain threats arising from increasing cross-border economic flows. For example, the health departments of two subnational governments, Yunnan province and Guangxi Zhuang autonomous region, have participated in the Mekong Basin Disease Surveillance (MBDS) network since 2001. MBDS is headquartered in the Thai health ministry and backed by international philanthropists, like Google and Rockefeller, the US Centers for Disease Control and Prevention, and the WHO. By building capacity, sharing intelligence and cooperating in pandemic preparedness and response, the MBDS implements the 2005 WHO International Health Regulations and its Asia Pacific Strategy for Emerging Diseases, which focus on transforming domestic governance to contain pandemics.[23] From 2006, multinational teams of health, customs, immigration and border officials have been created, focusing on 37 cross-border sites. During "public health emergencies of international concern", an emergency operating centre is established and teams deploy to help contain pandemics. Examples include outbreaks of dengue fever (on the Thai-Laotian border), typhoid (Vietnam-Laos), avian flu (Laos, Thai-Laos), swine flu and COVID-19.[24] This is a far cry from the 2003 SARS epidemic when Chinese officials covered up the outbreak for months.

Nonetheless, reflecting state transformation dynamics, different state apparatuses were clearly operating at cross-purposes early in the COVID-19 outbreak. Reflecting fragmentation and decentralisation, local governments initially prioritised economic growth – and public security bureaux, regime stability – while whistle-blowing health officials were arrested. However, the Politburo quickly recognised the severity of the crisis and demanded full compliance with global protocols, directing regulatory agencies to crack down on decentralised party-state actors. Commissions for Discipline Inspection revealed the pathologies of decentralisation, criticising local officials for "Disobeying the unified command and control of epidemic prevention and control, refusing to execute the superiors arrangement [sic]", lying, "Fraud, concealment, misrepresentation, omission ... delayed reporting ... and covering up".[25] Only through this struggle to cohere the party-state was robust compliance with WHO rules was eventually achieved.

Chinese agencies are also involved in maritime security governance, a fact missed in studies focusing on naval or coastguard aggression in the South China Sea. Reflecting the fragmentation and internationalisation of state apparatuses, even after four separate coastguard agencies were amalgamated into the China Coastguard in 2013, the Ministry of Transport's Maritime Safety Administration (MSA) persisted independently and participates in many international initiatives. These include the US-led West Pacific Naval Symposium, the Container Security Initiative, the Proliferation Security Initiative, the Regional Maritime Security Initiative, the International Maritime Organisation's International Ship and Port Facility Security Code programme (IMO-ISPFS) and the Japanese-led Regional Cooperation Agreement on Combating Piracy and Armed Robbery Against Ships in Asia.[26] Several of these focus on developing shared regulations and practices for domestic implementation; i.e. they operate by promoting state transformation.[27] For example, the US International Port Security Program (IPSP) involves member-states – including China – changing domestic governance to enact the IMO-ISPFS code, then submitting to inspections by the US Coastguard and US-authorised companies to ensure compliance. This harmonisation of port governance seeks to curtail the use of shipping for smuggling, trafficking in illegal goods, nuclear proliferation and terrorist activities. The MSA has also been involved in the IMO-led Cooperative Mechanism in the Straits of Malacca and Singapore, which has successfully built the coastguard capacity of littoral states to combat piracy there.[28]

Chinese security actors have also internationalised to combat banditry on the Mekong River, which threatens Chinese merchant shipping. Such activity has been led by China's Ministry of Public Security (MPS), a domestic policing agency. After a major incident in 2011, the MPS created a regional network with its counterparts in Thailand, Myanmar, Laos, Vietnam and Cambodia, headquartered at Yunnan's Guanlei Port, generating bimonthly multinational riverine patrols. Yunnan water police vessels participate in every patrol, with other states contributing ships on rotation.[29] A Chinese police official describes the vessels as operating like "one police force together".[30] Chinese participant-observers explain that the patrols effectively extend the Chinese police's jurisdiction beyond China's borders, enabling them to arrest suspected criminals, who are then handed over to the local authorities.[31] The network has also established river-side hotlines to allow sailors and local people to contact the police.[32] In 2016, the patrols reportedly yielded 9,926 arrests and 6,467 drug-related criminal cases, plus the seizure of 12.7 tons of drugs, 55.2 tons of precursor chemicals and large amounts of firearms and ammunition.[33] This network has recently been consolidated into the Lancang-Mekong Integrated Law Enforcement and Security Cooperation Centre (LM-LESC), based in Kunming. LM-LESC is a formal international organisation, headed by a Chinese secretary-general, with each member-state contributing a deputy secretary-general.[34] LM-LESC coordinates joint patrols, joint operations, intelligence and investigation support, law-enforcement capacity-building and information sharing.[35]

Even Chinese companies have become involved in governing NTS issues. Most notably, they are the primary agencies through which China's opioid substitution programme (OSP) has been implemented in Myanmar and northern Laos. Chinese agribusinesses are given subsidies and import tax breaks to encourage them to establish plantations that provide alternative livelihoods for opium farmers, thus reducing drug production. This policy originated bottom up, pioneered by Yunnanese counties in the early 1990s before being scaled up to the provincial and then national level as part of the "people's war on drugs" from 2004. However, reflecting fragmentation, the OSP is coordinated not by the MPS but rather the Ministry of Commerce (MOFCOM); and reflecting decentralisation, policy implementation and financing is devolved to the Yunnan bureau of commerce.[36] This has allowed corrupt local officials to direct funding towards agribusinesses linked to the local party-state, which have abused the OSP to establish plantations through land grabbing and forced displacement, in cahoots with corrupt officials in Laos and Myanmar, often in areas where opium cannot even be grown.[37] Coupled with a collapse in the price of rubber, the main substitution crop, this has fuelled deprivation and resentment, particularly in Myanmar, opium production actually increased during the OSP's most intensive phase.[38] Coupled with the behaviour of other local government and corporate actors, this has undermined security in the Sino-Myanmar borderlands.[39] Such examples demonstrate the impact of the political economy context in shaping governance outcomes.

The claim here, then, is not that transnational security governance is working optimally and we have no cause for concern; the point is that it exists and demands research as part of any attempt to understand, evaluate and improve Asian security order. Importantly, these same initiatives coincide with aggressive conduct by other Chinese agencies in the same policy domain, especially concerning maritime security. Realist ontologies lead analysts to focus exclusively on the bellicosity, assuming that this represents "China"; consequently, they overlook inconsistent behaviour entirely or argue that "China" is clearly not serious about cooperation because "it" is being uncooperative simultaneously. Such conclusions only hold if one (wrongly) believes that all actions taken by every party-state apparatus are tightly controlled and regulated by a top leadership with infinite oversight and control.[40]

A shift of optics, away from statist ontologies, is required to accurately describe, let alone evaluate, Asian security practices. Our conclusions may remain gloomy, but they will be reasoned from investigation and evidence, which is preferable to ignorance. Moreover, the existence of more cooperative actors and initiatives creates entry points for policy actors seeking to improve Asian security. They can work alongside agencies trying to collaborate with foreign counterparts, reinforcing them against their more hawkish compatriots. Conversely, a doom-and-gloom picture of "billiard-ball" states on a collision course is a counsel of despair, downgrading human agency and narrowing policy options to questions of deterrence and response – which may precipitate the very collision they are ostensibly seeking to avoid.

Implications for Asian security (2): the Belt and Road Initiative

The state transformation lens also provides a more accurate understanding of what statists generally gloss as "grand strategy". This task is particularly pressing today with respect to China's BRI.

Statists view the BRI as a new, more "proactive" Chinese "grand strategy", designed to produce "a more multipolar order, in Asia and globally".[41] This "well thought-out Chinese grand strategy" is ostensibly designed "to reclaim [China's] geopolitical dominance in Asia... [challenge] US dominance and... create a Chinese-centered order".[42] Described as a "geopolitical and diplomatic offensive",[43] or even "Chinese neo-imperialism",[44] the BRI aims at "nothing less than rewriting the current geopolitical landscape",[45] or even "world dominance".[46] Through it, China seeks "to re-constitute the regional order – and eventually global order – with new governance ideas, norms, and rules".[47]

However, through a state transformation lens, the picture looks very different. Far from being a top-down grand strategy, we can trace BRI's emergence through extensive bottom-up lobbying, aggregated into remarkably vague national guidelines. As my research with Jinghan Zeng shows, the BRI began as a vague slogan ("one belt, one road") in late 2013 and was only subsequently fleshed out by politico-economic actors lobbying for power and resources.[48] Provincial governments populated the emerging policy platform with their pet projects, some dating back to the late 1980s, and all of which are primarily intended to stimulate local economic growth rather than advance some geopolitical plan.[49] Their competitive lobbying and self-interested interpretation of Xi's vague slogan – not Xi's strategic vision – caused the BRI to expand from a programme aimed primarily at neighbouring Asian states to a global initiative open to all countries.[50] It generated policy guidelines that are little more than a wish list, encompassing practically every part of the party-state and neglecting to prioritise policies or resources.[51]

The BRI is so incoherent and lacking in top-down direction that not only is there no official map of the BRI, Beijing has even banned unofficial ones.[52] MOFCOM cannot even settle on a consistent definition of BRI countries, referring to both 59 and 61 "countries along the Belt and Road" in 2017, but 56 and 63 in 2018, for example,[53] despite the Office of the Leading Group for the BRI, under the State Council, listing 138 BRI countries.[54]

Unsurprisingly, the BRI's implementation does not follow the revisionist pattern suggested in statist accounts. Despite recurrent claims that BRI is about promoting "new norms" that challenge the liberal international order, one struggles in vain to identify *any* particular norms being developed or disseminated through the initiative. Official documents express values around economic integration and pluralism/multiculturalism, but this pro-market, "live-and-let-live" approach hardly constitutes an alternative China model, let alone a strident challenge to liberal order.[55] Scholarly and official discussion in China centres on what norms China *could* promote and what a specifically Chinese notion of global governance *could* involve.[56] The truth is that they do not yet know; they are trying to fill the void following Xi's vague pronouncements. So far, the debate contains "not much new".[57]

Nor does the economic activity at the real heart of the BRI demonstrate strategic direction. Outbound Chinese investment is not even being guided by the six broad "corridors" outlined in Beijing's main policy blueprint; it remains heavily concentrated in East Asia and developed economies, and non-BRI investment has grown faster than BRI investment.[58] MOFCOM states that only 13 per cent of outbound investment is going to BRI countries.[59] Ye's analysis of project documents released from 2014 to 2016 also shows that BRI activities were "not regulated or guided" by official policy frameworks.[60] Indeed, China's central bank governor has openly complained about projects that "do not meet our industrial policy requirements for outward investment", noting that "they are not of great benefit to China and have led to complaints abroad".[61]

If BRI projects are not being driven by grand strategy, what *is* driving them? Ye's analysis is again revealing: project documents show that "industrial overcapacities" were "the main motivation".[62] This finding reflects the BRI's true nature as a strategic-seeming overlay on an attempt to address structural contradictions in China's political economy, particularly massive surplus capacity, faltering growth and profitability, and excessive debt. The BRI is a "spatial fix" for these problems, seeking to externalise them and initiate a fresh round of capital accumulation.[63] It acts as a second round of post-global financial crisis stimulus for Chinese state-owned enterprises (SOEs), especially those in the saturated infrastructure sector, following the exhaustion of the first round amidst burgeoning overcapacity and the de facto bankruptcy of many local governments. Accordingly, construction contracts vastly outweigh productive investment – US$256 billion versus US$148 billion from 2014 to 2018 – and SOEs account for 96 per cent of construction projects and 72 per cent of direct investment.[64] BRI financing has even been appropriated for domestic use to "save loss-making SOEs".[65]

Accordingly, what is built in the name of the "Belt and Road" is determined not by a sinister geopolitical plan, but rather by the interests of Chinese (especially state-linked) corporate interests and how these intersect with interests on the recipient side. Chinese scholars and officials emphasise that the BRI is an initiative, an invitation to cooperate bilaterally, and not a strategy, which is unilaterally imposed. This is not mere sophistry. Even if there really was a secret blueprint of what "China" wanted to build (which there is not), it could not be built without the consent of foreign governments. Moreover, China's development financing really *is* recipient driven: would-be beneficiaries must identify the projects they want, then apply to Beijing for assistance. This model is explicitly reflected in the BRI, which involves would-be participants identifying their priorities, then bilateral discussions to see where Chinese interests and resources can contribute, generating a framework document setting priorities for cooperation. This document may be signed off by senior leaders, giving the impression of traditional, top-down interstate diplomacy; but its content and subsequent implementation are very much directed "bottom up" by actors on both sides. Chinese firms often lobby would-be recipients to seek Beijing's support for projects that they can implement, in the hope of winning the tied contract. Recipient governments may agree because the project is genuinely needed for economic development, but also as a means of dispensing patronage, accessing kickbacks or in combination with side payments like military assistance.[66]

These dynamics can generate diverse projects that, far from adding up to a strategic masterplan, are simply "incoherent": a "belt and road to nowhere", as one analyst observes.[67] Driven by need or greed, recipients can often pursue economically unviable projects. Meanwhile, weak and fragmented governance of outbound investment on the Chinese side permits irrational exuberance – particularly when risk is transferred through sovereign debt, creating serious moral hazard – while providing little meaningful assessment of economic or political risk in host countries and virtually no on-the-ground assessment of SOEs' conduct.[68] This explains the extravagance and irrationality of many high-profile BRI programmes and why several have gone seriously awry, notably in cases like Sri Lanka, Malaysia, Kenya, Myanmar and the Maldives, where heavily indebted governments have been forced to try to renegotiate projects or restructure their debts.

The realist claim that this results from Chinese "debt trap diplomacy" is a classic instance of realist lenses occluding more than they reveal.[69] This thesis assumes that "China" is a rational, unitary actor, engaged in long-range strategic planning that drives all parts of the party-state. The Chinese leadership has deliberately decided to offer unsustainable loans to poor countries, knowing that recipients will eventually experience a debt crisis, allowing China to extract concessions and possibly even seize key infrastructure like ports, thereby extending China's naval reach. Such claims collapse under empirical scrutiny.

Consider the most prominent example cited in support of this statist interpretation: Sri Lanka's Hambantota Port. Far from symbolising cunning "debt-trap diplomacy", this was a prime case of shoddy investment practices amidst extensive corruption.[70] Hambantota Port was not proposed by China but by Sri Lanka's Mahinda Rajapaksa regime, as part of a post-war spending spree designed to cultivate political support and service patronage networks. Indeed, the idea of building it had been circulating for decades; it was included in the country's 2002 development strategy; and construction began before the words "belt and road" were even uttered. Chinese SOEs competed fiercely for this lucrative project, while China's Export-Import Bank stood to make a substantial profit on the loans, while Colombo shouldered all the risk. However, the port was poorly conceived, prematurely launched to coincide with Rajapaksa's birthday, and created vast surplus capacity, resulting in persistent losses. Meanwhile, the Sri Lankan government suffered a severe debt crisis caused by excessive borrowing from Western financial institutions after US-led quantitative easing – not due to Chinese loans, which comprised just 6 per cent of the state's debt-servicing costs. Sri Lanka sought Chinese help, resulting in China Merchant Ports (CMP) leasing the port for 99 years from 2017, along with 1,235 acres of land, in exchange for US$1.1 billion. Colombo used this to service non-Chinese debts and bolster its dwindling foreign reserves. There was no debt-for-asset swap, as widely claimed – the original loans remain in place. Far from a successful case of "economic statecraft", this is a poor outcome for China. CMP – ultimately backed by state-owned banks – is now saddled with a white elephant that it is struggling to make profitable. Nor can China's navy use the port, as fancifully claimed: this is expressly forbidden in the lease agreement, and the Sri Lankan Navy's southern command is being relocated to Hambantota. Far from a case of skilful "debt-trap diplomacy", this is a case study of Chinese ineptitude, with an attempt to export surplus capacity and capital creating a "debt trap" for the Chinese state.

Nor is this case unique. As of 2014, China's overseas assets, totalling US$6.4 trillion, were yielding a net loss.[71] China is itself in a "debt trap" in countries like Venezuela, where it has lost US$20 billion of US$62.2 billion lent.[72] It will always be possible to apply a realist gloss to developments like this, by claiming that "China" would not endure such colossal losses without some long-term game plan; the theoretical assumptions of coherent, unitary, strategic state behaviour mean that, *somewhere, somehow*, there *must* be a strategic rationale. Through so-called realist lenses, the reality of fragmented, poorly coordinated and error-prone behaviour by Chinese party-state actors is transmuted into coherent, strategic behaviour. Such arguments reflect the triumph of deductive reasoning from faulty theory over empirical reality, and assumptions about how China's party-state operates that are belied by decades of scholarship by Chinese politics specialists.

A state transformation perspective, therefore, offers a vital reality check for statists when evaluating Xi Jinping's signature foreign policy. Far from being a "well-thought-out grand strategy", the BRI is revealed as a strategic sounding, but actually exceedingly vague and capacious, overlay for diverse, primarily economic interests. Given its personal association with Xi, the BRI certainly mobilises actors and resources across the party-state; but these actors are not simply following a top-down plan. They are debating, shaping and populating the party-state's loose policy platform, exploiting the initiative to pursue their own interests beneath the BRI's banner. The result is not coherent, strategic behaviour but rather in poorly coordinated, even incoherent conduct.

This view again implies a very different policy response from that proposed by realists. If the BRI is primarily shaped "bottom up", with prospective recipients playing a substantial role in designing projects, this creates an entry point for policy actors concerned about debt sustainability or the social and environmental consequences of mega-projects. Development agencies can intervene to help recipients better manage Chinese assistance and work with Chinese regulators to strengthen their oversight functions. NGOs and international organisations can help recipients build appropriate governance structures to regulate Chinese firms and mitigate negative consequences. This may yield better outcomes than a balancing approach, which seeks to derail the belt and road.

Conclusion

This chapter has critiqued the tendency in Asian security studies to cleave to traditional conceptualisations of the state and security. The pluralising tendencies of the broader security studies subfield seem largely to have passed Asia by, resulting in the continued use of statist ontologies and realist or quasi-realist assumptions. This leads to a narrow fixation on questions of the balance of power, strategy (grand or otherwise) and formal intergovernmental organisations. By showcasing research based on non-realist ontologies of the state, I showed how this blinds scholars to important developments in Asian security. My point is not that things like the military balance or great power rivalry do not exist or do not matter, nor that states can never act strategically. My point is rather that these dynamics are only one possible part of the security landscape in Asia. A realist lens may bring into focus "assertive" or "aggressive" conduct, but blur out of sight more cooperative behaviour by different parts of the same state. What looks like "grand strategy" through realist lenses may look very different through the prism of state transformation.

The importance of "getting Asia right", or at least not getting it wrong, is more important now than ever.[73] Statist and realist ontologies are not innocent or harmless. A particular understanding of the state and security entails a particular understanding of what is happening today in Asia and entails particular policy responses. For scholars of Asian security who uncritically adopt realist or quasi-realist understandings, there is a real danger of fuelling the very conflictual dynamics that their frameworks are supposed only to analyse.

Notes

1 Nicos Poulantzas, *State, Power, Socialism*, New Left Books, London, 1978; Bob Jessop, *State Theory: Putting the Capitalist State in Its Place*, Polity, Cambridge, 1990; Bob Jessop, *State Power: A Strategic-Relational Approach*, Polity, Cambridge, 2008.
2 The closest mainstream equivalent is Etel Solingen's work, which sees politics as involving struggles between pro- and anti-globalisation coalitions, but avoids this reductive binary approach.
3 Joel S. Migdal, *State in Society: Studying How States and Societies Transform and Constitute One Another*, Cambridge University Press, Cambridge, 2001, pp. 20, 22.
4 Bob Jessop, 2008, no. 1, pp. 36–37.

5 John Agnew, "The Territorial Trap: The Geographical Assumptions of International Relations Theory," *Review of International Political Economy*, 1, (1), 1994, pp. 53–80.
6 Bob Jessop, "Avoiding Traps, Rescaling States, Governing Europe," in Roger Keil and Rianne Mahon (eds.), *Leviathan Undone? Towards a Political Economy of Scale*, UBC Press, Vancouver, 2009, p. 99.
7 David Harvey, *A Brief History of Neoliberalism*, Oxford University Press, Oxford, 2005.
8 Philip G. Cerny, "Paradoxes of the Competition State: The Dynamics of Political Globalization," *Government and Opposition*, 32, (2), 1997, pp. 251–274.
9 Lee Jones, "Theorizing Foreign and Security Policy in an Era of State Transformation: A New Framework and Case Study of China," *Journal of Global Security Studies*, 4, (4), 2019, pp. 579–597.
10 Giandomenico Majone, "The Rise of the Regulatory State in Europe," *West European Politics*, 17, (3), 1994, pp. 77–101; Kanishka Jayasuriya, "Globalisation and the Changing Architecture of the State: Regulatory State and the Politics of Negative Coordination," *Journal of European Public Policy*, 8, (1), 2001, pp. 101–123.
11 Graham Harrison, *The World Bank and Africa: The Construction of Governance States*, Routledge, London, 2004; Navroz K. Dubash and Bronwen Morgan (eds.), *The Rise of the Regulatory State of the South: Infrastructure and Development in Emerging Economies*, Oxford University Press, Oxford, 2013.
12 Neil Brenner, *New State Spaces: Urban Governance and the Rescaling of Statehood*, Oxford University Press, Oxford, 2004; Michael Keating, *Rescaling the European State: The Making of Territory and the Rise of the Meso*, Oxford University Press, Oxford, 2013.
13 World Bank, ed., *East Asia Decentralizes: Making Local Government Work*, World Bank, Washington, DC, 2007.
14 Anne-Marie Slaughter, *A New World Order*, Princeton University Press, Princeton, NJ, 2004; Ulrich Brand, *The Internationalization of the State as the Reconstitution of Hegemony*, University of Vienna, Vienna, 2007; Alex Demirović, "Materialist State Theory and the Transnationalization of the Capitalist State," *Antipode*, 43, (1), 2011, pp. 38–59.
15 Christopher J. Bickerton, *European Integration: From Nation-States to Member States*, Oxford University Press, Oxford, 2012; Shahar Hameiri and Lee Jones, *Governing Borderless Threats: Non-Traditional Security and the Politics of State Transformation*, Cambridge University Press, Cambridge, 2015.
16 James N. Rosenau, *Distant Proximities: Dynamics Beyond Globalization*, Princeton University Press, Princeton, NJ, 2003.
17 Alexander S. Kuznetsov, *Theory and Practice of Paradiplomacy: Subnational Governments in International Affairs*, Routledge, Abingdon, 2015.
18 See for example Emil J. Kirchner, "Regional and Global Security: Changing Threats and Institutional Responses," in Emil J. Kirchner and James Sperling (eds.), *Global Security Governance: Competing Perceptions of Security in the 21st Century*, Routledge, London, 2007, pp. 11–12; Mely Caballero-Anthony, "Non-traditional Security and Infectious Diseases in ASEAN: Going Beyond the Rhetoric of Securitization to Deeper Institutionalization," *Pacific Review*, 21, (4), 2008, pp. 507–525.
19 Liselotte Odgaard, "China: Security Cooperation With Reservations," in Emil J. Kirchner and James Sperling (eds.), *Global Security Governance: Competing Perceptions of Security in the 21st Century*, Routledge, London, 2007, p. 216.
20 Daniel Flemes, "Network Powers: Strategies of Change in the Multipolar System," *Third World Quarterly*, 34, (6), 2013, pp. 1016–1017.
21 Shahar Hameiri and Lee Jones, no. 15.
22 Shahar Hameiri and Lee Jones, "The Political Economy of Non-Traditional Security: Explaining the Governance of Avian Influenza in Indonesia," *International Politics*, 52, (4), 2015, pp. 445–465.

23 MDBS Secretariat, "Mekong Basin Disease Surveillance," *MBDS Foundation*, 2019, www.mbdsnet.org/ (Accessed October 10, 2019).
24 William I. Long, "Cross-Border Health Cooperation in Complicated Regions: The Case of the Mekong Basin Disease Surveillance Network," in G. Shabbir Cheema, Christopher A. McNally, and Vesselin Popovski (eds.), *Cross-Border Governance in Asia: Regional Issues and Mechanisms*, United Nations University Press, Tokyo, 2011, pp. 93–121.
25 JQK News, "Hubei: Severely Punish Those Who Tell Lies, Ignore Human Life, Report Happiness to Superiors and Not Worry," *JQK News*, 2020, www.jqknews.com/news/378453-Hubei_severely_punish_those_who_tell_lies_ignore_human_life_report_happiness_to_superiors_and_not_worry.html (Accessed May 27, 2020).
26 Mingjiang Li, "China and Maritime Cooperation in East Asia: Recent Developments and Future Prospects," *Journal of Contemporary China*, 19, (64), 2010; Joshua H. Ho, "Combating Piracy and Armed Robbery in Asia: The ReCAAP Information Sharing Centre (ISC)," *Marine Policy*, 33, (2), 2009, pp. 432–434.
27 See Shahar Hameiri and Lee Jones, "Global Governance as State Transformation," *Political Studies*, 64, (4), 2016, pp. 804–806.
28 Joshua H. Ho, "Enhancing Safety, Security, and Environmental Protection of the Straits of Malacca and Singapore: The Cooperative Mechanism," *Ocean Development & International Law*, 40, (2), 2009, pp. 233–247; Nazery Khalid, "With a Little Help from My Friends: Maritime Capacity-Building Measures in the Straits of Malacca," *Contemporary Southeast Asia*, 31, (3), 2009, pp. 424–446.
29 Interviews with Yunnan-based experts on Chinese relations with Mekong countries, October 2018, and LM-LESC official, January 2019.
30 Interview with LM-LESC official, January 2019.
31 Interview with Yunnan-based experts, October 2018.
32 Interview with LM-LESC official, January 2019.
33 Yingqiu Pan and Guang Shi, "Forging a Secure Waterway," *China Report ASEAN*, 2017, https://chinareportasean.com/2017/02/22/forging-a-secure-waterway/ (Accessed February 20, 2020).
34 LM-LESC, "Organizational Structure," 2019, www.lm-lesc-center.org/pages_57_283.aspx (Accessed August 1, 2019).
35 LM-LESC, "Security Cooperation," 2019, www.lm-lesc-center.org/list51.aspx (Accessed August 1, 2019).
36 Xiaobo Su, "Nontraditional Security and China's Transnational Narcotics Control in Northern Laos and Myanmar," *Political Geography*, 48, (September), 2015, pp. 72–82.
37 Weiyi Shi, "Rubber Boom in Luang Namtha: A Transnational Perspective," *GTZ*, 2008, http://lad.nafri.org.la/fulltext/1599-1.pdf (Accessed November 1, 2015).
38 Kevin Woods and Tom Kramer, *Financing Dispossession: China's Opium Substitution Programme in Northern Burma*, Transnational Institute, Amsterdam, 2012; Tom Kramer et al., *Bouncing Back: Relapse in the Golden Triangle*, Transnational Institute, Amsterdam, 2014.
39 Shahar Hameiri, Lee Jones, and Yizheng Zou, "The Development-Insecurity Nexus in China's Near-Abroad: Rethinking Cross-Border Economic Integration in an Era of State Transformation," *Journal of Contemporary Asia*, 49, (3), 2019, pp. 473–499.
40 Lee Jones, no. 9.
41 Flynt Leverett and Bingbing Wu, "The New Silk Road and China's Evolving Grand Strategy," *The China Journal*, 77, 2016, pp. 110–132.
42 Abanti Bhattacharya, "Conceptualizing the Silk Road Initiative in China's Periphery Policy," *East Asia*, 33, (4), 2016, p. 2.
43 François Godement and Agatha Kratz (eds.), *"One Belt, One Road": China's Great Leap*, ECFR, Brussels, 2015, p. 2.

44 Tom Miller, *China's Asian Dream: Quiet Empire Building Along the New Silk Road*, Zed Books, London, 2017, p. 18.
45 Werner Fasslabend, "The Silk Road: A Political Marketing Concept for World Dominance," *European View*, 14, (2), 2015, pp. 293–302.
46 Theresa Fallon, "The New Silk Road: Xi Jinping's Grand Strategy for Eurasia," *American Foreign Policy Interests*, 37, (3), 2015, p. 140.
47 William A. Callahan, *China's Belt and Road Initiative and the New Eurasian Order*, Norwegian Institute of International Affairs, Oslo, 2016, p. 1.
48 Lee Jones and Jinghan Zeng, "Understanding China's 'Belt and Road Initiative': Beyond 'Grand Strategy' to a State Transformation Analysis," *Third World Quarterly*, 40, (8), 2019, pp. 1415–1439.
49 Tim Summers, "China's 'New Silk Roads': Sub-National Regions and Networks of Global Political Economy," *Third World Quarterly*, 37, (9), 2016, pp. 1628–1643; Gaye Christoffersen, "The Russian Far East and Heilongjiang in China's Silk Road Economic Belt," *China Policy Institute: Analysis*, 2016, https://cpianalysis.org/2016/04/25/the-russian-far-east-and-heilongjiang-in-chinas-silk-road-economic-belt/ (Accessed May 2, 2016); Lee Jones and Jinghan Zeng, no. 48.
50 Xianghong Zeng, "The Geopolitical Imaginations of the 'One Belt, One Road' Initiative and Regional Cooperation," *World Economics and Politics*, 2016, (1), 2016, pp. 46–71, 157–158.
51 See The National Development Reform Commission and Ministry of Foreign Affairs, "Vision and Actions on Jointly Building Silk Road Economic Belt and 21st-Century Maritime Silk Road," 2015, https://reconasia-production.s3.amazonaws.com/media/filer_public/e0/22/e0228017-7463-46fc-9094-0465a6f1ca23/vision_and_actions_on_jointly_building_silk_road_economic_belt_and_21st-century_maritime_silk_road.pdf (Accessed May 22, 2016).
52 Thomas P. Narins and John Agnew, "Missing from the Map: Chinese Exceptionalism, Sovereignty Regimes and the Belt Road Initiative," *Geopolitics*, early online, 2019, pp. 1–29.
53 The first figure refers to non-financial direct investment while the latter refers to contracted projects. Ministry of Commerce, *MOFCOM Department of Outward Investment and Economic Cooperation Comments on China's Outward Investment Cooperation in 2017*, MOFCOM, Beijing, 2018; Ministry of Commerce, *MOFCOM Department of Outward Investment and Economic Cooperation Comments on China's Outward Investment and Cooperation in 2018*, MOFCOM, Beijing, 2019.
54 Office of the Leading Group for the Belt Road Initiative, "Profiles," *Belt and Road Portal State Council Information Center*, 2019, https://eng.yidaiyilu.gov.cn/info/iList.jsp?cat_id=10076&cur_page=1 (Accessed October 10, 2019).
55 Lee Jones, "Does China's Belt and Road Initiative Challenge the Liberal, Rules-Based Order?," *Fudan Journal of the Humanities and Social Sciences*, 13, 2019, pp. 113–133.
56 See for instance Jinghan Zeng, "Chinese Views of Global Economic Governance," *Third World Quarterly*, 40, (3), 2019, pp. 578–594.
57 Michael D. Swaine, "Chinese Views on Global Governance Since 2008–9: Not Much New," *China Leadership Monitor*, 2016, https://carnegieendowment.org/2016/02/08/chinese-views-on-global-governance-since-2008-9-not-much-new-pub-62697 (Accessed October 11, 2019).
58 David Dollar, "Yes, China Is Investing Globally – But Not So Much in Its Belt and Road Initiative," *Brookings Institution: Order from Chaos*, 2017, www.brookings.edu/blog/order-from-chaos/2017/05/08/yes-china-is-investing-globally-but-not-so-much-in-its-belt-and-road-initiative/ (Accessed January 20, 2020); Maggie Xiaoyang Chen and Chuanhao Lin, *Foreign Investment Across the Belt and Road: Patterns, Determinants, and Effects*, World Bank, Washington, D.C., 2018, pp. 11–12.

59 Ministry of Commerce, *MOFCOM Department of Outward Investment and Economic Cooperation Comments on China's Outward Investment and Cooperation in 2018*.
60 Min Ye, "Fragmentation and Mobilization: Domestic Politics of the Belt and Road in China," *Journal of Contemporary China*, 28, (119), 2019, p. 12.
61 Emily Feng, "China Tightens Rules on State Groups' Foreign Investments," *Financial Times*, 2017, www.ft.com/content/3251987c-7806-11e7-90c0-90a9d1bc9691 (Accessed January 15, 2020).
62 Min Ye, no. 60, p. 12.
63 Lee Jones, "The Political Economy of China's Belt and Road Initiative," Paper presented at the *Fifth Australian International Political Economy Network Workshop*, 2019; see also Tim Summers, *China's Regions in an Era of Globalization*, Routledge, Abingdon, 2018.
64 Celia Joy-Perez and Derek Scissors, *Be Wary of Spending on the Belt and Road*, American Enterprise Institute, Washington, D.C., November 14, 2018, www.aei.org/publication/be-wary-of-spending-on-the-belt-and-road/.
65 Min Ye, no. 60, pp. 13–14.
66 Lee Jones, no. 63.
67 Graeme Smith, "The Belt and Road to Nowhere: China's Incoherent Aid in Papua New Guinea," *Lowy Interpreter*, www.lowyinstitute.org/the-interpreter/belt-and-road-nowhere-china-s-incoherent-aid-papua-new-guinea (Accessed June 25, 2018).
68 Shahar Hameiri and Lee Jones, "China Challenges Global Governance? The Case of Chinese International Development Finance and the Asian Infrastructure Investment Bank," *International Affairs*, 94, (3), 2018, pp. 573–593; Lee Jones and Yizheng Zou, "Rethinking the Role of State-owned Enterprises in China's Rise," *New Political Economy*, 22, (6), 2017, pp. 743–760.
69 Cf. Lee Jones and Shahar Hameiri, "Debunking the Myth of 'Debt-Trap Diplomacy'," in *Understanding the Politics of China's Belt and Road Initiative*, Chatham House, London, 2020.
70 See Ibid., ch. 3.
71 Feng Lu et al., "Why China? The Economic Logic Behind China's One-Belt-One-Road Initiative," in Binhong Shao (ed.), *Looking for A Road: China Debates Its and the World's Future*, Brill, Leiden, 2016, pp. 198–199.
72 Celia Joy-Perez and Derek Scissors, no. 64.
73 David C. Kang, "Getting Asia Wrong: The Need for New Analytical Frameworks," *International Security*, 27, (4), 2003, pp. 57–85.

6 Reflecting on US-China rivalries in post-conflict Sri Lanka

Ganeshan Wignaraja[1]

Introduction

Sri Lanka is once again on the radar of the world's great powers. As it cannot afford a significant military capability, Sri Lanka has historically pursued a non-aligned foreign policy of being friends with everyone and enemies with no one. After emerging from a costly 26-year civil conflict in 2009, this classic Asian small power experienced relative calm and graduated to middle-income economy status. Sri Lanka's post-conflict decade has coincided with heightened geopolitical competition between great powers, with the US seeing China's rise as a threat to its global economic and military dominance. Worsening great power relations during the COVID-19 global pandemic has prompted talk of a second cold war and preparedness for decoupling between the US and China.[2] Bitter disputes exist between the great powers in areas such as trade, investment, technology, security, Hong Kong and the origins of the coronavirus. Moreover, US-China rivalries have radiated to Sri Lanka with both attempting to incorporate the country into their sphere of influence. However, the policy implications for Sri Lanka are unclear.

This chapter reflects candidly on Sri Lanka's foreign relations with the US and China in the post-conflict period and the influence of domestic and international factors. Although some research exists on Sri Lanka-China relations[3], a comparative data-driven analysis of the country's engagement with both great powers is lacking.[4] Using the lens of international political economy, this chapter looks at Sri Lanka-great power relations covering the period from January 2010 to December 2020. The focus is on identifying Sri Lanka's economic and security priorities and the responses of great powers. The second section discusses why great powers may be interested in Sri Lanka. The third section assesses Sri Lanka's foreign trade and investment with great powers. The fourth section examines the effectiveness of development assistance from great powers to Sri Lanka. The fifth section charts assistance from great powers for Sri Lanka's national security capacity. The final section concludes by drawing lessons from Sri Lanka's experience on managing small power–great power relations in a scenario of a second cold war in a post-COVID world.

DOI: 10.4324/9781003106814-6

Why Sri Lanka matters to the US and China

Being a small power can matter to a significant extent in the contemporary international system.[5] There are several related reasons why the US and China might court a small power like Sri Lanka in the country's post-conflict period.

First, Sri Lanka occupies a strategic geographical location. The Indian Ocean has transformed into one of the world's busiest East-West trade and industrial corridors on the back of Asia's global rise over recent decades. It carries two-thirds of global oil shipments and a third of global bulk cargo. The spread of global supply chains to manufacturing hubs in China and suppliers in the rest of East Asia stimulated regional industrialisation and trade. A network of major ports and services activities followed, including trade logistics, finance, information technology and professional services. While the decade since the global financial crisis saw a slowdown, trade-led growth in the Indian Ocean was more robust than the world economy, benefiting from a rich natural resource base, vast fish stocks, a talent pool of educated youth, a rising China and India and smaller outward-oriented economies.[6] The region's historical dynamism suggests that it may recover faster than the world economy following the sudden stop in large swathes of the global economy in 2020 in the wake of the COVID-19-induced economic crisis.

The Indian Ocean's maritime security environment has also become dynamic. In particular, characterised by rising tensions between China and the US, problems between other regional economies and growing non-traditional security threats relating to maritime crime. Unsurprisingly, there is increasing international interest in expanding security cooperation with India, given a significant military capability.[7] The Trump administration withdrew from the Trans-Pacific Partnership (TPP) in January 2017 and developed a Free and Open Indo-Pacific Strategy (FOIP) in November 2017. Meanwhile, adopting a tough line on China in 2021, the Biden administration is also looking to contain China's military and economic power in Asia with the help of its allies – a key difference from the Donald Trump administration. The FOIP thus remains a broad concept emphasising maritime security, a liberal trading order and foreign aid. A fundamental tenant of the FOIP is the US viewing India as a key ally in its quest to counter a rising China and as a net security provider in the Indian Ocean.[8] Although Sri Lanka is not explicitly mentioned, some analysts also consider the country as an important partner in the FOIP.[9] The FOIP itself is partly a reaction to China's Belt and Road Initiative (BRI), an ambitious inter-continental programme for regional infrastructure connectivity launched in 2013, which would stretch from East Asia to Europe, significantly expanding China's economic and political influence.

A prime location in the centre of the Indian Ocean means that great powers consider Sri Lanka's role as an example of a small economy punching above its weight class.[10] Alice Wells, principal assistant secretary for South and Central Asian Affairs at the US State Department, recently observed that "Sri Lanka occupies some very important real estate in the Indo-Pacific region, and it's a country of increasing strategic importance in the Indian Ocean region".[11] The country is about ten nautical miles off the main East-West maritime trade route, which sees some 60,000 ships passing through annually, and only 34 nautical miles off the Southern coast of India with a large economy and a growing middle class of consumers. Furthermore, great powers have long eyed Trincomalee Harbour in North East Sri Lanka – reputed to be one of the world's deepest natural harbours – as a potential naval base, particularly for submarines. Trincomalee was home to the East Indies Station of the Royal Navy during Second World War and has become the Sri Lanka Navy's main base.

Second, Sri Lanka is an aspiring regional trading hub. The rise of Indian Ocean represents a huge regional economic opportunity for Sri Lanka, which was incorporated into the world economy as a plantation export economy during British rule in the 19th century. The economic policies of successive governments have attempted to add value to Sri Lanka's strategic location and put it on the commercial radar of great powers and their multinational corporations (MNCs). Following economic liberalisation in 1977 to become South Asia's most open economy, Sri Lanka successfully attracted foreign direct investment (FDI) and exported ready-made garments, thereby leveraging its advantages of preferential treatment under the Multi-Fibre Arrangement (MFA) and cheap labour.[12] More recently, Sri Lanka has aspired to become a major regional trading, logistics and finance hub, situated between the leading global hubs of Dubai and Singapore.[13] Major investments to handle containerised cargo since the early 1980s[14] has led to the emergence of Colombo Port as a pivotal South Asian port handling about half of all India's foreign transhipment trade.[15] The adjacent Colombo Port City is also being built on 249 hectares of reclaimed land from the sea and will eventually become triple A-grade commercial office space in Colombo and spur service-sector-led development.[16] To overcome the disadvantage of a small domestic market in the eyes of foreign investors, Sri Lanka began securing preferential market access to the dynamic Asia market through a strategy of bilateral free trade agreements (FTAs) with Asian powers like China, India, Singapore and Thailand.

Third, soft power strategies and domestic politics. Some commentators[17] note that Sri Lanka experienced a significant expansion of Chinese influence during the 2005–2015 regime of President Mahinda Rajapaksa. Development financing from Western countries dried up because of the country's graduation to middle-income status and concerns over human rights issues towards the end of the civil conflict. Human rights issues also led Sri Lanka to lose the coveted EU's Generalised System of Preferences plus facility (GSP+), which gave Sri Lankan exporters preferential access to the 27-nation bloc. China stepped in with commercial loans for infrastructure projects that were built by Chinese state-owned enterprises (SOEs) on a turnkey basis. Sri Lanka became an integral part of the Maritime Silk Road on the official BRI map,[18] and the Hambantota Port was considered a signature project (see later).

A coalition government led by President Maithripala Sirisena, between 2015 and 2019, swung the foreign policy pendulum back towards non-alignment, albeit with a tilt towards the West.[19] President Sirisena's government changed the pro-China policy of President Mahinda Rajapaksa while also attempting to mend the damage done to Sri Lanka's relations with the US, the European Union (EU) and

India. It renegotiated the Hambantota Port deal with China (see later), suspended other Chinese-funded infrastructure projects, decided to negotiate an International Monetary Fund (IMF) Extended Fund Facility and regained the EU's GSP+ facility.

The election of President Gotabaya Rajapaksa on 16 November 2019 appeared to signal another shift in the foreign policy pendulum. His government advocated the concept of "neutral non-alignment" to Sri Lanka's development advantage and invited great powers and others to invest in Sri Lanka rather than providing commercial loans. The new president's take on non-alignment might be informed by his strategic experience as a senior army officer and permanent secretary of defence during the civil conflict as well as his background as the brother of former President Mahinda Rajapaksa. At the time of writing, there were signs of renewed great power rivalries in pursuit of geopolitical influence in strategically located Sri Lanka particularly through so-called pandemic diplomacy of China and the US. Sri Lanka faces a delicate balancing act between great powers but it appears that President Gotabaya Rajapaksa has begun to follow in the footsteps of his brother's pro-China policy.

Fourth, Sri Lanka is a contributor to global public goods. Like other smaller nations in Asia, such as Singapore, Sri Lanka has actively supported multilateralism and a global rules-based order, which has traditionally balanced the interests of great and small powers alike. This commitment is rooted in Sri Lanka joining the United Nations in 1955 and being a founder member of the Non-Aligned Movement (NAM) in 1961. This meant that Sri Lanka was among a group of countries that did not want to be aligned with or against any major power. More recently, Sri Lanka played a key role in formulating the 1982 United Nations Convention on the Law of the Sea (UNCLOS), which provides customs and rules

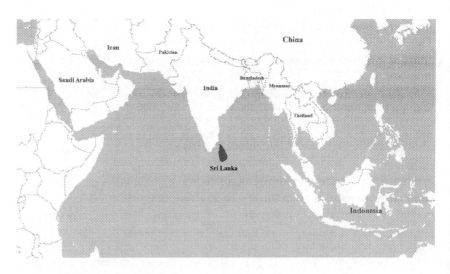

Map 6.1 Sri Lanka at a Glance

to maintain order and peaceful relations on the sea, and signed the 2016 Paris Agreement on Climate Change to tackle climate change and intensify the actions required for a sustainable low carbon future. Sri Lanka has also contributed about 18,000 troops to UN Peacekeeping operations, having first deployed a small continent of peacekeepers to the UN Mission in the Democratic Republic of Congo in 1960. This has reduced the burden on great powers to provide troops for peacekeeping operations.

The map shows the strategic location of Sri Lanka

Foreign trade and investment with great powers

Sri Lanka's twin priorities under this heading are to foster trade-led growth through exports and FDI and to avoid the country getting into a so-called middle-income trap (i.e. economic stagnation at middle-income levels and failing to transit to high-income status). There are positive and negative aspects of Sri Lanka's foreign trade and investment relations with great powers. From a low base, trade between Sri Lanka and both great powers grew in the post-conflict period but with differing implications for Sri Lanka's trade balance. However, bilateral FDI inflows from great powers into Sri Lanka significantly lag trade relations. Furthermore, despite years of trade talks, Sri Lanka lacks a bilateral FTA with either the US or China.

Sri Lanka-US trade and FDI

Sri Lanka's bilateral trade surplus with the US rose annually from US$1.7 billion to US$2.3 billion between 2010–2012 and 2017–2019 (see Table 6.1). During the pandemic, this figure fell to US$2.0 billion in 2020 reflecting a decline in US demand for Sri Lanka's exports. The US remains Sri Lanka's single largest export destination with a quarter of total exports. Garments dominate making up nearly three-quarters of Sri Lanka's exports to the US. Over time, the Sri Lankan garment industry shifted its competitive advantage on value addition rather than cheap production cost, focusing on product quality and the ability to manufacture niche items.[20] Many Sri Lankan garment firms have long-term manufacturing relations for leading US garment buyers/brands. Some large Sri Lankan garment firms have invested in plants in neighbouring Latin American countries such as Mexico, Haiti and Honduras to resourcefully use trade agreements to gain preferential access to the enormous high-income US market. MAS Holdings, Sri Lanka's largest garment firm, recently began manufacturing operations in the US by the acquisition of the business operations of Acme-McCrary Corporation, which is incorporated in North Carolina.[21]

However, US FDI inflows into Sri Lanka – totalling only about US$154 million during 2013–2019 (or only 2 per cent of cumulative FDI into Sri Lanka) – have been modest with very little going into the manufacturing sector (see Table 6.1). During the pandemic, US FDI to Sri Lanka fell to US$13 million in 2020 (down

Table 6.1 Indicators of US and China Ties with Sri Lanka (US$ Millions)

	The United States	China
Trade		
(1) Sri Lanka's Bilateral Deficit/Surplus		
Period Average (2010–2012)	1,732	(1,877)[1]
Period Average (2017–2019)	2,295	(3,952)[1]
2020	2,005	(3,366)[1]
(2) Per cent of Sri Lanka's Total Exports; Cumulative (2017–2019)	25	3
Foreign Direct Investment (FDI) to Sri Lanka		
(3) Cumulative FDI Inflows (2013-2019)	154	1,703
(4) Per cent of Sri Lanka's Total FDI Inflows (2013–2019)	2	24
Financial Development Assistance[2]		
(5) Cumulative Financial Development Assistance to Sri Lanka (2010–2019)	463	10,059
(6) Per cent of Sri Lanka's 2019 Gross Domestic Product (GDP)	0.6	12
Number of Tourist Arrivals to Sri Lanka		
(7) Cumulative Tourist Arrivals (2010–2019)	450,531	1,425,668
(8) Per cent of Sri Lanka's Total Tourist Arrivals (2010–2019)	3	9
Security Cooperation		
(9) Gift of Naval Vessels to Sri Lanka	1× Type 053H2G frigate	2× Hamilton Class Cutters
(10) Training for the Sri Lankan Military	Major US Navy exercises (e.g. Rim of the Pacific Exercise), regional dialogue	"Silk Route" Exercise, regional dialogue
(11) Defence Agreement(s) with Sri Lanka	Under discussion	NA
(12) Counter-Terrorism Support to Sri Lanka	Federal Bureau of Investigation (FBI) assistance	Security equipment and finance

Sources: USAID, Dept. of External Resources at the Ministry of Finance, Sri Lanka; ICT, Trade Map and IMF Direction of Trade Database; Central Bank of Sri Lanka.

Note:
1 ( ) indicates a trade deficit.
2 Heading covers grants and commercial loans.

from US$20 million in 2019). The low level of US FDI flows to Sri Lanka partly reflects Sri Lanka being geographically far from the US, lacking a country reputation among US MNCs as a location for manufacturing investment and having a very small domestic market of 21.8 million people with few active FTAs. It may also reflect US investors with an Asian presence viewing Sri Lanka as a riskier location for manufacturing activities than other locations in Southeast Asia. A perceived lack of political stability, given the legacy of a long civil conflict and the Easter Sunday attacks in 2019, is one issue.

Another may be that Sri Lanka is not regarded as a very friendly place to conduct business[22] according to the findings of international benchmarking exercises of the business environment across countries. For instance, Sri Lanka ranks 99th out of 190 countries in the World Bank's 2020 Doing Business Study, which provides objective measures of business regulations and their enforcement across 190 countries.[23] The country's poor ranking is indicative of a relatively cumbersome business environment compared to other upper-middle income Asian countries, which have successfully attracted significant US FDI inflows since the 1980s. According to the World Bank[24], Sri Lanka lags behind Malaysia and Thailand in important aspects of the business environment such as enforcing contracts, registering property and paying taxes.[25] Recognising these problems, Sri Lanka has made some recent progress in reforms to protecting minority investors, getting electricity connections and dealing with construction permits. But the digitisation of business regulations remains an unfinished agenda item.

The US-Sri Lanka bilateral Trade and Investment Framework Agreement (TIFA) signed in 2002 provides a framework for the two countries to discuss and resolve frictions at an early stage. Some 13 meetings have been held as of mid-2020. TIFAs are sometimes a prelude to a prized goal of a bilateral FTA with the US, given the enormous benefits of access to the world's largest market. There is a lengthy queue of countries seeking FTAs with the US, and the US seeks comprehensive FTAs, which involve substantial market opening of partner economies. Sri Lanka is not on the US FTA radar because of potential commercial issues such as a small domestic market, remoteness from the US and red tape affecting business.

Sri Lanka-China trade and FDI

A major challenge for Sri Lanka is a rising bilateral trade deficit with China, which doubled annually from US$1.9 billion to US$3.9 billion between 2010–2012 and 2017–2019. During the pandemic, this figure fell to US$3.4 billion in 2020. This large bilateral deficit is underpinned by a surge in capital goods and intermediate imports from China for infrastructure projects in Sri Lanka (see later). The import surge reflects a combination of long-term supplier relations between Chinese SOEs, heavy state subsidies to highly protected firms based in China and artificially low export prices, and the lack of a capital goods industry in Sri Lanka. Sri Lanka received US$1.7 billion of cumulative FDI inflows from China during 2013–2019 (or 24 per cent of total cumulative FDI inflows), which is higher than US FDI inflows, but nearly all is destined to infrastructure projects. The limited Chinese investor interest in Sri Lankan manufacturing seems linked to similar factors as those for US FDI inflows. Like with the US, there was a fall in Chinese FDI to Sri Lanka from US$46 million to US$15 million between 2019 and 2020.

Negotiations have been ongoing for a Sri Lanka and China FTA since 2014. But six rounds of talks stalled in 2017 due to disagreements regarding trade liberalisation under the proposed FTA. Sri Lanka had proposed a gradual trade opening with China by liberalising 90 per cent of tariff lines in a phased-out manner over a 20-year period. However, China has insisted on faster liberalisation of tariff lines between the two countries and objected to a review clause to reassess the FTA after 10 years.[26] Small and medium enterprises (SMEs) in Sri Lanka have expressed concerns about competition from cheap Chinese imports, which benefit unfairly from state subsidies, and have lobbied against fast trade opening. In 2021, President Rajapaksa's government has expressed interest in re-starting FTA talks with China in a bid for Sri Lankan exporters to gain market access to the dynamic Chinese market and to attract Chinese FDI to help upgrade Sri Lanka's manufactured exports beyond garments.

Tourism arrivals

In passing, it is worth mentioning tourism arrivals as an example of people-to-people movement from the great powers to Sri Lanka. Cumulative Chinese tourist arrivals to Sri Lanka (9 per cent of total tourist arrivals) were triple that of cumulative US tourist arrivals (3 per cent of total tourist arrivals) during the period 2010–2019. This difference may reflect factors such as increased marketing of Sri Lanka as a multi-dimensional tourism destination in China, the introduction of direct flights between China and Sri Lanka as early as 2006 and an increase in air connectivity of 18 weekly flights to four Chinese cities by 2016.[27] Furthermore, Sri Lanka is far from the US, there is an absence of direct flights to Sri Lanka making air travel quite expensive and US tourists have easy access to many cost-competitive holiday destinations in Latin America and the Caribbean. The closure of the airport in 2020 as a part of COVID-19 containment measures during the pandemic led to a collapse of tourism arrivals from the US and China.

Development assistance from great powers

Regarding development assistance, Sri Lanka's priorities are to address national development needs while avoiding geopolitical entanglements. The US is an older foreign aid provider to Sri Lanka than China. Both great powers have upped their support to Sri Lanka in the post-conflict period but with different foreign aid frameworks. In essence, the US provides relatively small grants, which do not have to be repaid by Sri Lanka, while China provides large commercial loans for infrastructure projects on which the capital and interest have to be repaid.

Lessons from the proposed MCC compact

Since 1956, the United States Agency for International Development (USAID) has provided development and humanitarian assistance to Sri Lanka. During the coalition government in Sri Lanka from 2015 to 2019, there was some shift in USAID priorities to strengthen democratic systems, promote sustainable economic growth and support marginalised and disaster-affected communities. Partly reflecting shifting US foreign aid priorities and Sri Lanka's graduation away from concessionary aid as a middle-income economy, however, USAID grants to Sri Lanka were relatively small totalling US$463 million during 2010–2019 (or about 0.5 per cent of Sri Lanka's 2019 GDP).

In 2005, President Mahinda Rajapaksa's government requested a Millennium Challenge Corporation (MCC) grant, but the MCC's response was muted. Fourteen years later, in a sign of increased US engagement to promote economic development, the MCC eventually approved a large compact programme for Sri Lanka in early 2019. Worth US$480 million (equivalent to US$22.43 for every Sri Lankan) over a 5-year period, the compact consisted of (1) a transport project to improve the road and bus network and (2) a land project to improve land administration. The MCC argues that the project brings several potential economic benefits to Sri Lanka.[28] One is that the money is an outright cash grant and does not have to be repaid to the MCC. Another is reducing distortions in the land market. Poor land administration in Sri Lanka means that there is a lot of litigation and the poor are affected disproportionately. Finally, it improves public transport, thereby reducing road congestion and enhances women's safety on buses.

Although Sri Lanka is a middle-income country, compacts are usually awarded to countries below middle-income status on the basis of them meeting MCC eligibility criteria of good governance, economic freedom and investment in its citizens. The delay in awarding a compact may be due to perceived gaps in governance and economic freedom in Sri Lanka during the civil conflict.

Sri Lanka's experience of MCC-type grant aid offers some sobering lessons for small powers in the developing world. The choice of projects included in the compact was based on a growth diagnostics study undertaken by foreign experts from Harvard University. It appears that insufficient or untimely consultations were undertaken with stakeholders in Sri Lanka including development partners or local think-tanks. For instance, there appeared to be little coordination on the transport project with multilateral development banks who dominate the transport development finance space in Sri Lanka. Furthermore, the land project was widely questioned as land ownership is a politically sensitive topic in Sri Lanka where land is a scarce commodity.[29] Improving agricultural productivity and irrigation systems may have been a better project because of its positive impact on improving depressed farm incomes and rural development.[30]

Another issue is that the administrative overhead seems high with some US$50 million (10 per cent of the total grant) allocated towards programme administration and oversight. While this might be standard MCC operating procedure, it seems unnecessarily high.[31] A rough rule of thumb from World Bank projects in Asia and the Pacific is that an overhead figure of 5–7 per cent should be sufficient for administrative overheads in aid programmes of this magnitude. A lower overhead means that more resources could be made available for development projects in Sri Lanka.

More generally, public communications throughout the process were surprisingly inadequate. The coalition government belatedly released the text of the compact agreement during the 2019 presidential election cycle. To further complicate matters, it seems that the presidential committee reviewing the compact in 2020 had a pre-determined political agenda, having only met once with the MCC Country Director and not met at all with the US Embassy.[32] Thus, in the absence of transparency, some members of the general public equated the compact as part of a sweetener for Sri Lanka to sign defence agreements with the US (see later).

In late October 2019, a couple of weeks before the presidential election, Sri Lanka's coalition government approved the compact and said that it will be submitted to parliament for enactment. Several opposition presidential candidates criticised the decision, and there was considerable activity on social media about the possible negative effects of the compact. In December 2019, following President Gotabaya Rajapaksa's election, a presidential committee was appointed to review the MCC compact. The final report of the presidential committee in June 2020 expressed reservations that certain clauses relating to land projects could not be legally implemented. The political ping pong over the MCC compact led to a loss of US patience with Sri Lanka. In mid-December 2020, the MCC Board of Directors decided to withdraw the compact from Sri Lanka and award it elsewhere. Sri Lanka's dysfunctional domestic politics and indecisiveness cost the country a significant US aid grant. Declining grant aid internationally and middle-income status means that Sri Lanka is unlikely to receive much grant funding in the future.

Hambantota Port – a Chinese debt trap?

Some observers trace the start of Chinese assistance for infrastructure development in Sri Lanka to the administration of President Mahinda Rajapaksa in the early 2000s. However, China's first infrastructure project in Sri Lanka dates to the 1970s in the form of outright grants, which included the construction of an international convention centre.[33] President Mahinda Rajapaksa's reign saw grant-based relations being upgraded to a commercial model that utilised interest-bearing loans and infrastructure-related FDI in transport, energy, telecommunications and water and sanitation projects. Furthermore, many of the early projects happened before the advent of the BRI in 2013. The total value of Chinese commercial loans, along with some infrastructure-related FDI, to Sri Lanka amounted to US$10.1 billion between 2010 and 2019 (or about 12 per cent of Sri Lanka's

2019 GDP).[34] This figure is over 20 times larger than grant-based development assistance provided by USAID during the same period.

The Hambantota Port was a signature project, predating the introduction of BRI in 2013. A decision was taken by President Mahinda Rajapaksa to accelerate the development of Hambantota – an economically backward region in southern Sri Lanka with high levels of youth unemployment – through infrastructure investment. A key project was a major transhipment port at Hambantota in the early 2000s, which was expected to become the country's second largest port after Colombo Port. With financing from the Export Import Bank of China (three fixed interest rate loans totalling US$1.4 billion), China Harbour Engineering Company (CHEC), a Chinese SOE constructed the port. It seems that comprehensive technical feasibility and market studies were not undertaken for the port project. Taking longer than expected to come on stream, the project incurred financial losses and put a strain on Sri Lanka's public finances. A chequered history has led some to portray Hambantota Port as a case study of unprofitable infrastructure investment and China's "debt-trap diplomacy".[35] It has been characterised as a strategic asset seizure, whereby China forcibly took control over Hambantota Port when the Sri Lankan government was allegedly unable to repay the loans that financed port construction.

Several clarifications are required of this misleading and dated narrative on the Hambantota Port project. First, a debt for equity swap implies that loans to China are forgiven or refinanced in exchange for equity. This is not what happened. In 2017, the coalition government of President Sirisena agreed to a straight infusion of equity in consideration for a 99-year lease. In accordance with a risk-sharing agreement, Sri Lanka received US$1.12 billion, which was used to bolster the country's foreign exchange reserves and retained ownership of the port.[36] Unlike the MCC agreement, the Hambantota agreement is not in the public domain but apparently provides for the Sri Lanka Navy to manage port security, thereby dispelling India's security concerns about China's strategic ambitions. After initially saying it was going to re-negotiate the Hambantota Port lease, President Gotabaya Rajapaksa's government backtracked under Chinese pressure and said it would honour it.

Second, the economic viability of Hambantota Port has improved significantly with the management of the project shifting to a different Chinese SOE, China Merchant Port Holdings Company Limited. This global port operator is not only developing Hambantota Port but also working to diversify the range of maritime services being offered (e.g. bunkering, ship repairing, sea marshals, crew changes, bonded warehousing and distribution). Once Hambantota Port becomes fully operational over the next few years, container traffic through Sri Lanka may double to some 16 million twenty-foot equivalent units (TEUs). The project also integrates port development with industrial development and services. The adjacent port-related industrial zone is hoped to facilitate the growth of the shipping industry and manufacturing through FDI. At 7 square kilometres, it is one of the largest industrial zones in South Asia and will provide modern infrastructure and incentives for export-oriented FDI and job creation. A business incubator and integrated logistics are included the project.

Third, whilst Sri Lanka may face a general foreign debt problem, this has little to do with Chinese loans. Hurley et al. assessed the likelihood of debt problems in a large sample of countries that received BRI investment from China but did not include Sri Lanka in the handful of countries they identified as being of particular concern.[37] The IMF's review of its extended fund facility in Sri Lanka in 2019 reported that Chinese commercial loans to Sri Lanka for infrastructure projects amounted to about US$5 billion (15 per cent of external debt) at the end of 2018.[38] To guard against the risk of a Chinese debt trap in the future, Sri Lanka should strengthen the debt-management system to reduce vulnerabilities and improve debt transparency with international assistance.[39] It should also request a short-term debt service suspension on Chinese debt to facilitate overall debt sustainability and increase its share of infrastructure financing from the Asian Investment and Infrastructure Bank (AIIB), which offers low-cost infrastructure finance at high procurement and environmental standards. In addition, Sri Lanka should adopt a more consistent policy framework for infrastructure projects made up of a supportive legal and regulatory structure, strong project management and transparent procurement procedures.[40]

Support from great powers to national security capacity

Sri Lanka's needs under this heading are partnerships to build national security capacity while minimising possible interference in Sri Lanka and avoiding militarisation of the Indian Ocean Region.[41] As it could not afford a significant military capability[42], Sri Lanka followed a non-aligned foreign policy alongside trying to improve its defence capability. China provided diplomatic support, armaments and military training during the civil conflict when the US was hesitant to step up due to human rights concerns.[43] However, since the conflict and particularly from 2015 onwards, under its FOIP, US bilateral security cooperation has increased.[44] These efforts have largely involved military equipment gifts, capacity building and policy dialogue, primarily in the maritime domain. This seems part of a trend where great and regional powers (e.g. Australia and India) are seeking to improve security ties with Indian Ocean littoral states such as Sri Lanka. This reflects rising maritime security threats in the Indian Ocean including piracy, climate change, illegal fishing, illegal immigration and drugs smuggling.[45]

Gifts of naval vessels

Until recently, Sri Lanka Navy was a relatively small naval force in terms of its power projection capabilities. During the conflict, the navy fought a sophisticated insurgency group with an effective sea wing. After the conflict, the navy focus changed to patrolling Sri Lanka's maritime boundaries against non-traditional security threats. The transnational nature of these crimes encouraged the US to provide military aid to improve the Sri Lanka Navy capacity to monitor Sri Lanka's exclusive economic zone. One gift in 2004 was a former medium endurance US Coast Guard cutter. Another gift in 2018 was a high endurance US Coast

Guard cutter (Hamilton class), which remains the largest vessel in Sri Lanka Navy's inventory (with a displacement of approximately 3,340 tons). These two US ships are appropriate to Sri Lanka's maritime security needs (drug interdiction, illegal immigrant interception and fisheries patrol) as they are designed for high-endurance, long-range missions.

China contributed to the Sri Lanka Navy's high-endurance capacity by gifting a Type 053H2G frigate, which is the second largest vessel by displacement. Whilst not the latest vintage of Chinese frigate, it is appropriate technology suited to Sri Lanka's maritime patrolling needs. The removal of the surface to air missile system before gifting makes it an offshore patrol vessel rather than a warship. Both the Chinese and US ships have hangars and landing pads for helicopters. This potentially adds air power to Sri Lanka's naval capabilities, which would increase the navy's maritime operational reach.

Joint training exercises and regional dialogue

The US also invited Sri Lanka to participate in the 2018 biennial Rim of the Pacific Exercise (RIMPAC), the world's largest maritime warfare exercise involving 26 countries. The invitation can be seen as a maturing of the Sri Lanka Navy's reputation as a professional maritime fighting force.[46] The US Marine Corps also trained with their Sri Lankan counterparts in 2016, and a naval exercise named CARAT (Cooperation Afloat Readiness and Training Exercise) was scheduled for 2019 but was cancelled after the 2019 Easter Sunday attacks in Sri Lanka.

Although the security relationship between China and Sri Lanka remains robust, there is little evidence of any significant bilateral military exercises since the two-staged "Silk Route" exercise in 2015. However, Chinese military personnel have frequently participated in other multilateral exercises hosted by Sri Lanka's armed forces such as "Cormoront Strike". In addition, Chinese military leaders along with their counterparts from the US, India, Australia and Japan are regular participants in the annual military forums hosted by the three branches of Sri Lanka's armed forces such as the Galle Dialogue (Sri Lanka Navy), Defence Seminar (Sri Lanka Army) and Colombo Air Symposium (Sri Lanka Air Force).

Defence cooperation agreements

While US-Sri Lanka cooperation on equipment and training has increased, Sri Lanka has hesitated to sign defence agreements with the US governing conduct, deployment and logistics. An Acquisition and Cross Servicing Agreement (ACSA) was first signed in 1995 and was renewed in 2007 and 2017. Nonetheless, ACSA and the far-reaching Status of Forces Agreement (SOFA) have become politicised domestically.[47] As the SOFA establishes the framework under which US military personnel can operate in Sri Lanka and how domestic laws can apply towards such personnel, the agreement has sparked worries about the risk of Sri Lanka's laws and sovereignty being undermined. In addition, the economic gain to Sri Lanka from such agreements seems unclear. While there is no evidence to support the claim, some are worried that such agreements are a possible stepping stone to a future agreement for a US military base in Sri Lanka. Finally, like with the MCC compact, critics say that there was insufficient consultation with parliamentarians and other stakeholders (e.g. the military) in Sri Lanka. At the time of writing, a SOFA with the US remains to be signed.

Interestingly, Sri Lanka has signed several Memorandum of Understanding (MOU), focusing on intelligence sharing and defence cooperation after the Easter Sunday attacks including ones with China. These non-US agreements, however, have not attracted the same level of scrutiny or opposition internally as the US SOFA. Given the fact that versions of the US ACSA were signed by multiple Sri Lankan administrations, it seems that the opposition to these agreements is motivated by local political concerns rather than on either principled or evidence-based aversions to security cooperation with the US.

Counter-terrorism support

Following the Easter Sunday attacks in 2019[48], both China and the US largely helped to aid local investigation efforts. Experts from the US Federal Bureau of Investigation and others shared their knowledge in explosives detection and forensic analysis. China's multi-pronged assistance included providing security and surveillance equipment, finance for the victims of the attacks and tourism promotion. The attacks highlighted gaps in Sri Lanka's internal state security structure. A pragmatic solution might be to use assistance from great powers to build the security sector's capacity to detect and deter future terror attacks.

Conclusion

This chapter discussed Sri Lanka's foreign relations with the US and China with a view to examining how great powers have responded to Sri Lanka's economic and security priorities. Great power interest reflects Sri Lanka's prime location as an aspiring trading hub in the Indian Ocean. Although Sri Lanka-great powers relations have intensified since 2010, their responses to Sri Lanka's priorities have been mixed. Trade has expanded, but Sri Lanka enjoys a trade surplus with the US while facing a problematic trade deficit with China. Far more glaring is that FDI inflows have lagged trade with the US and larger FDI flows from China are destined for infrastructure rather than manufacturing. Development assistance has increased, but Sri Lanka faces a dilemma of accessing small outright US grant aid versus a large volume of Chinese commercial infrastructure loans, which may pose the risks of a debt trap and geopolitical entanglements. China has been a visible security partner, and the US has upped its efforts to build Sri Lanka's defence capacity in the Indian Ocean maritime domain. But years of talks have not produced bilateral FTAs or major defence cooperation agreements with either great power.

Sri Lanka's experience provides important lessons for managing small power–great power relations for mutual benefit in a scenario of a second cold war in a post-COVID world.

First and foremost, building a resilient economy and society offers small powers the best chance of recovery from the COVID-19 economic shock and gains from relations with great powers than the alternatives. Under siege from protectionist lobbies and nationalist ideologies, some small powers are under pressure to turn inwards and adopt import substitution policies driven by controls and SOEs. However, the history of economic development is replete with cases of failed import substitution, which has led to poor allocation of resources, slow growth and black markets, amongst other issues.[49] Sudden and unplanned trade liberalisation can also cause the collapse of domestic industries, unemployment and import dependence. What is needed instead is a pragmatic, non-ideological approach to economic strategy in small powers, which combines market forces with state intervention in the form of macroeconomic policies, regulations and social welfare interventions to improve market outcomes.

In the case of Sri Lanka, such an approach to build a post-COVID-19 economy was identified in a recent report by an eminent persons' group of academics and business.[50] The key policy priorities suggested by the report are to (1) improve food security and provide enhanced social protection, (2) continue with macroeconomic stabilisation efforts and more effectively manage external debt through a new IMF programme and emergency assistance from other international financial institutions and bilateral donors, (3) undertake economic reforms including streamlining red tape and promoting digitisation of all public services, and (4) improve the coordination of economy policies through better institutions. These measures, along with improved regional economic cooperation in South Asia, should be kept in place for the medium term to put Sri Lanka on the road to recovery.

Second, great powers can support small powers to escape from a middle-income trap. The experience of high-performing Asian economies suggests that this requires actively transforming bilateral economic relations towards a different relationship from one based on aid and trade between great powers and small powers to a more dynamic one that eventually emphasises FDI, trade and aid.[51] At the heart of this transformation is a shift from traditional development assistance frameworks of providing grant aid or commercial borrowing for infrastructure towards diplomatic and economic cooperation. Transferring knowledge on good practices to sustain outward-orientation, target FDI and portfolio investment, streamline business procedures, capacity building for comprehensive FTA negotiations and improving macroeconomic management is a key aspect of such an approach. It may be prudent for small powers like Sri Lanka, on the cusp of the transition between lower and upper-middle-income status, to study Asian lessons of effective foreign aid management.

Third, there is a need to attempt the difficult task of decoupling security cooperation from economic relations in small power–great power engagement. An overemphasis on security cooperation between small powers and great powers can lead to intensifying geopolitical tensions and mistrust with regional powers such as India, which are important players in South Asia and the Indian Ocean Region.[52] In an ideal world, security cooperation with great powers should largely focus on developing regional public goods such as maritime patrol capabilities in small powers to tackle maritime crime and undertake search and rescue at sea.

Fourth, non-alignment remains a crucial principle to guide small power relations with great powers. Faced with rising geopolitical tensions between great powers, small powers like Sri Lanka face a quandary whether to continue balancing their great power engagement or change their alliance. Some have even been criticised for advocating non-alignment while tilting towards a great power on important international issues. Small powers should adhere to strict neutrality in foreign policy and "be careful not to choose sides among the big powers in the new strategic equilibrium of the Indian Ocean Region".[53] Codifying foreign policy in a written document, which defines national interests, goals for foreign engagement and principles, may make it easier for small powers to pursue non-alignment in consistent manner. More generally, small powers should lend their support to a multilateral and regional rules-based order, which is under increasing threat, as the optimal route to achieve global peace and prosperity. This means working closely with others in fora such as the United Nations, the Commonwealth and the Indian Ocean Rim Association.

In the final analysis, there is no one-size-fits-all approach to guiding effective small power–great power relations. These lessons need to be carefully tailored to the individual national circumstances, development strategies and capacity of small powers.

Notes

1 The views expressed here are solely mine. An earlier version of this paper was presented at the 2019 Berlin Conference on Asian Security (BCAS) organised by *Stiftung Wissenschaft und Politik* (SWP). I am most grateful to Indrajit Coomaraswamy, Felix Heiduk, Dinusha Panditaratne, a reviewer and BCAS 2019 participants for comments; to Malinda Meegoda for his input on security cooperation; and to Pabasara Kannangara and Chatuni Pabasara for research assistance.
2 M. A. Witt, "Prepare for the US and China to Decouple", *Harvard Business Review*, June 26, 2020, at https://hbr.org/2020/06/prepare-for-the-u-s-and-china-to-decouple
3 See for example S. Kelegama, "China-Sri Lanka Economic Relations: An Overview", *China Report*, 50 (2), 2014, pp. 131–149; G. Asirwatham, "Overview of Sri Lanka-China Relations", *The Prospector, LKI Blog on International Relations*, December 24, 2018, at www.lki.lk/blog/overview-of-sri-lanka-china-relations/; S. de Silva, "Trapped Between the Dragon and South Asia's Big Brother: The Case of Sri Lanka's Balanced Foreign Policy", *Sri Lanka Journal of Social Sciences*, 41 (2), 2018, pp. 69–81; R. Jayamaha, "Five Years into the Belt and Road Initiative: Potential Economic Benefits and Opportunities for Sri Lanka", RCSS Occasional Papers, Regional Centre for Strategic Studies, Colombo, 2019 (1); G. Wignaraja, D. Panditaratne, P. Kannangara, and D. Hundlani, "Chinese Investment and the BRI in Sri Lanka", Chatham House Research Paper, March 2020, at www.chathamhouse.org/publication/chinese-investment-and-bri-sri-lanka
4 Gunaratne provides a useful but descriptive historical overview of Sri Lanka's foreign policy with China, India and the US since independence. P. R. Gunaratne, "Sri Lanka's Foreign Policy: Colombo's Relations with Washington, Beijing and New Delhi", in T. Inoguchi (ed.), *The Sage Handbook of Asian Foreign Policy*, Sage Press, London, 2020, pp. 811–838.
5 T. Long, "Small States, Great Power? Gaining Influence Through Intrinsic, Derivative and Collective Power", *International Studies Review*, 19, 2017, pp. 185–205.

6 G. Wignaraja, "An Economic Analysis of Sri Lanka's Indian Ocean Opportunity", *Journal of the Indian Ocean Rim Studies*, 2 (1), 2019, pp. 132–149.
7 C. Raja Mohan, "Maritime Asia: An Indian Perspective", in G. Till (ed.), *The Changing Maritime Scene in Asia: Rising Tensions and Future Strategic Stability*, Palgrave Macmillan, Basingstoke, 2015, pp. 49–58.
8 A. Ayers, "The US Indo-Pacific Strategy Needs More Indian Ocean", Expert Brief, Council of Foreign Relations, January 22, 2019, at www.cfr.org/expert-brief/us-indo-pacific-strategy-needs-more-indian-ocean
9 J. Smith, "Sri Lanka: A Test Case for the Free and Open Indo-Pacific Strategy", The Heritage Foundation, Washington, DC, March 14, 2019.
10 See H. de Silva, "Sri Lanka's Role in the Indian Ocean and the Changing Global Dynamic", Speech at Public Forum on the Indian Ocean at the Institute of South Asian Studies, National University of Singapore, January 9, 2017, at www.mfa.gov.lk/depfm-isas/
11 US State Department, "Briefing with Alice G. Wells, Principal Assistant Secretary for South and Central Asian Affairs", January 24, 2020, at https://translations.state.gov/2020/01/24/principal-deputy-assistant-secretary-of-state-for-south-and-central-asian-affairs-alice-wells/
12 G. Wignaraja, *Trade Liberalization in Sri Lanka: Exports, Technology and Industrial Policy*, Macmillan Press, Basingstoke, UK, 1998; D. Lal and S. Rajapathirana, *Impediments to Trade Liberalization in Sri Lanka*, Trade Policy Research Centre, Thames Essays 51, Gower, Aldershot, 1989.
13 For a comprehensive analysis of the maritime trade dependence and prospects of Sri Lanka and maritime competitors such as Bangladesh and Myanmar, see J. Colombage and L. Edirisinghe, "Maritime Trade Dependence of Bangladesh, Myanmar and Sri Lanka", *Maritime Affairs (Journal of the National Maritime Foundation of India)*, online publication, October 3, 2018, pp. 85–98.
14 This investment includes building four new container terminals and deepening the main channel to handle large container ships.
15 Kannangara, P. "Sagarmala: India's New Port Development Strategy and Its Implications for Sri Lanka", *LKI Policy Brief*, February 13, 2019.
16 For an overview, and future scenarios, see LKI, "Port City SEZ – A Catalyst for Modern Services in Sri Lanka", Lakshman Kadirgamar Institute of International Relations and Strategic Studies, Colombo, 2020, at https://lki.lk/publication/port-city-sez-a-catalyst-for-modern-services-in-sri-lanka/
17 For example, J. Smith, no. 9.
18 See the map on the website for the First Belt and Road Forum for International Cooperation in 2017, at http://2017.beltandroadforum.org/GB/31/index.html
19 P. R. Gunaratne, no. 4.
20 R. Dheerasinghe, "Garment Industry in Sri Lanka: Challenges, Prospects and Strategies", *Central Bank of Sri Lanka Staff Studies*, 33 (1), 2009, pp. 33–72.
21 MAS Holdings NewsLine, 11 April, 2017, at http://newsline.masholdings.com/truly-global-mas-is-now-operational-in-the-americas/
22 I am grateful to former US Ambassador to Sri Lanka Robert Blake for this insight from his discussions with potential US investors.
23 World Bank, "Economy Profile Sri Lanka: Doing Business 2020", The World Bank, Washington, DC, 2020, at www.doingbusiness.org/content/dam/doingBusiness/country/s/sri-lanka/LKA.pdf
24 Ibid.
25 Kamardeen and Panditaratne provide a comprehensive assessment of the political background to FDI in Sri Lanka and how the Sri Lankan regulatory landscape needs to change to attract FDI that reflects domestic priorities. N. Kamardeen and D. Panditaratne, "The Regulation of Foreign Investments in Sri Lanka: A Policy-Based Perspective", LKI Working Paper, January 14, 2019, at https://lki.lk/publication/18132/

26 U. Moramudali, "Against the Tide: The Growth of China Sri Lanka Trade", *The Diplomat*, August 1, 2019.
27 News Release Sri Lankan Airlines, 28 January, 2016, at www.srilankan.com/en_uk/coporate/news-details/101.
28 See the author's video interview with MCC Country Director, Jenner Eldelman on October 24, 2019 at LKI in Colombo, www.youtube.com/watch?v=qjlShC3WL-8.
29 N. Gunatilleke, "MCC Land Compact Grant – More Knowledge and Study", *The Island*, July 15, 2019, at www.island.lk/index.php?page_cat=article-details&page=article-details&code_title=207504
30 G. Wignaraja, "Making the Millennium Challenge Corporation Compact Work for Sri Lanka", *Asia Pacific Bulletin No. 488*, September 18, 2019, East West Center.
31 Ibid.
32 Lankanewsweb, "US Debunks Presidential Committee Claims on MCC" 28 June, 2020, at www.lankanewsweb.net/67-general-news/64295-US-debunks-Presidential-committee-claims-on-MCC.
33 China's first infrastructure project in Sri Lanka dates to the 1970s in the form of outright grants, which included the construction of a convention centre. The iconic Bandaranaike Memorial International Conference Hall (BMICH), inaugurated in Colombo in 1973, was a Chinese gift to Sri Lanka emulating the design of the Great Hall of the People in Beijing. The two countries had enjoyed a warm relationship since Sri Lanka recognised the People's Republic of China (PRC) in January 1950 and supported China's accession to the UN. These developments and the historic barter trade deal – the Ceylon – PRC Rubber-Rice Pact of 1952 – led to China gifting the BIMCH to Sri Lanka. See G. Asirwatham, "Overview of Sri Lanka-China Relations", *The Prospector, LKI Blog on International Relations*, December 24, 2018, at www.lki.lk/blog/overview-of-sri-lanka-china-relations/
34 See G. Wignaraja et al., no. 3, for a comprehensive study of Chinese investment in Sri Lanka.
35 Chellaney was an early proponent of Sri Lanka falling into a Chinese debt trap. B. Chellaney, "China's Creditor Imperialism", *Project Syndicate*, December 20, 2017, at www.project-syndicate.org/commentary/china-sri-lanka-hambantota-port-debt-by-brahma-chellaney-2017-12?barrier=accesspaylog; Thorne and Spevack explore the link between China's investment in the Hambantota Port and geopolitical strategy. They argue that the terms of the 99-year lease on Hambantota Port favour China, that the investment generated political influence and that Chinese debt constricts Sri Lankan policy. D. Thorne and B. Spevack, "Harbored Ambitions: How China's Port Investments Are Strategically Reshaping the Indo-Pacific", *A Report by C4ADS*, Washington, DC, at https://static1.squarespace.com/static/566ef8b4d8af107232d5358a/t/5ad5e20ef950b777a94b55c3/1523966489456/Harbored+Ambitions.pdf; This narrative has been challenged by Weerakoon and Jayasuriya, Brautigam and Wignaraja et al., see D. Weerakoon and S. Jayasuriya, "Sri Lanka's Debt Problem Is Not Made in China", *East Asia Forum*, February 28, 2019; D. Brautigam, "A Critical Look at Chinese Debt Trap Diplomacy: The Rise of a Meme", *Area Development and Policy*, 5 (1), 2020, pp. 1–14; Wignaraja et al., no. 3.
36 See G. Wignaraja et al., no. 3.
37 J. Hurley, S. Morris, and G. Portelance, *Examining the Debt Implications of the Belt and Road Initiative from a Policy Perspective*, Centre for Global Development, Washington, DC, March 4, 2018, at www.cgdev.org/publication/examining-debt-implications-belt-and-road-initiative-a-policy-perspective (Accessed February 3, 2020).
38 International Monetary Fund, Asia and Pacific Dept., *Sri Lanka: Fifth Review Under the Extended Arrangement Under the Extended Fund Facility*, International Monetary Fund, Washington, DC, 2019, at www.imf.org/en/Publications/CR/Issues/2019/05/15/

Sri-Lanka-Fifth-Review-Under-the-Extended-Arrangement-Under-the-Extended-Fund-Facility-46900 (Accessed February 5, 2020).
39 G. Wignaraja et al., no. 3.
40 R. Jayamaha, no. 3.
41 For a discussion, see D. Panditaratne, "China's Commercial and Military Presence in the Indian Ocean: A Perspective from Sri Lanka", in *CNA Conference Reports Views of China's Presence in the Indian Ocean*, CNA, Washington, DC, 2020.
42 For cross-country data on defence spending, see M. Meegoda, "How Can Sri Lanka Navigate the Asian Arms Race Conundrum?", *LKI Policy Brief*, Lakshman Kadirgamar Institute of International Relations and Strategic Studies, December 19, 2018, at www.lki.lk/publication/how-can-sri-lanka-navigate-the-asian-arms-race-conundrum/
43 Nonetheless, there is a view that the US provided backroom help to Sri Lanka during the civil conflict such as military intelligence and encouraging active military assistance from Israel. R. Venugopal, "Global Dimensions of the Conflict in Sri Lanka", Queen Elizabeth House Working Paper No. 99, Oxford University, 2003.
44 J. Smith, no. 9.
45 G. Wignaraja, no. 6; A. Chatterjee, "Non-traditional Maritime Security Threats in the Indian Ocean Region", *Maritime Affairs (Journal of the National Maritime Foundation of India)*, 10 (2), November 6, 2014, pp. 77–95.
46 A relatively small group of some 25 officers from Sri Lanka's recent marine battalion participated in RIMPAC 2018.
47 S. Ramachandran, "Sri Lankans Up in Arms Over US Military Pacts", *The Diplomat*, August 15, 2019.
48 Gunaratna argues that these multiple suicide attacks represent a new phase of the so-called Islamic State's global expansion. R. Gunaratna, "Islamic State: A New Phase of Global Expansion", RSIS Commentary No. 081–24, April 2019.
49 J. N. Bhagwati, "Free Trade: Old and New Challenges", *Economic Journal*, 104 (423), March 1, 1994, pp. 231–246.
50 See Pathfinder Foundation, "Pathfinder Beyond the Box: A New Economic Visions for Post-COVID-19 Sri Lanka", 2020, at https://lki.lk/publication/lki-supported-pathfinder-foundation-to-prepare-action-oriented-recommendations-on-a-post-covid-19-sri-lankan-economy/
51 G. Wignaraja, J. Tyson, A. Prizzon, and D. W. te Velde, "Asia in 2025: Development Prospects and Challenges for Middle-Income Countries", Overseas Development Institute, London, September, 2018, at www.odi.org/publications/11202-asia-2025-development-prospects-and-challenges-middle-income-countries.
52 C. Raja Mohan, no. 7.
53 R. Yuanzhe, "Exploring Unknown Shores: China's Small State Diplomacy", *South Asia Scan*, Issue No. 7, May, Institute of South Asian Studies, National University of Singapore, 2020, p. 5.

Bibliography

Asirwatham, G., "Overview of Sri Lanka-China Relations", *The Prospector, LKI Blog on International Relations*, December 24, 2018, at www.lki.lk/blog/overview-of-sri-lanka-china-relations/

Ayers, A., "The US Indo-Pacific Strategy Needs More Indian Ocean", *Expert Brief, Council of Foreign Relations*, January 22, 2019, at www.cfr.org/expert-brief/us-indo-pacific-strategy-needs-more-indian-ocean

Bhagwati, J. N., "Free Trade: Old and New Challenges", *Economic Journal*, 104 (423), March 1, 1994, pp. 231–246.

Brautigam, D., "A Critical Look at Chinese Debt Trap Diplomacy: The Rise of a Meme", *Area Development and Policy*, 5 (1), 2020, pp. 1-14.

Chatterjee, A., "Non-traditional Maritime Security Threats in the Indian Ocean Region", *Maritime Affairs (Journal of the National Maritime Foundation of India)*, 10 (2), November 6, 2014, pp. 77–95.

Chellaney, B., "China's Creditor Imperialism", *Project Syndicate*, December 20, 2017, at www.project-syndicate.org/commentary/china-sri-lanka-hambantota-port-debt-by-brahma-chellaney-2017–12?barrier=accesspaylog

Colombage, J., and L. Edirisinghe, "Maritime Trade Dependence of Bangladesh, Myanmar and Sri Lanka", *Maritime Affairs (Journal of the National Maritime Foundation of India)*, online publication, October 3, 2018, pp. 85–98.

de Silva, H., "Sri Lanka's Role in the Indian Ocean and the Changing Global Dynamic", Speech at Public Forum on the Indian Ocean at the Institute of South Asian Studies, National University of Singapore, January 9, 2017, at www.mfa.gov.lk/depfm-isas/

de Silva, S., "Trapped Between the Dragon and South Asia's Big Brother: The Case of Sri Lanka's Balanced Foreign Policy", *Sri Lanka Journal of Social Sciences*, 41 (2), 2018, pp. 69–81.

Dheerasinghe, R., "Garment Industry in Sri Lanka: Challenges, Prospects and Strategies", *Central Bank of Sri Lanka Staff Studies*, 33 (1), 2009, pp. 33–72.

Gunaratna, R., "Islamic State: A New Phase of Global Expansion", RSIS Commentary No. 081–24, April 2019.

Gunaratne, P. R., "Sri Lanka's Foreign Policy: Colombo's Relations with Washington, Beijing and New Delhi", in T. Inoguchi (ed.), *The Sage Handbook of Asian Foreign Policy*, Sage Press, London, 2020, pp. 811–838.

Gunatilleke, N., "MCC Land Compact Grant – More Knowledge and Study", *The Island*, July 15, 2019, at www.island.lk/index.php?page_cat=article-details&page=article-details&code_title=207504

Hurley, J., S. Morris, and G. Portelance, *Examining the Debt Implications of the Belt and Road Initiative from a Policy Perspective*, Centre for Global Development, Washington, DC, March 4, 2018, at www.cgdev.org/publication/examining-debt-implications-belt-and-road-initiative-a-policy-perspective (Accessed February 3, 2020).

International Monetary Fund, Asia and Pacific Dept., *Sri Lanka: Fifth Review Under the Extended Arrangement Under the Extended Fund Facility*, International Monetary Fund, Washington, DC, 2019, at www.imf.org/en/Publications/CR/Issues/2019/05/15/Sri-Lanka-Fifth-Review-Under-the-Extended-Arrangement-Under-the-Extended-Fund-Facility-46900 (Accessed February 5, 2020).

Jayamaha, R., "Five Years into the Belt and Road Initiative: Potential Economic Benefits and Opportunities for Sri Lanka", RCSS Occasional Papers, Regional Centre for Strategic Studies, Colombo, 2019 (1).

Kamardeen, N., and D. Panditaratne, "The Regulation of Foreign Investments in Sri Lanka: A Policy-Based Perspective", LKI Working Paper, January 14, 2019, at https://lki.lk/publication/18132/

Kannangara, P., "Sagarmala: India's New Port Development Strategy and Its Implications for Sri Lanka", *LKI Policy Brief*, February 13, 2019.

Kelegama, S., "China-Sri Lanka Economic Relations: An Overview", *China Report*, 50 (2), 2014, pp. 131–149.

Lal, D., and S. Rajapathirana, *Impediments to Trade Liberalization in Sri Lanka*, Trade Policy Research Centre, Thames Essays 51, Gower, Aldershot, 1989.

Lee, Hsien Loong, "The Endangered Asian Century", *Foreign Affairs*, July/August, 2020.

LKI, "Port City SEZ – A Catalyst for Modern Services in Sri Lanka", Lakshman Kadirgamar Institute of International Relations and Strategic Studies, Colombo, 2020, at https://lki.lk/publication/port-city-sez-a-catalyst-for-modern-services-in-sri-lanka/

Long, T., "Small States, Great Power? Gaining Influence Through Intrinsic, Derivative and Collective Power", *International Studies Review*, 19, 2017, pp. 185–205.

Meegoda, M., "How Can Sri Lanka Navigate the Asian Arms Race Conundrum?", *LKI Policy Brief*, Lakshman Kadirgamar Institute of International Relations and Strategic Studies, December 19, 2018, at www.lki.lk/publication/how-can-sri-lanka-navigate-the-asian-arms-race-conundrum/

Moramudali, U., "Against the Tide: The Growth of China Sri Lanka Trade", *The Diplomat*, August 1, 2019.

Panditaratne, D., "China's Commercial and Military Presence in the Indian Ocean: A Perspective from Sri Lanka", in *CNA Conference Reports Views of China's Presence in the Indian Ocean*, CNA, Washington, DC, 2020.

Pathfinder Foundation, "Pathfinder Beyond the Box: A New Economic Visions for Post-COVID-19 Sri Lanka", 2020, at https://lki.lk/publication/lki-supported-pathfinder-foundation-to-prepare-action-oriented-recommendations-on-a-post-covid-19-sri-lankan-economy/

Raja Mohan, C., "Maritime Asia: An Indian Perspective", in G. Till (ed.), *The Changing Maritime Scene in Asia: Rising Tensions and Future Strategic Stability*, Palgrave Macmillan, Basingstoke, 2015, pp. 49–58.

Ramachandran, S., "Sri Lankans Up in Arms Over US Military Pacts", *The Diplomat*, August 15, 2019.

Smith, J., "Sri Lanka: A Test Case for the Free and Open Indo-Pacific Strategy", The Heritage Foundation, Washington, DC, March 14, 2019.

Thorne, D., and B. Spevack, "Harbored Ambitions: How China's Port Investments Are Strategically Reshaping the Indo-Pacific", A Report by C4ADS, Washington, DC, 2017, at https://static1.squarespace.com/static/566ef8b4d8af107232d5358a/t/5ad5e20ef950b777a94b55c3/1523966489456/Harbored+Ambitions.pdf

US State Department, "Briefing with Alice G. Wells, Principal Assistant Secretary for South and Central Asian Affairs", January 24, 2020, at https://translations.state.gov/2020/01/24/principal-deputy-assistant-secretary-of-state-for-south-and-central-asian-affairs-alice-wells/

Venugopal, R., "Global Dimensions of the Conflict in Sri Lanka", Queen Elizabeth House Working Paper No. 99, Oxford University, 2003.

Weerakoon, D., and S. Jayasuriya, "Sri Lanka's Debt Problem Is Not Made in China", East Asia Forum, February 28, 2019.

Wignaraja, G., "An Economic Analysis of Sri Lanka's Indian Ocean Opportunity", *Journal of the Indian Ocean Rim Studies*, 2 (1), 2019, pp. 132–149.

Wignaraja, G., "Making the Millennium Challenge Corporation Compact Work for Sri Lanka", *Asia Pacific Bulletin No. 488*, September 18, 2019, East West Center.

Wignaraja, G., *Trade Liberalization in Sri Lanka: Exports, Technology and Industrial Policy*, Macmillan Press, Basingstoke, UK, 1998.

Wignaraja, G., D. Panditaratne, P. Kannangara, and D. Hundlani, "Chinese Investment and the BRI in Sri Lanka", Chatham House Research Paper, March 2020, at www.chathamhouse.org/publication/chinese-investment-and-bri-sri-lanka

Wignaraja, G., J. Tyson, A. Prizzon, and D. W. te Velde, "Asia in 2025: Development Prospects and Challenges for Middle-Income Countries", Overseas Development Institute, London, September, 2018, at www.odi.org/publications/11202-asia-2025-development-prospects-and-challenges-middle-income-countries

Witt, M. A., "Prepare for the US and China to Decouple", *Harvard Business Review*, June 26, 2020, at https://hbr.org/2020/06/prepare-for-the-u-s-and-china-to-decouple

World Bank, "Economy Profile Sri Lanka: Doing Business 2020", The World Bank, Washington, DC, 2020, at www.doingbusiness.org/content/dam/doingBusiness/country/s/sri-lanka/LKA.pdf

Yuanzhe, R., "Exploring Unknown Shores: China's Small State Diplomacy", *South Asia Scan*, Issue No. 7, May, Institute of South Asian Studies, National University of Singapore, 2020.

7 India, Indo-Pacific Coalitions and China: From Alignment to Alliance?

Jagannath P. Panda

Introduction

India's China policy has for the past forty years centred around constructive, tactical economic engagement and managing its powerful neighbour's dramatic rise amidst perpetual security concerns. Under Prime Minister Narendra Modi, this delicate balancing has included a nationalistic outlook, too, which seeks to bring about "parity of power, both bilaterally and regionally", aiming to "position India as a peer partner rather than just a partner of China".[1] The Doklam stand-off in 2017 did precisely that. However, the altercation in the Galwan valley in June 2020, the deadliest clash along the Line of Actual Control (LAC) since 1975, has put a spanner in the works of this policy framework.[2] China's "peaceful rise" seems to have also run its course – all its recent highly aggressive foreign policy decisions and incursions in the neighbourhood bear testament to that.[3] Moreover, India's post-Galwan nationalistic anti-China narrative, coupled with the post-COVID-19 global backlash against China, is pushing to overhaul India's "China Connect" policy.[4]

Globally, the United States, India's "Comprehensive Global Strategic"[5] partner, has intensified its anti-China rhetoric. The US-China ties have faced some of the most challenging times in the "Asian Century". [6] In 2017, the United States named China (as well as Russia) a "revisionist power" in its National Security Strategy (NSS);[7] and in 2019, the US Department of the Treasury called it a "currency manipulator"[8]. The China threat has received bipartisan recognition in Washington; under new US President Joe Biden, US' China policies are unlikely to revert to positive impressions, even as a more calculated and smooth policy direction in dealing with Beijing is implemented. China, for its part, has time and again tried to upend the existing international order and challenge the *status quo*: China-centred financial institutions, such as the Asian Infrastructure Development Bank (AIIB) and the National Development Bank (NDB), are certainly challenging the US dominance of global economy. Overall, too, China seems to be successfully threatening global US hegemony. Thus, their ties today highlight "confrontationist-competitive" characteristics, a shift from the post-Cold War "cooperative-competitive" spirit.[9] The July 2020 release of the US official 'position' by former Secretary of State Mike Pompeo on the South China Sea that deemed Chinese claims in the region as "completely unlawful"[10] and escalation

DOI: 10.4324/9781003106814-7

in tensions post orders by the US government to Beijing to shut its Houston consulate, citing efforts to steal trade secrets, marked the further classification of this argument.[11] With new Secretary of State Anthony Blinken remarking that former US President Donald Trump's tough China approach was correct, a continuation of US-China rivalry can be anticipated.[12]

The US-China rivalry of today stems from the rapid expansion in capacity and influence of China which was not accompanied with political openness. In the late 1970s, Deng Xiaoping undertook a reform process that transformed the Chinese economy. In 2001, communist China was allowed entry into the US-led world trading order, as the West was under the impression that it would be able to integrate and mould China into its liberal, democratic fold. However, China's miraculous economic growth exceeded expectations. The rise of Xi Jinping as a strongman has only strengthened government controls amid a growing economy and modernised military; when he became President in 2013, China had the largest foreign exchange reserve in the world boasting of trillions of dollars and had established itself as an export and manufacturing powerhouse.[13] China is the world's second-largest economy and has been the "world's largest goods trading nation since 2013, accounting for 11.4 per cent of global goods trade in 2017".[14] Its increasing military posturing, in the Indo-Pacific for instance, has been a grave cause for concern for the United States, which was looking to reduce its presence in Asia and the Indo-Pacific. The Obama administration's "pivot"[15] to Asia, the Trump administration's "America First" policies along with its anti-China rhetoric and Biden's call to "renew" alliances and have America "lead again"[16] have only worsened the tensions between China and the United States. Consequently, a "bipartisan consensus", outlining the need for the United States to refigure its China policy, has emerged.[17]

As Sanjay Baru argues in his 2015 opinion piece in *The Hindu*, the path China decides to choose for itself will determine its relations with other nations. If Beijing is able to reject 'an imperialist view of history', it can work together with India and other nations in the multipolar world order.[18] This statement has held true with respect to development of relations between China and countries across the world. The crux of the problem is that China has upped its ante in recent times: it has blatantly disregarded the existing international norms; engaged in multiple conflicts at the same time even as a new pandemic has been raging the world, primarily, as a show of strength; and pursued a new, hard-line "wolf-warrior diplomacy". This has certainly led to a global backlash, and consequently its ties with several countries have been affected. For example, China-Australia ties are at an "all-time low"[19] after Australia called for an independent investigation into the origins of COVID-19.[20] China retaliated by placing tariffs on Australian barley and banning beef from major Australian exporters.[21] Australia called the economic threats by its largest trading partner a "wake-up call"[22] and said that it would not be "intimidated" by such behaviour.[23] After the COVID-19-induced slowdown, Japan in April 2020 earmarked a US$ 2.2 billion stimulus package to shift businesses out of China into neighbouring nations or back home to thus reduce dependency on China.[24] The first round of subsidies as part of this effort saw 57 Japanese companies in China receiving USD 535 million to shift to Japan while 30 others have been paid to expand production into Southeast Asian Nations like Vietnam and Thailand.[25] Moreover, incursion attempts by Chinese patrol ships into the Japan-administered Senkaku Islands (called Diaoyu in China) in the East China Sea (ECS) have soured the already tense Sino-Japanese relations. Other examples of China's increased belligerence include its military exercises near Taiwan, latest border disputes with Bhutan (as well as Nepal and India); maritime incidents in the South China Sea (SCS) and the National Security Law for Hong Kong.[26] Importantly, the incidents cannot be seen as either isolated or one-offs. They reflect China's readiness to engage in, or even create new, conflicts to pursue its own strategic needs, be they domestic or international, without much regard for the existing rules-based order.

This chapter highlights the impending transformation that is taking place in India's China policy after the Galwan clash that has changed existing perceptions, especially with regard to ties with its Indo-Pacific partner-states. It looks into the Quadrilateral Strategic Dialogue (Quad or "Quad 2.0") grouping which is leading to a greater framework of cooperation in Indo-Pacific (under a narrative of "Quad Plus"), as well as into other multilateral cooperation frameworks. It also analyses the new policy framework's likely focus on containing China's Belt and Road Initiative (BRI), rather than pursuing a blatant anti-China rhetoric, and opting for major changes to its "power-partner" parity with China. India's domestic policies such as the "Aatmanirbhar Bharat" scheme and its trilateral cooperative frameworks with Indo-Pacific partners, as well as the US-led Blue Dot Network (BDN), are examined as viable alternatives to counter China's BRI. The chapter studies India's Indo-Pacific overtures through a possible strategic manoeuvring in the SCS, advocating for a broader convergence with its Quad and Quad Plus partners in the region. The chapter concludes by calling for a more radical shift in India's foreign policy.

Delineating New Strategic Imperatives through Quad 2.0 and Quad Plus

India's foreign policy has undergone a remarkable shift under the Narendra Modi government but is still in transition: evolving from non-alignment[27] to multi-alignment, perhaps now tilting towards alliances in the post-Galwan period. Its "power-partner" framework juxtaposes China as a revisionist power in the Indo-Pacific with China as an economic partner in the multilateral domain.[28] The Galwan clash has seriously undermined the developmental partnership India and China share, and the necessity for India to reorient its defence and economic policies along nationalistic lines has heightened. In other words, a firm economic and security approach to China coupled with greater focus on an India-US alignment framework to promote an alliance-based understanding with Indo-Pacific partners has become a strategic imperative in India's foreign policy.[29]

Against this background, Quad 2.0 comprising India, the US, Japan and Australia is a significant entity that perhaps marks the "changing nature of diplomacy" in the post-COVID world.[30] The grouping initially began as a consultative forum to counter the increasing threat posed by Beijing's aggressive rise in the

Indo-Pacific.[31] Specifically, India's engagement to date must be seen through a "plural and compound" lens of India's evolving ties with major powers (or like-minded countries) and its strategic interests in the Indo-Pacific region without actually formally embracing an alliance structure.[32] This is set to change in light of the aforementioned recent events.

In the coming years, India can be expected to willingly embrace a US-led liberal, democratic world order that envisions a "Free and Open Indo-Pacific" (FOIP). For the Quad, this is not a new vision. Its official meetings since 2017 have always reposed their faith in international norms to promote peace, stability and prosperity in the Indo-Pacific (see Table 1).

Table 7.1 Quad's Official Consultations (2017–2019)

S. no	Date	Venue	Official representatives	Major issues discussed
1.	November 13, 2017	Philippines/ Manila, on the side-lines of the ASEAN summit.	Officials from India's Ministry of External Affairs (MEA), Australia's Department of Foreign Affairs & Trade (DFAT), Japan's Ministry of Foreign Affairs (MOFA) and the US Department of State	Rules-based order in the Indo-Pacific (e.g., respect for international law, freedom of navigation and overflight); enhancing connectivity; efforts to address the challenges of countering terrorism and upholding maritime security in the Indo-Pacific.
2.	June 7, 2018	Singapore, on the side-lines of the East Asia Summit	Foreign Ministry officials from India, Australia, Japan and the US	Shared objectives in the areas of connectivity and development, regional security, including counterterrorism and non-proliferation, humanitarian assistance and disaster relief (HA-DR), and maritime cooperation; support for a free, open, prosperous and inclusive Indo-Pacific; commitment towards a rules-based order in the Indo-Pacific.

S. no	Date	Venue	Official representatives	Major issues discussed
3.	November 15, 2018	Singapore	Officials from India's MEA, Australia's DFAT, Japan's MOFA and the US State Department	Cooperation in areas such as connectivity, sustainable development, counterterrorism, non-proliferation and maritime and cybersecurity.
4.	May 31, 2019	Bangkok	Officials from India's MEA, Australia's DFAT, Japan's MOFA and the US State Department	Same as above.
5.	September 26, 2019	New York, first ministerial-level meeting of the Quad, held on theside-lines of the UNGA	US Secretary of State Mike Pompeo, Indian External Affairs Minister Dr. S. Jaishankar and Foreign Ministers Toshimitsu Motegi of Japan and Marise Payne of Australia.	Same as above.
6.	November 4, 2019	Bangkok	Senior officials from the Ministry of External Affairs of India, Department of Foreign Affairs & Trade of Australia, Ministry of Foreign Affairs of Japan and Department of State of the United States of America	Same as above, plus: re-affirmed commitment to a free, open, prosperous and inclusive Indo-Pacific, reiterated support for ASEAN-centrality.

(*Continued*)

Table 7.1 (Continued)

S. no	Date	Venue	Official representatives	Major issues discussed
7.	September 25, 2020	Virtual	Senior officials from the Ministry of External Affairs of India, Department of Foreign Affairs & Trade of Australia, Ministry of Foreign Affairs of Japan and Department of State of the United States of America	Same as above, plus: discussed important of enhancing supply chain resilience in lieu of the COVID-19 pandemic.
8.	October 6, 2020	Tokyo, Japan, second ministerial-level meeting	Indian External Affairs Minister Dr. S. Jaishankar, US Secretary of State Mike Pompeo, Foreign Ministers Toshimitsu Motegi of Japan and Marise Payne of Australia	Same as above, plus: discussed post-COVID 19 international order, called for a coordinated response to financial problems due to the pandemic, agreed to hold these consultations regularly.
9.	December 18, 2020	Virtual	Senior officials from the Ministry of External Affairs of India, Department of Foreign Affairs & Trade of Australia, Ministry of Foreign Affairs of Japan and Department of State of the United States of America	Same as above.

S. no	Date	Venue	Official representatives	Major issues discussed
10.	February 18, 2021	Virtual	Indian External Affairs Minister Dr. S. Jaishankar, US Secretary of State Anthony Blinken, Foreign Ministers Toshimitsu Motegi of Japan and Marise Payne of Australia	Same as above, plus: highlighted their shared attributes as political democracies, market economies and pluralistic societies, noted that Indo-Pacific concept is gaining recognition internationally especially in Europe, discussed vaccination plans.

Source: Ministry of External Affairs (www.mea.gov.in)

India's foreign policy transformation is obviously a response to China's increasingly coercive and revisionist behaviour particularly in the SCS and the ECS. India should in the future be less worried about China's apprehensions of the Quad 2.0 as an Asian North Atlantic Treaty Organisation (NATO) and continue to bolster its strategic ties with like-minded countries such as the US.

India has in some ways already started that trend: For example, apart from being a Global Strategic Partner and Major Defence Partner (MDP)[33] of the United States, it has also signed with the US the Logistics Exchange Memorandum of Agreement (LEMOA) in 2016,[34] the Communications Compatibility and Security Agreement (COMCASA) in 2018,[35] the defence technology transfer pacts in 2019[36] and the Basic Exchange and Cooperation Agreement (BECA)[37].; and conducted the tri-service military exercise "Tiger Triumph".[38] India and Japan held their first 2+2 Foreign and Defence Ministerial Meeting on November 30, 2019 in New Delhi to "enhance the strategic depth of bilateral security and defence cooperation". The two nations welcomed the second Dharma-Guardian exercise in 2019 and the second "SHINYUU Maitri-2019" military exercise.[39] New Delhi in 2020 also successfully inked the long-pending Acquisition and Cross-Servicing Agreement (ACSA) with Japan.[40] India and Australia participated in their first-ever virtual summit in June 2020 and elevated their "bilateral Strategic Partnership concluded in 2009 to a Comprehensive Strategic Partnership (CSP)". Both sides agreed to "increase military inter-operability through defence exercises through their agreement concerning Mutual Logistics Support".[41] Furthermore, the inclusion[42] of Australia in the US-Japan-India joint maritime exercise Malabar has boosted the maritime security synergy of the Quad.

Technologically, upholding a firmer position against Huawei and recalibrating its 5G links can serve as a major cooperation area between India and partner nations to strengthen military information exchange and technological growth. India has now signed military logistics agreements – like ACSA – with Japan, US,

South Korea and France; this provides New Delhi a comprehensive network for military technology growth. Further, the UK Government's idea of a 5G club of 10 democracies, which would include India, amid the growing security concerns related to China's Huawei could also further this growth.[43] This so-called D10 club of democratic partners could likely see fruition post a potential expansion of the Group of Seven (G7) – at present comprising of the UK, the US, Germany, France, Japan and Canada. UK as 2021 G7 President has called for the inclusion of Australia, South Korea and India into the grouping which would find synergy with Biden's call for a 'summit of democracies'; however, Japan's reluctance for this expansion has at present stalled discussions.[44] In fact, the UK Government has asked Japan for assistance in building its 5G wireless networks without the Huawei technologies, citing NEC Corp and Fujitsu Ltd as alternative suppliers.[45] This signifies the beginning of modified 5G network supplying, which would only ameliorate India's 5G dilemma regarding its security and sovereignty concerns with China and provide safer and more transparent alternatives for New Delhi's technological advancement.

Meanwhile, the Quad Plus has emerged as a "conjectural framework", which has been increasingly deliberated upon in the international strategic circles after the former US Deputy Secretary of State Stephen Biegun invited "specific countries" in the Indo-Pacific to discuss issues related to countering the COVID-19 through weekly telephonic conversations held between March 20, 2020 and May 15, 2020.[46] Apart from four Quad members, the abstract alliance includes the Republic of Korea (ROK or South Korea), Vietnam, New Zealand, Brazil and Israel. While the Quad Plus narrative is aimed at discussing various responses to the pandemic, the former US Secretary of State Mike Pompeo's initiation of the meeting on May 11, 2020 signified a grander strategic intent.[47] For India, the endorsement of Quad Plus has only buttressed its embracement of an American world view and further helped defend a liberal and rules-based global order by countering China's revisionist policies. Most importantly, the Quad Plus proposition complements India's "inclusive" Indo-Pacific construct[48] by acknowledging the centrality of the Association of Southeast Asian Nations (ASEAN) and chalking out the boundaries of the Indo-Pacific from Africa to maritime Asia.

Moreover, the Quad Plus framework provides immense economic benefits to India and strengthens policies such as the Modi's "Atmanirbhar Bharat". It is an established fact that the global order is witnessing an economic crisis with alterations to the supply chain networks and prospects of infrastructure building. A major modification has been the increasing global desire to shift the supply chain networks away from China and reassessment of the projects under Beijing's grand infrastructural initiative, the BRI.[49] For this reason, as mentioned earlier, countries like Japan have set aside $ 2.2 billion of its Covid-19 stimulus to relocate production away from China.[50] The US is also working to shift its manufacturing out of China, while India is setting up local supply chain operations to reduce risks.[51] Australia, too, is seeking to diversify its trade and supply networks away from China on account of Beijing's coercive behaviour towards Canberra in retaliation to the latter's call for an independent inquiry.[52] If anything, the Quad Plus seems like a viable alliance to transform the supply chain networks away from Beijing, especially in the infrastructure, energy, business, trade, investment and technology sectors. More so, as the countries involved in the conjectural grouping hold integral and advantageous positions in the global supply chain networks. Against this scenario, India's embrace of an economic alliance structure like the Quad Plus would be economically beneficial in the post-COVID order, at a time when India's financial growth itself is witnessing a slowdown. The India-Japan-Australia led Supply Chain Resillience Initiative (SCRI) finds extensive synergy here for creating a sustainable post-pandemic global supply chain network.

Broadly, the Chinese incursion in Galwan has served for a stronger push for India to move towards an alliance system that need not be limited to an anti-China rhetoric; rather, it should be an organic evolution of synergies, which aim to promote and sustain a democratic, liberal and rules-based order. However, India might not want to consider an alliance with the Quad countries if they do not embrace a reciprocal partnership with India. Though the US showed India reciprocity by proposing the expansion of the Group of 7 (G-7) with India as a member – an idea that the UK is now further propagating[53] – New Delhi would want Washington to acknowledge its rising power status and growing global importance while retreating from its superpower-centric approach. Thus, India would prefer the US to limit its Trump era "America First" principle when considering rebuilding alliances and partnerships under Biden. India would also want the US to relook at the regional pockets of the Indo-Pacific, such as the Bay of Bengal and the Arabian Sea, as strategically significant maritime domains. Until now, these areas have held less strategic vitality for the US; however, to build an alliance system on equal footing which is advantageous for both sides, an expansion of Washington's Indo-Pacific vision is crucial. Similarly, New Delhi would also desire a reciprocal alliance with Tokyo and Canberra in order to fully embrace its Strategic and Global Partnership and Comprehensive Strategic Partnership with Japan and Australia, respectively, in true form.

Indo-Pacific Coalitions beyond the Quad/Quad Plus in the Face of Changing Realities

Of late, India has been looking to explore other Indo-Pacific coalitions apart from the Quad, including several multilateral and mini-lateral frameworks. But most of all, the trilateral groupings have been seen to be rather effective in building strategically significant partnerships that have catered to India's economic, diplomatic and security interests, as well as helped counter China's rising influence in the Indo-Pacific.

Indian Trilateralism in JAI and AJI

The Japan-America-India (JAI) trilateral was formally launched in June 2018 at the G-20 Summit in Buenos Aires.[54] The trilateral aims to enhance coordination in areas such as connectivity, maritime security, disaster relief and freedom of navigation, although it was mainly an economic network.[55] It also seeks for a "strategic capital" in the Indo-Pacific that brings about economic engagement between the three countries.[56] Notwithstanding the obvious economic benefits, the JAI trilateral is a strategic platform for all parties. It allows the US to expediently challenge China in its own backyard, and it is crucial in protecting Japan's interest in the SCS. And for India, too, the trilateral is crucial for protecting its interests in the Indo-Pacific. Similarly, the Australia-Japan-India (AJI) trilateral, introduced in June 2015,[57] has sought to balance Chinese aspirations by safeguarding sovereignty, equality, territorial integrity, self-determination and "open, inclusive, stable and transparent"[58] architecture in the Indo-Pacific region.[59] The AJI trilateral has consequently led to several bilateral foreign-secretary level meetings[60] – the respective 2+2 meetings between India and Japan[61], India and Australia[62] and Japan and Australia[63] – and helped fructify the trilateral's vision in turn. SCRI's timely establishment has given new direction to AJI which can emerge as a defining development for the trilateral's regional leadership goals.

Though it goes without saying that groupings such as the AJI have always tried to tread carefully so as to not showcase an anti-China hue, however, China's increasingly hostile posturing in recent times has allowed the US to pursue a more "transactional" approach to foreign policy in Asia and the Indo-Pacific.[64] Moreover, India, Japan and Australia are also aligning with the US view of China as a revisionist power. Naturally, there is a change in India's perception of these alliance structures in the Indo-Pacific. This is especially noticeable in case of India's strengthened ties with Australia in the AJI:[65] India and Australia have discovered new common grounds and enhanced economic, defence and strategic engagement (e.g. Australia's patronage of the India Economic Strategy, 2035).[66] India also re-evaluated its earlier policy and invited Australia for the Malabar exercises despite China's objections.[67] At their summit in 2020, the two countries also signed Mutual Logistics Support Agreement (MLSA) that would allow them to use the others military bases for logistics support, including food, water and petroleum. This bonhomie has benefitted India in the international area. For example, after the Pulwama terrorist attack in India-administered Kashmir, Australia implicitly supported India and condemned Pakistan. It also co-sponsored India's resolution in the United Nations (UN) to designate Masood Azhar, a Pakistani national, a terrorist.[68]

At the same time, China's coercive behaviour in recent times has opened the way for the international community, in particular India, Japan, the US and Australia, to embark on an openly confrontational China policy. This has also been a rallying point for the countries concerned to cooperate and collaborate through various frameworks. India, for instance, is looking to maximise on this opportunity and position itself as a balancing, emerging power. This is in contrast to India's traditional foreign policy approach that followed non-alignment. Its Indo-Pacific partners acknowledge India's clout in tackling China. For example, in his keynote speech at the Japan Symposium in February 2020, Japan's Ambassador to Australia, Reiichiro Takahashi, talked about "the importance of India to the region's future":[69]

> India is no longer an unaligned country in the old and immediate sense of the words, neither is it consumed by its relations with its immediate neighbours. India is implementing its Act East policy, and expanding its diplomatic presence across the region. This is a development that Japan wholeheartedly supports.

Thus, these partner states, including India, must look at ways to enhance strategic cooperation with other partners at the sub-regional level, too; for example, cooperation with the Pacific Island Countries could be explored through the AJI trilateral. They should also figure out ways to attract large-scale investment in the region so as to expand their supply chains beyond China. Other possibilities include building infrastructure and connectivity cooperation via programmes like the Japan-India Act East Forum,[70] the Australia-India Comprehensive Economic Cooperation Agreement (CECA)[71] and the Japan-Australia Economic Partnership (JAEPA).[72] The AJI trilateral must also boost deeper ties with states in the Asia-Africa region through developing more inclusive regional frameworks for cooperation in maritime, economic and information technology sectors.

BDN and India

Launched in November 2019, the BDN is a multi-stakeholder initiative by the US, Japan and Australia that primarily aims to advance an economic alliance framework for high-quality infrastructure promotion in the Indo-Pacific through public-private partnerships,[73] offering an alternative to the BRI. The network is a by-product of the US "pivot to Asia" policy and shares many of the goals of the Quad such as a free and open Indo-Pacific.[74]

India was invited to join the framework during Trump's official visit to India in February 2020, but India is yet to embrace the project.[75] It is hoped that in the post-COVID and post-Galwan foreign policy the option of joining the network will be explored more seriously. Already, under Modi, the foreign policy has moved away "from multi-alignment to pointed-alignment with a set of countries that are critical to India's economic and strategic interests in promoting an alternative supply-chain network", in an effort to break the dependency on China.[76] India's recent programmes such as Make in India, Digital India, Start-up India and *Aatmanirbhar Bharat* (Self-reliant India) have allowed greater foreign investments and bolstered India's economy. The Self-reliant India scheme in particular aims to emerge as "a vital link in the new post-Covid supply-chain networks" and make "India's foreign policy resilient".[77] The scheme is however still in its infancy, and the government must address the basic concerns, including misperceptions of investors and India's strategic trade partners, bureaucratic red tape, corruption and lack of synergy between government departments, to implement it successfully.[78] For instance, negotiations for an India-European Union (EU) Free Trade Agreement (FTA) were held back because Brussels was concerned that the policy reflected a protectionist trend.[79] In such a scenario and given India's apprehensions about the BRI, India joining the BDN "could mark the beginning of a new 'economic alliance'".[80]

Other Partnerships in the Indo-Pacific

It is crucial for India to explore economic and infrastructure partnerships and build deeper bilateral and trilateral ties with countries like Indonesia, the Philippines,[81] Vietnam, South Korea, as well as with the neighbouring island states in the Indian Ocean (particularly Mauritius, the Maldives, Seychelles and Sri Lanka)[82] so as to manage China's economic and diplomatic influence in Asia. In order to emerge as a regional power and expand its strategic clout in Asia, India's enhanced engagement with these states is crucial. The Quad Plus framework has proved immensely successful in engaging with the economies of South Korea, Vietnam and New Zealand in matters pertaining to COVID-19. In the post-COVID world, there is considerable scope to seek increased collaborations in devising strategies for inclusive economic growth and development. The disruption of global supply chains by the pandemic has left developing economies in a precarious position. If India and its allies are to ensure that China does not unduly assert itself in the region, they must engage with these states on a significantly sustained and deeper level in diplomacy, defence and security, as well as through calibrated developmental aid and technical partnerships. A combined approach of this nature is in line with Prime Minister Modi's goal of improving "Security and Growth for All the Region" (SAGAR)[83] in Southeast Asia and the islands of the Indian Ocean. The Indian Ocean islands in particular are of critical strategic importance: many strategists hypothesise that Beijing aims to secure ties with these islands to establish military bases that surround India.[84] To counter China's Maritime Silk Road, India and its allies must consistently pursue concerted diplomacy and build resilient ties with these island states.

Containing China's Military Build-up and India's Overtures in the SCS

China's stand on the Indo-Pacific in a post COVID order is going to grow increasingly assertive and hostile; a recent report by Chinese state-run media house *Global Times* attests to that. As per the report, the People's Liberation Army Navy (PLAN) is providing its marine corps "intensive training" and improving their aerial assault capabilities in an effort to "ready personnel in advance to maximize the power of the two recently launched Type 075 amphibious assault ships".[85] In May, the *PLA Daily* reported that the PLAN Marine Corps (PLANMC) was being readied into a "multidimensional integrated combat force".[86] China is preparing its marine corps for a larger role in the international arena (e.g. defending its overseas interests and bolstering its claims in the ECS, SCS and Taiwan Strait).

India's active involvement in the security and military maritime domain of the Indo-Pacific is becoming more and more vital, with the SCS starting to take center stage. The SCS is an area of extreme friability and vitality for all of India's Quad 2.0 partners; for India – over 55 per cent of India's trade passes through this contested region.[87] From a broader perspective, it is now extremely important for the United States and its allies in the Indo-Pacific to protect the freedom of navigation rights, Sea Lanes of Communication (SLOCs) and the United Nations Convention on the Law of the Sea (UNCLOS) from the rising China threat. The Quad partners have already been quite vocal against the Chinese military posturing in the region and have also conducted several joint naval exercises to contain this threat. Their alignment was reflected when, as a response to Beijing's refusal to adhere legal and diplomatic processes in accordance with the universally recognised principles of international law in the SCS, in 2017, the US, Australia and Japan demanded China (and Philippines) to abide by the 2016 Permanent Court of Arbitration (PCA) ruling on the SCS.[88] India, too, supported the PCA ruling in its official statement on July 12, 2016.[89]

The United States has been conducting regular Freedom of Navigation Operations (FONOPs) in the SCS for long in a bid to check China's military adventurism there. India and Japan have always attested the importance of freedom of navigation and overflight, lawful trade and peaceful resolution of disputes in accordance with international law.[90] The three countries have been conducting the Malabar naval exercises – which Canberra has now re-joined – in order to help maintain this rule of law. Australia, too, has emphasised on its freedom of navigation rights in the region.[91] The US and Australia have been conducting military exercises in the SCS despite China's objections (in April 2020, the two patrolled in an area that is claimed by Vietnam, Malaysia and China, where a Chinese vessel was suspected to be exploring for oil).[92] In its defence white paper in 2020, Japan has opposed "unilateral attempts to change the status quo by coercion" in the ECS and SCS and stressed on the need for multilateral security cooperation to strengthen its FOIP vision.[93] In an effort towards that vision, Japan's Maritime Self-Defence Force recently conducted trilateral military exercises with the Australia and the US in the SCS.[94]

Nonetheless, despite international criticism and efforts, China has continued its military build-up provocatively even as the world is battling the COVID pandemic. Still, the promise of the Quad Plus process has synergised the Indo-Pacific partners. Vietnam, a Quad Plus partner, has long protested China's expansionism in potentially energy-rich stretch in the SCS. In April 2020, Vietnam lodged an official protest with China after the sinking of its fishing boat, which the former claimed was rammed by a Chinese coast guard vessel near the Paracels; days after, Vietnam demanded that China respect its sovereignty after the latter established two districts in the Paracel and Spratly Islands.[95] China, on the other hand, has firmly opposed Vietnam's calls for Indian investment in oil and gas exploration in its Exclusive Economic Zone (EEZ) in the SCS.[96] Post-Galwan, India should explore wider collaboration with Vietnam (as also other Quad Plus countries) to counter the growing China challenge.

Further, strengthened security cooperation between the US and India would be helpful in containing, what the US has recently called, China's "bullying" and "unlawful behaviour" in the SCS.[97] This shift away from its so-called isolationist policies has rekindled hopes for a stronger commitment in the Indo-Pacific, assuaging its key allies in the region like India, Japan, South Korea and Australia.[98] India's post-Galwan policy trajectory must utilise this reinjection of US support and bolster its maritime cooperation in the SCS perhaps through an alliance structure including the US. In fact, former US Secretary of State Michael Pompeo recently stated the "PRC's predatory world view has no place in the 21st century",[99] which is in line with Modi's "age of expansionism is over" address to the Indian troops in July 2020.[100]

India should also boost its ties with the Philippines – a US treaty ally under the 1951 Mutual Defense Treaty. The Philippines has been concerned about China's recent naval drills in the SCS. India and the Philippines already have a bilateral defence cooperation that comprises "capacity building and training, exchange visits of delegations and naval and coast guard ship visits". In 2019, India participated with the navies of the US, the Philippines and Japan in their first joint naval exercise in the disputed SCS.[101] A new collaboration may well be on cards, as per the Philippine Defence Minister Delfin Lorenzana, who stated that India was "interested in carrying out navigation activities" in the SCS.[102]

As mentioned earlier, India is already strengthening its defence cooperation with Australia. Pursuing to involve Australia in the Malabar exercise is important in view of enhancing maritime security in the SCS. However, there needs to be a stronger synergy between the Quad nations not only bilaterally but also together as a unit to improve the social and economic conditions in the Indian Ocean Region (IOR) in general. The IOR is fast emerging as a global geopolitical and geo-economic hotspot,[103] and India and its allies will need to collaborate effectively not only to counter-balance China's increasing influence and aggressive militarisation in the region but also to preserve the health of the region. The "Blue Economy", for example, is an effective means to manage a sustainable maritime environment.[104] So, "coordinated and proactive growth" of the Indian Ocean economies must be built via sustainable practices.[105] The Quad nations must create a comprehensive strategy so as to tap the geopolitical, security and economic potential of the IOR without exploiting its abundant marine resources.

India: Alignments to alliances?

India's 'China Policy', as studied by Chinese scholar Li Li, in the post-Cold War era moved from a détente leading to cooperative partnership in 1996, antagonistic ties in 1998, comprehensive bilateral cooperation in 2003; from hereon, diplomatic growth successfully improved strategic, economic and political relations between the two nations.[106] However, over the past decade and especially post-Galwan, increasing Chinese belligerence in its immediate neighbourhood is threatening the peace and stability in India, Asia and the Indo-Pacific. In such a scenario, India cannot continue to rely on an appeasement policy towards China, as the Galwan clash has also shown. Modi's "Indo-Pacific Oceans Initiative (IPOI)" for a safe, secure and stable maritime domain is a step in the right direction that highlights India's willingness to counter China's aggressive behaviour.[107] India also hosted the fourth East Asia Maritime Security workshop with Australia and Indonesia in February 2020 to further similar goals.[108]

Nonetheless, it is important to note that for India, a shift away from simple alignment structures does not necessarily connotate an acceptance of alliances. Rather, as External Affairs Minister (EAM) Dr. S. Jaishankar has clarified, India will "never join an alliance system in the future as it never did in the past".[109] Instead, a stronger alignment framework that boasts of dual parity and mutual benefit, creating 'security coalitions' and 'communities' to match pace with realities of contemporary security environments can be expected to mark the future trajectory of Indian foreign policy.[110] With an 'element of bipolarity'[111] emerging between the US and China in the multipolar order of today, India's increasing proximity to the US in the wake of rising security threats from China highlight this very changing nature of India-China ties. But, as EAM Jaishankar stated in his address to the India Ideas Summit, the US still needs to "learn to work with a more multipolar world with more plurilateral arrangements" Building on his earlier comments of India not entering into alliances, the EAM stated that it is the US that needs to go "beyond alliances". [112]

In the last few years India has decisively moved away from non-alignment: "India has moved on from its non-aligned past. India is today an aligned state – but based on issues."[113] Under the Modi government, the country has not shied from building partnerships with specific aims or from asserting its desire to position itself as a global leader. India's policy of multi-alignment has surely helped strengthen security in the Indo-Pacific. But in the post-Galwan order, India needs to gradually move towards a 'multi-alignment plus alliance' formation that builds stronger, security driven alignments in order to prioritise not only economic benefits but also the protection of its core national interests.

Notes

1 India's China outlook has been a result of pragmatism, pursued for over four decades and modelled around the principle of economic engagement aimed to promote parity pf power that allows the emergence of India as a peer and not just partner to China. Read, Jagannath Panda, "Narendra Modi's China Policy: Between Pragmatism and Power Parity", Journal of Asian Public Policy, 9 (2), 2016, pp. 185–197, at https://doi.org/10.1080/17516234.2016.1165334 (Accessed July 17, 2020).
2 Rahul Singh, "A Timeline: India-China's Deadliest Border Clash Since 1975 Explained", Hindustan Times, June 17, 2020, at www.hindustantimes.com/india-news/a-timeline-india-china-s-deadliest-border-clash-since-1975-explained/story-9Ct6lHQKkRuXM-5w2K5xmwO.html (Accessed July 17, 2020).
3 Stanley Johnny, "Is China's 'Peaceful Rise' Over?" The Hindu, June 17, 2020, at www.thehindu.com/news/international/analysis-is-chinas-peaceful-rise-over/article31853332.ece (Accessed July 17, 2020).
4 Jagannath Panda, "India's China Policy Signals a Shift Post-Galwan", India Inc., June 28, 2020, at https://indiaincgroup.com/indias-china-policy-signals-a-shift-post-galwan/ (Accessed July 17, 2020).

5 "Joint Statement: Vision and Principles for India-U.S. Comprehensive Global Strategic Partnership", India's Ministry of External Affairs, February 25, 2020, at https://mea.gov.in/bilateral-documents.htm?dtl/32421/Joint+Statement+Vision+and+Principles+for+IndiaUS+Comprehensive+Global+Strategic+Partnership (Accessed July 17, 2020).
6 Jonathan Woetzel and Jeongmin Seong, "We've Entered the Asian Century and There Is No Turning Back", World Economic Forum, October 11, 2019, at www.weforum.org/agenda/2019/10/has-world-entered-asian-century-what-does-it-mean/ (Accessed July 17, 2020).
7 "National Security Strategy of the United States of America", The White House, December 2017, at www.whitehouse.gov/wp-content/uploads/2017/12/NSS-Final-12-18-2017-0905.pdf (Accessed July 17, 2020).
8 "Treasury Designates China as a Currency Manipulator", US Department of the Treasury, August 5, 2019, at https://home.treasury.gov/news/press-releases/sm751#:~:text=Under%20Section%203004%20of%20the,trade."%20Secretary%20Mnuchin%2C%20under (Accessed July 17, 2020).
9 US-China ties have imbibed a 'confrontationist-competitive' spirit, with competition between the two becoming the driving factor of their relations, unlikely to change with alterations in military capabilities, economic clout or political changes within national frameworks. Read, Jagannath Panda, "India's Strategic Moments in US-China Tug-of-War", The Asian Age, October 21, 2018, at www.asianage.com/360-degree/211018/indias-strategic-moments-in-us-china-tug-of-war.html (Accessed July 17, 2020).
10 Michael R. Pompeo, "U.S. Position on Maritime Claims in the South China Sea", US Department of State, July 13, 2020, at www.state.gov/u-s-position-on-maritime-claims-in-the-south-china-sea/ (accessed July 17, 2020).
11 Edward Wong, Lara Jakes and Steven Lee Myers, "U.S. Orders China to Close Houston Consulate, Citing Efforts to Steal Trade Secrets", The New York Times, July 22, 2020, at www.nytimes.com/2020/07/22/world/asia/us-china-houston-consulate.html (Accessed July 23, 2020).
12 "US secretary of state Blinken: Trump was right to take tougher approach on China ", Times of India, February 9, 2021, at https://timesofindia.indiatimes.com/world/us/us-secretary-of-state-blinken-trump-was-right-to-take-tougher-approach-on-china/articleshow/80763016.cms (Accessed March 2, 2021)
13 Jeffrey A. Bader, 'How Xi Jinping Sees the World . . . and Why', Brookings, February 11, 2016, at www.brookings.edu/research/how-xi-jinping-sees-the-world-and-why/ (Accessed July 17, 2020).
14 Jonathan Woetzel, Jeongmin Seong, Nick Leung, Joe Ngai, James Manyika, Anu Madgavkar, Susan Lund and Andrey Mironenko, "China and the World Inside the Dynamics of a Changing Relationship", McKinsey Global Institute, July 2019, at www.mckinsey.com/~/media/mckinsey/featured%20insights/china/china%20and%20the%20world%20inside%20the%20dynamics%20of%20a%20changing%20relationship/mgi-china-and-the-world-full-report-june-2019-vf.ashx (Accessed July 17, 2020). Marking its regional economic dominance in Asia, China even took over the US as the largest nation of trading goods in 2013; see, 'China Surpasses US as World's Largest Trading Nation', The Guardian, January 10, 2014, at www.theguardian.com/business/2014/jan/10/china-surpasses-us-world-largest-trading-nation (accessed July 17, 2020).
15 Hillary Clinton, "America's Pacific Century", Foreign Policy, October 11, 2011, at https://foreignpolicy.com/2011/10/11/americas-pacific-century/ (Accessed July 17, 2020).
16 Joseph R. Biden Jr., "Why America Must Lead Again", Foreign Affairs, 2020, at www.foreignaffairs.com/articles/united-states/2020-01-23/why-america-must-lead-again (Accessed March 2, 2021)

17 Extensively covering the underpinnings of the Trump administration's approach to China, this report analyses nuances attached to the US-China rivalry in a comprehensive manner: See "U.S.-China Rivalry in the Trump Era: A WPR Report", World Politics Review, May 2020, at https://s3.amazonaws.com/worldpoliticsreview/WPR-US-China-Rivalry-Trump-Era.pdf?utm_source=WPR+Free+Newsletter&utm_campaign=8517d6c23d-sw-floater-asia&utm_medium=email&utm_term=0_6e36cc98fd-8517d6c23d-64599302&mc_cid=8517d6c23d&mc_eid=7d06e1105d (Accessed July 17, 2020).
18 Sanjay Baru, "India and China in a multipolar world", The Hindu, May 11, 2015, at www.thehindu.com/opinion/lead/sanjaya-baru-writes-india-and-china-in-a-multipolar-world/article7190817.ece (accessed July 23, 2020). Read also, Sanjay Baru, "The Geo-economics of Multipolarity", in Sujan R. Chinoy and Jagannath Panda (ed.), Asia Between Multipolarism and Multipolarity, Knowledge World, New Delhi, 2020, pp. 3–19.
19 "Mutual Trust between Australia and China at All-Time Low", Global Times, June 25, 2020, at www.globaltimes.cn/content/1192669.shtml (Accessed July 17, 2020).
20 Stephen Dziedzic, "Australia Started a Fight with China over an Investigation into COVID-19 – Did It Go Too Hard?" ABC, May 20, 2020, at www.abc.net.au/news/2020-05-20/wha-passes-coronavirus-investigation-australia-what-cost/12265896 (Accessed July 17, 2020).
21 "China Punishes Australia for Promoting an Inquiry into Covid-19", The Economist, May 21, 2020, at www.economist.com/asia/2020/05/21/china-punishes-australia-for-promoting-an-inquiry-into-covid-19 (Accessed July 17, 2020).
22 Paul Karp, "China's Coercive Behaviour A 'Wake-Up Call', Australia's Former Top Public Servant Says", The Guardian, May 7, 2020, at www.theguardian.com/australia-news/2020/may/08/chinas-coercive-behaviour-a-wake-up-call-australias-former-top-public-servant-says (Accessed July 17, 2020).
23 "Australia Will Not Be 'Intimidated' Amid China Economic Threats: PM Scott Morrison", CNA, June 11, 2020, at www.channelnewsasia.com/news/world/australia-china-trade-scott-morrison-covid-19-12825200 (Accessed July 17, 2020).
24 Isabel Reynolds and Emi Urabe, "Japan to Fund Firms to Shift Production out of China", Bloomberg, April 8, 2020, at www.bloomberg.com/news/articles/2020-04-08/japan-to-fund-firms-to-shift-production-out-of-china (Accessed July 17, 2020).
25 Simon Denyer, "Japan helps 87 companies to break from China after pandemic exposed overreliance", The Washington Post, July 21, 2020, at www.washingtonpost.com/world/asia_pacific/japan-helps-87-companies-to-exit-china-after-pandemic-exposed-overreliance/2020/07/21/4889abd2-cb2f-11ea-99b0-8426e26d203b_story.html (Accessed July 23, 2020).
26 This essay makes arguments regarding a prospective end of foreign policy restraint that Beijing has been following until now, by extensively analysing the ways in which China is willing to aggressively engage with countries: See Kurt M. Campbell and Mira Rapp-Hooper, "China Is Done Biding Its Time: The End of Beijing's Foreign Policy Restraint?" Foreign Affairs, July 15, 2020, at www.foreignaffairs.com/articles/china/2020-07-15/china-done-biding-its-time?utm_medium=newsletters&utm_source=twofa&utm_campaign=China%20Is%20Done%20Biding%20Its%20Time&utm_content=20200717&utm_term=FA%20This%20Week%20-%20112017 (Accessed July 17, 2020).
27 India's foreign policy practice post-independence was broadly a result of the continuous interaction between its domestic circumstances and the international environment. This practice, known as non-alignment, was on the one hand, a factor to the sensitivities India held towards its colonial legacy of anti-imperial sentiments primarily present in the political spectrum of the country, which led New Delhi to keep itself outside the gambit of the Cold War. On the other hand, it was a result of India's dwindling

economy post its independence in 1947, coupled with its nationalistic inclinations during that time. Non-alignment remained the central component in India's foreign policy practice and a defining element of India's identity in the global politics for a long time. It had allowed India to follow a path of strategic autonomy while providing it a room to manoeuvre according to its national interests. However, the administration under Prime Minister Narendra Modi in its first phase indicated towards a move away from this rhetoric. India's strategic position *vis-à-vis* China's evolving regional posture of assertiveness and the mounting uncertainty in the recent construct of the Indo-Pacific compelled New Delhi to look towards alignment. This enabled India to seek economic and security cooperation with favourable regional partners to allow itself to exercise greater strategic autonomy. Please read, Sumit Ganguly and Manjeet S. Pardesi, "Explaining Sixty Years of India's Foreign Policy", India Review, 8 (1), 2009, pp. 4–19; Harsh V. Pant and Julie M. Super, "India's 'Non-Alignment' Conundrum: a Twentieth-Century Policy in a Changing World", International Affairs, 91 (4), 2015, pp. 747–764.

28 Please read, Jagannath P. Panda, "China as a Revisionist Power in Indo-Pacific and India's Perception: A Power-Partner Contention", Journal of Contemporary China, May 19, 2020, pp. 12–16.

29 Jagannath Panda, no. 4. See also, Yaroslav Trofimov, "India Sees Opportunity as U.S. Remakes Its Alliances", The Wall Street Journal, January 22, 2020, at www.wsj.com/articles/india-sees-opportunity-as-u-s-remakes-its-alliances-11579717050 (accessed July 23, 2020)

30 "Transcript of Media Briefing by Foreign Secretary and Secretary (East) in Manila (November 13, 2017)", Ministry of External Affairs, India, November 13, 2017, at https://mea.gov.in/media-briefings.htm?dtl/29114/transcript+of+media+briefing+by+foreign+secretary+and+secretary+east+in+manila+november+13+2017. (Accessed July 18, 2020).

31 Jesse Barker Gale, "The Quadrilateral Security Dialogue and the Maritime Silk Road Initiative", CSIS Briefs, April 02, 2018, at www.csis.org/analysis/quadrilateral-security-dialogue-and-maritime-silk-road-initiative. (Accessed July 18, 2020).

32 Jagannath P. Panda, "India's Call on China in the Quad: A Strategic Arch between Liberal and Alternative Structures", Rising Powers Quarterly, 3 (2), August 2018, p. 83.

33 "Joint Statement: the United States and India: Enduring Global Partners in the 21st Century", The White House, June 07, 2016, at https://obamawhitehouse.archives.gov/the-press-office/2016/06/07/joint-statement-united-states-and-india-enduring-global-partners-21st. (Accessed July 18, 2020).

34 "Secretary Pompeo, Secretary of Defense Esper, Minister of External Affairs Jaishankar, & Indian Minister of Defense Singh", US Embassy and Consulates in India, December 18, 2019, at https://in.usembassy.gov/secretary-michael-r-pompeo-secretary-of-defense-mark-t-esper-minister-of-external-affairs-subrahmanyam-jaishankar-and-indian-minister-of-defense/ (Accessed July 18, 2020).

35 "Joint Statement on the Inaugural India-U.S 2+2 Ministerial Dialogue", Ministry of External Affairs, September 06, 2018, at https://mea.gov.in/bilateral-documents.htm?dtl/30358/Joint+Statement+on+the+Inaugural+IndiaUS+2432+Ministerial+Dialogue. (Accessed on July 18, 2020)

36 "Joint Statement on the Second India-U.S. 2+2 Ministerial Dialogue", Ministry of External Affairs, December 19, 2019, at https://mea.gov.in/bilateral-documents.htm?dtl/32227/Joint+Statement+on+the+Second+IndiaUS+2432+Ministerial+Dialogue. (Accessed on July 18, 2020)

37 "Documents announced during the 3rd India – US 2+2 Ministerial Dialogue", Ministry of External Affairs, October 27, 2020, at https://mea.gov.in/bilateral-documents.htm?dtl/33143/Documents+announced+during+the+3rd+India++US+2432+Ministerial+Dialogue (Accessed March 2, 2021)

38 "Exercise Tiger TRIUMPH", US Embassy and Consulates in India, November 13, 2019, at https://in.usembassy.gov/tiger-triumph/. (Accessed on July 18, 2020)
39 "Joint Statement: First India-Japan 2+2 Foreign and Defence Ministerial Meeting", Ministry of External Affairs, India, November 30, 2019, at www.mea.gov.in/bilateral-documents.htm?dtl/32131/Joint+Statement++First+IndiaJapan+2432+Foreign+and+Defence+Ministerial+Meeting (Accessed July 21, 2020).
40 "India, Japan sign key pact for reciprocal provision of supplies, services between defence forces", hindustan Times, September 10, 2020, at www.hindustantimes.com/india-news/japan-s-pm-shinzo-abe-speaks-on-phone-with-narendra-modi-lists-elevation-of-global-partnership-between-the-two-countries-as-a-key-achievement/story-dgAYdfesU7Vtz2Miua6z7M.html
41 "Joint Statement on a Comprehensive Strategic Partnership between Republic of India and Australia", Ministry of External Affairs, India, June 04, 2020, at www.mea.gov.in/bilateral-documents.htm?dtl/32729/Joint_Statement_on_a_Comprehensive_Strategic_Partnership_between_Republic_of_India_and_Australia (Accessed July 18, 2020).
42 "Australia joins Exercise MALABAR 2020", Department of Defence Ministers, November 3, 2020, at www.minister.defence.gov.au/minister/lreynolds/media-releases/australia-joins-exercise-malabar-2020#:~:text=Australia%20has%20joined%20key%20regional,of%20regional%20peace%20and%20security.
43 "The UK Is Proposing to Expedite the Process of the D10 (Democratic Ten) Structure, which Includes India", The Economic Times, May 30, 2020, at https://cio.economictimes.indiatimes.com/news/government-policy/uk-plans-new-5g-club-of-10-democracies-including-india-report/76102203 (Accessed July 18, 2020). To gain a more elaborate understanding of the D10 framework and why it is a vital for democracies involved, read, Erik Brattberg and Ben Judah, "Forget the G-7, Build the D-10", Foreign Policy, June 10, 2020, at https://foreignpolicy.com/2020/06/10/g7-d10-democracy-trump-europe/ (accessed July 23, 2020)
44 Jagannath Panda, "Motives for Tokyo's reluctance on an expanded G7", Asia Times, January 29, 2021, at https://asiatimes.com/2021/01/motives-for-tokyos-reluctance-on-an-expanded-g7/ (Accessed March 2, 2021)
45 "U.K. Asks Japan for Huawei Alternatives in 5G Networks", The Hindu, July 19, 2020, at www.thehindu.com/news/international/uk-asks-japan-for-huawei-alternatives-in-5g-networks/article32128118.ece (Accessed July 19, 2020).
46 "Cooperation among Select Countries of the Indo-Pacific in Fighting COVID-19 Pandemic", Ministry of External Affairs, India, May 14, 2020, at https://mea.gov.in/press-releases.htm?dtl/32691/Cooperation_among_select_countries_of_the_IndoPacific_in_fighting_COVID19_pandemic (Accessed April 18, 2020).
47 "Secretary Michael R. Pompeo's Videoconference with Partners on COVID-19", US Department of State, May 11, 2020, at www.state.gov/secretary-michael-r-pompeos-videoconference-with-partners-on-covid-19/. (Accessed July 18, 2020).
48 "Prime Minister's Keynote Address at Shangri La Dialogue (June 01, 2018)", Ministry of External Affairs, India, June 01, 2018, at https://mea.gov.in/Speeches-Statements.htm?dtl/29943/Prime+Ministers+Keynote+Address+at+Shangri+La+Dialogue+June+01+2018 (Accessed July 18, 2020).
49 Kirk Lancaster, Michael Rubin and Mira Rapp-Hooper, "What the COVID-19 Pandemic May Mean for China's Belt and Road Initiative", Council on Foreign Relations, March 17, 2020, at www.cfr.org/blog/what-covid-19-pandemic-may-mean-chinas-belt-and-road-initiative (Accessed July 18, 2020).
50 Japan Sets Aside ¥243.5 billion to Help Firms Shift Production out of China," Japan Times, April 09, 2020, at www.japantimes.co.jp/news/2020/04/09/business/japan-sets-aside-%C2%A5243-5-billion-help-firms-shift-production-china/ (Accessed July 18, 2020).

51 Andrea Shalal, Alexandra Alper and Patricial Zengerle, "U.S. Mulls Paying Companies, Tax Breaks to Pull Supply Chains from China", Reuters, May 18, 2020, at www.reuters.com/article/us-usa-china-supply-chains/u-s-mulls-paying-companies-taxbreaks-to-pull-supply-chains-from-china-idUSKBN22U0FH (Accessed July 18, 2020); Nishtha Yadav, "Why Businesses in India Are Building Local Supply Chain Capacity," India Briefing, April 08, 2020, at www.india-briefing.com/news/businesses-india-building-local-supplychain-capacity-20154.html/ (Accessed July 18, 2020); Danish Khan, "Lava Plans to Move Export Manufacturing Base to India", The Economic Times, May 16, 2020, at https://economictimes.indiatimes.com/tech/hardware/lava-plans-to-move-export-manufacturing-base-to-india/articleshow/75766598.cms (Accessed July 18, 2020).
52 Paul Karp, "Coalition Eyes Australian 'Economic Sovereignty' with Boost to Manufacturing", The Guardian, May 19, 2020, at www.theguardian.com/business/2020/may/20/coalition-eyes-australian-economic-sovereigntywith-boost-to-manufacturing (Accessed July 18, 2020).
53 "Telephone Conversation between Prime Minister and President of USA", Ministry of External Affairs, India, June 02, 2020, at www.mea.gov.in/press-releases.htm?dtl/32719/Telephone_conversation_between_Prime_Minister_and_President_of_USA (Accessed July 18, 2020).
54 Yashwant Raj, "With a Three-Way Fist-Bump, JAI Trilateral Goes Annual", Hindustan Times, June 28, 2019, at www.hindustantimes.com/india-news/with-a-three-way-fist-bump-jai-trilateral-goes-annual/story-74tmrMfCBwxFng1njyyfaN.html (Accessed July 19, 2020).
55 Jagannath Panda, "'JAI', the Quad and China: Understanding the Undercurrents", SWP Working Paper, German Institute for International and Security Affairs, November 2019, at www.swp-berlin.org/fileadmin/contents/products/projekt_papiere/BCAS_2019_Panda_Quad_and_China.pdf (Accessed July 18, 2020).
56 Ibid.
57 David Lang, "Security Interests Draw Japan, Australia and India Closer", Japan Times, July 8, 2015, at www.japantimes.co.jp/opinion/2015/07/08/commentary/japan-commentary/security-interests-draw-japan-australia-india-closer/#.XsntkC2B3fY (Accessed July 18, 2020).
58 "Joint Statement – First India-Japan 2+2 Foreign and Defence Ministerial Meeting", no. 36.
59 Jagannath Panda, "Australia-India-Japan Trilateral Must Overcome Connect Contradiction", in Lucy West (ed.), Australia-Japan-India Trilateral Dialogue 2019: Leadership, Partnership and ASEAN Centrality in the Emerging Indo-Pacific, Griffith University, Queensland, 2020, pp. 4–6.
60 Dipanjan Roy Chaudhury, "Australia, Japan and India Trilateral in Delhi on December 12", The Economic Times, July 12, 2018, at https://economictimes.indiatimes.com/news/defence/australia-japan-and-india-trilateral-in-delhi-on-december-12/articleshow/61840323.cms?from=mdr (accessed July 18, 2020).
61 "Joint Statement – First India-Japan 2+2 Foreign and Defence Ministerial Meeting", no. 36.
62 "India-Australia Foreign and Defence Secretaries' Dialogue (2+2)", Ministry of External Affairs, India, December 9, 2019, at www.mea.gov.in/press-releases.htm?dtl/32178/indiaaustralia+foreign+and+defence+secretaries+dialogue+2432 (Accessed July 18, 2020).
63 "Eighth Japan-Australia Foreign and Defence Ministerial Consultations ('2+2')", Ministry of Foreign Affairs of Japan, October 10, 2018, at www.mofa.go.jp/a_o/ocn/au/page3e_000949.html (Accessed July 18, 2020).
64 Mark Beeson, "Donald Trump and Post-Pivot Asia: The Implications of a 'Transactional' Approach to Foreign Policy", Asian Studies Review, 44 (1), 2020, pp. 10–27,

at https://doi.org/10.1080/10357823.2019.1680604 (Accessed July 18, 2020); John Ikenberry, "The Plot against America Foreign Policy: Can the Liberal Order Survive?" Foreign Affairs, 96 (2), 2017, at https://scholar.princeton.edu/sites/default/files/gji3/files/may-june_2017_foreign_affairs.pdf (Accessed July 18, 2020).

65 Aakriti Bachhawat, "No Longer in a Cleft Stick: India and Australia in the Indo-Pacific", The Strategist, June 25, 2019, at www.aspistrategist.org.au/no-longer-in-a-cleft-stick-india-and-australia-in-the-indo-pacific/ (Accessed July 18, 2020).

66 "Government Response to an India Economic Strategy to 2035: Factsheet", Australian Department of Foreign Affairs and Trade, at www.dfat.gov.au/sites/default/files/government-response-to-an-india-economic-strategy-to-2035.pdf (Accessed July 18, 2020).

67 Sudhi Ranjan Sen and Archana Chaudhary, "India to Ignore Chinese Objections, Invite Australia for Malabar Naval Exercise", The Print, July 10, 2020, at https://theprint.in/defence/india-to-ignore-chinese-objections-invite-australia-for-malabar-naval-exercise/457960/ (Accessed July 18, 2020).

68 Aakriti Bachhawat, no. 60.

69 "Ambassador's Keynote Speech to the Japan Symposium 2020", Perth US Asia Centre, February 2020, at https://perthusasia.edu.au/events/%EF%BC%88perth-usasia-centre%EF%BC%89ambassadors-address-to-the-ja.aspx (Accessed July 21, 2020).

70 "Launch of India-Japan Act East Forum", Ministry of External Affairs, India, December 5, 2017, at www.mea.gov.in/press-releases.htm?dtl/29154/Launch_of_IndiaJapan_Act_East_Forum (Accessed July 18, 2020).

71 "Australia-India Comprehensive Economic Cooperation Agreement", Department of Foreign Affairs and Trade, Australia, at www.dfat.gov.au/trade/agreements/negotiations/aifta/Pages/australia-india-comprehensive-economic-cooperation-agreement (Accessed July 18, 2020).

72 "Japan-Australia Economic Partnership Agreement", Department of Foreign Affairs and Trade, Australia, at www.dfat.gov.au/trade/agreements/in-force/jaepa/Pages/japan-australia-economic-partnership-agreement (Accessed July 18, 2020).

73 Jagannath P. Panda, "India, the Blue Dot Network, and the 'Quad Plus'", Journal of Indo-Pacific Affairs (*JIPA*), July 17, 2020, at www.airuniversity.af.edu/JIPA/Display/Article/2278057/india-the-blue-dot-network-and-the-quad-plus-calculus/ (Accessed July 22, 2020).

74 Jagannath P. Panda, "Wealth, Welfare and Win Must Guide India-US Indo-Pacific Partnership", Wion, February 22, 2020, at www.wionews.com/opinions-blogs/wealth-welfare-and-win-must-guide-india-us-indo-pacific-partnership-282124 (Accessed July 19, 2020).

75 Nayanima Basu, "Blue Dot Network – US Answer to China's Belt & Road Initiative that India's 'Interested' in", The Print, March 10, 2020, at https://theprint.in/theprint-essential/blue-dot-network-us-answer-to-chinas-belt-road-initiative-that-indias-interested-in/378457/ (Accessed July 19, 2020).

76 Jagannath Panda, "Modi's 'Self-Reliant India' Has Key Foreign Policy Aspects", Asia Times, July 13, 2020, at https://asiatimes.com/2020/07/modis-self-reliant-india-has-key-foreign-policy-aspects/ (Accessed July 19, 2020).

77 Ibid.

78 Gautam Chikermane and Rishi Agrawal, "To Convert Atmanirbhar Bharat into Reality, Modi Needs to Wage a War", ORF, July 4, 2020, at www.orfonline.org/expert-speak/to-convert-atmanirbhar-bharat-into-reality-modi-needs-to-wage-a-war-69171/ (Accessed July 19, 2020).

79 "India's Atmanirbhar Policy Shows Protectionist Trend, Hampers Negotiations for FTA: EU Officials", The Wire, July 14, 2020, at https://thewire.in/external-affairs/india-atmanirbar-eu-summit-fta-covid-vaccine (Accessed July 19, 2020).

80 Jagannath P. Panda, no. 69.

81 Dipanjan Roy Chaudhary, "India Seeks to Widen Indo-Pacific Partnership with Philippines amid China's Aggression," The Economic Times, June 13, 2020, at https://economictimes.indiatimes.com/news/defence/india-seeks-to-widen-indo-pacific-partnership-with-philippines-amid-chinas-aggression/articleshow/76362720.cms (Accessed July 19, 2020).

82 Ian Hall, "India's Clever Alliances with Island States: A Multifaceted Outreach with Indian Ocean Neighbours Provides Useful Lessons in Navigating China's Dominance," The Interpreter, November 5, 2019, www.lowyinstitute.org/the-interpreter/india-s-clever-alliances-island-states (Accessed July 19, 2020).

83 "Text of the PM's Remarks on the Commissioning of Coast Ship Barracuda," Narendra Modi, March 12, 2015, at www.narendramodi.in/text-of-the-pms-remarks-on-the-commissioning-of-coast-ship-barracuda-2954 (Accessed July 19, 2020). For an evaluation of the policy and the extent to which it has successfully delivered security and growth in the region, see Jivanta Schottli, "'Security and Growth for All in the Indian Ocean' – Maritime Governance and India's Foreign Policy," India Review, 18 (5), January 27, 2020, at https://doi.org/10.1080/14736489.2019.1703366 (Accessed July 19, 2020).

84 Lora Saalman, "India's 'So-Called' String of Pearls," Carnegie Endowment for International Peace, June 5, 2012, at https://carnegieendowment.org/2012/07/05/india-s-so-called-string-of-pearls-pub-48794 (Accessed July 19, 2020).

85 Liu Xuanzun, "China Expands Marine Corps' Aerial Assault Capabilities Following Type 075 Ship Launch", Global Times, April 27, 2020, at www.globaltimes.cn/content/1186938.shtml (Accessed July 17, 2020).

86 "China's Marine Corps Preparing and Training for Global Role", Janes, May 13, 2020, at www.janes.com/defence-news/news-detail/2020/05/15/7bbbfe95-2cfb-4d3f-bdda-5ef0af5f04a9 (Accessed July 17, 2020).

87 "Question No.808 Trade Through South China Sea", Ministry of External Affairs, India, February 8, 2017, at www.mea.gov.in/rajya-sabha.htm?dtl/28041/QUESTION+NO808+TRADE+THROUGH+SOUTH+CHINA+SEA (Accessed July 17, 2020).

88 Charlotte Gao, "US, Australia, Japan Jointly Challenge China on South China Sea Issue", The Diplomat, August 09, 2017, at https://thediplomat.com/2017/08/us-australia-japan-jointly-challenge-china-on-south-china-sea-issue/. (Accessed July 18, 2020).

89 "Statement on Award of Arbitral Tribunal on South China Sea under Annexure VII of UNCLOS", Ministry of External Affairs, India, July 12, 2016, at https://mea.gov.in/press-releases.htm?dtl/27019/Statement_on_Award_of_Arbitral_Tribunal_on_South_China_Sea_Under_Annexure_VII_of_UNCLOS. (Accessed July 18, 2020)

90 "Joint Statement: First India-Japan 2+2 Foreign and Defence Ministerial Meeting", no. 36.

91 "Australian Warships 'Challenged' by Chinese Navy in South China Sea," The Guardian, April 19, 2018, at www.theguardian.com/australia-news/2018/apr/20/australian-warships-challenged-by-chinese-navy-in-south-china-sea. (Accessed July 18, 2020.)

92 Rozanna Latiff, "Australia Joins U.S. Ships in South China Sea amid Rising Tension", Reuters, April 22, 2020, at www.reuters.com/article/us-china-security-malaysia/australia-joins-u-s-ships-in-south-china-sea-amid-rising-tension-idUSKCN2240FS (Accessed July 22, 2020).

93 "2020 Defense of Japan", Ministry of Defense, Japan, July 2020, at www.mod.go.jp/e/publ/w_paper/pdf/2020/DOJ2020_Digest_EN.pdf (Accessed July 22, 2020).

94 Jesse Johnson, "MSDF Joins Exercises with U.S. and Australia on Doorstep of South China Sea", July 21, 2020, at www.japantimes.co.jp/opinion/2020/07/21/commentary/world-commentary/risk-many-freedom-navigation-operations/#.Xxfwn8dR02w (Accessed July 22, 2020).

95 "Vietnam Protests China's Expansion in Disputed East Sea", Vietnam Insider, April 20, 2020, at https://vietnaminsider.vn/vietnam-protests-chinas-expansion-in-disputed-east-sea/ (Accessed July 18, 2020).
96 This paper extensively analysis the complex India-China relations under the banner of the SCS, CPEC and BRI: Rumel Dahiya and Jagannath Panda, "A Tale of Two Disputes: China's Irrationality and India's Stakes", IDSA, June 29, 2015, at https://idsa.in/policybrief/ATaleofTwoDisputesChinasIrrationalityandIndiasStakes_rdahiya_290615 (Accessed July 17, 2020). Also see "China Objects to Vietnam's Call for India to Invest in Oil and Gas in South China Sea", The Economic Times, January 12, 2018, at https://energy.economictimes.indiatimes.com/news/oil-and-gas/china-objects-to-vietnams-call-for-india-to-invest-in-oil-and-gas-in-south-china-sea/62468024 (Accessed July 22, 2020).
97 Michael R. Pompeo, no. 10
98 Shishir Gupta, "US Backs ASEAN on South China Sea, Challenges China's Predatory World View", Hindustan Times, July 14, 2020, at www.hindustantimes.com/world-news/us-backs-asean-on-south-china-sea-challenges-china-s-predatory-world-view/story-QhWynYN2lGFvVofSh5aWBN.html (Accessed July 17, 2020).
99 Michael R. Pompeo, no. 10.
100 "'Age of Expansionism Is Over': PM Modi Sends Message to China", The Times of India, July 4, 2020, at https://timesofindia.indiatimes.com/india/age-of-expansionism-is-over-pm-modi-sends-message-to-china/articleshow/76778542.cms (Accessed July 17, 2020).
101 "India Joins Philippines, US, Japan in South China Sea drills", The Economic Times, May 9, 2019, at https://economictimes.indiatimes.com/news/defence/india-joins-philippines-us-japan-in-south-china-sea-drills/articleshow/69256405.cms?utm_source=contentofinterest&utm_medium=text&utm_campaign=cppst (Accessed July 22, 2020).
102 "India Is Interested in Navigation in the South China Sea Region: Philippines", The Economic Times, July 7, 2020, at https://economictimes.indiatimes.com/news/defence/india-is-interested-in-navigation-in-the-s-china-sea-region-philippines/articleshow/76825668.cms?from=mdr (Accessed July 17, 2020).
103 Christian Bouchard and William Crumplin, "Neglected No Longer: the Indian Ocean at the Forefront of World Geopolitics and Global Geostrategy", Journal of the Indian Ocean Region, 2010, 6 (1), pp. 26–51, at https://doi.org/10.1080/19480881.2010.489668 (Accessed July 17, 2020).
104 "What Is the Blue Economy?" World Bank, June 6, 2017, at www.worldbank.org/en/news/infographic/2017/06/06/blue-economy (Accessed July 17, 2020).
105 Lyndon E. Llewellyn, Susan English and Sharon Barnwell, "A Roadmap to a sustainable Indian Ocean Blue Economy", Journal of the Indian Ocean Region, 2016, 12 (1), pp. 52–66, at https://doi.org/10.1080/19480881.2016.1138713 (Accessed July 17, 2020).
106 Li Li, "India's Security Concept and Its China Policy in the Post-Cold War Era", The Chinese Journal of International Politics, 2008, 2 (2), pp. 229–261, at https://doi.org/10.1093/cjip/pon009; For a comprehensive understanding of China's New Security Concept in the post-Cold War era that has sought to reassure nations that its rise in economics and military is a 'peaceful' one, read, Elizabeth Freund Larus, "China's New Security Concept and Peaceful Rise: Trustful Cooperation or Deceptive Diplomacy?", American Journal of Chinese Studies, 2005, 12 (2), pp. 219–241, at www.jstor.org/stable/44288800. Accessed 23 July 2020.
107 "PM Modi Proposes Indo-Pacific Oceans Initiative", The Economic Times, November 5, 2019, at https://economictimes.indiatimes.com/news/politics-and-nation/pm-modi-proposes-indo-pacific-oceans-initiative/articleshow/71915838.cms; "PM Modi Proposes New Initiative to Secure Maritime Domain in Indo-Pacific", The Times of India,

November 4, 2019, at https://timesofindia.indiatimes.com/india/pm-modi-proposes-new-initiative-to-secure-maritime-domain-in-indo-pacific/articleshow/71910705.cms (Accessed July 17, 2020).

108 "India's Indo-Pacific Ocean's Initiative Aims Maritime Security Pillar for Inclusive Region", The Economic Times, November 21, 2019, at https://economictimes.indiatimes.com/news/defence/indias-indo-pacific-oceans-initiative-aims-maritime-security-pillar-for-inclusive-region/articleshow/72153070.cms (Accessed July 17, 2020).

109 "India will never join any alliance: Jaishankar", The Asian Age, July 21, 2020, at www.asianage.com/india/all-india/210720/india-will-never-join-any-alliance-jaishankar.html (accessed July 23, 2020); For an explainer on why India has historically moved away from alliance frameworks, read, " Why India avoids alliances ", The Economist, June 21, 2018, at www.economist.com/the-economist-explains/2018/06/01/why-india-avoids-alliances (accessed July 23, 2020)

110 Thomas S. Wilkins, "'Alignment', not 'alliance' – the shifting paradigm of international security cooperation: toward a conceptual taxonomy of alignment", Review of International Studies, 2012 (1), pp. 53–76, at www.jstor.org/stable/41485490 (accessed July 23, 2020)

111 "India will never join any alliance: Jaishankar", see note 104

112 "US has to learn to work with more multipolar world: S Jaishankar at India Ideas Summit", The Times of India, July 22, 2020, at https://timesofindia.indiatimes.com/videos/news/us-has-to-learn-to-work-with-more-multipolar-world-s-jaishankar-at-india-ideas-summit/videoshow/77114801.cms (Accessed July 23, 2020).

113 "Raisana Dialogue: India an Aligned State Based On Issues, Says Vijay Gokhale", Business Standard, January 10, 2019, at www.business-standard.com/article/news-ani/raisana-dialogue-india-an-aligned-state-based-on-issues-says-vijay-gokhale-119011001464_1.html (Accessed July 22, 2020).

8 Major power competition and Southeast Asia

Institutional strategies and resources

Alice D. Ba

Introduction

In Asia, where the interests of major powers intersect and compete, major powers have been both recurrent policy challenges and points of academic debate. Times of heightened major power competition can pose particular challenges. In these debates, small and medium powers can be easily dismissed as peripheral players and as actors with limited strategic agency. In Asia, Southeast Asian states, which include some of Asia's smallest powers, are understood to experience a greater sense of vulnerability to strategic pressure or imposition, resulting in starker choices (e.g. between "balancing" and "bandwagoning"), especially at times of heightened great power competition.

Yet, studies on Southeast Asia also highlight more complicated realities where states have pursued a mix of simultaneous state engagements that neither fully embrace nor fully deny both status quo and rising powers. Despite some important variation, investigations into the foreign policies of individual Southeast Asian states similarly suggest more proactive efforts to expand the strategic space in which they operate. In these efforts, regional institutions and institutional strategies have become an important instrument in the Southeast Asian foreign policy toolbox.

This chapter focuses on the role of regional institutions, especially the role of the Association of Southeast Asian Nations (ASEAN) in Southeast Asian states' strategic response to major power changes in Asia. Few Asian states may be as vested in regional arrangements as Southeast Asia's small and medium powers, which spearheaded the creation of a web of ASEAN-linked institutional frameworks and connections over the course of the 1990s and 2000s. These frameworks, in turn, have given states powers of voice and agenda-shaping that exceed similarly situated powers in other regions. Nonetheless, shifting great power dynamics does affect opportunities and constraints in the pursuit of state and regime goals. Meanwhile, the intensification of US-China tensions since 2010 and especially since 2017 has put greater pressure on individual states, renewing questions about the ability of both Southeast Asian states and their institutional strategies to manage and mediate their major power relations.

DOI: 10.4324/9781003106814-8

128 *Alice D. Ba*

This chapter enters into the previous discussions by considering the distinctive attributes of regional institutions in service of state interests and as responses to the challenges posed by large powers, especially in light of contemporary US-China developments. In particular, the chapter asks, what do regional institutions add to the mix of strategies available to Southeast Asia's small and medium powers in their response to major power challenges? What significance does the current US-China rivalry have for institutional strategies in Southeast Asia? How different is the current challenge compared to previous great power challenges? In answering these questions, this chapter considers the geopolitical and normative features distinctive to Asia's geopolitical space, as well as how Southeast Asia is situated in that space.[1] While discussions have given much attention to the challenges posed by a rising China, not enough attention has been given to Asia's other attributes. These attributes affect not only the nature of geopolitical challenges faced by states but also how regional institutions look and work in response to those challenges.

This chapter proceeds as follows. It begins by first situating institutional strategies with reference to the strategies employed by Southeast Asia's small to medium powers, as well as the particular significance of ASEAN to Southeast Asian states. This first section also introduces some of the distinctive attributes of both ASEAN and multilateralism more generally, as a strategic response to major power challenges. The second section then considers how best to conceptualise the major power challenge in Southeast Asia. The third section then considers institutional strategies at a time of intensified US-China rivalry and with an eye to drawing connections between the past and present periods. It highlights important parallels between different periods in terms of challenges faced, but also shifts in emphasis in both institutional strategy and the kinds of strategic effects sought.

Starting points for thinking about regional institutions in Southeast Asian strategies

Two observations offer starting points for thinking about Southeast Asian state strategies:

1 Southeast Asian states are all small to medium powers.
2 National autonomy is a core strategic value.

The fact that Southeast Asian states are all small to middle powers offers one of the most important starting points for thinking about state strategies. While there is debate about how best to define "small" and "medium" powers, the characteristic of concern here is that compared to other states in, or operating in, Asia, Southeast Asian states lack the same kinds of material resources available to other states operating in Asia. Further, home to some of the region's later developing economies, Southeast Asia as a region also has a greater need for developmental investment and is thus more dependent on extra-regional partners.[2] A greater sense of political and domestic insecurity can also add to states' general sense of constraint, if not vulnerability to other states. In general, Southeast Asian states are considered neither "major powers" nor "regional powers", in that they fall well short of the ability to reorder relations on a regional scale.[3] In Southeast Asia, a historical and persistent strategic narrative of being smaller powers amongst much larger ones also adds a different, reinforcing dimension to conceptions of Southeast Asian states as being "smaller states".

A strong commitment to national autonomy offers a second, related starting point for thinking about Southeast Asian states' institutional strategies. This normative commitment manifests in at least two ways when it comes to national security strategies. It manifests in a strong defence of sovereignty norms, including non-interference being one of the more defining norms associated with Southeast Asian institutional strategies and ASEAN being its most important institutional expression.[4] Second, as several recent studies highlight, Southeast Asian states have tended to gravitate towards strategies that expand their space of manoeuvre.[5] While their positionality as small and medium powers may require them to turn to larger powers for economic or security goods, they also try to avoid situations of over-reliance on any one actor. Thus, states will generally prefer less-exclusive approaches to their security relations.

Similarly, while these powers' structural condition undoubtedly means that they are more materially limited in the kinds of tools available to them, it does not necessarily follow that such states lack either agency or influence in shaping larger power effects, especially at the local and regional levels. In particular, one of the more important tools and avenues by which smaller powers have sought to play more proactive strategic roles has been through international institutions. Studies, for example, have expanded on the work done by Andrew Cooper, Richard Higgott and Kim Nossal who drew attention to how international institutions offer non-major powers opportunities to promote alternative ideas that range from the narrowly functional to the more order-transformative, as well as to mobilise new coalitions and mediate differences between states.[6]

There are practical reasons, as well as historical reasons specific to Southeast Asia, for the importance attached to regional institutions and especially ASEAN in Southeast Asia. It is useful to briefly outline some of these reasons at the outset as it helps to establish how institutional strategies differ from other strategies and why smaller states might find them attractive as responses to major power challenges. It also serves to highlight some of the more context-specific purposes and imperatives attached to institutional strategies in Southeast Asia. These starting points also offer baselines for considering how these strategies have changed or not in the face of contemporary challenges.

Generally speaking, regional institutions have distinctive attributes that set them apart from other state strategies and lend them strategic value, especially to the small to medium powers of Southeast Asia. Moreover, these attributes have tended to be reinforced by the institutional norms and practices associated with ASEAN and ASEAN-linked institutions (most notably, ASEAN Regional Forum [ARF], the ASEAN Plus Three [APT], the East Asia Summit [EAS] and the ASEAN Defence Ministers Plus [ADMM Plus], which include participation from other states in Asia, including the United States and China). Amongst the attributes of greatest importance, regional institutions provide sovereignty-enhancing platforms, an attribute enhanced by the norms and expectations of time and place. Reflective of post-Second World War norms of sovereign equality, regional institutions importantly offer smaller powers a place at the table. They also help equalize, or at least soften, power disparities by giving participating states recognition and political standing based on sovereignty, less on power.

The distance between small and large powers is additionally narrowed by region-specific norms, practices and conditions that also condition institutional strategies pursued by both ASEAN and non-ASEAN states. In particular, ASEAN's early initiative in creating expanded frameworks creates a situation that may be distinctive to Asia – namely the fact that Southeast Asia's small and medium powers, through ASEAN, enjoy an advantaged positionality within both individual institutional frameworks and the larger matrix of overlapping frameworks. That positionality – what states now call "ASEAN Centrality" – has given smaller states even greater standing and ability to shape regional security agendas than what they typically enjoy in global institutions, for example. Further, ASEAN's consensus decision-making practices, which also serve to reinforce ASEAN's non-interference norms, effectively give even the smallest ASEAN state the power to block or highly constrain regional initiatives.

This advantaged positionality has, for Southeast Asian states, reinforced the sovereignty-enhancing attributes of regional institutions in service of national autonomy, which remains one of the most important values guiding how states approach their various relations inside and outside ASEAN. This positionality also contributes to why for Southeast Asian states, more so than for other powers in Asia, regional institutions have generally been accorded greater prominence in most states' conceptualisation of strategy and approaches to national and regional security.

A second important attribute distinguishing regional institutions is their multiple actor quality. As multiple actor platforms, regional institutions, by design, offer opportunities to work with other actors. This has at least two important strategic effects of particular value to small and medium powers. First, working with other states can amplify the interests and perspectives of smaller states in ways that might not be possible in purely bilateral settings. Second, the multilateral character of regional institutions means that relations and pressures are not dyadic in the sense of being one on one, thus easing the effects of asymmetric relations. Here, as well, this attribute is reinforced by region-specific principles and practices. In Asia, Southeast Asian states' early strategic emphasis on political inclusion and engagement in the creation of regional frameworks beyond ASEAN has meant that nearly every state in East and South Asia, as well as every state with a significant operating presence in Asia, today regularly participates in one or several regional frameworks in which ASEAN enjoys centrality.

While multilateralisation, in general, and the regularisation of multi-actor regional cooperation, in particular, tends to complicate major power agendas with its normative demand that major powers work with others, ASEAN-associated frameworks – by increasing the number and diversity of participating states – tend to take it up another level. They do so not only by introducing potentially different centres of power but also by expanding and complication the mix of interests and agents involved.

This particular strategic effect, it should be noted, is also additionally intensified by some distinctive geopolitical conditions. First is the fact that the region is characterised by several larger powers plus the United States. China and Japan, for instance, both actively pursue regional agendas, including bids for hegemonic status. India has also become more actively involved. As Jürgen Haacke, for example, has noted, the presence of multiple competing large powers may be a defining condition of Southeast Asian strategies.[7] Further, in Asia, these larger powers are also joined by several other powers that also have some geopolitical weight – the so-called "middle powers" – including Australia and South Korea. Such conditions create both opportunities and constraints that may not be true of smaller powers pursuing institutional strategies in other regions where there is, for example, only one major power of relevance, no middle powers, or only smaller powers.

Summing up, the distinguishing features that make regional institutions attractive strategic pathways and instruments for Southeast Asia's small and middle powers are as follows:

1 **Regional Institutions as Sovereignty-Enhancing Platforms** have mitigated the distance between small and large states in international organisations and expanded opportunities for Southeast Asia's small to middle powers to exercise their voice.
2 **Regional Institutions as Multiple Actor Platforms** serve to diffuse power via the multilateralisation of interests and processes.
3 **The Advantaged Positionality of the ASEAN or what states now call "ASEAN Centrality"** has reinforced and intensified the dynamics associated with both of the previous points. To the extent that this positionality is seen as critical to states' ability to exercise their voice and autonomy, ASEAN Centrality has now been codified and elevated to the level of strategic principle.

These attributes are not without problems, and those problems tend to be reinforcing. For example, precisely because institutional strategies depend on other states, the varied priorities of fellow members – ASEAN and non-ASEAN – may limit strategic options and effects. The challenge of collective action is additionally complicated by ASEAN's practice of consensus – which, in effect, requires unanimity among participating states. Pluralism, as noted earlier, can diffuse power and influence, but it can also complicate collective action.

This problem also extends to ASEAN itself, which, as a 10-member organisation, contains several internal fault lines. These include the geographic and developmental divide between maritime and mainland states, historical distrust between mainland states and differences among the maritime states whose nationalist conflicts of the 1960s provided an important precipitating context for

ASEAN's creation in 1967. Linked to a history of great power competition in Asia, divisions were also sources of vulnerability – openings for "Balkanization" (divide and rule) by external powers. Bridging these divisions has thus provided a key defining strategic imperative and priority of ASEAN as an institutional strategy since 1967.

Southeast Asia's major power challenges: a bit of Déjà Vu?

Despite their ubiquity, "power transition" characterisations about Asia tend to be conceptually challenged. In addition to the difficulties of pinpointing the point of "transition",[8] the term can both presume too much and overstate the great power changes and order-level effects that follow from changing balances of power. In Asia, for example, the "rise of China" has been associated with integration as much as with its "selective contestation" of existing arrangements.[9]

A better way to conceptualise Asia's geopolitical conditions may be to think about Asia's shifting great power conditions in terms of "great power competition", rather than "transition". There are empirical and analytical reasons for doing so. For example, "major power competition" captures something important about the current strategic context, but at the same time, offers more fluid and dynamic ways to think about Asia's strategic context and state strategies. It also avoids limiting conclusions about what will or should follow (e.g. a Chinese order versus a US order).

"Great power competition" also allows consideration of how the current moment may not be as distinct as sometimes portrayed. For instance, this is far from the first time that Southeast Asian states have been challenged by great powers or great power competition. Being in the shadow of larger powers has actually been an important constant of Southeast Asian states' geopolitical reality. In this regard, great power competition defined the two most formative periods of contemporary states' existence, namely the era of European imperial expansion when Southeast Asia found itself divided among competing European powers and, most notably, the Cold War when Southeast Asia found itself the object of competition between the United States, former Soviet Union and China. Both these periods also factored large in the understood threats from great power "Balkanisation" that provided one of the key strategic justifications for ASEAN in 1967.

Post-Cold War Asia offers a third period associated with great power competition. Specifically, the removal of Cold War strategic overlays was seen to unleash old and new rivalries between Asia's major powers.[10] Major power competition across these periods also shared the similarity of there being more than one competitive dyad at play. During the Cold War, the operative dyads were between the United States and Soviet Union, between the United States and China and between China and the Soviet Union. During the post-Cold War period, the two competitive dyads in play were between the United States and China and between China and Japan. Reflective of Asia's specific conditions (e.g. there being more than one major power), the presence of more than one competitive dyad in each of these periods also potentially affected how competition played out. While not unconnected, dyads in each period did have their own stand-alone driver that created more complex power structures in Asia than, for example, regions defined by only one competitive major power relationship. In short, viewed through the lens of great power competition, current 21st-century US-China tensions and dynamics are not sui generis so much as they are distinct expressions of more historically enduring conditions. This also expands opportunities to compare and contrast current conditions and strategies with past periods.

This said, differences also matter. For one, there have been important differences in the nature of the major power competition. Most notably, the Cold War era exhibited clearer strategic divisions between competing major powers. In contrast, the competition that characterised the immediate post-Cold War era was more abstract and more ambiguous, as evidenced by increasing characterisations of Asia in terms of "strategic uncertainty",[11] a conceptualisation that gained analytic traction as Asia transitioned into a second decade without major conflict. In underscoring the unknown, "strategic uncertainty" offered more open-ended assessments of major power relations.

Just as importantly, relations between Asia's non-major powers were also different in each era. The Cold War era was a period in which Southeast Asian states were less established as political units. There was also much more limited interdependence between the different contending poles as well as between other Asian states. This is in marked contrast to the growing ties and interdependence, as well as greater confidence of Southeast Asian states, that characterised the post-Cold War Asia.

Both these differences have affected the institutional strategies pursued. For example, during the Cold War, when major power competition was both explicit and intense and when states were less established, ASEAN's institutional response had previously been more indirect – for example, through the cultivation of national and regional stability and unity, and by providing a platform from which to assert principles of regional and national autonomy. For ASEAN's newer members, as well, and especially Vietnam, joining ASEAN offered a way to navigate the consequences of US-China-Soviet dynamics (competition and rapprochement) at the tail end of the Cold War.

In contrast, conditions of greater strategic uncertainty and heightened nationalist confidence widened strategic possibilities in the first post-Cold War period. Interdependence also created different imperatives, producing adaptations to existing institutional strategies. In particular, it produced a more proactive strategy aimed at addressing the uncertainties of greatest concern. Vis-à-vis the United States, the ending of the Cold War jeopardised the provision of key security and economic goods. Vis-à-vis China, rapprochement with Vietnam and the former Soviet Union eliminated the key strategic rationale for relations. Institutional strategies offered ways to stabilise major power commitments. Guided by the strategic logic of inclusion – a non-exclusionary approach to trade, development, and security relations and cooperation – institutional strategies sought broadly to "diversify",[12] "hedge"[13] and "omni-enmesh"[14] so as to expand their options and mitigate their vulnerabilities vis-à-vis the changing policies of any one power – be it the United States or China.

Regional institutional strategies at a time of US-China competition

The above thus offer starting points for thinking about institutional strategies and the geopolitical space in which those strategies operate, as well as what current geopolitical challenges might signify. The period begins around 2010, as the South China Sea took on new geopolitical significance as an increasingly charged site of US-China maritime competition. The period is similar and different from the major power challenges of past periods of major power competition.

At one level, the current period bears greatest similarity to the Cold War period. Since 2017, US-China competition has both intensified and expanded into a range of issue realms, transforming major power competition to more explicit rivalry. Moreover, the current period of major power competition stands out for the speed by which relations have deteriorated, especially since 2017.

For Southeast Asian states, the comprehensive competitive dynamics of US-China relations challenge security in more than one way. The spectre of military incidents and conflict posed by US-China maritime tensions risks drawing Southeast Asian states into more direct conflict scenarios. The erosion of the economic pillar of US-China relations, once a reliable foundation for US-China relations, poses a particular challenge for Southeast Asian states. In Southeast Asia, the comprehensive challenge posed by US-China tensions threatens security at all levels – domestic (e.g. regime interests) and regional (e.g. the challenge to ASEAN unity as especially exemplified by past challenges to fashion an ASEAN consensus on the South China Sea), as much the international systemic great power level.

Cold War analogies, however, only go so far as they can overly minimise critical economic and political differences in world and Asian contexts.[15] These contextual differences are important because they condition how other states respond and, in turn, how major power competition plays out. First and foremost, the high levels of interdependence that characterises contemporary Asia, for example, complicate any effort by major powers to compel states to "pick a side". A good example is the US-China "trade war" pursued under US President Trump sought to "decouple" both the United States and Asian partners from the Chinese economy. While, in the short term, Southeast Asia's newer emerging markets (e.g. Vietnam and Cambodia) might benefit from the prospect of diverted production and investment, more established Southeast Asian economies are more vested in current arrangements domestically and economically. For these states, the trade war jeopardises a range of established interests associated with complex production networks and supply chains, on which domestic and strategic livelihoods depend.

Further, for Southeast Asian states, there are also other risks and spillover effects. For one, the US-China trade war undercuts global demand, resulting in global and regional economic contraction. In 2019, the first full year of the US-China trade war, Asia-Pacific trade and services, by volume and value, experienced its worst year since the 1997–1998 Asian Financial Crisis.[16] Such developments are of particular concern for Southeast Asian economies which are more dependent on trade than most countries and for which the trade war threatens economic growth associated with regime stability.[17] For another, trade is just one dimension of Southeast Asian concern. In particular, Southeast Asia's infrastructure needs remain high.[18] This makes China a valued partner beyond trade, especially given its "Belt and Road" initiative (BRI) and its creation of the Asian Infrastructure Investment Bank [AIIB]), both of which prioritize infrastructure connectivity. Notwithstanding the belated attention of the United States to this area, US infrastructure investments pale in comparison. The economics of Southeast Asian development thus increases the risks of trying to decouple or distance from China's economy as the United States would prefer.

Meanwhile, Southeast Asian economies, themselves, are also vulnerable to aggressive US trade policies. For example, the United States, with the election of President Trump, identified as many as four Southeast Asian economies (Vietnam, Malaysia, Thailand and Indonesia) as potential candidates for trade investigation and tariffs.[19] In mid-2019, President Trump labelled Vietnam "almost the single worst abuser of everybody" and levied 400% on its steel imports.[20] The United States has also imposed human rights sanctions on Cambodia and Myanmar and threatened Brunei with the same.

Thus, economic interdependence and economic development make for very different conditions today than during the Cold War. Extensive links with both the United States and China create powerful incentives for states to work against the imposition of such a choice. Moreover, because this dilemma is broadly shared across the region, Southeast Asian states are not alone in their desire to maintain relations with both sides or in wanting to avoid destabilising conflict between two important partners. In particular, they are joined by several "middle powers" of consequence and that are similarly tied to both the United States and China. Both these conditions – high levels of interdependence plus the multiplicity of middle powers in East Asia, regional institutions – make regional institutions of continued but also different relevance as platforms to work with others, similarly interested in managing the effects of major power competition.

Another critical difference between today's Asia and the Asia of the Cold War is the prominence of regional institutions – a legacy of the first post-Cold War period. Moreover, there is not just one major regional framework, but instead, several, with the most prominent of them again being anchored to ASEAN. While ASEAN is often criticised for its "alphabet soup" of institutions, the fact that there are several working frameworks also allows states to adapt different frameworks for different purposes.

This said, the new era also brings different institutional politics. For example, while the proliferation and normalisation of regional institutions as forums for diplomacy and regional cooperation mean that neither the United States nor China can easily ignore them, major power attention can also produce mixed effects. On the one hand, both have adapted their institutional engagements to accommodate Asia's post-Cold War multilateral norms. While both may have been originally ambivalent or resistant to regional institutions, both have also come to realise that not participating risks losing support from key regional states in Southeast Asia.

For example, the US decision to increase its engagement with ASEAN institutions in 2010 was born largely of these pressures and the concern that it could not afford to stay out of institutions like the East Asia Summit, given China's participation.

On the other hand, heightened institutional engagements have also rendered institutional arrangements into arenas and instruments for competition, as well as cooperation. Not only have the United States and China taken greater initiative within existing arrangements, but over the past decade, both have also actively pursued alternative institutional initiatives outside ASEAN frameworks. The more active institutional initiative taken by the United States and China also contrasts with the more passive and even resistant role they took in the first post-Cold War period. China's initiatives, especially, have grown in number and ambition. These include the Asian Infrastructure Investment Bank, its "Belt and Road Initiative(s)", the Beijing Xiangshan Forum and the Conference on Interaction and Confidence-Building Measures in Asia (CICA), all of which involve a larger, more central role for China than provided in current ASEAN-linked arrangements and frameworks.

Chinese initiatives and expanded engagement with ASEAN in general, however, have also fuelled US concerns that China is trying to push the United States "out of Asia". The result has been greater institutional initiative from the United States. Most notably, the US push for a Trans-Pacific Partnership (TPP) under US President Barack Obama offered a US-styled economic framework that would have exerted strong competitive pressures on both participating and non-participating states to shift trade, investment and production commitments in ways that made the Chinese economy less central. More recently, the United States under President Donald Trump has aggressively pursued reconfigured cooperation under a "Free and Open Indo-Pacific" (FOIP), an initiative that makes "geopolitical competition between free and repressive visions of world order" its centrepiece and explicitly accuses China of "leveraging military modernisation, influence operations, and predatory economics to coerce neighbouring countries to reorder the Indo-Pacific region to their advantage".[21]

These dynamics create different kinds of challenges for Southeast Asian states on the institutional front. For one, US-China competition risks politicising regional institutions in ways that could undermine their strategic value, which draws largely from its ability to provide an inclusive, neutral space for Asia's diverse actors. That risk became most evident in 2010, when US and Chinese participants verbally clashed over the South China Sea during a meeting of the ARF, which became a site for similar exchanges in the years that followed.

For another, US-China institutional competition challenges ASEAN unity, which again for Southeast Asian states is a top priority. In particular, US-China competition can aggravate some of the intra-ASEAN fault lines highlighted earlier. The fault line between maritime and mainland Southeast Asia is of special concern, as it corresponds with other divisions, namely the line between the China-proximate/oriented and the US-oriented and, most recently, how vested they are in the South China Sea dispute, a dispute that has regularly challenged states' ability to achieve consensus in ASEAN. Roughly corresponding with the developmental divide in ASEAN between ASEAN's founding states and members that joined in the 1990s (the exception being Thailand), this fault line is also made salient by Chinese regional initiatives, especially infrastructure and developmental initiatives in the Mekong.

Continuity and change mark states' responses to the challenges of major power competition in the current era and their efforts to adapt institutional strategies to contemporary circumstances. One important continuity is states' continued reliance on existing ASEAN-linked regional institutions to simultaneously engage both the United States and China, though there is now greater emphasis on the importance of ASEAN institutions providing neutral platforms from which to pursue a middle course that is neither fully "pro" nor "against" either side.[22] Whilst not completely new, it still contrasts with the previous period when greater emphasis was placed on mitigating unilateral pressures from any one state.

The current emphasis is also different from the Cold War period when states relied on regional institutions (then, it was only ASEAN) to project a more autonomous space between contending powers. Today's institutional strategy is more outward-looking; it is also more active. During the Cold War, states were more internally and intra-regionally focused and looked to ASEAN, primarily as a means to create geopolitical space for national development. In contrast, today's institutional strategy extends beyond Southeast Asia, with ASEAN and ASEAN-linked institutions providing cooperative pathways in support of common security agendas.

Today's institutional strategy is also more active in the sense that states are also using ASEAN platforms to pursue more proactive diplomatic interventions in response to some of the more fractious effects of recent major power initiatives. Three examples serve to illustrate this. The first is ASEAN's role in launching and then facilitating the Regional Comprehensive Economic Partnership (RCEP) negotiations. Launched in 2012, RCEP negotiations helped to offset the Obama-era pursuit of the TPP, excluding China. While the TPP, at the time, promised participating states more certain gains, there were strategic reasons to continue negotiating RCEP. In particular, as a regionally inclusive framework, RCEP offered a way to reassure China about 1) ASEAN states' commitment to their economic relations and 2) their continued interest in China-inclusive regional integration. Similarly, with the Trump administration's inauguration of the US-China trade war in 2018, ASEAN states redoubled their attention to RCEP as a means by which to mitigate the trade war's negative effects on the region as a whole.[23] That renewed attention helped rejuvenate lagging talks, the result being the successful conclusion of RCEP negotiations 16 months later.

A second example may be found in ASEAN states use of ASEAN Plus One platforms to pursue new defence diplomacy and non-traditional security cooperation with both the United States and China. This role has become increasingly important at a time when the usual avenues for military confidence building between the United States and China have weakened. For example, in 2018, ASEAN states inaugurated the first ASEAN-China maritime exercises. Following China's disinvitation from US-led biennial RIMPAC exercises, ASEAN-China maritime exercises, even if more limited, served to counter any possible perception of ASEAN states supporting anti-China exercises. Similarly, in 2019, lest the United States view ASEAN-China maritime exercises negatively, ASEAN states also launched the first ASEAN-US Maritime Exercises. These examples serve to illustrate some careful choreography on ASEAN's part and one way that states have sought to negotiate a more autonomous, if not neutral, position via the pursuit of multiple, non-exclusive engagements.

ASEAN has also provided a platform from which to offer a more "open and inclusive" conception of the Indo-Pacific than that offered by the US FOIP strategy under Trump. While some in ASEAN feared that a direct ASEAN approach would lend legitimacy to the divisive conception pushed by the Trump administration, the "ASEAN Outlook on the Indo-Pacific" (pushed especially by Indonesia) is nevertheless a good example of how some states envisage opportunities for ASEAN to more actively engage and recast major power initiatives along less dangerous and divisive lines.

In a similar vein, the current era has also seen a more active defence of "ASEAN Centrality". While ASEAN states have long resisted efforts to seize the institutional initiative from them, the principle of ASEAN Centrality is now about more than defending ASEAN's privileged seat in regional institutions. Specifically, ASEAN Centrality is also being invoked – notably by both ASEAN states and other Asian powers (e.g. India and South Korea) as a necessary alternative to the more controversial and divisive initiatives associated with the major powers.

Conclusion

For ASEAN states, more so than for other non-great power actors – for example, Australia, New Zealand and South Korea – institutional strategies have offered one of the more important ways to offset the extreme asymmetries that characterise some bilateral relations in support of national autonomy priorities. This chapter has highlighted important attributes associated with regional institutions that smaller states may find especially attractive, given their greater material limitations. For Southeast Asia's small and medium powers, ASEAN, since its founding in 1967, has been especially central in their historical efforts to manage major powers and major power competition. The intensification of US-China competition, especially since 2017, has raised questions, however, about both ASEAN and the institutional strategies that states have relied on.

This chapter has shown that Southeast Asian states are no strangers to major power competition. Consideration of past periods offers ways to think about institutional strategies over time. This chapter has highlighted some similar strategic imperatives that drive institutional strategies across time – in particular, the strong value placed on national autonomy and a strong interest in mitigating the vulnerabilities associated with depending on any one power for security or economic goods. At the same time, this has not meant that great power competition is exactly the same or that institutional strategies have been static.

While the current period of US-China competition may, on the surface, bear greatest resemblance to the divisive dynamics of the Cold War, critical changes have also taken place that, at least for now, mitigate against "Cold War" scenarios.

These include the high degrees of intra-Asian interdependence, the prominent diplomatic presence of more than one regional institution, the unique positionality of ASEAN in Asia and also important changes at the state level. These changes tend to support the continued importance of institutional strategies in conjunction with other strategies, though they are not without their vulnerabilities to US-China competition. For example, precisely because both relationships are so important, any mismanagement by ASEAN or by individual states risks destabilising support from critical domestic constituencies that could compel states to adopt less ASEAN-centric strategies. The challenge to ASEAN unity also remains very real and highly vulnerable to major power interventions. Similarly, should it be the case that enough states in or out of ASEAN decide to prioritise non-ASEAN options, this could also undermine the value of ASEAN to Southeast Asian states.

Still, as highlighted in this chapter, there are strong national- and regional-based incentives for states to take more proactive efforts to mitigate the destabilising effects of US-China competition for the Asian region, and Southeast Asia, in particular. It is often said that Southeast Asian states, above all, want to avoid being put in a position of having to make an impossible choice between the United States and China. This impossible choice is often characterised as one in which Southeast Asian states have no role in constructing. Yet, as illustrated here, this is not entirely true as some states have turned to ASEAN as a means to push back against artificially constructed "dichotomous choices" and to create alternative security paths. Ideally, those paths would be inclusive of both the United States and China but if not, then institutions might still offer paths that can simultaneously engage both at the same time or, at a minimum, provide opportunities to work with Asia's many other actors to create alternative mechanisms and relationships that can help offset their common vulnerability to US-China dynamics.

Notes

1 This book focuses on East Asia defined as Northeast Asia plus Southeast Asia, but as the discussion highlights, this arena is evolving and contested precisely because of some of the geopolitical attributes associated with "East Asia".
2 In contrast, "major powers are largely independent of other actors' support and enjoy greater chances to achieve a favorable outcome[s]" *vis-à-vis* other states. See, for example, Renato Corbetta and William J. Dixon, "Multilateralism, Major Powers, and Militarized Disputes", *Political Research Quarterly*, 57 (1), March 2004, p. 5.
3 See, for example, Ibid.; Sandra Destradi, "Regional Powers and Their Strategies: Empire, Hegemony and Leadership", *Review of International Studies*, 36 (4), October 2010, pp. 903–930; Derrick Frazier and Robert Stewart-Ingersoll, "Regional Powers and Security: A Framework for Understanding Order Within Regional Security Complexes", *European Journal of International Relations*, 16 (4), December 2010, pp. 731–753.
4 See Amitav Acharya, *Constructing a Security Community in Southeast Asia: ASEAN and the Problem of Regional Order*, Routledge, London, 2001.
5 See, for example, John Ciorciari, *The Limits of Alignment: Southeast Asia and the Great Powers Since 1945*, Georgetown University Press, Washington, DC, 2009; Aileen Baviera, "President Duterte's Foreign Policy Challenges", *Contemporary Southeast Asia*, 38 (2), 2016, pp. 202–208; Jürgen Haacke, "The Nature and Management of

Myanmar's Alignment with China: The SLORC/ SPDC Years", *Journal of Current Southeast Asian Affairs*, 30 (2), 2011, pp. 105–140; Antonio Fiori and Andrea Passeri, "Hedging in Search of a New Age of Non-Alignment: Myanmar Between China and the USA", T*he Pacific Review*, 28 (5), 2015, pp. 679–702; Le Hong Hiep, "Vietnam's Hedging Strategy Against China Since Normalization", *Contemporary Southeast Asia*, 35 (3), 2013, pp. 333–368. For a discussion on similar dynamics in states' approaches to recent major power economic initiatives, see Alice D. Ba, "Beyond Dichotomous Choices: Responses to Chinese Initiative in Southeast Asia", in Hannes Ebert and Daniel Flemes (eds.), *Regional Powers and Contested Leadership*: Palgrave MacMillan, Berlin Heidelberg, 2018, pp. 189–227.

6 Cooper, Higgott, and Nossal focus on middle powers, which in their reconceptualization, are defined by their multilateral behaviour. See Andrew F. Cooper, Richard A. Higgott, and Kim R. Nossal, *Relocating Middle Powers: Australia and Canada in a Changing World Order*, University of British Columbia Press, Vancouver, 1993; Jonathan H. Ping, *Middle Power Statecraft: Indonesia, Malaysia and the Asia-Pacific*, Routledge, London, 2017; Ralf Emmers and Sarah Teo, "Regional Security Strategies of Middle Powers in the Asia-Pacific", *International Relations of the Asia Pacific*, 15 (2), 2016, pp. 185–216.

7 Jürgen Haacke, "The Nature and Management of Myanmar's Alignment with China: The SLORC/ SPDC Years", *Journal of Current Southeast Asian Affairs*, 30 (2), 2011, pp. 105–140; see also, Mohammad Salmon, "Strategic Hedging and Unipolarity's Demise: The Case of China's Strategic Hedging", *Asian Politics & Policy*, 9 (3), 2017, pp. 354–377.

8 Steve Chan, *China, the U.S., and the Power-Transition Theory: A Critique*, Routledge, London and New York, 2008. See also, Richard Ned Lebow and Benjamin Valentino, "Lost in Transition: A Critical Analysis of Power Transition Theory", *International Relations*, 23 (3), 2009, pp. 389–410.

9 For two recent discussions on China's "selective contestation" of key arrangements and practices, see Matteo Dian and Hugo Meijer, "Networking Hegemony: Alliance Dynamics in East Asia", *International Politics*, 57, 2020, pp. 131–149; and Rosemary Foot, "China's Rise and US Hegemony: Renegotiating Hegemonic Order in East Asia?", *International Politics*, 57, 2020, pp. 150–165. See also, Evelyn Goh, "Contesting Hegemonic Order: China in East Asia", *Security Studies*, 28 (3), 2019, pp. 614–644. For a discussion on early integration logics that were associated with ASEAN linked institutional strategies, see Alice D. Ba, "Who's Socializing Whom: Complex Engagement in Sino-ASEAN Relations", *Pacific Review*, 19 (2), 2006, pp. 157–169.

10 Aaron Friedberg, "Ripe for Rivalry: Prospects for Peace in Multipolar Asia", *International Security*, 18 (3), Winter 1993–1994, pp. 5–33.

11 See discussions in, for example, Yuen Foong Khong, "Coping with Strategic Uncertainty: The Role of Institutions and Soft Balancing in Southeast Asia's Post-Cold War Strategy", in A. Carlson, P. J. Katzenstein, and J. J. Suh (eds.), *Rethinking Security in East Asia: Identity, Power and Efficiency*, Cambridge University Press, New York, 2004; see, also, Alice D. Ba, "Asia's Regional Security Institutions", in Rosemary Foot, John Ravenhill, and Saadia Pekkanen (eds.), *Oxford Handbook on the International Relations of Asia*, Oxford University Press, Oxford, 2014, pp. 667–689.

12 Alice D. Ba, "Between China and America: ASEAN's Great Power Dilemmas", in Evelyn Goh and Sheldon Simon (eds.), *China, the United States and Southeast Asia: Contending Perspectives on Politics, Security, and Economics*, Routledge, Abingdon and New York, 2008, pp. 107–127.

13 Cheng-Chwee Kuik, "Power Transitions Threaten ASEAN's Hedging Role", *East Asia Forum Quarterly*, January/March 2018, pp. 22–23.

14 Evelyn Goh characterizes it as a strategy of "omni-enmeshment". See Evelyn Goh, "Great Powers and Hierarchical Order: Analyzing Southeast Asian Regional Security Strategies", *International Security*, 32 (3), 2007/2008, pp. 113–157.

15 For one discussion, see Bilahari Kausikan, "New Cold War or Not New Cold War?" *Global Brief Magazine*, June 30, 2020, https://globalbrief.ca/2020/06/new-cold-war-or-not-new-cold-war/
16 See Graham Ong-Webb, "Southeast Asia in 2019: Adjustment and Adaptation to China's Regional Impact", *Southeast Asian Affairs*, 2020 (1), 2020, pp. 1–17.
17 See, for example, Ibid.; "Trump's China Tariff Escalation to Further Shrink Thai Exports", *The Nation (Thailand)*, August 2, 2019; Mari Pangestu, "China – US Trade War: An Indonesian Perspective", *China Economic Journal*, 12 (2), 2019, pp. 208–230.
18 See Asian Development Bank, "Meeting Asia's Infrastructure Needs", Asian Development Bank, Manila, 2017.
19 See, for example, Karlis Salna and Harry Suhartono, "Indonesia Worried About Being Added to Trump's Trade Hit List", *Bloomberg*, May 14, 2019; Masuyuki Yuda, "Trump Squeezes Thailand in Trade Row Over Chemicals Ban", *Nikkei Asian Review*, December 17, 2019.
20 Michelle Jamrisko, "Vietnam Is a Trade War Winner: Now It Has to Figure Out How to Stay Ahead", *Bloomberg*, October 29, 2019.
21 See Summary of the 2018 National Defense Strategy of the United States of America; see, also, Ian J. Storey and Malcolm Cook, "The Trump Administration and Southeast Asia: America's Asia Policy Crystalizes", *ISEAS Perspective*, November 29, 2018.
22 See, for example, Cheng-Chwee Kuik, no. 14; Evelyn Goh, "Southeast Asian Strategies Toward the Great Powers: Still Hedging After All These Years?" *The Asean Forum*, February 22, 2016, www.theasanforum.org/southeast-asian-strategies-toward-the-great-powers-still-hedging-after-all-these-years/
23 See, for example, the comments of Vivian Balakrishnan, foreign minister of Singapore, which chaired ASEAN in 2018. Jessica Donati, "Asian Nations Push Back at US on Trade, Sanctions", *Wall Street Journal*, August 5, 2018.

9 From appeasement to soft balancing

The Duterte administration's shifting policy on the South China Sea *imbroglio*

Renato Cruz De Castro

Introduction

Three weeks prior to his fifth official visit to Beijing, President Rodrigo Duterte announced that he would bring up with President Xi Jinping the July 12, 2016, United Nations Convention on the Law of the Sea (UNCLOS) awards to the Philippines. He sounded resolute to defend the Philippines' territorial rights in the West Philippine Sea, as provided by the 2016 UNCLOS awards that invalidated China's expansive maritime claim in the disputed waters.[1] He explained that it was about time for him to raise the issue with China since he had only 3 years left in office.[2] He added that he could not accept China's sweeping, expansive, and illegal claims in the contested waters.[3] Likewise, President Duterte said he would push for the immediate adoption of the Code of Conduct (CoC) of Parties in the South China Sea dispute. This is supposed to reduce tension and minimise the hostile encounters and risky miscalculation that ensue because of China's delaying tactics. He reasoned out that he wanted the CoC because he did not want "trouble" for the Philippines.

The highly anticipated Duterte-Xi summit in Beijing, however, produced modest results for the resolution of the South China Sea dispute.[4] President Duterte was steadfast in declaring that the PCA award is "final, binding, and not subject to appeal." However, he found himself paralysed when President Xi reiterated China's position of ignoring the awards and consequently said that he would no longer raise the issue in their future meetings. After raising high expectations on the UNCLOS ruling, he ended up agreeing to continue the constructive bilateral dialogues with China and to work for the CoC's completion by 2022. He was also amenable to meeting his Chinese counterpart frequently, strengthening communication, and bolstering diplomatic ties to achieve win–win benefits for the two countries.[5] Concluding his 5-day official visit to China, he declared that he would heed President Xi's suggestion to "set aside disputes, eliminate external interference, and concentrate on conducting cooperation, making pragmatic efforts and seeking development."[6] President Duterte's meekness when confronted by President Xi is part of his efforts to ease the growing tension in Philippine-China relations.

DOI: 10.4324/9781003106814-9

From July to August 2019, the Armed Forces of the Philippines (AFP) and the Department of National Defence (DND) issued alarmist statements on China's audacious encroachments on the country's doorstep. Since July 2019, the AFP has closely monitored Chinese naval presence and movements in Philippine waters.[7] It maintained that the People's Liberation Army's Navy (PLAN) reneged on an earlier promise made by the Chinese ambassador in Manila that the Philippines would be informed in advance of any movement of PLAN vessels in the country's territorial waters.[8] The defence secretary recommended the filing of a diplomatic protest by the Department of Foreign Affairs (DFA) on the suspicious and unlawful transits of Chinese warships in Philippine waters including the passage of two Chinese survey ships in the country's exclusive economic zone (EEZ).[9]

Nevertheless, President Duterte, noting the futility of confronting China, opted for regularly scheduled bilateral consultations between the two countries conducted in an avowedly friendly atmosphere. In the aftermath of his last visit to China, the *Straits Times* observed,

> Before he left for Beijing, Mr. Duterte raised expectation on the matter (China's militarization of the seven South China Sea land features), even though it was unclear what he sought by pressing the arbitration victory into his six-year term. He had largely avoided the subject, opting instead to curry favour from [sic: with] China.[10]

These divergent statements and positions emanating from President Duterte, the AFP, and the DND reflect an internal division in the current administration. The debate involves key government officials who want to balance China's growing naval power in the South China Sea and those who believe that the path of peacefully resolving the territorial row is through diplomacy and economic cooperation. The latter group wants to continue the administration's appeasement policy on China, while the former group urges the government to challenge China's growing naval presence in the South China Sea. This clash of opinions drove the Duterte administration to incrementally (and reluctantly) adopt a policy of soft balancing on China.

This chapter examines the gradual transition in the Duterte administration's policy on China from appeasement to soft balancing.[11] It raises the following main question: How does the Duterte administration apply a policy of soft balancing on China? It also addresses these relevant questions: What is the difference between appeasement and soft balancing? How did the Duterte administration pursue a policy of appeasement? What led to its efforts to shift its China policy from appeasement to soft balancing? What is the future of its soft-balancing policy on China?

Pursuing an appeasement policy

In the later part of 2016, the Duterte administration revealed its intention to change the Philippines' confrontational foreign policy on China. Cabinet officials observed with envy how China helped build infrastructure projects in the poor regions of Southeast Asia when it extended US$6 billion to finance Laos' railway system and Cambodia's first oil refinery. The Philippines had struggled against its more prosperous Southeast Asian neighbours in competing for foreign investments primarily because of the country's lack of infrastructure. President Duterte and his economic advisers noted how Chinese investments boosted infrastructure development in Myanmar, Laos, and Cambodia.[12] They were equally enticed by the Belt and Road Initiative (BRI) plans for increased connectivity among Southeast Asian countries through roads, railways, sea routes, airways, and the internet to promote unimpeded trade, policy coordination, and financial integration.[13] Thus, the key approach of the Duterte administration regarding the South China Sea dispute was to shift the previous administration's confrontational policy on China to a more conciliatory bilateral consultation.[14] President Duterte made clear his intention to improve relations with China in a press conference and met with the Chinese ambassador to the Philippines immediately after his election in May 2016.[15]

The rapprochement with China became evident during the Philippine government's handling of the arbitral ruling on the South China Sea *imbroglio*. In January 2013, the Philippines directly confronted Chinese expansive claims in the disputed waters by filing a statement of claim against China in the Arbitral Tribunal of the UNCLOS. After a 3-year wait, the tribunal at The Hague in the Netherlands handed down its awards on the maritime dispute between the Philippines and China on July 12, 2016. The five-judge arbitral tribunal unanimously ruled in favour of the Philippines on almost all of its claims against China. It determined that China's claim to historic rights through its nine-dash line in the South China Sea is contrary to international law.[16]

Despite the Philippines' overwhelming legal triumph over China, the Duterte administration met the eagerly anticipated decision with sober, cautious, and even muted reaction. In June 2016, China issued a foreign ministry statement admonishing the Philippines to discontinue the arbitration formalities.[17] The Duterte administration heeded this call with a very understated response to the awards. Although the domestic reaction was overwhelmingly positive and jubilant, then Foreign Secretary Perfecto Yasay Jr. simply said that he welcomed the ruling and advised his fellow citizens to exercise moderation and sobriety. The Philippines did not even ask China to abide by the UNCLOS award. Instead, it merely called on the concerned countries to exercise restraint and urged a peaceful settlement of the dispute through consultations among the parties in keeping with international law.[18]

To earn China's confidence, President Duterte commented that the award to the Philippines is purely a bilateral issue between the Philippines and China and is not a concern of the ASEAN.[19] Foreign Secretary Yasay amplified the same sentiment by saying that

> the relationship between the two countries (China and the Philippines) was not limited to the maritime dispute. There were other areas of concern in such fields as investment, trade, and tourism and discussing them could open the doors for talks on the maritime issues.[20]

The pivot to China

In September 2016, President Duterte veered away from the U.S. and gravitated towards China in an effort to generate a windfall of Chinese economic assistance for the development of the country's infrastructure. On September 12, 2016, he announced without warning that U.S. Special Operations Forces in Mindanao must leave the country. He argued that there could be no peace in this southern Philippine island as long as American troops are operating there.[21] The following day, he disclosed that the Philippine Navy (PN) would terminate joint patrols with the U.S. Navy in the Philippines' EEZ to avoid upsetting China.[22]

In October 2016, President Duterte designated China for his first official visit outside the Association of Southeast Asian Nations (ASEAN) member-states.[23] Accompanied by 250 Filipino businesspersons, President Duterte went to Beijing to seek a new partnership while tension between the Philippines and the U.S. was mounting.[24] During the first meeting, President Xi stressed to President Duterte the need for practical bilateral cooperation between the two disputing countries. He suggested that the Philippines and China must thoroughly coordinate their development strategies and cooperate with each other within the framework of the BRI.[25] Both leaders issued a joint communiqué that laid down 13 areas for comprehensive cooperation and signed memorandums of cooperation in economics and trade, investment, financing, and construction of infrastructure.[26] Accordingly, the total amount of money committed by China to boost economic cooperation between the two countries amounted to US$13.5 billion, of which US$9 billion was allocated for infrastructure development in the Philippines.[27]

In a sense, instead of rectifying the perceived imbalance in the Philippines' relations with the two major powers, President Duterte merely replaced the U.S. with China as the Philippines' most important bilateral partner. Not surprisingly, President Duterte has steadily become apathetic to increased Chinese island-building activities in the South China Sea. Initially, he was lured by the Chinese promise of trade concessions, grants, loans, and investments. His administration adopted hook, line, and sinker of Beijing's official line "that after several years of disruption caused mainly by 'non-regional countries (Japan and the U.S.),' the South China Sea has calmed with China and Southeast Asian countries agreeing to peacefully resolve [their] disputes."[28]

Linking the BRI with the Build, Build, Build initiative

The Duterte administration points to poor infrastructure as the main reason why the Philippines has economically lagged behind by its neighbours in Southeast Asia.[29] Therefore, infrastructure development is perceived as necessary since "it will create employment, vitalize the regions, and reduce inequality, and poverty."[30] From its perspective, the Philippines would benefit from the BRI, particularly in the revival of the maritime silk route, as it dovetails with the Philippine government's massive infrastructure build-up scheme.[31] Accordingly, the Duterte administration's economic strategy of sustained and inclusive economic growth is anchored on an unprecedented infrastructure programme that would require Php8.4 trillion (an estimated US$17 billion) over the next 5 years. The Philippines had eyed a sizeable portion of the estimated US$1 trillion that China is investing in infrastructure projects in 60 countries to develop land and maritime routes following the old Silk Road network that once connected China to Central Asia and Europe.

In November 2018, during President Xi's visit to Manila, the Philippines and China signed a Memorandum of Understanding (MOU) on the BRI that will be in force until the end of President Duterte's term in 2022. Under said MOU, the Philippines and China have agreed to encourage infrastructure cooperation and interconnectivity in transportation, telecommunication, and energy sectors.[32] In the aftermath of the signing of the MOU, however, Finance Secretary Dominguez found himself on the defensive as he parried criticism against the agreement alleging that the Philippines may fall prey to the so-called Chinese debt diplomacy and compromise the country's sovereignty in exchange for investments for its infrastructure programme.[33]

Broken promises?

As an archipelagic country that is detached from continental Asia, it is still unclear how the Philippines could tap into the BRI fund. When the BRI was unveiled in 2013, the Philippines was not a party to the initiative. The exclusion was caused by the tension between the two countries over the South China Sea dispute.[34] China removed the Philippines from the list of countries that were projected to be part of a web of six economic corridors linking China with its neighbouring sub-regions.[35] China only accepted the Philippines as a promising participant in the BRI after President Duterte effected his appeasement policy on China in the latter part of 2016.

However, by the time the Philippines became a BRI participant in 2017, the initiative suffered a major setback as projects from Pakistan to Tanzania and Hungary were cancelled, renegotiated, or delayed. The problem sprang from the disputes about costs or complaints from the host countries alleging that they got too little financial returns from infrastructure projects built by Chinese companies and financed primarily by Chinese loans.[36] Some participating countries bemoaned the fact that China not only provided funding but also supplied Chinese project managers, equipment, construction materials, and even workers. This, in turn, triggered public backlash and questions over the actual benefits of BRI projects, especially with regard to domestic job creation. Conspicuous BRI-financed high-speed rail projects in Thailand and Indonesia have also been marred by significant delays due to implementation problems ranging from land acquisition to cost over-runs and other constraints.[37]

In August 2018, Finance Secretary Carlos Dominguez confirmed the slow entry of Chinese public-sector investments. He admitted that there had been "roadblocks" to the inflow of Chinese Official Development Assistance (ODA), particularly Beijing's hesitation to co-finance certain projects with other lenders and its insistence on the use of renminbi instead of dollar in ODA disbursement.[38] He also revealed that securing ODA from China had been delayed because of the reorganisation of the Chinese government in early 2018.[39] Prior to President Xi's visit to the Philippines on November 20, 2018, Filipino economic managers divulged that among the 10 big-ticket projects in the country that China promised to finance, the Philippines and China have so far concluded only one loan agreement – the US$62.09 million Chico River Pump Irrigation Project.[40]

The shortfall on expected Chinese public investment to the country coincided with a series of untoward incidents between Philippine and Chinese forces in the South China Sea. The appeasement policy is based on a quid pro quo with China. President Duterte unravelled his predecessor's balancing policy on China's maritime expansion in the South China Sea. This was done primarily in exchange for the infusion of Chinese investment and aid into the Duterte administration's 5-year massive infrastructure-building programme and for moderating Chinese heavy-handed behaviour vis-à-vis the Philippines in the South China Sea.

In mid-June 2018, then Philippine Foreign Affairs Secretary Alan Peter Cayetano disclosed that the Philippines informed China of the four "red lines" in the two countries' territorial disputes.[41] In the same month, the Philippine government issued a formal demand that the Chinese Coast Guard avoid the Philippines' traditional fishing grounds and stop the harassment of Filipino fishermen in the Scarborough Shoal. This was triggered by TV reports that Chinese coast guard personnel were boarding Filipino fishing vessels, inspecting the fish caught, and confiscating the fishermen's best catch.

In late July 2018, the Philippine government expressed its concern to China over the increase in offensive Chinese radio warnings against Philippine aircraft and ships flying and sailing, respectively, near Chinese reclaimed and fortified islands in the South China Sea. An internal AFP report leaked to the Associated Press revealed that Philippine Air Force (PAF) planes patrolling the South China Sea had received at least 46 warnings from Chinese naval outposts in the artificial islands where more powerful communication and surveillance equipment have been installed along with weapons such as anti-aircraft guns and surface-to-air missiles. On August 15, 2018, President Duterte criticised China for its island-building activities and called on it to temper its behaviour in the South China Sea. Many analysts regarded these statements as the sternest from the president after dramatically cosying to China and downgrading security relations with the U.S.[42]

Keeping the Philippine-U.S. Alliance intact

In late 2016, President Duterte announced his startling plan to separate from the U.S. by unilaterally abrogating the 1951 Mutual Defence Treaty (MDT), the 1997 Visiting Forces Agreement (VFA), and the 2015 Enhanced Defence Cooperation Agreement (EDCA). Propitiously, the 5-month siege of Marawi City in 2017 and the Philippine military's glaring weakness in both conventional and unconventional warfare gave the U.S. the opportunity to bring the Philippines back "onside, rather than pushing it further into China's embrace."[43] Stabilising the Philippine-U.S. alliance became Washington's urgent strategic priority. In the face of Philippine-China rapprochement, the management of the U.S.-Philippine alliance depends on two key security issues – the South China Sea dispute and the growing threat from the so-called Islamic State of Iraq and Syria (ISIS) in Mindanao.

The siege of Marawi City also provided the AFP the rationale for opposing President Duterte's October 2016 plan to expel American Special Forces from Mindanao. There is currently between 200 and 300 American troops deployed in the Philippines serving in advisory capacity in the AFP's post-Marawi City counter-insurgency/counter-terrorism operations.[44] President Duterte relented to the AFP's desire to keep American troops in its camps because the U.S. contributes intelligence and military hardware to support its operations against insurgents and terrorist groups in Mindanao.[45] The Pentagon also transferred 10 new reconnaissance planes worth US$30 million to the AFP under the Obama administration's US$425 million Maritime Security Initiative (MAI) that includes intelligence, surveillance, and reconnaissance equipment.[46]

In November 2017, President Duterte admitted that he is in friendly terms with Washington again and is allowing the AFP to engage the U.S. military in more vigorous joint military exercises including joint counter-terrorism training, amphibious, and live-fire exercises. In a side meeting during the ASEAN summit in Manila, U.S. President Donald Trump and President Duterte reaffirmed their commitment to MDT and the implementation of the 2014 EDCA. The two leaders also tackled proposals for the U.S. to help modernise the AFP and develop its capacity and capability for maritime security, domain awareness, and rapid humanitarian response.[47]

In August 2018, Assistant Secretary of Defence Randall Schriver visited Manila to assure the Philippines of American security commitment. In his meeting with key Philippine defence and military officials, Mr. Shriver underscored the value of frequent subject matter expert exchanges and joint training activities between the two countries' militaries, the U.S. support to the AFP's counter-terrorism operations in Mindanao, and the Philippine-U.S. cooperation to counter violent extremism.[48] He said that combined military activities such as *Balikatan* and *Kamandag* enhance the interoperability between U.S. and Philippine armed forces. Lastly, he reiterated the U.S.'s support to the AFP modernisation programme and acknowledged the increasing importance of the Philippine-U.S. alliance to the stability in Indo-Pacific region.[49]

During his March 2019 visit to Manila, Secretary of State Michael Pompeo declared, "As the South China Sea is part of the Pacific; any armed attack on Philippine forces, aircraft or public vessels in the South China Sea will trigger mutual defence obligations under Article 4 of our mutual defence treaty."[50] He reiterated American support for and defence of the Philippines in the light of the latter's concern about Chinese island-building activities and the militarisation of these land features in the South China Sea. During a separate conversation, Secretary Pompeo told President Duterte, "Our commitments under the treaty are clear. Our obligations are real. The South China Sea is certainly part of an important body of water for freedom of navigation."⁵¹ He also stressed that the Trump administration has made true commitment to ensure that "the South China Sea remains open for the security of the countries in the region, of the world, and for commercial transit."⁵²

The crisis in Philippine-U.S. security cooperation in late 2016 was effectively managed despite the AFP's shift of focus from external defence and maritime security to counter-terrorism and humanitarian assistance and disaster relief (HADR). Supporting the shared interest of counter-terrorism and HADR enabled the U.S. military to strengthen the pro-American elements in the Philippine government and the AFP that mitigated or thwarted President Duterte's efforts to "separate" from the U.S. and to gravitate closer to China. The urban battle during the siege of Marawi City bared the need for the alliance to adjust to the operational requirements to address the threats to Philippine security and brought back President Duterte onside the U.S., rather than pushing him to the arms of China. Currently, Philippine-U.S. security partnership hinges on continuous engagements but with a refocused agenda. It teetered on the brink of a total breakdown after President Duterte's announcement of crossing the Rubicon in October 2016, relative to his charting of an independent course for Philippine foreign policy. After keeping its alliance with the U.S. intact and seeking a clear security guarantee from the U.S., the Duterte administration has begun applying a soft-balancing policy on China despite the Philippine-China rapprochement.

The security partnership with Japan: soft balancing on the side?

Even after President Duterte declared his symbolic break from the U.S. in October 2016, Japan has continued to maintain its healthy and cordial relationship with the Philippines. In essence, Japan became an important counter-vailing force to the pervasive Chinese influence on the Philippines because of President Duterte's pursuit for a new economic partnership with China. In addition, the functioning security partnership forged with Japan has enabled the Philippines to effectively play its classic diplomatic gambit of pitting one great power against the other, which is a form of soft balancing.

During his working visit to Japan from October 25 to 27, President Duterte witnessed the signing for the lease of five Japan Self-Defence Force's (JSDF's) TC-90 maritime reconnaissance planes to monitor Chinese activities in the South China Sea.⁵³ The leasing of the five TC-90 planes at US$7,000 per plane a year was one of the important decisions of the Duterte administration in terms of territorial defence as the AFP lacks valuable assets for maritime domain awareness.⁵⁴ President Duterte also raised the prospects of the Philippines and Japan holding military exercises in the future.⁵⁵

From January 12 to 13, 2017, Prime Minister Shinzo Abe went on a state visit to Manila at a time when the Philippines assumed taking a hostile posture towards the U.S. The Philippines was his first stop in a four-nation diplomatic swing to bolster Japan's trade and security engagements amidst China's increasing economic and diplomatic influence in Southeast Asia. Prime Minister Abe and President Duterte pledged to deepen their maritime security cooperation and help resolve the South China Sea dispute peacefully. Since both the Philippines and Japan are maritime nations, Prime Minister Abe promised to support the Philippines' capacity building in the field of maritime security.[56]

In March 2018, Japan completed its delivery of five TC-90s to the PN. The five donated reconnaissance aircraft augmented the PN's six 40-year-old Britten-Norman Islanders that are being used in maritime patrol, surveillance, HADR, and rapid assessment missions. The provision of the TC-90s alleviated the PN's limited ability to conduct regular and routine patrols in the South China Sea, given its few and obsolete air assets. The planes made possible for the PN to conduct more extensive and wider maritime domain awareness operations. Under its acquisition programme, the PN plans to purchase more advanced maritime patrol aircraft, in particular, two long-range reconnaissance aircraft.[57] Along with Prime Minister Abe's pledges of more grants and investment, the donation of the five TC-90 reconnaissance aircraft to the PN was part of Tokyo's efforts to assist the Philippines economically and militarily to counter-balance China's political influence over the Duterte administration. Interestingly, the transfer of these reconnaissance planes to the PN proved that maritime security cooperation between Japan and the Philippines is developing smoothly regardless of the Sino-Philippine rapprochement.

Japan also delivered 10 Multi-Role Response Vessels (MRRV) to the Philippine Coast Guard (PCG). The PCG already commissioned six of these vessels and the last four were transferred to the Philippines before 2018 ended. According to the PCG, the MRRVs would be used for routine search-and-rescue and law-enforcement operations. However, Philippine defence officials also indicated that these vessels could also be deployed by the PN to combat piracy and patrol the country's extensive EEZ in the South China Sea.[58] In accepting this security hardware, the Duterte administration, in effect, regards Japan as a balancer between the U.S. and China in the Philippines' diplomatic gambit to diversify its foreign relations that include ties with Japan, China, and even Russia.[59]

In the aftermath of the Marawi City siege by Islamist extremists in 2017, Japan has committed to fund and establish PCG radar stations on the islands in the Sulu and Celebes Seas to monitor the movement of terrorist groups transiting between Indonesia and the southern island of Mindanao.[60] It also plans to train the local coast guard personnel who will operate these stations. Prime Minister Abe also offered US$2 million to help the Philippines rebuild Malawi City, which was extensively damaged during the street-to-street fighting between the AFP and the Islamist militants.[61] Japan's provision of four radar stations is part of a wider ODA package that includes helicopter parts for the PAF, funding for infrastructure projects such as railroads, and financial assistance for the rehabilitation of Marawi City. These loans and grants heighten Japan's economic and security ties with the Philippines. From Japan's point of view, the Philippines remains a key factor in preventing China's political and diplomatic influence from spreading into the Western Pacific.[62]

Pursuing ASEAN's soft-balancing approach

The idea of an ASEAN-China CoC originated on September 2, 2002, after the two parties signed the "Declaration on a Code of Conduct (DoC) of Parties in the South China Sea." The DoC is primarily a political statement of broad principles of behaviour devised to stabilise the situation in the South China Sea and prevent the accidental outbreak of conflict in the disputed areas. ASEAN's goal is to transform the DoC into a legally binding CoC and not just a general statement of principles. The association prioritises the drafting and conclusion of a binding code, which will represent the commitment of its member-states and China to a rules-based system, as opposed to a power-based, regional order. The CoC will not only be a set of norms, rules, and procedures to guide the conduct of parties in the South China Sea but will also represent a confidence-building mechanism to create a conducive environment for the peaceful resolution of disputes in accordance with international law.

On May 18, 2017, China and the 10 member-states of ASEAN suddenly announced that they had finally agreed on a framework for a CoC on the South China Sea. At a press briefing after the China-ASEAN foreign ministers' meeting, Chinese Foreign Minister Wang Yi said that he would like to wrap up the deliberations on a CoC, indicating that China is positive towards the conclusion of a CoC.[63] On August 6, 2017, the foreign ministers of the ASEAN member-states and China endorsed the framework of the CoC negotiation. The agreement on a framework is a small step forward in the conflict-management process for the South China Sea dispute.

The agreed framework does not define the geographic scope of the South China Sea and is simply focused on the prevention, management, and settlement of dispute in the disputed waters of the South China Sea.[64] However, it does not contain any specific reference to the binding dispute mechanisms included in the UNCLOS.[65] ASEAN insists that the CoC must be legally binding. However, Beijing wants the adherence to the CoC to be voluntary like in the 2002 DoC.[66] Furthermore, it is silent on the need to put in place an effective regime to manage South China Sea disputes, especially on fishery management and oil and gas development.[67] It falls short of outlining a detailed and coordinated system to manage maritime resources.[68] Expectedly, the negotiation for a CoC will be a long and protracted process and possibly as frustrating since ASEAN and China are still in a quandary about whether the final CoC will be legally binding or not.

The framework agreement aims to exclude the U.S. and Japan as external actors "who interfere" in the dispute and to marginalise ASEAN's role in the South China Sea dispute. It emphasises that the maritime dispute is between the Southeast Asian claimant states and China.[69] ASEAN will play a limited role in the conflict management, and most importantly, there will be no interference from external powers such as the U.S. and Japan. Chinese Vice Foreign Minister Liu Zhenmin succinctly stated, "We hope that our consultations on the code are not subject to any outside interference."[70] Foreign Minister Wang also reaffirmed this position while he was in Manila. This position, however, makes the future of the negotiation for a CoC a hostage to an externality that is beyond the control of both China and the ASEAN member-states.

As the country coordinator of the ASEAN-China Dialogue, President Duterte declared that the Philippines would push for the early adoption of the CoC in the South China Sea with the relevant parties.[71] He added that the path to peacefully resolving the South China Sea disputes is through cooperation, rather than confrontation. China's Premier Li Keqiang said on November 13, 2018, in Singapore that his country hopes to complete the CoC negotiations within 3 years.[72]

President Duterte also planned to discuss with President Xi the expeditious negotiations and conclusion of the CoC. He commented that the "absence of the CoC that is to be observed by affected countries has caused numerous conflicts in the subject waters that could have been prevented by a document that will regulate their actions."[73] President Xi welcomed the Philippine president's efforts to hasten the conclusion of a CoC, which he described as a creative way to set rules for the resolution of the South China Sea dispute.

However, the Chinese leader also stressed that the CoC negotiation should "exclude external disturbances in order to focus on cooperation and developments to safeguard regional peace and stability."[74] This implies that what will be concluded in 2022 will be different from what the ASEAN envisioned in 2002. Similarly, it begs the question of whether or not the contents of the CoC will be the set of rules and norms that the ASEAN has sought since the mid-1990s with binding legal effects. The ASEAN's original intent was to use the CoC as a means of effecting a soft-balancing policy on China. The 2022 CoC, however, will probably contain provisions that will enable China to assume a leadership role vis-à-vis the ASEAN member-states. It will also ensure that there will be no need for countries outside the region to be involved in the dispute.[75] Such a scenario would eventually allow Beijing to establish a Sino-centric regional order in Southeast Asia.[76]

Conclusion

In late 2016, President Duterte started pursuing an appeasement policy on China relative to the South China Sea *imbroglio*. He distanced his country from its longstanding treaty ally, while cosying up to a regional power aspiring to reconfigure the maritime territory of East Asia. He also set aside the 2016 UNCLOS decision on the South China Sea dispute. Initially, the Duterte administration was convinced that its appeasement policy on China was worth pursuing because it would make the Philippines a beneficiary of the latter's emergence as a global economic power. However, China has not reciprocated the latter's appeasement policy as it has delayed the funding of various infrastructure projects under the Philippine government's "Build, Build, Build" programme. Moreover, the coercive actions of the PLAN against Philippine military aircraft and ships operating in the South China Sea have not stopped.

Eventually, the Philippines has slowly and reluctantly adopted a policy of soft balancing. The Duterte administration applies soft balancing by a) fostering a security partnership with Japan, b) maintaining its defence alliance with the U.S., and c) pushing for the immediate passage of the ASEAN-China CoC. In 2016, the Duterte administration's goal was to foster closer Philippine-China economic diplomatic relations that could moderate Chinese coercive moves in the South China Sea. Three years after experimenting with an appeasement policy, the current administration's objective vis-à-vis China has changed. The goal now is to restrain Chinese aggressive behaviour in the South China Sea through its alliance with the U.S., its security arrangements with Japan, and a more active participation in the ASEAN. Hopefully, these efforts can temper or modify this emergent power's heavy-handed behaviour towards the Philippines relative to the South China Sea dispute.

Notes

1 Robert Sutter and Chin-Hao Huang, "Broad Confidence, Coercive Advances, Complicated Regional Responses," *Comparative Connections: A Triannual E-Journal of Bilateral Relations in the Indo-Pacific* 21 (2), September 2019, p. 59. http://cc.pacforum.org/2019/09/broad-confidence-coercive-advances-complicated-regional-responses/ (Accessed May 29, 2020).
2 Manila Bulletin, "Duterte to Rush Conclusion of Code of Conduct in South China Sea," *Manila Bulletin*, Manila, August 8, 2019, p. 2.
3 Ibid., p. 2.
4 Robert Sutter and Chin-Hao Huang, no. 1, p. 59.
5 Xinhua News Agency, "2nd Ld.-Writethru-China Focus: Xi, Duterte Meet on Pushing Forward Ties," *Xinhua News Agency*, August 30, 2019, Beijing, p. 1.
6 Raul Dancel, "Duterte, Xi Jinping 'Agree to Disagree' on South China Sea Issue: They Fail to See Eye to Eye on 2016 Ruling Agree to Continue Talks, Says Philippine Envoy," *The Straits Times*, Singapore, August 31, 2019, p. 1.
7 Robert Sutter and Chin-Hao Huang, no. 1, p. 58.
8 Philippine News Agency (PNA), "AFP Makes Adjustments amid China Warships Passage in PH Waters," *Philippine News Agency*, Manila, August 16, 2019, p. 1.
9 Third Anne Peralta Malonzo, "Wesmincom: Passage of Chinese Warships in Sibutu Strait Not Innocent," *SunStar Philippines*, Cebu City, August 15, 2019, pp. 1–2.
10 Raul Dancel, no. 6. p. 2.
11 Professor Paul defined soft balancing as restraining the power or aggressive policies of a state through international institutions, concerted diplomacy *vis-à-vis* limited, informal ententes, and economic sanctions in order to make its aggressive actions less legitimate in the eyes of the world. Hence, its strategic goals are more difficult to obtain. According to him, soft-balancing strategies shy away from formal hard-balancing alliances where allies cooperate in using their military resources against a specific state or states, and usually obligates one or more of the signatories to use force, in specified circumstances. Instead of formal alliances, soft balancing often develops limited diplomatic coalitions, or ententes to balance a powerful threatening state, and often uses international institutions to apply soft balancing to reduce the threatening state's aggressive behavior. T.V. Paul, *Restraining Great Powers: Soft Balancing from Empires to Global Era*, Yale University Press, New Haven and New York, 2018, p. 20.
12 Michael Delizo, "China Sees Key Role for Philippines in Belt and Road Initiative," *TCA Regional News*, Chicago, December 2016, p. 2. https://search.proquest.com/docview/1845008451/fulltext/220E06A5 (Accessed May 29, 2020).
13 Ibid., p. 2.
14 The National Institute for Defence Studies, *East Asian Strategic Review 2017*, The Japan Times, Tokyo, 2017, p. 134.

15 Ibid., p. 134.
16 Permanent Court of Arbitration, "The South China Sea Arbitration, The Republic of the Philippines versus the People's Republic of China," Press Release, The Hague, July 12, 2016, p. 1.
17 The National Institute of Defence Studies, no. 14, p. 139.
18 Ibid., p. 140.
19 Oxford Daily Brief Service, "Philippines: New Foreign Policy May Be Destabilizing," *Oxford Daily Brief Service*, 16, 2016, Oxford, p. 2.
20 Jose Katigbak, "Philippines Eyes Talks with China Sans Preconditions," *The Philippine Star*, Manila, September 18, 2016, p. 1. www.philstar.com/headlines/2016/09/18/1624973/philippines-eyes-talks-china-sans-preconditions?utm_source=Arangkada+News+Clips&utm-campaign (Accessed May 29, 2020).
21 David Cagahastian, "Malacanang Clarifies Duterte Statement on Kick out of U.S. Troops in Mindanao," *BM News*, September 13, 2016, Blackburn, p. 3.
22 Trefor Moss, "Philippine President's Shift on U.S. Alliance Worries Military: His Willingness to Upend Alliance with the U.S. Has Dumbfounded Even Those in His Inner Circle," *The Wall Street Journal*, September 16, 2016, New York, p. 1. www.wsj.com/articles/philippine-presidents-shift-on-u-s-alliance-worries-military-1474058666
23 The National Institute for Defense Studies, no. 14, p. 134.
24 Neil Jerome Morales and Karen Lema, "The Philippines Is Preparing a Major Pivot Toward China amid Tension with the U.S.," *Business Insider*, October 11, 2016, New York, p. 1. www.businessinsider.com/the-philippines-is-preparing-a-major-pivot-toward-china-2016-10?source=Arangkada+News+Clips&utm_campaign=2df . . .
25 National Institute for Defence Studies, no. 14, p. 87.
26 Ibid., p. 88.
27 Ibid., p. 88.
28 Robert G. Sutter and Chin-Hao Huang, no. 1; Robert G. Sutter and Chin-Hao Huang, "Beijing Presses Its Advantages," *Comparative Connections* 18 (3), January 2017, p. 43. http://cc.pacforum.org/wp-content/uploads/2017/01/1603_china_sea.pdf (Accessed May 29, 2020).
29 MENA Report, "Philippines' DuterteNomics in China Launched," *MENA Report*, May 16, 2017, Amman, p. 1. https://search.proquest.com/docview/1899178166/fulltext/220E06A5 (Accessed May 29, 2020).
30 Ibid., p. 2.
31 MENA Report, "Philippines: PH to Benefit from Belt and Road Initiative," *MENA Report*, June 21, 2017, Amman, p. 1. https://search.proquest.com/docview/1912008204/fulltext/220E06A5
32 Business Mirror, "Phil, China MOU on Belt and Road Initiative Expires at End of Duterte's Term in 2022," *Business Mirror*, November 27, 2018, Manila, p. 1.
33 Ibid., p. 1.
34 Michael Delizo, no. 12, p. 2.
35 Joel Wuthnow, *Chinese Perspectives on Belt and Road Initiative: Strategic Rationales, Risks, and Implications*, National Defense University Press, Washington, D.C., 2017, pp. 4–5.
36 Mayvelin Caraballo, "China ODA Impact Uncertain – Nomura," *TCA Regional News*, April 18, 2018, Chicago, p. 1.
37 Euben Paracuelles, "ASEAN Stands to Gain from Belt and Road Initiative Despite Challenges," *The Business Times*, May 17, 2018, Manila, p. 1.
38 Ian Nicolas Cigaral, "Diokno: Xi Jinping's Manila Visit to Pressure China's Bureaucracy to Hasten Infra Projects," *Philippine Star*, November 14, 2018, Manila, pp. 1–2.
39 Ibid., p. 1.
40 Ibid., p. 1.
41 Sarah Zheng, "Manila's Tough Talk on South China Sea Aimed at Easing Fears at Home, Analysts Say: Duterte Is Under Pressure to Take Hard Line on China Over Its Military Moves in Disputed Waters," *South China Morning Post*, June 2, 2018, Hong Kong, p. 1.

42 Jim Gomez, "Duterte: China Should Temper Its Behavior in Disputed Waters," *Bloomberg*, August 14, 2018, New York, p. 1. www.bloomberg.com/news/articles/2018-08-14/duterte-china-should-temper-i (Accessed May 29, 2020).
43 Ely Ratner, "Why Trump Was Right to Invite Duterte to the White House," *Politico Magazine*, May 3, 2017, Arlington County, p. 2. www.politico.com/magazine/story/2017/05/03/trump-invite-duterte-white-house-philippines-215095 (Accessed May 29, 2020).
44 Jessica Donati and Gordon Lubold, "World News: U.S. Elevates Philippine War Effort," *Wall Street Journal*, January 20, 2018, New York, p. 1.
45 Sheldon Simon, "U.S.-Southeast Asian: Regional Skepticism," *Comparative Connections* 19 (2), September 2017, p. 45. http://cc.pacforum.org/wp-content/uploads/2017/09/1702_US-SEA.pdf (Accessed May 29, 2020).
46 Ibid., p. 47.
47 The White House, "Joint Statement Between the United States of America and the Republic of the Philippines," Office of the Press Secretary, November 13, 2017, p. 2.
48 U.S. Embassy in the Philippines, "Assistant Secretary of Defence Randall Schriver Visits Manila, Underscores U.S. Commitment to the Philippines," *U.S. Embassy in the Philippines News*, August 17, 2018, p. 1.
49 Ibid., p. 2.
50 Ankit Panda, "In Philippines, Pompeo Offers Major Alliance Assurance on South China Sea," *The Diplomat*, March 4, 2019, Washington, p. 1. https://search.proquest.com/docview/2187567015?accountid=190474 (Accessed May 30, 2020).
51 Manila Bulletin, "Lorenzana Says 67-yr Old MDT Could Become Cause, Not Deterrent, for Chaos," *Manila Bulletin*, March 5, 2019, Manila, p. 2. https://search.proquest.com/docvie/2188186454?accountid=190474
52 Ibid., p. 2, and Mike Yeo, "Japan to Bolster Philippine Maritime Security with TC-90 Aircraft," *Defence News*, October 30, 2016, p. 1.
53 Ministry of Foreign Affairs, "Japan-Philippines Joint Statement," Issued in Tokyo, October 26, 2016.
54 Rene Acosta, "Duterte Pushes for Contracts to Modernize Armed Forces," *New Nations*, October 27, 2016, London, p. 1.
55 Anonymous, "Duterte Says Open to Idea of Military Exercises with Japan," *Kyodo News*, October 27, 2016, Tokyo, p. 1.
56 Catherin Valente, "Abe Offers PhP430 B Package," *TCA Regional News*, January 13, 2017, Chicago, p. 2. https://search.proquest.com/docview/1857825130?accountid=28547 (Accessed May 30, 2020).
57 Mike Yeo, "Japan to Bolster Philippine Maritime Security with TC-90 Aircraft," *Defence News*, October 30, 2017, Vienna, Virginia, p. 1. https://www/defensenews.com/global/asia-pacific/2017/10/30/japan-to-bolster-philippin (Accessed May 30, 2020).
58 Prashanth Paramesaran, "A Big Week for Japan-Philippines Defence Ties," *The Diplomat*, March 29, 2018, Washington, p. 2. https://thediplomat.com/2018/03/a-big-week-for-japan-philippines-defense-ties/ (Accessed May 30, 2020).
59 The National Institute for Defence Studies, no. 14, p. 136.
60 Tim Kelly and Nobuhior Kubo, "Japan to Build Four Radar Stations for the Philippines to Counter Piracy Surge, Sources Say," *The Japan Times*, November 11, 2017, Tokyo, p. 1. www.japantimes.co.jp/news/2017/11/11/national/politics-diplomacy/japan-build- (Accessed May 30, 2020).
61 Ralph Jennings, "Japan Deepens Economic Support for Philippines in Rivalry with China," *Voice of America News*, November 3, 2017, Washington, p. 3. https://search.proquest.com/docview/1959227775/fulltext/19E45C6176B14116PQ/14?a . . . (Accessed May 30, 2020).
62 Tim Kelly and Nobuhior Kubo, no. 60, p. 2.
63 The National Institute for Defence Studies, no. 14, p. 141.

64 Carlyle Thayer, "A Closer Look at the ASEAN-China Single Draft South China Sea Code of Conduct," *The Diplomat*, August 3, 2018, Washington, p. 1. https://thediplomat.com/2018/08/a-closer-look-at-the-asean-china-single-draft-south-china-sea-code-of-conduct/ (Accessed May 30, 2020).
65 Ibid., p. 1.
66 Sheldon Simon, no. 45, p. 46.
67 Gregory Poling, "South China Sea Code of Conduct Still a Speck on the Horizon," *Asian Maritime Transparency Initiative*, September 6, 2018, Washington, D.C., p. 3. https://amti.csis.org/south-china-sea-code-conduct-still-speck-horizon/ (Accessed May 30, 2020).
68 Ibid., p. 3.
69 Sheldon Simon, no. 45, p. 45.
70 Ankit Panda, "China, ASEAN Come to Agreement on a Framework South China Sea Code of Conduct," *The Diplomat*, May 19, 2017, Washington, D.C., pp. 1–2. http://thediplomat.com/2017/05/china-asean-come-to-agreement-on-a-framework-south-china-sea-code-of-conduct/ (Accessed May 29, 2020).
71 Xinhua News Agency, no. 5, p. 1.
72 The National Institute for Defence Studies, *East Asian Strategic Review 2019*, Urban Connections, Tokyo, 2019, p. 106.
73 Manila Bulletin, "Duterte Lands in Beijing for 5th China Trip," *Manila Bulletin*, August 28, 2019, Manila, p. 1.
74 Cao Deshing, "Xi Encourages Progress on South China Sea," *China Daily International Edition*, August 30, 2019, Beijing, p. 1.
75 The National Institute for Defence Studies, *NIDS China Security Report 2019: China Strategy for Reshaping the Asian Order and Its Ramifications*, The National Institute for Defence Studies, Tokyo, 2019, p. 35.
76 Ibid., p. 35.

Bibliography

Acosta, Rene. (2016) "Duterte Pushes for Contracts to Modernize Armed Forces." *New Nations*, October 27: 1.
Anonymous. (2016) "Duterte Says Open to Ideas of Military Exercises with Kapan." *Kyodo News*, October 27: 1.
Business Mirror. (2018) "Phil, China MOU on Belt and Road Initiative Expires at Duterte's Term in 2022." *Business Mirror*, November 27: 1.
Cagahastian, Davis. (2016) "Malacanang Clarifies Duterte Statement on Kick out of U.S. Troops in Mindanao." *BM News*, September 13: 1.
Cao, Deshing. (2019) "Xi Encourages Progress on South China Sea." *China Daily International Edition*, August 30: 1.
Caraballo, Euben. (2018) "ASEAN Stands to Gain from Belt and Road Initiative Despite Challenges." *The Business Times*, May 17: 1.
Caraballo, Mayveilin. (2018) "China ODA Impact Uncertain – Nomura." *TCA Regional News*, April 18: 1.
Dancel, Raul. (2019) "Duterte, Xi Jinping Agree to Disagree on South China Sea Issue: They Fail to See Eye to Eye on 2016 Ruling Agree to Continue Talks, Says Philippine Envoy." *The Straits Times*, August 31: 1.
Delizo, Michael. (2016) "China Sees Key Role for Philippines in Belt and Road Initiative." *TCA Regional News*, December: 2.
Donati, Jessica, and Gordon Lubold. (2018) "World News: U.S. Elevates Philippines War Effort." *Wall Street Journal*, January 20: 1.

Gomez, Jim. (2018) "Duterte: China Should Temper Its Behavior in Disputed Waters." *Bloomberg*, August 14: 1.

Jennings, Ralph. (2017) "Japan Deepens Economic Support for Philippines in Rivalry with China." *Voice of America*, November 3: 1.

Katigbak, Jose. (2016) "Philippines Eyes Talks with China sans Precondition." *The Philippine Star*, September 18: 1.

Kelly, Tim, and Nobuhior Kubo. (2017) "Japan to Build Four Radar Stations for the Philippines to Counter Piracy Surges, Sources Say." *The Japan Times*, November 11: 1.

Malonzo, Third Anne Peralta. (2019) "Wesmincom: Passage of Chinese Warships in Sibutu Strait Not Innocent." *SunStar*, August 15: 1–2.

Manila Bulletin. (2019) "Duterte Lands in Beijing for 5th China Trip." *Manila Bulletin*, August 28: 1.

Manila Bulletin. (2019) "Dutetrte to Rush Conclusion of Code of Conduct in the South China Sea." *Manila Bulletin*, August 8: 1.

Manila Bulletin. (2019) "Lorenzana Says 67-yr Old MDT Could Become Cause, Not Deterrent, for Chaos." *Manila Bulletin*, March 5: 2.

MENA Report. (2017) "Philippines: DuterteNomics in China Launched." *MENA Report*, May 16: 1.

MENA Report. (2017) "Philippines: PH to Benefit from Belt and Road Initiative." *MENA Report*, June 21: 1.

Ministry of Foreign Affairs. (2016) *Japan-Philippines Joint Statement*. Press Statement, Tokyo: Ministry of Foreign Affairs.

Morales, Neil Jerome, and Karen Lema. (2016) "The Philippines Is Preparing a Major Pivot Toward China Amid Tension with the U.S." *Business Insider*, October 11: 1.

Moss, Trefor. (2016) "Philippine President's Shift on U.S. Alliance Worries Military: His Willingness to Upend Alliance with the U.S. Has Dumbfounded Even Those in His Inner Circle." *The Wall Street Journal*, September 16: 1.

Oxford Daily Brief Service. (2016) "Philippines: New Foreign Policy May Be Destabilizing." *Oxford Daily Brief*: 2.

Panda, Ankit. (2017) "China, ASEAN Come to Agreement on a Framework South China Sea Code of Conduct." *The Diplomat*, May 19: 1.

Panda, Ankt. (2019) "In Philippines, Pompeo Offers Major Alliance Assurance on South China Sea." *The Diplomat*, March 4: 1.

Paramesaran, Prashanth. (2018) "A Big Week for Japan-Philippines Defence Ties." *The Diplomat*, March 29: 2.

Paul, T.V. (2018) *Restraining Great Powers: Soft Balancing from Empires to the Global Era*. New Haven and New York: Yale University Press.

Permanent Court of Arbitration. (2016) *The South China Sea Arbitration: The Republic of the Philippines versus the People's Republic of China*. Press Release, The Hague: Permanent Court of Arbitration.

Philippine News Agency. (2019) "AFP Makes Adjustments amid China Warships Passage in PH Waters." *Philippine News Agency*, August 16: 1.

Poling, Gregory. (2018) "South China Sea Code of Conduct Still a Speck on the Horizon." *Asian Maritime Transparency Initiative*, September 6: 1.

Ratner, Ely. (2017) "Why Trump Was Right to Invite Duterte to the White House." *Politico Magazine*, May 3: 2.

Simon, Sheldon. (2017) "U.S.-Southeast Asia: Regional Skepticism." *Comparative Connections*, September: 45.

Sutter, Robert G., and Chin-Hao Huang. (2017) "Beijing Presses Its Advantages." *Comparative Connections*: *A Triannual E-Journal of Bilateral Relations in the Asia-Pacific* 18, no. 3 (January): 43.

Sutter, Robert G., and Chin-Hao Huang. (2019) "Broad Confidence, Coercive Advances, Complicated Regional Responses." *Comparative Connections: A Triannual E-Journal of Bilateral Relations in the Indo-Pacific* 21, no. 2 (September): 59.

Thayer, Carlyle. (2018) "A Closer Look at the ASEAN-China Single Draft South China Sea Code of Conduct." *The Diplomat*, August 3: 1.

The National Institute for Defence Studies. (2017) *East Asian Strategic Review 2017*. Tokyo: The Japan Times.

The National Institute for Defence Studies. (2019) *East Asian Strategic Review 2019*. Tokyo: Urban Connections, 2019.

The National Institute for Defence Studies. (2019) *NIDS China Security Report 2019: China Strategy for Reshaping the Asian Order and Its Ramifications*. Tokyo: The National Institute for Defense Studies.

The White House. (2017) *Joint Statement Between the United States of America and the Republic of the Philippines*. Press Release, The White House, Washington, D.C.: Office of the Press Secretary, 2017.

U.S. Embassy in the Philippines. (2018) *Assistant Secretary of Defence Randal Schiver Visits Manila Underscores U.S. Commitment to the Philippines*. Press Release, Manila: U.S. Embassy in Manila, 1.

Valente, Catherin. (2017) "Abe Offers PhP430B Package." *TCA Regional News*, January 13: 1.

Wuthnow, Joel. (2017) *Chinese Perspectives on Belt and Road Initiative: Strategic Rationales, Risk, and Implications*. Washington, D.C.: National Defense College.

Xinhua News Agency. (2019) "2nd Ld-Writethru-China Focus: Xi, Duterte Meet on Pushing Forward Ties." *Xinhua News Agency*, August 30: 1.

Yeo, Mike. (2016) "Japan to Bolster Philippine Maritime Security with TC-90 Aircraft." *Defence News*, October 30: 1.

Zhang, Sarah. (2018) "Manila's Tough Talk on South China Sea Aimed at Easing Fears at Home, Analysts Say: Duterte Is Under Pressure to Take Hard Line on China Over Its Military Moves in Disputed Waters." *South China Morning Post*, June 2: 1.

10 Beyond strategic hedging

Mahathir's China policy and the changing political economy of Malaysia, 2018–2020

Hong Liu

Introduction: towards a Constructivist approach to Malaysian foreign policy

In Mahathir Mohamad's controversial political manifesto entitled *The Malay Dilemma*, published in 1970, 11 years before taking up his first prime ministership (1981–2003), he highlighted the substantial economic disparities between the Malays and the ethnic Chinese, calling for the Malaysian government's affirmative actions to provide protection and comprehensive support for the Malays who are "sons of the land." The implementation of the New Economic Policy (NEP) since the early 1970s has significantly reduced the economic gaps between these two major ethnic groups and helped bring about a reasonably large Malay middle class, with some of them emerging as key players in the local political economy.[1]

While the dilemmas faced by the Malays identified initially by Mahathir might have largely faded away half a century after *The Malay Dilemma*'s publication, the deep-seated question about national and ethnic identity remains at the core of Malaysia's politics and directly or indirectly impact upon its diplomacy. The country has now faced new sets of dilemmas that are intricately embedded in the domestic and international political economy within a fast-changing region symbolised by the rise of China and its growing clout in the region as well as intensifying US-China confrontations, especially over the past decade. While China was amidst the turmoil of the Cultural Revolution in 1974 when the two countries established diplomatic relations, it has risen to become the second largest economy in world. In the meantime, the beginning of the Trump administration in early 2017 witnessed the escalation of the American-China rivalries in almost all spheres, ranging from diplomatic and trade to technological and ideological. The global COVID-19 pandemic has further fuelled the competitions between the two major powers in both the international and regional arenas. All these have inevitably affected Malaysia's foreign policy options, including its relations with China and the US.

Malaysia's foreign policy choices, therefore, are increasingly shaped through a complex process of (re)negotiations among different stakeholders, both internally and externally. As two of the three largest trading partners of Malaysia, both China and the US have significant impact upon the country's reindustrialisation

DOI: 10.4324/9781003106814-10

and its trade, which account for 130.50 per cent of its total gross domestic product (GDP) in 2018, according to the World Bank national accounts data.² As one of the most dynamic economies in Southeast Asia, Malaysia's domestic politics, including racial politics, are also to affect China's grand strategies such as the Belt and Road Initiative (BRI) that was launched in late 2013 and, to a lesser extent, America's Indo-Pacific Strategy, which was the Trump administration's defining foreign policy towards the region with the key goal of containing China.³

It was against such a fluid domestic and global milieu that the 92-year-old Mahathir rose to power once again, after winning, quite unexpectedly, the nation's 14th General Election in May 2018. Although Mahathir 2.0 was short-lived in its political life, ending on 29 February 2020 due to internal frictions within the ruling coalition,⁴ as this chapter argues, his foreign policy towards China represented some major departures from both his first prime ministership and his immediate predecessor, Najib Razak (2009–2018), and heralded some key characteristics that have an impact upon Malaysia's future diplomacy.

The existing literature concerning Southeast Asian nations' China policy over the past two decades has been dominated by the "strategic hedging" framework. The concept of strategic hedging is introduced as "a core strategy for second-tier states operating in the current deconcentrating unipolar system with the United States as system leader,"⁵ and it has been suggested that "Southeast Asian states have sought to maintain their strategic autonomy by adopting hedging strategies to secure economic and security benefits from different partners".⁶

In a number of studies, Kuik has argued that

> the enduring uncertainty at the systemic level has compelled the states to hedge by pursuing contradictory, mutually counteracting transactions of 'returns-maximizing' and 'risk-contingency' options, which seek to offset the potential drawbacks of one another, as a way to project a non-taking-sides stance while keeping their own fallback position at a time when the prospect of power structure is far from clear.⁷

A recent study on Mahathir's China policy after 2018 also contended that "Malaysia has demonstrated a cautious hedging strategy that overall tends to acquiesce toward China, even in areas of tension."⁸

The strategic hedging thesis, in its own right, has provided some instrumental insights in explaining the rationality and choices of foreign policy behaviours of smaller powers such as those in Southeast Asia in avoiding "bandwagoning," which is "often defined as the opposite of balancing, or the choice of allying with the stronger or threatening side."⁹ However, there is a need to consider other alternatives beyond Neo-realism and Neo-liberalism, which focus on the state's material power and serve as main theoretical foundation of strategic hedging.¹⁰

This chapter is not only informed by a recognition of the political economy's significant role in shaping foreign policies, but it is also inspired by the Constructivist approach in International Relations (IR), which "emphasizes the social and relational construction of what states are and what they want."¹¹ Contrast to materialism interpretation, Constructivism looks at "international politics not just about materials forces such as power and wealth but is also shaped by subjective and intersubjective factors, including ideas, norms, culture and identity." This approach is particularly relevant for third world countries where "ideas and ideologies are far more important than power or wealth." This is perhaps a reason that Constructivism has gained "popularity in Southeast Asia," with scholars looking to the local historical resources as a basis for IR theorising.[12]

From the perspective of China-Southeast Asian relations, there has been a growing body of research analysing the motivations and impacts of China in its overseas expansion. Such studies tend to view actors within China as the major variable behind China's foreign policy and foreign direct investment (FDI) in the region. First, much of the debate has pinpointed the Chinese state as the primary determinant undergirding the BRI, which, as Xi Jinping's signature foreign policy design since its launch in 2013, has constituted a core of China's diplomacy towards the region.[13] Second, the state-centric perspective has been augmented by other studies on the multitude of actors shaping China's economy. They posit that the BRI is driven by other Chinese players such as the state-owned enterprises (SOE), private firms and less well-capitalised Chinese entrepreneurs. To ensure access to overseas energy supply, Beijing has been utilising diplomatic instruments and policy banks to help its national firms – primarily the SOEs – tap into the oil and gas fields in Russia-Central Asia, Middle East-North Africa and South America.[14]

These two strands of work tend to understand Chinese outward expansion mainly from the perspective of the Chinese actors, giving little attention to the responses formulated and implemented by players in the BRI recipient states such as Malaysia who have their own agendas in their engagement (or disengagement) with China. Therefore, a perspective from Southeast Asia is imperative to decipher the on-the-ground intricacies of the region's diplomacy towards China.[15]

With the previous brief discussion on various approaches to a rising China in Southeast Asia and Malaysian foreign policy, this chapter addresses the following questions: How did the "China factor" contribute to Malaysia's domestic political transformation leading to the re-emergence of Mahathir in May 2018? What were Mahathir's and his government's policies towards China (and by extension, the US-China rivalries)? What were key elements in Mahathir's foreign policy that are not adequately explained by the dominant framework of strategic hedging? How did domestic political economy and other social factors shape his perceptions and policy choices with respect to international power politics (and vice versa)? What are the implications of Malaysia's experiences under Mahathir 2.0 for a better understanding of the local initiatives and interests of small powers in responding to and affecting great power politics?

This chapter is organised into three main sections. The first part briefly discusses the factors leading to Mahathir's resurgence, including the role of the opposition alliance's anti-China rhetoric before and during the general election. The second section examines complex domestic factors and variables in shaping Malaysia's engagements with China and its stance in the great power politics, under the

New Foreign Policy Framework announced in June 2019. The third part analyses Malaysia's policies towards the BRI through a case study of the East Coast Rail Link (ECRL) project as well as Mahathir's positions on Huawei, which has been a hotly disputed issue between the US and China in recent years. Apart from exploring the implications of Malaysia's dilemmas in a broader context of international political economy, the concluding section highlights the importance of going beyond strategic hedging by giving greater attention to significant roles of local agency (interests, institutions and players) in engaging great power politics, which in turn points to the validity of Constructivism in deciphering Southeast Asian foreign policies towards a rising China. In short, this chapter goes beyond the existing debates between rebalancing and hedging theses and aims to place the emphasis on how small and middle powers articulate and advance their own interests amidst intensified great power contestations.[16] Data for this chapter are mainly drawn from relevant policy documents and speeches published in Malaysia, China and other countries, which are supplemented by the author's own fieldworks in Malaysia and China including interviews with stakeholders in both countries.[17]

The China factor and Mahathir's re-emergence

Mahathir's China policy during his second term between May 2018 and February 2020 started from the fact that China had been a major economic force in Malaysia. The governmental statistics showed that China became Malaysia's largest investor in 2016, contributing an investment totalling US$1.6 billion (equivalent to 17.5 per cent of the country's total FDI inflow). China was Malaysia's largest trading partner for the tenth consecutive year in 2018, with bilateral trade increasing by 15 per cent from US$63.6 billion in 2017 to US$77.7 billion in 2018.[18] Chinese FDI has eclipsed those from the Netherlands (11.7 per cent of inward FDI), Germany (9.5 per cent of inward FDI), the UK (9.5 per cent of inward FDI), Korea (8.0 per cent of inward FDI) and Singapore (7.7 per cent of inward FDI). Chinese investment is especially noticeable in large-scale, capital-intensive infrastructure projects.

The United Malays National Organisation (UMNO) that had been in power after the country's independence in 1957 was a key player in the ruling coalition (the Barisan Nasional or the National Front) of the Malay, Chinese and Indian political and business elites, which had controlled the country's political and economic resources for more than half a century. It was, therefore, a big surprise that UMNO and its allies were voted out in the 14th General Election. The UMNO-led coalition lost power not only at the federal level but also in several important states, including Johor, its birthplace and traditional vote bank.

While there were complex factors leading to UMNO's defeat, such as "credible personalities" embodied in Mahathir and pre-electoral coalitions,[19] the disquiet surrounding the Najib administration's management of the BRI and its relations with China was one of the more prominent factors in unseating the ruling coalition. Indeed, one of the main pleads of the Mahathir campaign was against the growing visibility of China in the country, exemplified not only in the massive scale of trade and investment but also in major real-estate projects such as the Forest City, a mega private housing project in a man-made island built by a mainland Chinese developer, with a targeted number of housing of more than 300,000 residents upon completion (most of whom are expected to be from China). Mahathir severely criticised large-scale projects like Forest City and pleaded to review all China investments if he won. "Here we gain nothing from the [Chinese] investment," Mahathir said. "We don't welcome that." With reference to the Forest City project, he claimed that "We don't have enough people with wealth to buy all those very expensive flats, so you're bringing in foreigners. No country wants to have an influx of huge numbers of foreign people into their country."[20] To be sure, the anti-China rhetoric was primarily aimed at outing Najib Razak, the then prime minister who was perceived to be corruptive and who had maintained close ties with China.[21]

As a reflection of growing influence of foreign affairs upon the 14th General Election[22], the China factor had also been politicised in Malaysia's ethnic politics surrounding the election. The Malaysian Chinese Association (MCA), which was the key ethnic Chinese party in the BN government, had been a strong supporter of the BRI, even making it one of the ten pledges in the election campaigning in 2018, in addition to setting up a BRI unit within the party to promote Chinese business participate in the BRI.[23] The MCA's attempt to play the China card, however, did not seem to work in its favour; it antagonised the other Chinese opposition party during the election campaign, which accused the MCA for using the poster of Chinese leader's handshaking with its chairman during the campaign. The 2018 election saw the worst performance of the MCA since independence, winning only one seat in the federal government, a big drop from the previous general election.

In any event, Mahathir's success at mobilising electoral support underlined how the controversies surrounding the BRI and Sino-Malaysian diplomacy had meshed with Malaysia's complex, multi-layered politics, indirectly inducing regime change. The background leading to Mahathir's re-emergence demonstrated that Malaysia has its own political and economic goals that may not be in line with China's foreign political and economic objectives, and when the divergence emerges, the former tends to assume a bigger role in determining the outcome.

Malaysia's foreign policies, therefore, should be understood in the interlinked context of both internal political economy and global power relations. In the process of formulating and implementing these policies, local imperatives – the interests, agency and mechanisms of Malaysia – should not be overlooked. What is important is how these local imperatives are articulated and institutionalised and how they are presented to major powers, which in turn shape the outcomes of diplomacy and international politics.

New foreign policy frameworks and Mahathir's positions towards China

When Mahathir assumed power after the May 2018 Election, he had to face the realities that would prevent him from translating his anti-China election campaign rhetoric into policy. Instead, domestic priorities served as the guiding principle of his positions towards China and big power politics, and the great powers possibly had to make some concessions in confronting these domestic-driven foreign policy agendas.

Mahathir's top domestic agenda after taking over the government was to ensure regime legitimacy and stability, especially for a coalition government (*Pakatan Harapan* or Hope Alliance) in which his own party, *Parti Pribumi Bersatu Malaysia* (known simply as Bersatu), was the minority, and a majority party in the alliance, *Parti Keadilan Rakyat* (People's Justice Party), led by Anwar Ibrahim who was slated to take the premiership within 2 years. In the meantime, he had to ensure that the influence of his predecessor, Najib Razak, and the UMNO, would be curtailed. His foreign policy had to facilitate or at least be broadly consistent with this political agenda.

This agenda had been reaffirmed by the new Foreign Policy Framework of the New Malaysia launched in June 2019.[24] In his preface to the policy document, which was the first such foreign policy document in the independent Malaysia, Mahathir highlighted that "we must continue to speak against injustices and in defending the rights of the oppressed. Malaysia must be effective in influencing and making decisions that impact our national interests." At the document's launch, Mahathir emphasised both continuity and change:

> We are living in a world where changes take place at a rapid pace. These changes bring both challenges and opportunities. It is, therefore, only logical that Malaysia does not stick to the traditional methods of engagement and instead proactively seek to explore new approaches.[25]

More specifically, this new framework adopts three broad categories of national interests:

> which are security, economic and identity. In terms of security, this Framework highlights the changes in issues pertaining to territorial dispute and the South China Sea, migration and irregular movement of people, cyber security and terrorism. In the economic dimension, this Framework discusses changes in emphasis that will be affected in issues related to Industrial Revolution 4.0, digital economy, ASEAN and fairer systems of international trade and finance. In the context of identity, this Framework elaborates on the changes in emphasis that will happen with regard to issues of human rights, assistance in post-conflict and post-disaster situations, memberships in international organisations, the Muslim world, South-South Cooperation, relations with major powers and international treaties and agreements.

Pertaining to economic interests, there was a profound reason that would prevent Mahathir's anti-China rhetoric (such as on Chinese investments) from being implemented. China continued to be a key economic partner for Malaysia after the establishment of the new regime. According to the then Deputy Prime Minister

Wan Azizah Wan Ismail who spoke in October 2019, total trade between Malaysia and China in 2018 was valued at RM325.53 billion (US$77.72 billion), an increase of 8.1 per cent from 2017.[26] Malaysia has been closely integrated with global supply chains. Over 82 per cent of large firms in Malaysia and nearly half of all small- to medium-sized enterprises participate in global value chains. Besides, Malaysia had a high degree of exposure to the Chinese economy, with China being both its largest trading partner and a top source of tourists.[27]

In terms of security, being a pragmatist, Mahathir had tried to contain potential conflicts with China over the South China Sea issue, for which Malaysia is a claimant over the disputed territories. Mahathir had proposed the non-militarisation of the disputed waterway and for it to be turned into a region of peace, friendship and trade.

> Essentially, the South China Sea should be a sea of cooperation, connectivity and community-building and not confrontation or conflict. This is in line with the spirit of Zone of Peace, Freedom and Neutrality (ZOPFAN). Malaysia will actively promote this vision in ASEAN according to the Framework.[28]

Indeed, this position was also in concordance with the so-called Mahathir Doctrine, which was thought to include the principles of neutral and non-alignment, mutual respect for mutual gain in any cooperative endeavour; the importance of the "prosper-thy-neighbour" philosophy, and a formula for reforming the Security Council.[29] Aware of his country's limitations and domestic priorities, Mahathir remarked candidly in September 2019: "You don't just try and do something which would fail anyway, so it is better to find some other less violent ways not to antagonize China too much, because China is beneficial for us."[30]

Finally, in terms of identity, as a long-time advocate of the so-called "Asian Values" and South-South Cooperation, Mahathir saw his country's foreign policy partially through the lens of civilisation, though this did not mean that the country would automatically side with China in its confrontation with America. It has been pointed out that "Mahathir's contributions [during his first prime ministership] to a wider East Asian regionalism are a lasting legacy,"[31] and this legacy was extended to his second term. His Foreign Minister Saifuddin Abdullah described in June 2019 that the Sino-Malaysian bilateral relations as being "also civilizational, it's a very unique kind of relations." He was quoted as saying

> Malaysia wants to learn more from China, especially in new technologies, robotics, Artificial Intelligence (AI), even in agriculture, we are sending our people to learn from your research and development. Between Malaysia and China, our relations go beyond political, bilateral and trade – it is also civilizational.[32]

In a broader sense, Mahathir's policy towards China could be understood in this historical continuity of "moral balance" and "a strongly organic concept of regionalism."[33]

The intertwining of economy and diplomacy: from ECRL to Huawei

As mentioned earlier, domestic political economy, alongside key issues such as economy, security and identity, played a main role in shaping Mahathir's foreign policies, which are beyond the strategic hedging framework. We illustrate our argument by examining the changing fate of the East Coast Rail Link (ECRL) with respect to Sino-Malaysian ties and Mahathir's views on China's telecom giant Huawei as a part and parcel of the US-China trade after 2017.

The case of ECRL's renegotiation project demonstrates the supremacy of domestic agendas in shaping Malaysia's China policy and Mahathir's skilful manoeuvre of big power politics to advance his country/party's own political interests. ECRL was initially orchestrated by the China Communications Construction Company (CCCC), an SOE, with strong endorsement by Najib Razak when he was in power. Najib considered that the ECRL project would be a "game changer" on the East Coast, driving an additional economic growth rate of 1–1.5 per cent per year in Pahang (his home state), Negeri Terengganu and Kelantan states[34] and connecting them with Selangor, the country's most prosperous state. With state-owned CCCC as the main contractor and with 85 per cent of the construction cost financed by soft loans from Beijing, ECRL was valued at a sum of US$18.2 billion. It had been fast-tracked by the government to commence construction in July 2017 rather than in late 2017 as initially expected.[35] ECRL had also been given top priority by CCCC, its leaders believed that ECRL, the largest railway project in Southeast Asia, would create demonstration effects that would advance its business prospects in Southeast Asia as well as other countries involved in the BRI.[36] The 600-km mega-project boasted a strong pro-Malay undertone as almost the entire stretch of the railway would pass through the three ethnic Malay-heavy states of Pahang, Terengganu and Kelantan.

Geopolitics is another important dimension of ECRL, which helps explain partially China's strong interest in continuing this project with smaller profit margins. Upon completion, it will connect Pahang's Kuantan Port (jointly managed by a Malaysian conglomerate and Guangxi Beibu Gulf International Port Group, a China SOE) to Port Klang on the west coast. This potential land bridge could provide a "significant resolution" to China's over-reliance on the Strait of Malacca, what it calls the "Malacca Dilemma."[37] As some 80 per cent of current Chinese energy needs pass through this narrow waterway, this new network will create alternative trade routes, but with significant Chinese involvement, as China now has a direct interest in both the Kuantan Port and ECRL itself. While a combined sea and land route via Kuantan Port and ECRL is estimated to cost more (in bulk cargo per ton) than the existing sea route via Singapore, the travel time can be shortened by 30 hours (18 per cent reduction from current levels).[38] The shorter travel time is useful for the movement of time-sensitive goods such as exotic food and biomedical products.

During his official visit to China in August 2018, in which he openly criticised "new colonialism" in a joint press conference (with Chinese Premier Li Keqiang) and stressed that "free trade should also be fair trade,"[39] Mahathir announced that ECRL would be "deferred until such time we can afford, and maybe we can reduce the cost also if we do it differently." He said on another occasion that Malaysia might cancel the project altogether.[40] While Mahathir's decision to shelf ECRL had been interpreted as a cost-cutting measure, its more important goal was likely to shrink the economic base of the Najib clique. More practically, ECRL's shelving (or de facto renegotiation) did not negate the fact that despite losing the control over the federal government, UMNO and Malaysian Islamic Party (PAS) had reinforced their grip on the state assemblies of the three east coast states, in addition to defeating most of Mahathir's allies vying for federal seats there. To bolster his legitimacy, Mahathir needed voters from these states with some segments of the Malay-heavy constituencies potentially tapping into ECRL's spillover effects, including allocating more contracts to the Malays.

Against this background of the renegotiation, as a seasoned politician, Mahathir changed his tone about China and the BRI. Speaking in Beijing in April 2019, during his second official visit to Beijing after reassuming power, he pledged to support the BRI, calling for "longer, bigger" trains to bridge the distance between the East and the West: "I am fully in support of the Belt and Road Initiative. I am sure my country, Malaysia, will benefit from the project." Considering the BRI would improve ease of travel and communication, he said that "the Belt and Road idea is great. It can bring the land-locked countries of Central Asia closer to the sea. They can grow in wealth and their poverty [will be] reduced."[41]

After a lengthy process of negotiations, China agreed in July 2019 to cut the cost of ECRL project by one-third, down to 44 billion ringgit (US$10.7 billion), with the Export-Import Bank of China financing 85 per cent of the loan. Malaysia would save about 12.6 billion ringgit in financing costs, reduced to 24 billion ringgit from 36 billion ringgit. In addition, China was set to purchase an additional 1.9 million tons of palm oil from Malaysia over the next 5 years.[42] Mahathir had revealed earlier that Malaysia hoped to take advantage of the ECRL renegotiation to sell more palm oil to China. It was indeed a big boost to Malaysia, as the European Union had passed an act earlier in the year to phase out palm oil from renewable fuel by 2030 over deforestation concerns, which in turn would severely affect the livelihood of the Malaysian farmers, thus weakening Mahathir's power base.[43] What was equally important for the relaunched project, therefore, was that that "at least" 40 per cent of civil works would be handed to local contractors.[44]

It should be pointed out, however, that Mahathir's newly found support for the BRI was not unconditional. While trade and investment from China were sought after for the purpose of boosting economic development and political legitimacy at home, Mahathir attempted to contain China's ideological influences *and* maintain Malaysian national identity. He argued that Malaysia is a multiracial country where racial sensitivities remain prevalent, as he declared in his keynote address at the ISIS Praxis conference held in Kuala Lumpur on October 21, 2019:

> We do not want our people to think that after being influenced by the West before, we have now become influenced by China. I believe that China will have a great influence over the whole world in the future, but for the moment, it is not for us to promote Chinese ideas and ideologies,

Commenting on a comic circulated in schools to promote China's BRI, titled *Belt and Road initiative for Win-Winism*, Mahathir replied that it was not good to influence the minds of Malaysian youths:

> The young people must understand the problems, strategies and the policies of their own country first, so that when they come up against other people, they know their place. As much as we do not want the influence of the West in our strategies in our school, we also do not want other countries to have undue influence over our young people.[45]

It was perhaps against this background of Mahathir's concern that this comic (in both Chinese and English) was banned from circulation a few days after his remarks. Ironically, this comic was presented by Mahathir himself to the Chinese president during his official visit to Beijing in April 2019.

For China, the renegotiation was necessary for both economic and geo-strategic reasons: the trade volume between the two countries stood at US$108.6 billion (RM455.8 billion) at the end of 2018, equivalent to 20 per cent of the total trade between China and ASEAN countries.[46] More importantly, the geopolitical significance of the BRI projects was most clearly reflected in ECRL. As mentioned, connecting the Kuantan Port to Port Klang could resolve China's perennial "Malacca Dilemma." The success of Malaysia would serve as a meaningful showcase for the 60-plus countries alongside the BRI. From a diplomatic perspective, Mahathir's affirmative and non-confrontational position on the South China Sea and China's ethnic minorities issues in Xinjiang – considered by Beijing to be core national interests – might also be a conducive reason for China in looking for long-term foreign policy goals in the region rather than short-term economic gains/losses.

In short, as the then Deputy International Trade and Industry Minister Ong Kian Ming put it,

> ECRL is a very interesting test case not just for Malaysia in the context of BRI, but globally, in finding sustainable ways to make sure that the project can be manageable in terms of financing and risk mitigation in the long-term.[47]

The re-launching of the ECRL project has demonstrated the complex intertwining of domestic political economy and diplomacy. In particular, Malaysia had successfully projected its own interest upon China, which was willing to make concessions based upon its long-term economic and geostrategic considerations.

Mahathir's skilful manoeuvring ensured the negotiation in Malaysia's national interests, which also facilitated his own political agendas (e.g., in reducing Najib's influences in some regions alongside the ECRL).

The global economy has been significantly affected by the US-China trade war since 2017, which is in itself a component of great power rivalries that has continued to shape the world. As a small power, Malaysia has, just like other countries in the region, been caught in the middle and faces major dilemmas whether to choose sides. As Joseph Liow pointed out in his study of Sino-Malaysian relations in the 1990s, "small states do matter in international relations, as they are often the battlefield upon which evolving major power rivalries are played out."[48] For one thing, alongside China and Singapore, America is one of the three largest trading partners to Malaysia. Whilst in the initial months of the American-China trade tensions, Malaysia had hoped that the country would benefit from the spillover effects of more factories moving out from China, though the results might not be that promising and clear-cut due to a complex set of reasons beyond Malaysia's control.[49]

Since the early phase of the trade war, the Chinese telecom giant Huawei has been in the centre of the confrontation, with its products and services being blacklisted by the US and some of its Western allies such as Australia and the UK. Malaysia's attitudes to the trade war and the Huawei ban, therefore, could be seen as a test case of its strategic positioning in the great power rivalries. Traversing through the dilemmas, Mahathir again skilfully turned the disputes to his own agenda of promoting reindustrialisation and the fourth industrial revolution.

Mahathir stated in October 2019 that Malaysia's economic growth relies on trade, and so the country needs markets and "cannot afford to make enemies."[50] While lamenting how Malaysia had been "caught in the middle" and could be hit with trade sanctions amidst rising protectionism, highlighted by the US-China trade war, he was disappointed with the proponents of free trade who were now indulging in restrictive trade practices on a "grand scale": "Economically we are linked to both markets, and physically we are also caught in between for geographical reasons. There are even suggestions that we ourselves would be a target for sanctions."[51]

Two major considerations shaped Mahathir's positions on Huawei. The first was his view on free trade from which Malaysia has benefitted greatly, and the other was his domestic development agenda of moving the country in the global chain of technological innovation, major Chinese tech corporations such as Huawei and Alibaba thus present viable opportunities for Malaysia to cooperate with.[52] Mahathir, therefore, believed strongly that the Trump administration's decision to ban Huawei was "not the way to go." In his keynote speech at the Nikkei Future of Asia Conference in May 2019, Mahathir said China currently boasted "the best technology in the world" and that the US had to accept the new status quo:

> We have to accept that the US cannot forever be the supreme nation [with] the best technology. . . . [The West] must accept that this capability can also be found in the East. But if they want to have a situation where they are always ahead, and if not [they] will ban you, [they] will send warships to your country, that is not competition. That is threatening people.[53]

Mahathir's supportive view of Huawei, among the strongest from an Asian leader, was echoed by the public and private sectors in the country. In June 2019, the then Foreign Minister Saifuddin Abdullah said that when Malaysia was facing the problem in selling palm oil to Europe, China added the volume of purchase of palm oil from Malaysia. "When some countries in the West go against Huawei, Malaysia reciprocated by saying 'No, we will continue using Huawei'."[54] In a similar vein, the then Finance Minister Lim Guan Eng told an audience in Kuala Lumpur in August 2019:

> I am happy that Huawei has its regional hub located in Kuala Lumpur, with more than 2,500 employees throughout Malaysia. Reputed as the leader in 5G technology, Huawei and other technology companies have a role to play in aiding Malaysia in implementing Industry 4.0 technology, especially 5G, throughout our society. We will continue to facilitate Chinese investment into Malaysia particularly the high-tech Industries and innovation-based services.

He added that Malaysia was keen to learn from Chinese advances in artificial intelligence (AI), advanced materials, robotics and cloud computing.[55] According to Malaysia-China Business Council (MCBC) Chairman Tan Kok Wai,

> China has made tremendous progress on new and pioneering technologies where we can learn so much from, especially when we are formulating plans to move forward to meet the challenges of the Fourth Industrial Revolution (IR4.0) and China will be an important partner to help us achieve the goal.[56]

Apart from engaging with Huawei, Mahathir's Malaysia was also tapping on the e-commerce sector with assistance from Alibaba in developing warehousing technology and from Tencent Holdings in mobile payments. During his official trip to China in August 2018, Mahathir made a point of visiting Alibaba headquarters in Hangzhou and took a high-speed train ride from there to Shanghai. Impressed with the company's use of modern technology, he remarked that "Malaysia could tap on your innovative ideas so that we can benefit too from modern technology."[57] In the meantime, unlike infrastructure projects that are more prone to disputes and competing interests from local and national forces, technological innovation projects, for instance, by Alibaba and Huawei, similar to private investment projects in the manufacturing sector, encountered less problems at home.[58]

Concluding remarks[59]

Lasting for only 22 months, the Mahathir 2.0 administration was short-lived. But his China policy has shown some important departure from his predecessor and highlighted the importance of going beyond the conventional approach of strategic hedging. This chapter has demonstrated the complicated domestic political and economic interests in shaping Mahathir's policies towards China (and to some extent, the US-China rivalries). Despite its power, wealth and technical expertise, China cannot forge ahead without understanding the aspirations of the Malaysian stakeholders and accommodating the latter's interests in the foreign policy formulation and implementation. As we have shown elsewhere, BRI projects require these stakeholders' cooperation (or at the very least, non-hindrance), and China's interactions with Southeast Asia have been shaped by the latter's own social, political and economic interests and agendas.[60] The articulation, institutionalisation and implementation in the foreign policy arena of these interests, furthermore, validate the Constructivist approach to international relations, especially among non-Western nations.

This chapter has underlined the value and necessity of looking beyond conventional literature that depict smaller countries such as Malaysia as merely on the receiving end of the bigger powers' diplomacy or just reacting through rebalancing or hedging strategies. ECRL's re-launching and Mahathir's support for Huawei (despite of the US ban and threat of trade sanctions) reinforced our earlier argument that Malaysia's foreign policy towards a rising China is contingent upon three key conditions: fulfilment of Malaysia's long-standing pro-ethnic Malay policy (including through Malays' involvement in the BRI-related projects such as ECRL), supporting the country's economic development and reindustrialisation, and advancement of geopolitical interests for both Malaysia and China.[61] These key conditions, moreover, can be translated into foreign policy options partly because China, based upon its own long-term economic and geo-strategic considerations, has been willing to accommodate Malaysia's domestic interests and minimise the potential tensions.

Our cases have also shown that a seasoned politician such as Mahathir has the capacities of skilfully converting the dilemmas the country faces to operational policy options to advance not only the country's own economic development agendas but also the political interests of the respective (dominant) groups in their quest for power. In terms of the influence of personality on foreign policy, Mahathir 2.0 represents a continuity from his first premiership and a discontinuity from his immediate predecessor.[62] It is, therefore, imperative to pay greater attention to local interests, initiatives, identity, ideology, agencies and institutions – all these are important elements in the Constructivist approach to international relations – in taking advantage of the changing global and regional environments for smaller powers' own agendas. It is from the conjuncture of all these factors and various interests that we should take our analysis of Malaysia's policy towards China beyond "strategic hedging."

Notes

1 Harold Crouch, *Government and Society in Malaysia*, Cornell University Press, Ithaca, 2019 [1996]; Edmund Terence Gomez and K. S. Jomo, *Malaysia's Political Economy: Politics, Patronage and Profits*, Cambridge University Press, Cambridge, 2000.
2 World Bank, "Trade (% of GDP)-Malaysia," https://data.worldbank.org/indicator/NE.TRD.GNFS.ZS?locations=MY (Accessed July 18, 2020).
3 There are numerous studies on the BRI from a diplomatic and strategic perspective, see for example, Suisheng Zhao (ed.), *China's New Global Strategy: The Belt and Road*

Initiative (BRI) and Asian Infrastructure Investment Bank (AIIB), vol. 1, Routledge, Oxon, 2020; Xue Gong, Joseph Liow, and Hong Liu (eds.), *Research Handbook on the Belt and Road Initiative,* Edward Elgar Publishing, Cheltenham, 2021. For a recent study on the Indo-Pacific strategy, see Andrew Scobell, "Constructing a U.S.-China Rivalry in the Indo-Pacific and Beyond," *Journal of Contemporary China*, 30(127), 2021, pp. 69–84.
4 The events leading to the downfall of Mahathir are too complex to detail here. See Jonathan Head, "How Malaysia's Government Collapsed in Two Years," March 5, 2020. www.bbc.com/news/world-asia-51716474 (Accessed May 25, 2020).
5 Vander Vennet and M. Salman, "Strategic Hedging and Changes in Geopolitical Capabilities for Second-Tier States," *Chinese Political Science Review*, 4(6), 2019, pp. 86–134.
6 Ann Marie Murphy, "Great Power Rivalries, Domestic Politics and Southeast Asian Foreign Policy: Exploring the Linkages," *Asian Security*, 13(3), 2017, pp. 165–182.
7 Cheng-Chwee Kuik, "How Do Weaker States Hedge? Unpacking ASEAN States' Alignment Behavior Towards China," *Journal of Contemporary China*, 25(100), 2016, pp. 500–514. In a related study, he argues that weaker states such as Malaysia do not hedge against any single actor *per se*; rather, they seek to hedge against a range of risks associated with uncertain power relations." Kuik, "Malaysia Between the United States and China: What Do Weaker States Hedge Against?" *Asian Politics & Policy*, 8(1), pp. 155–177. See also Rebecca Strating, "Small Power Hedging in an Era of Great-Power Politics: Southeast Asian Responses to China's Pursuit of Energy Security," *Asian Studies Review*, 44(1), 2020, pp. 97–116; Suisheng Zhao and Xiong Qi, "Hedging and Geostrategic Balance of East Asian Countries Toward China," *Journal of Contemporary China*, 25(4), 2016, pp. 485–499.
8 Zachary Abuza, "Malaysia: Navigating Between the United States and China," *Asia Policy*, 27(2), 2020, pp. 115–134.
9 Ann Marie Murphy, no. 7. See also Moch Faisal Karim and Tangguh Chairil, "Waiting for Hard Balancing? Explaining Southeast Asia's Balancing Behaviour Towards China," *European Journal of East Asian Studies*, 15(1), 2016, pp. 34–61. Jürgen Haacke, "The Concept of Hedging and Its Application to Southeast Asia: A Critique and a Proposal for a Modified Conceptual and Methodological Framework," *International Relations of the Asia-Pacific*, 19(3), 2019, pp. 375–417.
10 In his review of the key features of Constructivism and its differences with other prevailing IR theories, Ian Hurd argues that "A contrasting approach to "social construction" in world politics is the position known as "materialism," which suggests that material objects (bombs, mountains, people, oil, and so on) have a direct effect on outcomes that is unmediated by the ideas people bring to them. Neorealism and neoliberalism are explicitly materialist approaches to world politics. They seek to explain international patterns and behaviours as the result of purely material forces, particularly the military hardware, strategic resources, and money that they see as constituting "power."" See Ian Hurd, "Constructivism," in Christian Reus-Smit and Duncan Snidal (eds.), *The Oxford Handbook of International Relations*, Oxford University Press, Oxford, 2009, p. 300.
11 Ian Hurd, no. 11, p. 299.
12 Amitav Acharya and Barry Buzan, *The Making of Global International Relations*, Cambridge University Press, Cambridge, 2019, pp. 232–234, 248. For an attempt to understand Southeast Asian policies toward China from a Constructivist perspective, see Hong Liu, "An Emerging China and Diasporic Chinese: Historicity, State, and International Relations," *Journal of Contemporary China*, 20(72), 2011, pp. 813–832.
13 See, for example, Alice D. Ba, "Is China Leading? China, Southeast Asia and East Asian Integration," *Political Science*, 66(2), 2014, pp. 143–165; Mark Beeson, "Can ASEAN Cope with China?" *Journal of Current Southeast Asian Affairs*, 35(1), 2016,

pp. 5–28; Weifeng Zhou and Mario Esteban, "Beyond Balancing: China's Approach Towards the Belt and Road Initiative," *Journal of Contemporary China*, 27(112), 2018, pp. 487–501. For an historical and network perspective on Sino-Southeast Asian relations, see Hong Liu, "Sino-Southeast Asian Studies: Towards an Alternative Paradigm," *Asian Studies Review*, 25(3), 2001, pp. 259–283; and Hong Liu, "Transnational Asia and Regional Networks: Toward a New Political Economy of East Asia," *East Asian Community Review*, 1(1), 2018, pp. 33–47.

14 Monique Taylor, *The Chinese State, Oil and Energy Security*, Palgrave Macmillan, New York, 2014. On Chinese capital in Southeast Asia, see Hong Liu and Zhou Yishu, "New Chinese Capitalism and the ASEAN Economic Community," in Yos Santasombat (ed.), *The Sociology of Chinese Capitalism in Southeast Asia*, Palgrave Macmillan, New York, 2019, pp. 55–73.

15 For recent studies on Southeast Asian responses to China's BRI, see Hong Liu and Guanie Lim, "The Political Economy of a Rising China in Southeast Asia: Malaysia's Response to the Belt and Road Initiative," *Journal of Contemporary China*, 28(116), 2019, pp. 216–231; Agatha Kratz and Dragan Pavlićević, "Norm-Making, Norm-Taking or Norm-Shifting? A Case Study of Sino – Japanese Competition in the Jakarta – Bandung High-Speed Rail Project," *Third World Quarterly*, 40(6), 2019, pp. 1107–1126; Alice D. Ba, "China's 'Belt and Road' in Southeast Asia: Constructing the Strategic Narrative in Singapore," *Asian Perspective*, 43(2), 2019, pp. 249–272; Felix Heiduk and Alexandra Sakaki, "Introduction to the Special Issue – China's Belt and Road Initiative: The View from East Asia," *East Asia*, 36(2), 2019, pp. 93–113; Hong Liu, Xin Fan, and Guanie Lim, "Singapore Engages the Belt and Road Initiative: Perceptions, Policies, and Institutions," *Singapore Economic Review*, 66(1), 2021, pp. 219–241; Hong Liu, Kong Yam Tan, and Guanie (eds.), *The Political Economy of Regionalism, Trade, and Infrastructure: Southeast Asia and the Belt and Road Initiative in a New Era*. World Scientific, Singapore, 2021.

16 Due to space constraint, this chapter focuses on Malaysia's China policy *per se* and only briefly touches upon its stances on US-China confrontations. For more extensive discussions on the issue, see David Shambaugh, "US-China Rivalry in Southeast Asia: Power Shift or Competitive Coexistence?" *International Security*, 42(4), 2018, pp. 85–127; Zachary Abuza, no. 9.

17 Some of the materials for this chapter are derived from Hong Liu and Guanie Lim, "A Nanyang Approach to the Belt and Road Initiative," in Yongnian Zheng and Litao Zhao (eds.), *Chineseness and Modernity in a Changing China: Essays in Honor of Professor Wang Gungwu*, World Scientific, Singapore, 2020, pp. 253–286.

18 Tham Siew Yean, "A Misguided 'Fear of China' Threatens Malaysia's Economy," October 2, 2019. www.eastasiaforum.org/2019/10/02/a-misguided-fear-of-china-threatens-malaysias-economy/ (Accessed October 20, 2019); Panos Mourdoukoutas, "Malaysia Cannot Escape from China – It's Too Late," *Forbes*, April 20, 2019. www.forbes.com/sites/panosmourdoukoutas/2019/04/20/malaysia-cannot-escape-from-china-its-too-late/#7e8819a3e2e9 (Accessed March 15, 2020).

19 On the 2018 General Election, see Bridget Welsh, "'Saviour' Politics and Malaysia's 2018 Electoral Democratic Breakthrough: Rethinking Explanatory Narratives and Implicatons," *Journal of Current Southeast Asian Affairs*, 37(3), 2018, pp. 85–108; Walid Jumblatt Abdullah, "The Mahathir Effect in Malaysia's 2018 Election: The Role of Credible Personalities in Regime Transitions," *Democratization*, 26(3), 2019, pp. 521–536; Andreas Ufen, "Opposition in Transition: Pre-electoral Coalitions and the 2018 Electoral Breakthrough in Malaysia," *Democratization*, 27(2), 2020, pp. 167–184.

20 "Mahathir to Review China Investments if He Wins Malaysia Election," *South China Morning Post* (hereafter *SCMP*), April 9, 2018; "Mahathir Vows to Review China Investments," *Straits Times*, April 10, 2018. For a more detailed discussion on the

Forest City project and how it has been intertwined with domestic politics, see Hong Liu and Guanie Lim, no. 16.
21 Mustafa Izzuddin, "Malaysia in 2018: A Sea Change in an Election Year," *Asian Survey*, 59(1), 2019, pp. 147–155.
22 C.f., David Han, "The Impact of Foreign Policy on GE14," *The Round Table*, 109(2), 2020, pp. 173–192.
23 James Chin, "The Malaysian Chinese Association, Set Adrift in need of a Direction," October 20, 2018. www.channelnewsasia.com/news/commentary/mca-malaysian-chinese-association-party-election-results-shift-10875556 (Accessed July 21, 2020). On MCA's relations with China, see Chow Bing Ngeow, "Barisan Nasional and the Chinese Communist Party: A Case Study in China's Party-Based Diplomacy," *The China Review*, 17(1), 2017, pp. 53–82.
24 Ministry of Foreign Affairs of Malaysia, *Foreign Policy Framework of the New Malaysia: Change in Continuity*, Federal Government Administrative Centre, Putrajaya, June 2019.
25 Tashny Sukumaran, "Mahathir to Update Malaysia's Foreign Policy, Including on South China Sea and International Muslim Cooperation," *SCMP*, September 18, 2019.
26 "DPM: Malaysia Welcomes More FDI from China." www.malaymail.com/news/money/2019/10/18/dpm-malaysia-welcomes-more-fdi-from-china/1801659 (Accessed October 21, 2019).
27 Calvin Cheng, "Is Malaysia Benefitting from the US – China Trade War?" www.eastasiaforum.org/2019/08/05/is-malaysia-benefitting-from-the-us-china-trade-war/. (Accessed October 21, 2019).
28 The ZOPFAN agreement to "keep Southeast Asia free from any form or manner of interference by outside powers" was signed by Indonesia, Malaysia, the Philippines, Thailand and Singapore in 1971. On the South China Sea issue in the context of China's foreign policy toward Southeast Asia, see for example, Taomo Zhou and Hong Liu, "Chinese Foreign Policy: Southeast Asia," in Weiping Wu and Mark Frazier (eds.), *The SAGE Handbook of Contemporary China*, Sage Publications, Los Angles and London, 2018, vol. 1, pp. 610–630.
29 Rizal Abdul Kadir, "Mahathir Doctrine' Keeps South China Sea Peaceful," *New Straits Times*, May 6, 2019.
30 "Malaysia PM Says Can't Provoke Beijing on South China Sea, Uighur Issue." www.reuters.com/article/us-malaysia-china-idUSKBN1WD0BY (Accessed on October 25, 2019).
31 Jörn Dosch, "Mahathirism and Its Legacy in Malaysia's Foreign Policy," *European Journal of East Asian Studies*, 13(1), 2014, pp. 5–32.
32 "Interview: Malaysia-China Ties Go Beyond Common Diplomatic Relations, Set to Grow Stronger: Malaysian FM." www.xinhuanet.com/english/2019-06/15/c_138144378.htm (Accessed May 12, 2020).
33 Anthony Milner, "Long-term Themes in Malaysian Foreign Policy: Hierarchy Diplomacy, Non-interference and Moral Balance," *Asian Studies Review*, 44(1), 2020, pp. 117–135.
34 Xiekui Zhang, Wei Song, and Lu Peng, "Investment by Chinese Enterprise in Infrastructure Construction in Malaysia," *Pacific Focus*, 35(1), 2020, pp. 109–140.
35 Lin Say Tee, "Flushed with Construction Jobs," *The Star*, March 11, 2017.
36 "Malaixiya Donghaiantielu Xiangmukaigong Zhilichengwei Shifangongcheng" (East Coast Rail Link to Become a Model Project), *Xinhua Silk Road*, August 14, 2017. http://silkroad.news.cn/Company/Cases/ppjs/45238.shtml (Accessed October 5, 2019).
37 Leslie Lopez, "Malaysia's East Coast Rail Line Touted as a Game Changer," *Straits Times*, December 22, 2016. China has been heavily dependent on Middle Eastern oil, with up to 80 per cent of its energy supply passing through the Malacca Straits, and as

early as in 2003, the then President of China, Hu Jintao, identified the need to mitigate the "Malacca Dilemma." B. A. Hamzah, "Alleviating China's Malacca Dilemma." http://isdp.eu/alleviating-chinas-malacca-dilemma/ (Accessed November 27, 2019).
38 Leslie Lopez, no. 38.
39 Lucy Hornby, "Mahathir Mohamad Warns Against 'New Colonialism' During China Visit," *Financial Times*, August 20, 2018; Chun Han Wong, "Malaysia Can't Afford $22 Billion Beijing-Backed Projects, Mahathir Tells China," *Wall Street Journal*, August 21, 2018.
40 Goh Sui Noi, "East Coast Rail Link and Pipeline Projects with China to Be Deferred: Malaysian PM Mahathir," *Straits Times*, August 21, 2018. In June 2018, Mahathir had criticised the project: "It was an unjustified, hefty lump sum price which lacked clarity in terms of technical specifications, price and by extension, economic justification."
41 "'The Belt and Road Initiative is Great': Malaysia PM Mahathir." www.channelnewsasia.com/news/asia/mahathir-endorse-belt-and-road-china-11481782 (Accessed October 21, 2019).
42 Anisah Shukry, "Malaysia Restarts Rail Project With China After Cost Cut." www.bloomberg.com/news/articles/2019-07-25/malaysia-restarts-rail-link-project-with-china-after-cost-cut (Accessed October 21, 2019).
43 Amy Chew, "Malaysia and Indonesia Threaten Boycott of EU Products, Say Millions of Farmers Risk Losing Livelihoods Due to Palm Oil Curbs," *SCMP*, March 22, 2019.
44 Tashny Sukumaran, "Local Contractors to Play Bigger Role in Reworked China-backed Rail Project," *SCMP*, November 19, 2019.
45 "PM Reiterates Support for BRI." www.nst.com.my/news/nation/2019/10/531975/pm-reiterates-support-bri (Accessed October 25, 2019).
46 Royce Tan, "Growing Importance of Malaysia-China Ties," *The Star*, August 6, 2019.
47 "ECRL Could Be Case Study for Malaysia's Involvement in BRI." https://themalaysianreserve.com/2019/10/01/ecrl-could-be-case-study-for-malaysias-involvement-in-bri/ (Accessed October 23, 2019).
48 Joseph Chin Yong Liow, "Malaysia-China Relations in the 1990s: The Maturing of a Partnership," *Asian Survey*, 40(4), 2000, pp. 672–691.
49 Tham Siew Yean, et al., "US – China Trade War: Potential Trade and Investment Spillovers into Malaysia," *Asian Economic Papers*, 18(3), 2019, pp. 117–135.
50 Tashny Sukumaran, "Mahathir Fears Malaysia Will Be Target of Sanctions amid US-China Trade War," *SCMP*, October 21, 2019.
51 "Keynote Address by Prime Minister Tun Dr Mahathir Mohamad at ISIS Malaysia Praxis Conference 'Malaysia Beyond 2020'." www.bernama.com/en/news.php?id=1781294 (Accessed October 25, 2019).
52 Barry Naughton, "Chinese Industrial Policy and the Digital Silk Road: The Case of Alibaba in Malaysia," *Asia Policy*, 27(1), 2020, pp. 23–39; M. F. Vila Seoane, "Alibaba's Discourse for the Digital Silk Road: The Electronic World Trade Platform and 'Inclusive Globalization'," *Chinese Journal of Communication*, 13(1), 2020, pp. 68–83.
53 Tashny Sukumaran, "Mahathir Stands Up for Huawei," *SCMP*, May 30, 2019.
54 "Interview: Malaysia-China Ties Go Beyond Common Diplomatic Relations, Set to Grow Stronger: Malaysian FM." www.xinhuanet.com/english/2019-06/15/c_138144378.htm (Accessed November 21, 2019).
55 "Malaysia Benefits from BRI, Seeks More Cooperation with China: Officials." www.chinadaily.com.cn/a/201908/08/WS5d4bde6fa310cf3e35564a36.html. (Accessed November 21, 2019).
56 Royce Tan, "Growing Importance of Malaysia-China Ties," *The Star*, August 6, 2019.
57 "Malaysia's PM Mahathir Tours China's Alibaba Headquarters, Hopes to Tap on Group's Innovative Ideas," *Straits Times*, August 18, 2018.
58 Miao Zhang, "Beyond Infrastructure: Re-thinking China's Foreign Direct Investment in Malaysia," *The Pacific Review*, 2020, doi: 10.1080/09512748.2020.1791237

59 An earlier version of this chapter was presented at the 15th Berlin Conference on Asian Security (November 10–11, 2019). The author is grateful for Guanie Lim for his collaboration as well as the constructive comments by the conference participants and Felix Heiduk. This research is supported by an NTU research grant (#04INS0000136C430). The author is solely responsible for the views and any remaining errors of this chapter.

60 An earlier version of this chapter was presented at the 15th Berlin Conference on Asian Security (November 10–11, 2019). The author is grateful for Guanie Lim for his collaboration as well as the constructive comments by the conference participants and Felix Heiduk. This research is supported by an NTU research grant (#04INS0000136C430). The author is solely responsible for the views and any remaining errors of this chapter. Liu, "Opportunities and Anxieties for the Chinese Diaspora in Southeast Asia," *Current History*, 115(784), 2016, pp. 311–318; Hong Liu and Els van Dongen, "China's Diaspora Policies as a New Mode of Transnational Governance," *Journal of Contemporary China*, 25(102), 2016, pp. 805–821; James Chin and Taufiq Tanasaldy, "The Ethnic Chinese in Indonesia and Malaysia: The Challenge of Political Islam," *Asian Survey*, 59(6), 2019, pp. 959–977.

61 Hong Liu and Guanie Lim, no. 16.

62 Khadijah Md. Khalid remarked that "Unlike Mahathir, who was deeply ideological and thus had a dualistic vision of the global order, Najib is not interested in the Cold War rivalry that plagued much of the world until the collapse of the Soviet Union. Najib is therefore a classic post-Cold War leader, acutely aware of the realignment taking place with the seeming decline of a unipolar world – in which the U.S. keeps hegemony – toward a more multipolar system." Khalid, "Malaysia's Foreign Policy under Najib: A Comparison with Mahathir," *Asian Survey*, 51(3), 2011, p. 452.

11 Midfield or margin?

Myanmar and neighbours in the game

Thi Thi Soe San

Introduction

For quite some years now, there has been constant reference to the 'new Great Game' on the Eurasian land mass and surrounding seas and oceans. The 'unipolar moment' (if it ever existed) at the end of the Cold War was brief. The advent of China as a major power came fast, followed by the 're-booting' of a newly assertive Russia. Add to that the rapid emergence of middle powers like India, Japan, South Korea and Australia, and suddenly it has evolved into a multi-player game.

How all this plays out will affect everyone, and it is a crucial task to observe, assess and respond to it, as individual countries and collectively. The arena or chessboard on which the great power rivalry is being performed is vast. It has been variously termed the Asia Pacific, the Indo-Pacific and East Asia. The South China Sea is one region where the drama is persistently intense. Myanmar is neither a littoral state nor a claimant, and even its diplomatic engagement as through the Association of Southeast Asian Nations (ASEAN) remains muted. It could be said that here Myanmar occupies a marginal role. On the other hand, when it comes to the Bay of Bengal and the Indian Ocean, Myanmar's position is unparalleled. At the juncture and nexus of many regions, it commands a central strategic position.

This chapter looks at how Sino-American rivalry has played out in the troublous south-eastern part of the Asian continent. Particularly in the turbulent country of Myanmar. With the competition intensifying in the 21st century, it also looks at the choices available for Myanmar and the rest of the region. There is agreement now that the tectonic disruptions following the COVID-19 pandemic will only accelerate trends and processes already underway. Forebodings of a new Cold War may not be that far-fetched.

Southeast Asia in the Great Game and Myanmar's foreign policy

Southeast Asia has become an important sub-arena where the Game is being played with some intensity. Having been a battleground during Second World War and the Cold War, the primary concern now is to avoid a replay of outright

DOI: 10.4324/9781003106814-11

and widespread hostilities. The South China Sea remains a flashpoint and it has sorely tested relationships within ASEAN. The responses of two countries – Cambodia and Vietnam – show up in stark contrast. China's Belt and Road Initiative (BRI) has three economic corridors involving Southeast Asian countries (Bangladesh-China-India-Myanmar, China-Myanmar and China-Indochina Economic Corridor) and the Lancang-Mekong Cooperation Mechanism spanning mainland Southeast Asia. All the countries are extensively involved, although in differing ways and responses, 'for richer or for poorer'. But beyond that concern, the competition for facilities, resources, infrastructure projects and, above all, political leverage, is relentless – despite the fact that sometimes there is contestation and there are setbacks and pushbacks like public protests.[1] In addition, the competition now even extends to regional institutions, that is, the Quadrilateral Security Dialogue. The next step will possibly be China's mobilisation of the so-called Community of Common Destiny.

The motives, directions, strategies and actions of the two 'majors' – China and the US – are continually studied and debated. As Felix Heiduk has argued in the introduction to this edited volume, while there is a lively debate regarding the possible outcome of the Sino-American rivalry, worries about the negative impact of the US-China rivalry are widely shared in Southeast Asia. Not to be left out, the middle powers are coming on strong. South Korea, for example, has launched strategic relationships with many ASEAN countries and South Korea's president visited Laos, Cambodia and Myanmar recently. Having taken part in the founding of the Non-Aligned Movement (NAM), Myanmar followed a policy of strict neutrality throughout the period of the Cold War. When it ended and the ideological contest drew to a close, the competition gradually broadened out to the many-sided game that is in play today. Like a number of other countries, Myanmar has been taciturn about declaring sides – an approach that has been called 'hedging'.[2] However, the Myanmar case is complicated by the motives and methods of the two political camps – the National League for Democracy (NLD) and the military. At this instance, it should be noted that the NLD does *not* represent the entirety of the civilian democratic stream.

Myanmar's foreign policy can be said to have been shaped by its mixed experiences with the two major powers over the past three-quarters of a century. The bitter and painful memories of the Second World War could by themselves have led to a policy of neutrality; the Cold War and the proximity to China only strengthened this propensity.[3] In the present time, strange as it may seem, for practical purposes, Myanmar can be said to have not one but three foreign policies. When a civilian government came into office in 2016, the ruling NLD deployed its own foreign policy (even though it has not been written down). The military, and the parties and governments thereof, also has its respective foreign policy, which is slightly more institutionalised.[4] Then there is the 'public' foreign policy, which may not be official or formal, but nonetheless has a clout of its own.[5] This lends credence to the weak/fragile state concept. Relations with China are a prime illustration of this state of affairs, which is steadily taking root. The self-interest and the haphazardness in China 'policy' are readily apparent. To put it another way – public opinion, informed and uninformed – matters equally as much, and more than in countries with stronger and less-divided states.

Following from this, when it is said that 'Myanmar' favours or aligns with this power or that power, one has to disaggregate and specify which 'Myanmar'. The Myitsone dam project illustrates this well again: the contract for it was signed by the then-military junta, but in 2011, it was suspended following public agitation. This has obviously led to relations with China becoming strained.[6] Other BRI projects that have followed have displayed a tendency of both the civilian government and military increasingly becoming reticent about information disclosures. The only possible answer to this is better and wider public consultations – something the NLD government is very reluctant to do.

Myanmar: destined to be a perpetual arena in the Great Game?

The regional fortunes of the US and China (and Britain and Japan for that matter) have oscillated in the land called Burma/Myanmar for the past century or so. Another way of saying this is that Myanmar is no stranger to having foreign powers wage a war on its soil. The relationship between the three countries dates back to early modern times. In the 19th century, Burma/Myanmar had been one of the destinations in Southeast Asia for the ethnic Chinese diaspora. The earliest American contacts had been through Christian (largely Baptist) missionaries. The political affiliation of the Chinese community in Burma in those days had been with the Nationalist (*Kuomintang/Guomindang*) Party and the Communist Party of China (CPC) was not present in Burma.

All three countries were belligerents in the Second World War. Burma is interesting in that its participation was divided into both sides: the main nationalist movement led by Aung San and the 'Thirty Comrades' sided with Japan. Virtually all the non-Bamar ethnic people supported the Allied cause and many fought against the Japanese. This was one of the early manifestations of divided loyalties in Burma. Japan's war against China had started in 1931, and by 1937, the entire coastline including seaports were in Japanese hands. To help the beleaguered Chinese government, the US had to ship essential war materiel to the port of Rangoon (Yangon) and then overland by the famed 'Burma Road' to the wartime capital of Chongqing. When Japan entered the World War and invaded Southeast Asia, including Burma, one of its objectives was to cut off the Burma Road. From December 1941 when Japanese forces and the Burma Independence Army entered Burma, the country became one of the major theatres of war. Chinese nationalist forces led by American General Joseph Stilwell played a part throughout the war – in the withdrawal as well as in the eventual recapture of essentially northern Burma.

The Burma Communist Party (BCP, later CPB) had been established in 1939, and throughout the war, it was part of the anti-fascist coalition. It had a strong power base, both politically and militarily. But in 1947 it was ousted from the national coalition – the Anti-Fascist People's Freedom League (AFPFL) – which was to have ominous consequences for the country. After suffering the depredations of the Second World War, the colony of Burma/Myanmar gained independence in 1948. An invitation to join the British Commonwealth was declined. Just 2 months later, a Communist rebellion began. In 1949, the Chinese Communists won the civil war in China, and the People's Republic was proclaimed. Burma was one of the first countries to recognise the new communist state. The cold war had already begun, and the stage was set for more conflicts in East Asia. Also, in January 1949, ethnic Karen (Kayin) rebel forces launched their bid for greater autonomy.

Although officially neutral in the Cold War, Burma leaned towards the West, as evidenced by continuous programmes of military assistance from the UK and later the US. Even in the period of outright military junta rule, there was military cooperation with many countries, notably with what was then West Germany.[7] Burma was one of the founding members of the NAM and a signatory at the Bandung Conference in 1955. An unexpected problem arose, growing out of the Cold War, and all three countries were embroiled again. It was the matter of the Chinese nationalist troops that remained in Burma's Shan state. They were referred to as *Kuomintang/Guomindang* (KMT) troops. As with French Indochina, communist revolution and the means to stem it rose to the top of policy priority lists across the West. The American OSS, and later its successor, the CIA, saw in the KMT forces an asset in the containment of 'Red' China – notwithstanding the fact that they were in the territory of a neutral Burma. The issue was brought to the United Nations (UN), and Burma demanded that they be removed, with the US bearing a great part of the culpability and responsibility. In the US, there was friction between the State Department and the Central Intelligence Agency. Ultimately, in 1960, the Burmese government invited People's Republic of China (PRC) units to take part in a joint operation to drive the KMT out from their last positions close to the Mekong river.[8]

Despite the heightened tension, relations with the US were never severed. Small-scale military assistance and training continued. At that time, Burma even sent its troops to join UN peacekeeping forces in the Congo. Following persistent political troubles and crises, the Burmese military under General Ne Win staged a coup in March 1962. The 1947 quasi-federal constitution was abrogated, and democracy came to an abrupt full stop. An era of repressive military dictatorship was ushered in, the effects of which linger to this day. Two ominous events took place in the 1960s; although the main drama was elsewhere, both had an impact on Burma. The first was the Second Indochina War. In 1965, US combat units began operations in Vietnam. That same year, Burma's dictator Ne Win paid a state visit to the US and was received by President Lyndon B. Johnson. Although Burma was on the margins of the battlefront, it too was fighting a communist insurgency. The two motivations met and clicked, and the spigots were opened for military assistance.

The second event was the Cultural Revolution, which engulfed China for a decade. China (or 'Red China' at that time) was closed off and regarded with suspicion and even hostility by the Burmese government and public alike, for its overt support for the Communist insurrection. Attempts to export the Cultural

Revolution to Burma in 1967 backfired badly – there were anti-Chinese riots across the country, with fatalities and destruction of property. The PRC government maintained a hardline stance and relations fell to an all-time low.

The next year, light infantry units trained and equipped along US Army lines pursued the BCP in the Pegu (Bago) Yoma forests. Thakin Than Tun, the leader of the BCP, was assassinated in the jungle by one of his own men (later known to be a government mole), and the Communist forces were hounded out of their strongholds in the Bago Yoma, a forested range of hills in south-central Myanmar. The moving of the base of the Communist insurrection to the north-east, adjacent to the border with China was a curtain-raiser on a new battleground and new interface, which continues in one form or another to this day – the plethora of ethnic-based insurrections with ties to China.

Table 11.1 Burma Communist Party

Active period	Party	Turning points
1939–1989	Burma Communist Party (BCP) (Front party – National Unity Front – NUF)	Armed rebellion and destructive civil war Rationale for growth of Burma Army Ne Win used BCP as rationale for his 'socialism' Relations with China and the US
Key aspects	Began with strong popular support – urban and rural Strong pro-Beijing line and purges Maoist ideology – uncompromising and unreformable Ultimately lost touch with Myanmar public and its needs	
Ending	Military defeat and rolling up of underground network Inability to come to grips with ethnic nationality issues Loss of intellectual edge	

A multi-party system was revived only in 1988. Approximately 240 parties registered, but the number that actually contested the 1990 elections was only a little more than 50. However, a democratic system did not ensue from those elections; instead, junta rule continued until the end of 2010. A majority of the parties were de-registered in the wave of repression following 1990, and those that remained – like the NLD – faced severe repressive measures.

A junta-directed National Convention that commenced in 1993 dragged on for 13 years, culminating in a draft constitution. The constitution was adopted after a deeply controversial referendum in May 2008, a week after a devastating cyclone hit Lower Myanmar. Political party registration re-commenced in early 2010, but the NLD did not re-register. Nonetheless, 36 parties did register and ran in the elections held on November 10, 2010.

The period from around 1990 to 2011 had been one of persistent courtship, ingress and expansion by China. Its protective role against Western measures at the UN Security Council was used as a masthead, and the Myanmar Junta knew that it needed the political cover and economic assistance. Other nations like India and Japan began their re-engagement but were no match for China in terms of clout. In a period marked by government opacity, civil society was the watchdog and gadfly keeping tabs on Chinese inroads.[9]

The elections of November 2010 marked a return to a multi-party system and the advent of a semi-elected government (albeit under the controversial 2008 constitution). However as mentioned previously, the NLD did not contest those elections. The following year, armed conflict resumed with the Kachin Independence Organization (KIO) in the far north, bringing a 17-year ceasefire to an end. Then, following public agitation, the president suspended the Chinese-run Myitsone dam project on the Ayeyarwady river. This led to a chill in bilateral relations and a fall in investments.[10] The NLD entered the by-elections of April 2012 and won a number of seats in the Union Parliament – including one held by its leader Aung San Su Kyi. This ushered in a *return to electoral democracy* followed by a (short) period of rosy ebullience in relations with the West.

However, this is an era of electoral politics, with an electorate emerging from decades of dictatorship. Populism holds sway and beyond garnering votes, parties and politicians have little regard for public opinion. There seems to be little thought as to the direction in which the country is going or needs to go. Civil society is not strong or big enough; it is divided and mostly involved in niche issues. The crony private sector is flourishing and growing stronger, keeping to its rentier, extractivist and exclusivist ways. On top of it all, all these stakeholders are discrete and inward-looking. One donor has asked how a democracy can be built if people do not talk to each other. In other words, Myanmar seems to be losing its way. After expending much time and suffering, a semi-democracy has been gained. But beyond this, there is neither road nor chart.

But with Myanmar's history of a 70-year civil armed conflict, electoral victories do not ensure the return of peace. Relying upon majoritarian politics and mono-ethnic nationalism can actively deter a peace settlement with the ethnic nationalities and, by extension, the hoped-for federal system. Moreover, it can only render an even more tenuous and fragile 'peace' following ceasefires negotiated with ethnic paramilitaries that began in 1989. The weight of majoritarian politics has defeated every exercise in peace-making, including the current Panglong Peace conference that had its third session in July 2018. It is like a balloon with not enough helium in it – it will not rise. Thus, Myanmar can be described as a land of many nationalisms but with no nation. Seventy-one years after independence, nation-making has not only stalled, it has even regressed. There is a long list of countries that had been mapped into existence by colonial powers and eventually became independent states. Their post-colonial record in building states and nations has been patchy, and there is a voluminous literature on the whys and wherefores. Myanmar is in the category that has fared poorly. The most eloquent testament to this lies in the longest-running civil war in the world – beginning a bare

3 months after independence in 1948 and stretching up to the present day. In the early decades, this conflict was partly fuelled by ideology and partly ethnic based. Following the collapse of the BCP in 1989, it has become a solely ethnic-oriented war, with religious overtones. Economic motivations are of much lesser importance in Myanmar's civil war.

Belt and Road Initiative and the China Myanmar Economic Corridor

> Yunnan has little industry. For the Belt and Road to really go ahead in Myanmar, the industrial weight of Sichuan, Chongqing and even Shanxi has to come in.
> – Senior academic at Sichuan University, 2019

In September 2018, the Memorandum of Understanding (MoU) for the China Myanmar Economic Corridor (CMEC) was signed without any details being made public. It is an important component of the BRI. But the Corridor will have implications far beyond infrastructure and economic development. China expects more trouble to arise from the South China Sea and, therefore, wants to use Myanmar to by-pass it. Hence, it is not just the chokepoint at the Straits of Malacca that is troubling them. This means that Myanmar assumes even more importance from China's perspective.

Fingar and Oi have outlined what is happening now with the BRI:

> The scope of this undertaking is breathtaking, but six years on, it seems to have garnered more skepticism and animosity than affection or soft power. Indeed, China's relationship with more or less all countries is more fraught today than it was before Xi launched the BRI.[11]

Table 11.2 presents the variation in attitude among stakeholders within the country.

Table 11.2 Attitudes towards the Belt and Road Initiative among Domestic Stakeholders

< MOST IN FAVOUR				LEAST IN FAVOUR >
Ethnic armed organisations, particularly, United Wa State Army/ Northern Brotherhood	China-linked businesses and regional governments with which they are heavily involved	Incumbent National League for democracy government	Central military	Majority of civil society organisations, including environmental movement, ethnic-cased civil society

Source: Author's own compilation.

A very pertinent starting question would be, If there are to be benefits for Myanmar, how will these be shared? Vertically (between stratas) and horizontally (between sub-national entities and ethnicities)? How will it impact upon the ending of the civil war and the hoped-for federal system? How will it affect the regional balance of power? It is a matter of some doubt whether these and similar concerns are even being considered in the halls of Naypyidaw. On the CMEC as well as in other spheres, a more consultative, inclusive and participatory approach is urgently required. What is at stake is more than just overcoming crises and the prospects at the next elections in 2020. It is ultimately directed towards building a viable, plural and federalist democracy, and a more equitable and tolerant society.

Of China's four existing mega-projects in Myanmar, the Myitsone dam is stalled. China is keen to resume work but is not pushing decisively. The Letpadaung copper mine is operating – under heavy security guard. The oil and gas pipeline from the Bay of Bengal coast to south-west China is also functioning. The Kyaukphyu deep sea port and adjoining Special Economic Zone (SEZ) are going ahead, and China's investment price tag was US$7.5 billion. Aung San Su Kyi's economic adviser has faulted this as being too high and it has been scaled down to US$1.3 billion.[12] Other voices warn of a debt trap, although China dismisses this. Looking at the recent experiences of Pakistan and Sri Lanka, one might argue that these cases might be perceived by many as warning signs.[13]

For China, there is ample reason for Myanmar, this country to its south-west which it had called the 'land of the southern barbarians' in ancient times, to be incorporated into its BRI, troublesome as it may be. Myanmar is now more or less a democracy again, after a long and arduous struggle. But it is poorly governed, and the military still has political ambitions of its own. Of added relevance are the country's remnants of its authoritarian past: an entrenched military, widespread cronyism and big business, ethnic conflicts and the resurgence of the politicization of religion and religious militancy. Peace is still elusive; mistrust is high, and big-scale corruption is rife. Nonetheless, China is prepared to take the risk and move in on a bigger scale.

One is tempted to conclude that the dragon shall have the last laugh, but it is most likely not going to be smooth sailing along the way. The degree of mistrust regarding China's intentions is high, and its public relations are poor. The key 'deliverable' will be the degree and nature of traction it has upon the Myanmar military. And when all is done, what will be China's 'value added' on Myanmar? This storyline will stretch over a number of years, and it will be messy and truncated. Keeping in mind that the MoU has only set things in motion – its full trajectory is still uncertain and remains to be seen.

This is mainly because other players are joining the infrastructure 'game'. For example, US scholars such as David M. Lampton have stated that with regard to China's high-speed rail, the US should think about getting more involved in such projects, either alone or in consortia with other countries. Regardless of further questions over whether infrastructure projects like high-speed rail links are a reasonable technological decision for some ASEAN country like Laos, connectivity is increasingly linked to geopolitics. Hence, if you do not build high-speed railways in Laos, you are not going to connect to the ASEAN countries further to the south. Not only that, each of the countries in the region has to decide – in light of the US-China bilateral relationship becoming more difficult – whose technology (particularly key technologies like 5G) they are going to buy.[14]

Like China, India has been playing both the military and the NLD, hedging its bets. Of late, the relationship with the military has picked up. Looking for new partners abroad, the military had been turning away from its former mentor and supplier China. But following the carnage in northern Rakhine, doors that had been kept open in the West slammed shut. Therefore, India became a ready alternative. India could have played an important role in using its influence in Myanmar to further democracy and human rights. However, it has clearly valued its economic and strategic interests over its concerns for humanitarian causes. Myanmar is crucial for the Modi government's Act East policy with the India-Myanmar-Thailand Asian Trilateral Highway, and the Kaladan multimodal project, a road-river-port cargo transport project. In the capital of the violence-affected Rakhine state, India has invested heavily in the construction of the Sittwe deep water port since 2016. The proposed SEZ by India will rival the Chinese SEZ located 80 km south of strategically located Sittwe. However, in the face of the CMEC MoU and other Chinese-led large-scale initiatives, competition with China in Myanmar has constrained India's influence. In fact, India has lost out to a considerable extent to China in recent years in terms of infrastructure projects.

The role of the US

> Competition with the US will intensify. But we do not expect Myanmar to take any side.
>
> – Scholar at a leading think-tank in Beijing

The US has been through more of a helter-skelter ride than most others in its 60-odd years of diplomatic relations with Myanmar. In the current period, at one end there is sometimes talk that the US and China should collaborate on finding solutions for Myanmar. At the same time, there is profound distrust of the US's intentions from the Chinese side. In particular, there is widespread belief that a policy of containment of China is being pursued. Regarding the BRI, the official US position (or at least that of the State Department) is that the US does not fundamentally oppose the BR and that it is for partner countries like Myanmar to decide from themselves whether and how they join BRI projects according to their needs and after diligent assessment. However, monitoring of BRI projects (now the CMEC) continues unabated. This is done by most of the major missions stationed in Myanmar. More so,. S technical expertise is provided to Myanmar in order to support the assessment, or at times even the renegotiation, of BRI projects. For example, according to media reports, US experts supported Myanmar officials in their efforts to renegotiate and thus effectively to scale back, the Chinese financed

Kyaukpyu deep port project in Rakhine state.[15] Due in part to recently enacted legislation, US direct investment does not amount to much. The US is instead concentrating on technical assistance, as well as education, democracy and peace promotion, and to some extent on support for public health. Even though direct military cooperation is proscribed, there are active programmes like those at the Asia-Pacific Center for Security Studies, Honolulu.[16]

The bitter divide(s) in Myanmar and the patent, chronic inability to bring peace warrant a comparison with earlier experiences of the US in the region. In particular, Vietnam's case is of interest here, as the Cold War was on and the US could not afford to lose a non-communist client. Hence, it was sucked into what became an 'unwinnable' war. For Myanmar today, in place of the Cold War, there is the great power contest. It is no longer ideological, but national aspirations and geopolitical interests are at stake – and these are even more potent potential drivers of internal division and conflict in the country.

As to how the pandemic has affected the two nations and their rivalry, Bates Gill stated that both countries' constructive response over the long term to the devastating human and economic toll of the pandemic is more important than shifting blame to the other. He further said that Germany's Foreign Minister Heiko Maas spoke for many world leaders when he noted that China took 'very authoritarian measures, while in the US the virus was played down for a long time. . . . These are two extremes, neither of which can be a model for Europe'.[17]

Competing strategic projects

The investment competition is not a new phenomenon in Southeast Asia. When Japan rose to become an economic power in Asia in the 1960s, not only was there an investment push to the South, but the Asian Development Bank was set up, with the position of chairman always held by a Japanese. Interestingly, China is now doing the same with the Asian Infrastructure Investment Bank. With the end of the Indochina wars, the economic and strategic value of the region found new expression in the Mekong River Commission, the first of many acronymic groupings centred on the Mekong river. Beijing has come up with one of the many branches of the Belt and Road in the Form of the Lancang-Mekong Cooperation.

ASEAN may mean different things to different viewers; the northern tier or mainland Southeast Asia is where the competition appears to be most intense. ASEAN 'togetherness' is both a cause and a result of this – something that is increasing despite the variation in the political systems and economic development in the ten countries of the Association. Despite the apparent incapacity at higher levels, Myanmar continues to be wooed from all sides. The US does not have significant infrastructure, manufacturing or other 'hardware' projects in Myanmar, and its overall aid profile is low. The big projects which can be seen as 'competing' are all with other countries. Japan and Korea have the largest shares, with India involved in self-centred connectivity projects. Three sectors or regions with projects in competition with one another are illustrated in Table 11.3.

Table 11.3 Three Sectors or Regions with Projects in Competition with One Another

	By China	By others
Rakhine state	Kyaukphyu deep sea port and industrial zone	Kaladan Multimodal Waterway (India)
Railways	Mandalay-Ruili high-speed rail (feasibility study stage)	Yangon Circular Rail line and later Yangon-Mandalay Rail line upgrading (Japan International Cooperation Agency, Japan)
Port/SEZ in delta	New Yangon City and Port (Kungyangon) planning stage	Thilawa Port and SEZ near Yangon (Japan)

Railways were especially important in Burma/Myanmar's colonial and post-independence periods. From around the beginning of this century, with the improvement of the highway system and the influx of modern buses and trucks, road transport has risen to pre-eminence. Spurred on by its own connectivity interests,[18] China has been pushing high-speed rail for some years now. Mandalay would be the hub, with spokes reaching out in all four directions, including north-east to the border with Yunnan province. Progress has been slow, with a feasibility study for the new Lashio-Muse railway line only recently completed. In the meantime, Japan International Cooperation Agency (JICA) has already launched the upgrading of the Yangon Circular Line, to be followed by the Yangon-Mandalay line, which is a primary artery.

For India, besides matching China's game plan in connecting to the Bay of Bengal, the Kaladan Multimodal Waterway is strategic in its own right, offering a maritime link and outlet to the land-locked North-East. The seaport is Sittwe, which is also the capital of Rakhine state. The construction timetable for this waterway has been held up, by armed conflict with the Arakan Army (AA), an ethnic armed organisation fighting the central government, which has labelled it a terrorist organisation. Evidence is circumstantial, but there are allegations that China is using the AA as its proxy in Rakhine state.[19]

In a recent article of *Foreign Affairs* magazine, Cambodian opposition leader-in-exile Sam Rainsy stated that locations conceded to Chinese projects in his country are being developed into military installations. The key term is 'dual use' – whereby an ostensible tourist resort could quickly be converted into a naval port facility, and a nearby airport to serve tourist arrivals becomes a fighter airbase.[20] This is not a new development in the world, and that is why items like high-speed rail and SEZs need to be assessed in terms of possible military use as well.

Conclusion

The 'Great Game' is nothing new to Myanmar – and by this, I mean the entire country and not just the policy-making crowd. As mentioned earlier, Burma/

Myanmar had been buffeted by the Cold War, but its internal disputes and conflicts were far more damaging. Now with the Great Game Redux, the larger public would want no part in it. Certainly, there are constituencies – political, business and ethnic – that would lean towards either major power, but these do not amount to much when set against native, public opinion (or wisdom). In the final tally, this may be the decisive factor.

One reason going for Myanmar is its size. It happens to be the largest country in mainland Southeast Asia in terms of land area. In a private conversation, friends from Laos and Kyrgyzstan felt they had no option but to go along with China. Not so in the case of Myanmar. It may be the size of a province in China, but with a different history and civilisation, it will not fit into any Chinese pocket easily.

The present-day Chinese expansionism is primarily economic rather than military or political. One observes this in Africa. Most of the attention on China is towards the big-ticket infrastructure projects. But at the same time, the 'small fry' from China is all over the country now, especially after the easing of visa requirements. This resembles Chinese population incursions into the Russian Far East. One recent middle-sized development is the new town of Shwe Kokko on the Thai-Myanmar border in Kayin state. It is a collaboration between a Kayin militia and a Chinese developer. Whether this represents a natural process or a slow swallowing by a pythonic entity is open to dispute. Besides the opposition from local public opinion, things might come to a head in a collision between Myanmar and Han Chinese nationalisms.

Expanding economic traffic with China is almost a *fait accompli*, considering the multifarious connectivities. Even if the Chinese state were not to figure so prominently, the individual entrepreneur would still be pulling bilateral trade relations. Of the factors standing in the way, the one that China understands the least is Myanmar's political pluralism. Of countries that share land borders with China, Laos and Vietnam are communist one-party states, and Cambodia has recently dispensed with its political opposition parties. Myanmar, on the other hand, has had a long experience with a system of democracy, however imperfect or factious or debilitating it may be.

It may be far more prudent for what may be called the Chinese world to follow what the earlier Chinese diaspora to Southeast Asia had done. Becoming acculturated, blending into local society, and contributing more than taking. Employing economic and infrastructural muscle to draw disparate nations and peoples into its orbit is much less likely to succeed.

The competition between the two powers is largely over public opinion in Myanmar. China is ahead in many sectors, but its public relations is poor. The US has an advantage in sectors like education, health and civil society-building and has also been encouraging American companies to target Mandalay, which is the pivot of the Chinese economic presence in Myanmar. Public opinion in large part remains cautious and wary of China's activities, and this will be difficult to change. Key challenges persist, such as that of achieving and maintaining peace. Elections will be held in 2020, but it is hard to envisage the outcome being a government strong and capable enough, and an environment conducive enough, to attain the elusive peace.

Myanmar's chronic problems are of domestic origin and have little to do with foreign influences or great power rivalry. All the powers and countries engaged with Myanmar know this, and there is a certain amount of anxiety in their dealings. They could spend a lot of time and effort countering one another, but by far the best course would be to help engender a Myanmar state that can come to terms with itself and is capable of setting things in order. All else proceeds from this.

Future configurations and postscript

Very recently, writing in ISEAS perspectives, Malcolm Cook and Hoang Thi Ha have come up with very blunt assessments:

> A more aggressive unilateralist China, a more unpredictable unilateralist USA, and deepening US-China rivalry have ended the post-Cold War order that benefited Southeast Asia and ASEAN. Southeast Asian states should consider joining more or establishing such minilateral informal coalitions in response to destabilizing actions from China, the USA, and the US-China rivalry.[21]

In their view, the coronavirus pandemic has exposed the global governance failings due to the US-China rivalry that has been exacerbated by the pandemic. They added that as the US-China rivalry deepens and expands, more such informal, issue-specific coalitions that do not include either superpower will be required to protect participating states' shared interests and the regional and global multilateral institutions placed under strain by China, the US and the US-China rivalry.[22]

Similarly, Drew Thompson has reminded that Southeast Asian states retain considerable agency to choose their own course and preserve their sovereign choices, however, albeit in a more complex environment.[23] He added that those states should not exclusively perceive US-China competition as a threat forcing them to choose sides in order to survive. If Southeast Asian states are to thrive, they must choose themselves, make choices based on their interests, rather than those of the US or China, diversify their economic relationships to enhance resilience and independence.

Events of 2020 are nothing less than seismic. The worst pandemic in a century has brought with it bewildering and frightening impacts, not least of which are in the face-offs between the two great powers and between them and other powers. A big reset is in the process of unfolding. Sino-American rivalry is taking on new dimensions and spilling over to tensions with other nations. Earlier alliances and alignments are undergoing upheavals. But superpowers will not give up their predominance easily, and how the picture turns out will be something to watch closely in this time of turbulence.

The stakes are high for both big powers – and for all others too for that matter. Besides having to battle the pandemic, both are facing severe pressures on the home front as well. Even before this happened, opinions in Southeast Asia were not favourable towards either power, and this could well take a turn for the worse.

Notwithstanding the (sensible) call for togetherness in the face of the plague, countries generally are farther apart than they had been. If the big powers pitch their capacious tents again (as China is already doing) and expect others to come in, they are looking at a long and hard road ahead. For the US, there is a chance for change in the 2020 elections. As for China, such opportunities are markedly less. Centralised control has been reinforced, and the legitimacies – personal (Xi Jinping) and institutional (CPC) – have to be upheld.

Reverting to a time-honoured and timeless choice, which of these two paths will the countries of Southeast Asia follow? A divided country like Myanmar could go either way or remain as it is now. Will reason and good sense prevail in much of Southeast Asia? Opinion polls are revelatory to a certain extent. But across the region it is a running battle between governments which are overtly authoritarian or inclining towards it, and a more enlightened, open and caring public and civil society.

The trajectories posited by history, culture and religion are not deterministic anymore. The big powers, at the very least, would love to strengthen their spheres of influence. At a time like this, when both have stumbled badly, there is an opportunity for the 'lesser' powers to strike out a path of their own, without being in thrall to either.

Notes

1 "Thousands Protest Against Myanmar Mega-Dam", *The ASEAN Post*, April 23, 2019. At https://theaseanpost.com/article/thousands-protest-against-myanmar-mega-dam
2 "State of Southeast Asia", *2020 Survey Report, ISEAS*, Singapore, January 16, 2020. At www.iseas.edu.sg/wp-content/uploads/pdfs/TheStateofSEASurveyReport_2020.pdf
3 HongweiFan and Yizheng Zou,"Burma-China Early Approach and Implications for Contemporary Bilateral Relations", *Asian Perspective*, 43 (3), 2019, pp. 459–480. doi: 10.1353/apr.2019.0021.
4 "Myanmar: The Military Regime's View of the World", International Crisis Group (ICG), Report No.28, December 7, 2001. At www.crisisgroup.org/asia/south-east-asia/myanmar/myanmar-military-regimes-view-world
5 "Explaining Myanmar's Foreign Policy Behaviour: Domestic and International Factors", *Mizzima*, December 8, 2016. At http://mizzima.com/news-opinion/explaining-myanmar%25E2%2580%2599s-foreign-policy-behaviour-domestic-and-international-factors
6 "Myanmar's Myitsone Dam Dilemma", *The Diplomat*, March 11, 2019. At https://thediplomat.com/2019/03/myanmars-myitsone-dam-dilemma/
7 Jörn Dosch and Satswan S. Sidhu, "The European Union's Myanmar Policy: Focused or Directionless?", *Journal of Current Southeast Asian Affairs*, 43 (2), 2015, pp. 85–112.
8 Robert H. Taylor,"Foreign and Domestic Consequences of the KMT Intervention in Burma", Data Paper No. 93, Southeast Asia Program, Department of Asian Studies, Cornell University, Ithaca, New York, 1973.
9 In this regard, one can observe a constant litany from China about Western agency being behind civil society 'troublemaking'. However, members of local civil society resent this very much

10 "China's Investment in Myanmar Declines in 2016–2017 Fiscal Year", *Xinhua*, March 7, 2017. At www.xinhuanet.com//english/2017-03/07/c_136109783.htm
11 Thomas Fingar and Jean C. Oi, "China's Challenges: Now It Gets Much Harder", *The Washington Quarterly*, 43 (1), March 19, 2020, pp. 67–84.
12 "Kyaukpyu Port to Become Model Project in China-Myanmar BRI Cooperation", *Xinhua*, January 18, 2020. At www.xinhuanet.com/english/2020-01/18/c_138716099.htm
13 Yan Naing, "Rescuing Myanmar from the Chinese Debt Trap", *The Irrawady*, August 21, 2020. At www.irrawaddy.com/opinion/guest-column/rescuing-myanmar-chinese-debt-trap.html
14 David M. Lampton, "All (High-Speed Rail) Roads Lead to China", Freeman Spogli Institute, Asia-Pacific Research Center, 2020. At https://aparc.fsi.stanford.edu/content/high-speed-rail-creates-both-potential-and-problems-china-explains-mike-lampton
15 Ben Kesling and Jon Emont, "U.S. Goes on the Offensive Against China's Empire-Building Funding Plan", *The Wall Street Journal*, April 9, 2019. At www.wsj.com/articles/u-s-goes-on-the-offensive-against-chinas-empire-building-mega-plan-11554809402
16 "Comprehensive Security Sector Development in Myanmar", The Asia-Pacific Center for Security Studies (APCSS), September 5, 2014. At https://apcss.org/category/workshop/
17 Bates Gill, "China's Global Influence: Post-COVID Prospects for Soft Power", *The Washington Quarterly*, 43 (2), 2020, pp. 97–115.
18 Kaho Yu, "The Belt and Road Initiative in Southeast Asia after COVID-19: China's Energy and Infrastructure Investments in Myanmar" *ISEAS Perspective*, No.39, 6 April, 2021.
19 Sudhi Ranjan Sen, "India Accuses China of Helping Rebel Groups on Myanmar Border", *The Japan Times*, December 7, 2020. At www.japantimes.co.jp/news/2020/12/07/asia-pacific/china-india-myanmar-border/
20 Sam Rainsy, "China Has Designs on Democracy in Southeast Asia", *Foreign Affairs*, June 10, 2020. At www.foreignaffairs.com/articles/china/2020-06-10/china-has-designs-democracy-southeast-asia
21 Cook and Hoang Thi Ha, "Beyond China, the USA and ASEAN: Informal Minilateral Options", *ISEAS*, No. 63, 2020.
22 Ibid.
23 Drew Thompson, "Intensifying U.S.-China Competition Creates New Challenges for Southeast Asia", *Global-Is-Asian*, May 29, 2020. At https://lkyspp.nus.edu.sg/gia/article/intensifying-u.s.-chinacompetition-creates-new-challenges-for-southeast-asia?fbclid=IwAR3O6w-HN2z4b8y60F8Tlp8W4brcj40IE7RSDj6Gc9qb1_mYrRD-W3clmRIE

Bibliography

Bates Gill, "China's Global Influence: Post-COVID Prospects for Soft Power", *The Washington Quarterly*, 43 (2), 2020, pp. 97–115.
Chao Yian Ping, "Wang Gungwu: Even if the West Has Lost Its Way, China May Not Be Heir Apparent", *ThinkChina*, May 18, 2020, at www.thinkchina.sg/wang-gungwu-even-if-west-haslost-its-way-china-may-not-be-heir-apparent
"China's Investment in Myanmar Declines in 2016–2017 Fiscal Year", *Xinhua*, March 7, 2017, at www.xinhuanet.com//english/2017-03/07/c_136109783.htm
"Comprehensive Security Sector Development in Myanmar", *The Asia-Pacific Center for Security Studies (APCSS)*, September 5, 2014, at https://apcss.org/category/workshop/
Cook and Hoang Thi Ha, "Beyond China, the USA and ASEAN: Informal Minilateral Options", ISEAS, Singapore, No. 63, 2020.

David M. Lampton, "All (High-Speed Rail) Roads Lead to China", Freeman Spogli Institute, Asia-Pacific Research Center, 2020, at https://aparc.fsi.stanford.edu/content/high-speed-rail-creates-both-potential-and-problems-china-explains-mike-lampton

Drew Thompson, "Intensifying U.S.-China Competition Creates New Challenges for Southeast Asia", *Global-Is-Asian*, May 29, 2020, at https://lkyspp.nus.edu.sg/gia/article/intensifying-u.s.-chinacompetition-creates-new-challenges-for-southeast-asia?fbclid=IwAR3O6w-HN2z4b8y60F8Tlp8W4brcj40IE7RSDj6Gc9qb1_mYrRDW-3clmRIE

"Explaining Myanmar's Foreign Policy Behaviour: Domestic and International Factors", *Mizzima*, December 8, 2016, at http://mizzima.com/news-opinion/explaining-myanmar%25E2%2580%2599s-foreign-policy-behaviour-domestic-and-international-factors

Frank Bekkers, "Geopolitics and Maritime Security", *Hague Centre of Strategic Studies*, 2019.

Hongwei Fan and Yizheng Zou, "Burma-China Early Approach and Implications for Contemporary Bilateral Relations", *Asian Perspective*, 43 (3), 2019, pp. 459–480. doi: 10.1353/apr.2019.0021

"Kyaukpyu Port to Become Model Project in China-Myanmar BRI Cooperation", *Xinhua*, January 18, 2020, at www.xinhuanet.com/english/2020-01/18/c_138716099.htm

Maung Aung Myo, "Myanmar as a Geopolitical Pivot in Indo-Pacific Region", *National Defense University Magazine*, 2015.

"Myanmar: The Military Regime's View of the World", International Crisis Group (ICG), Report No. 28, December 7, 2001, at www.crisisgroup.org/asia/south-east-asia/myanmar/myanmar-military-regimes-view-world

"Myanmar's Myitsone Dam Dilemma", *The Diplomat*, March 11, 2019, at https://thediplomat.com/2019/03/myanmars-myitsone-dam-dilemma/

Robert H. Taylor, "Foreign and Domestic Consequences of the KMT Intervention in Burma", Data Paper No. 93, Southeast Asia Program, Department of Asian Studies, Cornell University, Ithaca, New York, 1973.

Shibashis Chatterjee, "The Look East Policy and India's Northeastern States", Graduate School of Nanyang Technological University, Singapore, March 2014.

"State of Southeast Asia", 2020 Survey Report, ISEAS, Singapore, January 16, 2020, at www.iseas.edu.sg/wp-content/uploads/pdfs/TheStateofSEASurveyReport_2020.pdf

Thomas Fingar and Jean C. Oi, "China's Challenges: Now It Gets Much Harder", *The Washington Quarterly*, 43 (1), March 19, 2020, pp. 67–84.

"Thousands Protest Against Myanmar Mega-Dam", *The ASEAN Post*, April 23, 2019, at https://theaseanpost.com/article/thousands-protest-against-myanmar-mega-dam

Zbigniew Brzezinski, *The Grand Chessboard- American Primacy and Its Geostrategic Imperatives*, Basic Books, New York, 1998.

12 The role of domestic political constraints in navigating great power relations

The case of South Korea

Seo-Hyun Park

Introduction

Is South Korea wavering?[1] As the rivalry between China and the United States heats up, in what ways will Seoul be forced to rethink its strategic commitments as a U.S. ally? Are South Koreans more likely to accept Chinese influence, especially when compared to recent instances of anti-American and anti-Japanese mobilisations? These questions – and similar queries about East Asian and Southeast Asian countries neighbouring China – appear to motivate many of the current policy discussions, domestic political discourse, and scholarly debates on Asian security.

Predictions of Seoul's predicament – caught between the two Great Powers of China and the United States – notwithstanding, it is important to recognise that the role of the United States, South Korea's only formal ally, and its policies remain sizeable in shaping perceptions of threat in South Korea and framing domestic political mobilisations by elites and publics alike. This is not to say that South Korea has not sought to adjust its foreign policy stances or to hedge against future trade-offs in terms of security choices with the increasing power and influence of China.[2] But, as Lim and Cooper show, many Asian governments have tended to exhibit path-dependent tendencies rather than outright hedging behaviours, even as some allies are expressing more reservations about their treaty obligations and the U.S.'s security commitments to the region.[3]

One useful way to identify such path dependence is to analyse the change (or lack thereof) in the framing of important foreign policy debates. It is telling that some of the most salient and widespread political mobilisations in South Korea have occurred in the face of tensions within the South Korea-U.S. alliance relationship. No comparable political frames or mobilisations – in terms of resonance and significance – have emerged yet with respect to South Korea-China bilateral relations. This lack of politicisation so far, I suggest, is not an indication of South Korea's acquiescence to China's leadership role. Rather, somewhat paradoxically, it signals the still-dominant frames of security thinking and policy centred on the U.S.-led regional security structure since 1945. South Korean political leaders continue to mobilise political support and incite serious opposition by signalling their strength of commitment to South Korea's alliance relations with the United States.

DOI: 10.4324/9781003106814-12

In this chapter, I illustrate how such domestic political constraints – in addition to the external structural pressures – shape South Korean leaders' choices in formulating their Great Power strategies. Drawing on my earlier work on historical patterns of contesting Great Power influence in Japan and Korea,[4] I show that political leaders in South Korea must carefully navigate a "socially shared discourse" which "are themselves embedded within a historical and cultural context"[5] when discussing foreign policy agendas – in particular, alliance-management issues. The rhetorical choices that leaders make are not theirs alone to freely create or manipulate. By invoking specific concepts and vocabulary, political leaders are either confirming or contesting pre-existing frames used to mobilise specific stances on how to think about alliance relations with the United States.

Within these established scripts of alliance contestation, leaders have varying degrees of political manoeuvrability based on the strength of their rule. I argue that leaders operating under conditions of political strength have more freedom to sidestep or shift existing framing contests, while challenged leaders in positions of weakness become entrapped in polarising rhetorical and physical mobilisations. In other words, strong regimes are frame-makers, while weak regimes are frame-takers.

In the following section, I provide an overview of key foreign policy debates that have been largely centred on "Great Power relations" in South Korea during and after the Cold War – and how they continue to be directly and indirectly deployed in contemporary crisis situations. I then turn to a discussion of possible alternative interpretations of alliance tensions between South Korea and the United States and the importance of understanding the rhetorical choices of political leaders and the context in which they were used. Next, I demonstrate the effects of such domestic political constraints on South Korea's foreign policy outcomes by comparing two South Korean presidencies – that of Roh Moo-hyun (2003–2008) and Moon Jae-in (2017-present).

Overview of key South Korean foreign policy debates

South Korea-China relations

Although China and South Korea fought on opposite sides during the Korean War, and despite ensuing ideological, military, and political divisions during the Cold War, expressions of anti-China sentiments were rare and did not coalesce into political movements or mobilisations in South Korea. This was in sharp contrast to the widespread voicing of anti-Japanese sentiments. Relations between Seoul and Beijing began to thaw in the 1980s, with the Chinese ignoring the Soviet decision to boycott the 1984 Summer Olympics in Los Angeles and supporting the 1988 Seoul Games as well. Following Deng Xiaoping's policy of economic opening, China began trading with South Korea, and by 1985, total China-South Korea trade ($1.16 billion) surpassed that between China and North Korea ($488 million).

Fuelled by South Korean President Roh Tae-woo's policy of "Nordpolitik," South Korea and China normalised diplomatic relations in 1992. Since that time, the two countries have significantly expanded their economic ties, and Beijing has supported Seoul on a number of significant political issues, such as Seoul's membership to the United Nations in 1992 and South Korea's commitment to a nuclear-weapons-free Korean peninsula – both against the wishes of its long-time ally, Pyongyang.

But by the late 1990s, there were signs that the "honeymoon period" was coming to an end, as friction began to mount over trade disputes. In the so-called "garlic battle" between South Korea and China, tensions erupted as the South Korean government, in the face of upcoming National Assembly elections in April 2000, sided with its farmers to levy higher tariffs on cheaper garlic imports from China in November 1999. The Chinese government was swift and strategic in its retaliatory measures, responding with sanctions on South Korean mobile phone handsets and polyethylene packing plastic, two key export items from South Korea to China.[6] While other bilateral issues, such as history and border disputes, economic tensions, and disagreement on North Korea policy, have begun to escalate over time, we have yet to see fully formed, tightly organised, and recurring movements or strategic debates on South Korea-China relations or South Korea's identity vis-à-vis China.

South Korea-U.S. relations

Where we *do* see more established and regularised patterns of political mobilisation, often tied to concerns of national identity and the language of nationalism, is in South Korea's relations with its larger, more powerful ally, the United States. Since the outbreak of the Korean War in June 1950, the United States became South Korea's primary benefactor during the Cold War, providing military and economic aid to the impoverished, newly independent nation. South Korea became part of the American-led hub-and-spokes regional security order aimed against the Soviet Union, China, North Korea, and other communist countries. The centrepiece of this regional security structure was the San Francisco Peace Treaty signed in 1951, which the United States helped negotiate to formally conclude the Second World War in Asia. As a result of this treaty,

> Washington extended its security umbrella over Tokyo in exchange for Japan's disarmament, pacification, and guaranteed alignment with the 'free world.' In effect, this bargain saw the US stepping into the breach between Japan and China as an 'outside arbiter play[ing] a policing role' – by making Japanese defense dependent on itself, the US extended a 'dual reassurance,' simultaneously guaranteeing China and Japan their security against each other, obviating the need for them to engage either in direct security competition or reconciliation.[7]

The United States also acted as a mediator and enforcer between Japan and South Korea, utilising both pressure and persuasion to facilitate cooperation between the two "quasi-allies," each allied to the United States, but not to each other.[8]

In addition to this post-war security bargain at the regional level, several political bargains or "social contracts" were struck domestically as well. In South Korea, the Cold War ideological and military competition with North Korea just across the border meant that conditions were ripe for the creation of a "national security state," in which authoritarian or military leaders were able to seize and sustain power by highlighting the threat of communism and prioritising stability over democracy-building or human rights, for example. Under the National Security Law (*Gukka Boan Beop*), in effect since 1948, any individuals engaging in activities compromising the safety of the state could be prosecuted. In practice, amongst those prosecuted were political dissidents or pro-democracy student activists who were accused of propagating pro-North Korea or pro-communist messages. Crucially, and relevant for contemporary intra-alliance tensions, expressions of anti-Americanism or even criticisms of the South Korea-U.S. alliance were included among these anti-state activities, which is why some of the long-held grievances and critiques of South Korea's stance towards the United States bubbled to the surface and coalesced into political movements in the 1990s, following South Korea's democratisation.[9] In this sense, some of the national identity politics surrounding South Korea's relations with the United States in recent decades may be seen as delayed responses to political oppression under successive military regimes during the Cold War.

A second social bargain of sorts in post-war South Korea was the economic and political mobilisation in support of the "developmental state." In South Korea and elsewhere, such widespread support for government-led large-scale economic development projects occurred in the context of the Cold War and domestic political unrest and were led by revolutionary regimes who often couched their policies in nationalist rhetoric promising to "catch up" with the West and to achieve "advanced country" status.[10] The role of the United States looms large here once again because of the massive amounts of American aid given to South Korea as well as the indirect support of anti-democratic but anti-communist political leaders by Washington in the name of stability.

It is this widespread belief in the U.S.'s pervasive influence, both real and imagined, in South Korean domestic politics that continues to motivate salient and intense political contests between the generally security-minded conservatives, who fear rocking the boat and support the status quo on alliance ties with the United States, on the one hand, and liberals who seek to reduce some of the structural inequalities and promote greater voice opportunities in intra-alliance interactions, on the other. In other words, the United States remains central to post-Cold War identity politics in South Korea because of its role – actual and perceived – in creating the conditions for these long-standing political-economic cleavages to emerge and endure. Moreover, such identity politics have become reinforced and further entrenched as South Korean political leaders have often utilised anti-communism and alliance ties to the United States as a tool of political mobilisation and of silencing the opposition.

Contesting established Great Power relations in post-Cold War South Korea

By some accounts, it is not surprising that we see greater pushback in South Korea against the idea of remaining strategically dependent on the United States since the 1990s. While South Korean alignment choices during the Cold War were largely determined by the dictates of power asymmetry and the communist threat, in the post-Cold War period, we should perhaps expect to see increasing attempts at foreign policy autonomy, especially given the overall decline in threat perception towards North Korea.[11]

While decreasing perceptions of threat and military dependence on the United States may have generally increased the likelihood of questioning existing alliance relations, the empirical reality paints a mixed picture. Alliance cohesion between South Korea and the United States was at its height in the late 1990s and early 2000s, even as South Korean views of North Korea were undergoing dramatic change during South Korean President Kim Dae-jung's "Sunshine Policy" initiative. Although anti-Americanism on the part of South Koreans was commonly blamed for the tensions in South Korea-U.S. alliance relations in the mid-2000s, with some speculating that the alliance itself may be in jeopardy, alliance cooperation continued, and overall bilateral relations appeared to strengthen since the second half of the 2000s. And, despite much domestic political tensions, and continued deterioration in relations with China, over the deployment of the U.S. missile defence system (THAAD or "Theater High Altitude Area Defense") in South Korea in 2017, there was little spillover into South Korea-U.S. alliance relations. In sum, structural dependence or threat levels do not directly lead to South Korean attitudes or responses towards alliance cooperation.

Others look to domestic political factors to explain the vicissitudes of alignment behaviour. Often highlighted is the role of political leadership since the political interests and preferences of specific leaders or coalitions can be critical for the state of alliance relations at a given time. Specifically, progressive or Left-leaning parties in South Korea, it is sometimes argued, tend to be more nationalistic and have relied on anti-American or anti-foreign rallying calls to advocate for less dependence on Great Powers, more sovereign autonomy, and democratic consolidation.[12]

Yet, it is worth noting that some of the strongest instances of bilateral coordination on North Korea policy and other forms of alliance cooperation occurred under governments representing the South Korean Left. For example, it was under the Kim Dae-jung government that collaboration ensued with the United States in curtailing North Korean development and testing of ballistic missiles. Additional positive externalities from this "Perry Process" included the U.S.-DPRK Joint Communique (October 12, 2000), in which Pyongyang agreed to a moratorium on launching "long-range missiles of any kind while talks on the missile issue continue,"[13] the creation for the first time of an official U.S.-Japan-South Korea consultative mechanism called the Trilateral Coordination and Oversight Group (TCOG), and continued dialogue with China and Russia on North Korea-related issues, which would help pave the way for the Six Party Talks format later. More recently, the progressive Moon government finalised the deployment of THAAD, with President Moon maintaining close ties with the Trump administration, initiating and mediating dialogue between Washington and Pyongyang. Thus, it appears ideological orientation of the party or political leader is by itself not a reliable predictor of the nature of alliance cooperation we can expect to see.

I argue instead that the nature of South Korean alignment behaviour results from the type and intensity of alliance contestation. The kinds of outcomes political leaders can deliver and the degree and duration of political backlash they face can affect both immediate- and long-term alliance relations. A key intervening variable here is regime strength. Depending on the degree of external pressure and how much political (including intra-party and inter-party) competition they face, political leaders can become either entrapped in or shield themselves from alliance contestation based on pre-existing political frames.

The role of domestic political constraints in navigating Great Power relations

As I have shown here and elsewhere, alliance management occurs in a dense social environment – local and global – and the type and degree of alliance cooperation as an outcome is shaped by the particular rhetorical framing of the government's response and of the cooperation agenda itself. But this framing is not controlled – or even controllable – solely by either the government or the public. It is important to note that the framing of political debates is not easily manipulated by any one individual, even a member of the powerful political elite or a vested interest group. As sociologist Charles Tilly reminds us, political claims and contests occur along recurring repertoires of mobilisation. Political leaders can participate in framing contests, but not necessarily on their own terms. Political struggles for legitimacy and political survival are largely a series of short-term-based decisions by competing elites – particularly in a democratic setting. In order to legitimate themselves, political leaders deploy certain resonant rhetorical frames based on "shared scripts" or cultural understandings.[14] These scripts, moreover, become remobilised and routinised over time. Tilly argues that repeated performances of political contention take on certain repertoires, where claims are often made on behalf of and against identifiable pairs: "bosses and workers, peasants and landlords, rival nationalist factions, and many more."[15]

In South Korean political debates, the structural environment of the Cold War and the U.S.'s strategic, political, and economic dominance in East Asia in the post-1945 period meant that the political legitimacy of any serious political contender hinged on their view of Korea-U.S. alliance relations, which would have a bearing on their stance on national security and ability to maintain economic growth and stability. Thus, many of the important post-war foreign policy debates in South Korea have readily organised themselves into a contest between the two alternatives: stability-maintaining versus change- and autonomy-promoting (or, as they are often described, pro-U.S. versus anti-U.S.) frames of mobilisation.

Repeatedly, in South Korea, leaders must confront framing of their policies by the media, pundits, and the public as being sufficiently sensitive to alliance relations with the United States. South Korean leaders themselves will also often claim that they are undoing a past administration's set of policies that veered too "pro-" or "anti-" American. But political leaders are not passive onlookers either; they do have a role to play in shaping public opinion and provoking mobilisations. Depending on the context, their entrance into a particular debate – on alliance relations, for example, may have important effects on the intensity and duration of political mobilisation. Leaders cannot completely create or control public opinion, but their rhetorical choices can restrain or amplify existing political frames.

While it may be impossible to avoid these pre-existing rhetorical frames altogether, not all instances of these framing contests lead to contentious alliance-management or cooperation problems. The vulnerability – and manoeuvrability – of leaders depends on the degree of challenge they face from both structural pressures and domestic political competition. In sum, vulnerable leaders dealing with unfavourable policy changes or demands from the United States and increased factional or inter-party competition are likely to be entrapped in pre-existing frames, while leaders operating from positions of strength have the luxury of substituting or side-lining ready-made frames waiting to be activated.

A tale of two governments: frame-takers and frame-makers

The effects of rhetorical framing under differently politically situated leaders can be illustrated through a comparison of two similar, Left-leaning governments in South Korea under Roh Moo-hyun in the mid-2000s and Moon Jae-in in the late-2010s. Both South Korean presidents faced newly elected U.S. presidents (George W. Bush and Donald J. Trump. respectively) who wanted to dramatically alter American policy on North Korea specifically and non-proliferation in general ("axis of evil" and Proliferation Security Initiative, or PSI, under Bush; "fire and fury" and abrogation of JCPOA and other multilateral mechanisms under Trump). Both Roh and Moon were under pressure to satisfy new alliance commitments, such as dispatching combat troops to Iraq as part of the "coalition of the willing," in the mid-2000s, and deploying the U.S.'s global missile defence system known as THAAD, in the late-2010s. While both presidents ultimately complied with U.S. demands, only Roh was plagued by sustained domestic contestation of alliance relations and tensions in relations with the United States until the end of his tenure. In contrast, the Moon administration appears to have largely weathered the THAAD storm, with no serious spillover effects on alliance relations.[16]

What explains these different outcomes in the degree of domestic contestation over alliance cooperation? The external challenges owing to North Korean provocations and U.S. policy changes were arguably comparable in both 2003 and 2017. The key difference was in the intensity of domestic political competition faced by Roh and Moon, which determined the strength of their rule and legitimacy as well – and by extension, their position as frame-takers or frame-makers.

As a relative newcomer to party politics and underdog contender in the 2002 presidential race, Roh Moo-hyun mobilised his political base with a newly enforced vision of foreign policy autonomy, distancing himself not only from the Grand National Party (GNP) conservatives but also more moderate candidates from his own Democratic Party. While his "autonomous defense" policy was initially popular, it also generated intensely polarising debates about the future of South Korea-U.S. alliance cooperation. When Roh agreed to dispatch more combat troops to Iraq, at the request of the United States, his political position was doubly weakened, with increasing attacks from the Left and the Right. Having engaged in the autonomy versus alliance debate himself as a presidential candidate, Roh, as president, could not free himself from the further framing of his policy choices in those terms, even as he tried to use alternative language and adopt more "moderate" positions on alliance ties.[17]

Moon Jae-in was elected president in a special election held in May 2017, following the impeachment of former President Park Geun-hye. As a presidential candidate, he had largely opposed the full installation of THAAD on South Korean soil, but found himself in a bind as the decision to deploy the first artillery in Seongju was made prior to his coming to power. In September 2017, President Moon chose not to reverse that decision and authorised the deployment of additional launchers. He addressed the nation in a televised speech in response to critical public opinion and several protests, involving violent encounters between citizens and the police. Harsh retaliation followed from the Chinese government and its citizens, including cancelling of Chinese tour groups, suspension of diplomatic talks, and boycotts and bans of Korean products and businesses.[18] Despite the resulting economic hardship due to these developments, frustration and anxiety on the part of Korean citizens have not snowballed into pro-alliance or anti-alliance mobilisations on a grand scale.

Key reasons include (a) a weakened conservative opposition due to its own internal divisions and lack of a clear centralised message and (b) the Moon administration's careful avoidance of language that might be construed as "anti-American." In fact, many of Moon's earlier diplomatic achievements were based on a basic framework of close coordination with the United States. Furthermore, Moon, during his presidency, not only allowed the TMD deployment but also announced major weapons purchases from the United States, a move many interpret as his government's attempt to counter and placate Trump administration officials' exorbitant demands for an increase in Seoul's contribution to keeping U.S. troops on the Korean peninsula.

In fact, despite a series of foreign policy and domestic political crises, Moon's party was able to weather the storm by winning the large majority in the most recent parliamentary elections. On April 16, 2020, the reigning Democratic Party and its satellite party, the Citizens Party, together captured 180 seats out of a total 300 in the National Assembly. To put this victory in context, winning three-fifths of all seats gave President Moon and his party the largest majority in more than three decades of South Korean democracy. The opposition Liberty Korea Party and Unity Party won 103 seats. Perhaps especially encouraging for the current government is the fact that 66.2 per cent of eligible voters cast votes during this election, the highest turnout in the past 20 years.[19]

Because President Moon has been manoeuvring from a position of relative strength, especially when compared to previous presidents (even at its lowest, his approval rating was generally in the 40 per cent range), he has been able to largely sidestep or neutralise polarising rhetorical contests surrounding alliance cooperation issues. Even as he faced steady criticism on his domestic and foreign policies, he has yet to see the type of anti-American and pro-American mobilisations and counter-mobilisations that paralysed South Korean politics during the negotiations over dispatching South Korean troops to Iraq in support of the U.S.'s war in the Middle East in 2003–2004. But, it is not difficult to imagine a counterfactual scenario, where such intense alliance-related domestic legitimacy politics could have accelerated, had the Democratic Party suffered electoral defeat, forcing a significantly weakened and vulnerable President Moon to participate in a contest of political frames not of his choosing. That during the general election campaign, President Moon was repeatedly attacked by his conservative rivals for "coddling the nuclear-armed North Korea and undermining the alliance with Washington by taking Seoul too close to Beijing," provides some tell-tale signs.[20]

Current and future sources of alliance politicisation

Discord on North Korea policy

There are at least three outstanding alliance cooperation issues that could have an impact on President Moon's political manoeuvrability, despite his high approval ratings domestically.[21] North Korea policy is perhaps the issue with the greatest stakes and vulnerability, as it has become Moon's signature platform, which has brought him significant international and domestic attention. While talks with North Korea are on hold, Moon is attempting to manage both China and the United States by making nominal contributions to U.S.-led efforts while reassuring Beijing of its non-aggressive aims. Korean officials have sought to highlight the fact that the missiles deployed in Seongju are terminal missiles, as opposed to forward base missiles, and, therefore, targeting only North Korea and not China. Beijing, however, has responded that THAAD is not a military issue but a political one. The Chinese view is that South Korea has joined the U.S.'s policy of encircling China with threatening weapons.

In response, some conservatives in South Korea have vocally pushed for maintaining the intelligence-sharing agreement with Japan (GSOMIA) and strengthening the U.S.-South Korea alliance. In October 2019, Hwang Gyo-an, then head of the conservative Liberty Korea Party, announced his party's policy agenda, which included a call to join the U.S.'s Indo-Pacific Strategy. The Moon government, meanwhile, has maintained a cautious stance. In November 2019, Seoul expressed support for the ASEAN position on the Indo-Pacific, which states that ASEAN countries will focus on economic cooperation without endorsing either Chinese or American policies of security competition or expansion in the region.

The Moon government has also increased its efforts towards its "New Southern Policy" (*Shin nambang jeongchaek*), which seeks to connect the Korean peninsula to Southeast Asia and drawing North Korea into regional economic cooperation projects.[22]

Defence burden-sharing negotiations

Another ongoing alliance-management issue is the difficult negotiations over defence burden-sharing. In his quest to get U.S. allies to pay more for U.S. troops, often voicing his zero tolerance for "free-riders," American President Donald Trump has reportedly demanded that South Korea agree to an unprecedented fivefold increase in its annual contribution to the upkeep of 28,500 U.S. Forces in Korea. This is an additional upcharge on top of the 8 per cent increase in Seoul's portion, already negotiated in the 2019 Special Measures Agreement (SMA). In the past, the South Korean government generally paid between 40 and 50 per cent (over $800 million annually) of the total non-personnel costs of maintaining U.S. troops on the Korean peninsula. South Korean officials have also emphasised that Seoul contributes to the alliance in multiple ways, beyond the SMA. For example, South Korea's defence spending is 2.6 per cent of its gross domestic product (GDP), the largest percentage among all U.S. allies. The South Korean government is also paying $9.7 billion, or about 90 per cent of the total cost of constructing Camp Humphreys, the U.S.'s largest overseas base, and purchased almost $20 billion worth of U.S. military hardware from 2012 to 2016, which accounts for about 80 per cent of South Korea's total defence imports.[23]

It was also common practice to negotiate 5-year agreements to minimise intra-alliance disruption or tensions and to signal strong alliance cohesion to rivals. But, with the last SMA set to expire in February 2019, and with continued U.S. demands for increased financial contribution from South Korea, the two sides agreed to a 1-year deal in which Seoul agreed to pay $927, an increase of $70.3 million from the previous agreement.[24] Although these kinds of pressure tactics from the United States are not new to South Korean diplomats, the White House's "new categories of expenses" present a new set of problems. In addition to traditional labour costs, the Trump administration now reportedly wants Seoul to pay for joint military exercises, the deployment of bombers and other strategic assets, and even costs to support on-base American civilian workers and family members of U.S. troops. The $5 billion price tag is even higher than the 2020 budget of $4.46 billion allocated by the Department of Defence for the costs of maintaining troops in South Korea.[25] Of the total, $2.1 billion is slotted for personnel costs. In a March 14, 2019, editorial, the *Wall Street Journal* argued that

> Mr. Trump's persistent monetary demands send a message that U.S. support for allies is always negotiable and might be withdrawn at a moment's notice. They also suggest that American support is about money, not shared security. Is the U.S. military a mercenary corps?[26]

Fears are increasing in South Korea of a potential withdrawal of U.S. troops.[27] Some conservatives have suggested that South Korea acquiesce to American demands and prepare for eventual troops withdrawal by demanding the ending of U.S.-guided restrictions on long-range missiles (currently set at 800 km) and allowing South Korea to possess nuclear submarines.[28] Others have gone as far to suggest that the South Korean government should present a counterproposal for a withdrawal of 10,000 U.S. troops from South Korea, should American pressures for unreasonable payment hikes continue.[29]

Leading up to the April elections, President Moon saw his approval ratings falter, as U.S. pressure continued, negotiations stalled, and about 4,000 South Korean employees in U.S. bases were furloughed. On April 11, 2020, Trump reportedly rejected a deal that would have had South Korea pay a sum amounting to a 13 per cent increase.[30] South Korean Foreign Minister Kang Kyung-wha has repeatedly stated that the South Korean government is ready to pay more, but within the limits of national capacity. She emphasised that Seoul's position throughout the SMA negotiations, which have stalled for the past 6 months, has been to ask for a reasonable and equitable increase.[31] According to a recent survey by the Korean Institute for National Unification (KINU), 96.5 per cent of respondents supported maintaining or reducing the current level of burden-sharing expenses.[32]

Pressures for troops dispatch in support of allied missions

A third source of intra-alliance tensions, with the potential for considerable domestic political consequences, and related to the burden-sharing issue, is the 2019 U.S. request for South Korean troops in the Middle East. After months of internal discussions, Seoul, on January 21, 2020, announced its plan to send troops to the Strait of Hormuz to safeguard its citizens and vessels passing through the strategic waterway amidst heightened tensions between the United States and Iran. The South Korean Ministry of National Defence announced that it would expand the operational area of its pre-existing anti-piracy mission in the Gulf of Aden, rather than send new troops. The Defence Ministry also emphasised that the 300-strong Cheonghae Naval Unit would work independently of the U.S.-led International Maritime Security Construct (IMSC) based in Bahrain,[33] although two liaison officers will be sent to the coalition to coordinate information-sharing.[34]

This configuration is widely interpreted as a compromise solution by a reluctant Seoul amidst U.S. pressure to join the American-led coalition since the attacks on oil tankers in the summer of 2019 and South Korea's strategic and economic interests in the Middle East.[35] Government data indicates that nearly 70 per cent of South Korea's oil imports pass through the Strait of Hormuz, with 170 South Korean ships sailing through the area about 900 times a year. It is estimated that about 25,000 South Koreans reside in the Middle East, including Iran.[36] While a State Department spokesperson said that the United States "welcomes and appreciates the ROK decision" and added that it "is a demonstration of the strength of the US-ROK alliance and our commitment to cooperate on global security concerns," the Iranian Ministry of Foreign Affairs has called South Korea's decision unacceptable and that Iran considers the presence of foreign forces in the region a threat.[37]

This is the first overseas troops dispatch requested by the United States in support of alliance commitments since the Iraq War, during which President Roh was heavily criticised from all sides and eventually impeached before being reinstated.[38] In addition to sending non-combat and combat troops to Iraq, South Korea has also sent C-130 Hercules transport aircraft and provided medical support for the U.S.-led coalition during the Gulf War, deployed troops to Afghanistan in December 2001 following the terror attacks of 9/11, and participated in peacekeeping operations in southern Lebanon and Kuwait.[39] While both the ruling Democratic Party and the right-wing opposition Liberty Korea Party have acknowledged that the government acted in the Korean national interest, the latter, joined by other smaller conservative parties, such as the Baruenmirae Party, have demanded that the government seek parliamentary approval. In contrast, the progressive left-wing Justice Party and the Peace Party have opposed the decision outright and criticised the government for bypassing proper parliamentary procedures.[40] According to Ahn Gyu-baek, the Chair of the National Defence Committee, the original legislation approving the dispatch to the Middle East included a contingency clause allowing the expansion of the mission's operational scope in the case of contingencies such as kidnapped citizens or ships.[41] The South Korean Defence Ministry has also stated that parliamentary approval for the mission's extension is not required, given past precedents where parliamentary authorisation was not needed to deploy troops to Libya and Yemen in 2011, 2014, and 2015 in order to rescue South Korean citizens.[42]

As the earlier discussion shows, the major issues of the day in South Korean foreign policy debates revolve around alliance-management and cooperation issues and evoke polarising frames established during the Cold War. Even in the post-Cold War period, South Korean leaders walk a tightrope between divided public opinion and managing existing defence commitments and expectations.

Conclusion

Along with fraught reports on climbing tensions in South Korea-U.S. relations, explicit or implicit assumptions are made about the fraying of the alliance and South Korea's turn towards China. In fact, an increasingly common refrain from Asian and American experts is that they expect South Korea and other smaller states to be more deferential to Great Powers (formerly, the United States, and perhaps currently or in the near future, China) – either out of strategic necessity or ingrained cultural attitudes. While it is true that there is not yet a repertoire of mobilisation frames for or against modern-day China, we should not lose sight of the fact that the language used to describe pro-U.S. attitudes, such as *sadae* (Revering the Great), was politically mobilised initially in the late nineteenth century by reformist elites who wanted to reduce dependence on and interference from Qing China. It is also worth noting that the percentage of South Koreans, for example, who had favourable views of China fell from 66 per cent in 2002 to 38 per cent in 2018, according to the Pew Research Center. Perhaps more importantly, South Korea currently ranks second (60 per cent), behind Japan (78 per cent), in terms of highest percentage of respondents with an unfavourable view of China. (In 2002, 31 per cent of South Koreans responded that they had an unfavourable view of China.[43]) These and other public opinion polls show that South Koreans are neither uniquely anti-American nor pro-Chinese. Public opinion is neither consistent nor irreversible.

What this also demonstrates is that deference towards Great Powers is neither automatic nor obvious. We should not assume that acceptance of hierarchical relations is either culturally innate to the region or structurally determined by asymmetrical distributions of power. Hierarchy and political dominance, like any other form of power, has always been politically contested, even in cases we are most likely to uncritically accept as hierarchy-prone, such as the Sino-centric tributary system in pre-modern Asia or the U.S.-led hub-and-spokes system following the Asia-Pacific War.[44] Major structural changes and external pressures (e.g. the U.S.-China trade wars and competition for influence in Asia) are interpreted through domestic political lenses and relations with the so-called Great Powers are likely to be entangled in issues of political legitimacy and national identity. This is why external observers may need to look deeper into domestic and regional contexts that do not necessarily align with global security frames.

For example, even though U.S.-China competition is typically analysed as a "post-Cold War" phenomenon, relations with the United States and China in post-Cold War South Korea are still embroiled in polarising debates about the legacies of the Cold War – in particular, the "national security state" and economic development under authoritarian rule. Political leaders, activists, and the media all discuss the necessity (or not) of "undoing" past policies that have veered too pro-U.S. or anti-U.S. In other words, current polarisation is deeply embedded in the region's Cold War history and the U.S.'s role in it.

One of the reasons why conservatives (or "the establishment") in South Korea are too often easily equated with harbouring pro-U.S. and pro-Japan attitudes is that many conservative political leaders and parties in the past have heavily relied on American and Japanese political and economic support for their success and legitimacy. Some of the most notorious anti-democratic laws such as the Cold War-era National Security Law banned any kind of criticism against the U.S. or the military alliance, equating anti-American or anti-alliance sentiments with pro-communism and treason. To provide some context, conservative voices dominated politics, the news media, business interests, and other elite groups in South Korea for much of the Cold War.

> It was not until 1998 that South Korea elected its first left-leaning president, the Nobel Peace Prize laureate Kim Dae-jung. . . . Older South Koreans have tended to vote conservative, criticizing anything less than unequivocal support for the alliance with Washington as 'pro-North Korean.' But postwar generations of South Koreans have more readily seen a need for diplomacy with North Korea and have voiced skepticism over the power of the chaebol . . . that have dominated the economy.[45]

It is safe to say then that current debates about the role of the United States in South Korean politics are part and parcel of the process of democratisation and reckoning in South Korea, in an effort to contest past legacies of the national security state and developmental authoritarianism.

This particular domestic political context, however, does not necessarily travel outside everyday politics in South Korea. While leaders may find it politically beneficial to piggyback on public sentiments and perceptions of structural inequality, the politicisation of history or alliance-management issues, accompanied by a "use it and leave it" mentality, it may also lead to domestic and international backlash. Policy-makers should consider the unintended spillover effects of domestic political competition. Messages intended primarily for domestic audiences are not always carefully interpreted – or even considered at all – by outside observers. What is critical then is the creative reimagining or reorientation of past political frames, especially ones that have settled into divisive or polarising routines or repertoires. For example, South Korean policy choices may be opened up further by avoiding essentialist anti-U.S. versus pro-U.S. or anti-Japan versus pro-Japan frames in favour of broader debates about positioning itself as a secondary versus middle power, regional versus global power, a system-supporting role or an agent of change.

Notes

1 This question is older than a decade and has generated multiple policy and scholarly discussions in both South Korea and the United States. See, for example, Ho-ki Kim, "Ije Miguk eun eopda? Sungmi eseo banmi kkaji, Han-guk-in ui bokjaphan simri bunseok [Is the United States No More Now? From Adulation to Anti-Americanism, An Analysis of the Complex Sentiments Held by Koreans]," *Shin Dong-a*, January 2003; Yong-Sup Han (ed.), *Jaju nya dongmaeng inya: 21segi Hanguk anbo oegyo ui jinro* [Self-Reliance or Alliance? Korea's Security and Foreign Policy in the 21st Century], Oruem, Seoul, 2004; Eric V. Larson et al., *Ambivalent Allies? A Study of South Korean Attitudes Toward the U.S.*, Rand Corporation, Santa Monica, March 2004.
2 G. John Ikenberry, "Between the Eagle and the Dragon: America, China, and Middle State Strategies in East Asia," *Political Science Quarterly*, 131 (1), 2016, pp. 9–43; Evelyn Goh, "Contesting Hegemonic Order: China in East Asia," *Security Studies*, 28 (3), 2019, pp. 614–644.
3 Darren J. Lim and Zack Cooper, "Reassessing Hedging: The Logic of Alignment in East Asia," *Security Studies*, 24, 2015, pp. 696–727.
4 Seo-Hyun Park, *Sovereignty and Status in East Asian International Relations*, Cambridge University Press, New York, 2017.
5 Stefano Guzzini, "Which Puzzle? An Expected Return of Geopolitical Thought in Europe?" in Stefano Guzzini (ed.), *The Return of Geopolitics in Europe? Social Mechanisms and Foreign Policy Identity Crises*, Cambridge University Press, Cambridge, 2012, p. 15.
6 Jae Ho Chung, "From a Special Relationship to a Normal Partnership? Interpreting the 'Garlic Battle' in Sino-South Korean Relations," *Pacific Affairs*, 76 (4), Winter 2003–2004, pp. 549–568.
7 Barry Buzan and Evelyn Goh, *Rethinking Sino-Japanese Alienation: History Problems and Historical Opportunities*, Oxford University Press, Oxford, 2020, p. 140.
8 Victor D. Cha, *Alignment Despite Antagonism: The United States-Korea-Japan Security Triangle*, Stanford University Press, Stanford, 1999.

9 Katharine H. S. Moon, *Protesting America: Democracy and the U.S.-Korea Alliance*, University of California Press, Berkeley, 2012.
10 Meredith Woo-Cumings, "Introduction: Chalmers Johnson and the Politics of Nationalism and Development," in Meredith Woo-Cumings (ed.), *The Developmental State*, Cornell University Press, Ithaca, 1999. In the same volume, T. J. Pempel, however, suggests that "developmental regimes" might be a more appropriate label, given that these governments often had the backing, either explicit or tacit, of various sectors and interest groups in society. See "The Developmental Regime in a Changing World Economy," in Meredith Woo-Cumings (ed.), *The Developmental State*, Cornell University Press, Ithaca and London, 1999, pp. 137–181.
11 On the role of structural dependence and threat perceptions in shaping alignment behavior, see Victor D. Cha, no. 8; Stephen M. Walt, *The Origins of Alliance*, Cornell University Press, Ithaca, 1990. Audrye Wong argues that the strength/weakness of threat from North Korea serves as an important mediating variable for South Korea's relations with China and the United States. See Audrye Y. Wong, "Comparing Japanese and South Korean Strategies Toward China and the United States: All Politics Is Local," *Asian Survey*, 55 (6), November-December 2015, pp. 1241–1269.
12 Ho-ki Kim, no. 1; Sook-Jong Lee, "Allying with the United States: Changing South Korean Attitudes," *The Korea Journal of Defense Analysis*, 17 (1), 2005, pp. 93–95; Katharine H. S. Moon, "Korean Nationalism, Anti-Americanism and Democratic Consolidation," in Samuel S. Kim (ed.), *Korea's Democratization*, Cambridge University Pres, New York, 2003, pp. 135–158.
13 U.S. Department of State, "U.S.-D.P.R.K. Joint Communique," available at https://1997-2001.state.gov/www/regions/eap/001012_usdprk_jointcom.html (Accessed October 30, 2019).
14 Charles Tilly, *Contentious Performances*, Cambridge University Press, New York, 2008, pp. 14–15; Sidney Tarrow, *The Language of Contention: Revolutions in Words, 1688–2012*, Cambridge University Press, New York, 2013, p. 17.
15 Charles Tilly, no. 14, p. 14.
16 The recent series of political mobilisations in support of or opposition to the current government in South Korea are not directly related to THAAD or alliance relations with the U.S., although here too, we can argue that President Moon's weakened political position (compared to earlier in his tenure) is a crucial factor in explaining his inability to sidestep the pro-Japan vs. anti-Japan framing.
17 For an extended discussion of the domestic politics of alliance cooperation in East Asia, see Seo-Hyun Park, "Rhetorical Entrapment and the Politics of Alliance Cooperation: Explaining Divergent Outcomes in Japan and South Korea during the Iraq War," *International Relations*, 31 (4), 2017, pp. 484–510.
18 Adam Taylor, "South Korea and China Move to Normalize Relations after THAAD Dispute," *The Washington Post*, October 31, 2017; Jin Kai, "Time for China to Rethink South Korea Relations?" *The Diplomat*, August 9, 2016.
19 "Chongseon: ibeon seon-geo gyeol-gwa eseo jumok hal 5gaji [The General Election: 5 Things to Note About These Recent Election Results]," *BBC News Korea*, April 16, 2020. Available at: https://www.bbc.com/korean/news-52306788.
20 Choe Sang-Hun, "In South Korea Vote, Virus Delivers Landslide Win to Governing Party," *The New York Times*, April 15, 2020.
21 Moon's approval rating shot up to 55 per cent in April 2020, an increase of more than 10 percentage points since January. Min Joo Kim and Simon Denyer, "South Korea's Ruling Party Wins Landslide in Elections Dominated by Coronavirus," *The Washington Post*, April 15, 2020.
22 With his state visit to Thailand, Myanmar, and Laos in early September 2019, he became the first South Korean president to visit all ten ASEAN countries during his term as president. This was partially in preparation for the Korea-ASEAN Special

Summit scheduled for November 25–27, 2019. Some had held out hope that North Korean leader Kim Jong Un might attend, and that the strengthening of economic and political ties with ASEAN may aid Moon's vision of the Korean peninsula serving as an economic hub (less reliant on trade with Great Powers) and also to help diversify South Korea's economic options in the midst of the trade wars between the U.S. and China, China's retaliatory measures after the deployment of THAAD, and Japan's economic restrictions due to political tensions over the history problem. The Blue House has announced its plans to increase Korea-ASEAN trade to $200 billion (about the volume of China-ASEAN trade) from $160 billion in 2019. Seoul is also negotiating free trade agreements with Indonesia, Malaysia, and the Philippines. One result of the recent state visit to Myanmar was the creation of a Korea Desk within the Myanmar government for Korean firms. In Thailand, Brand K was introduced as a platform for South Korean small and medium sized businesses to launch their innovations locally. See Hyeok-cheol Kwon, "Jisomia, gunsa anin jeongchi munjeda [GSOMIA, A Political, Rather than a Military, Issue]," *Hangyoreh 21*, November 29, 2019.

23 Emma Chantlett-Avery, "U.S.-South Korea Alliance: Issues for Congress," *Congressional Research Service: In Focus*, June 23, 2020. Available at https://crsreports.congress.gov/product/pdf/IF/IF11388 (Accessed July 6, 2020); Jesse Johnson, "Trump's Push for Seoul to Pay More for U.S. Troops Throws Alliance into Question and Puts Tokyo on Notice," *The Japan Times*, November 3, 2019.

24 Hae Won Jeong, "What Are the Implications of South Korea's Decision to Send a Naval Unit to the Strait of Hormuz?" *The Diplomat*, January 28, 2020.

25 On this point, see "Saseol: Bangwibi bundamgeum 5 bae olliraneun miguk-ui gapjil [Editorial: The U.S.'s Heavy-Handed Power Play of Demanding a Fivefold Increase in Defense Burden]," *Kyunghyang Shinmun*, September 25, 2019.

26 "Editorial: The Wrong Way to Make Allies Pay More," *The Wall Street Journal*, March 14, 2019.

27 Ki-ho Kim, "Bangwibi galdeung euro olhae juhan migun jisang-gun jeongtu budae eopseojil su do [U.S. Ground Combat Troops May Leave This Year Due to Defense Burden Conflict]," *Shin Dong-a*, February 23, 2019.

28 Jeong-uk, Kim, "Anbo jokswae pul-eo haekjam jang-geo-ri misail deung 'goseumdochi gukbang' gatchueoya [Remove Security Constraints and Create 'Porcupine Defense' Stance Equipped with Nuclear Submarines and Long-Range Missiles]," *Seoul Economic Daily*, July 5, 2020; Eo-yeong Ha, "Guk-hoe gukbang wiweonjang, 'mal do an doeneun bang-wi-bi yogu, miguk do algeot [National Assembly Defense Committee Chair Says 'U.S. Probably Knows that Defense Spending Request Does Not Make Sense]," *Hangyoreh 21*, November 22, 2019.

29 Dae-ro Pak, "Mi bangwibi gwadohan yogu e juhan migun 1man myeong gamchuk yeokjeanhaeya [Must Offer Counterproposal to Reduce 10,000 U.S. Troops If the U.S. Makes Excessive Demands for Payment]," *Newsis*, July 1, 2020.

30 Seong-ho Pak, "Teureompeu, bang-wi-bi 13% insang Han-guk je-an geobu [Trump Rejects Korean Proposal of 13% Increase]," *MBC News Today*, April 11, 2020.

31 Su-yun Kang and Ji-hyeon Kim, "Kang Kyung-wha oegyo, 'gongpyeong han bangwibi bundam, 4cha hyeopsang im hal geot ['Will Head to Fourth Round of Negotiations, Asking for Equitable Defense Contribution,' Says Foreign Minister Kang Kyung-wha]," *Joongang ilbo*, June 18, 2020; "Gyochak sangtae Hanmi bangwibi hyeopsang [Stalemate in Korea-U.S. Defense Contribution Negotiations]," *Dong-A Ilbo*, May 7, 2020; Yu-jeong Lee and Da-yeong Kim, "Kang Kyung-wha, 'Buk mi daehwa momenteom itgi wihae noryeok hal geot ['Will Make Effort to Continue Momentum for North Korea-U.S. Talks,' Says Kang Kyung-wha]," *Joongang ilbo*, July 2, 2020.

32 "Tong-il yeon-gu-won tong-il uisik josa 'Guk-min 96.5%, Hanmi bang-wi bundamgeum yuji ddoneun jul-yeo-ya ['96.5% of Citizens Say Maintain or Reduce Spending on U.S.-Korea Defense Burden-Sharing,' According to Attitudes Toward Unification Survey], *Maeil Kyungje Shinmun*, June 25, 2020.

33 As of March 2020, the IMSC has eight members (Albania, Australia, Bahrain, Lithuania, Saudi Arabia, United Arab Emirates, United Kingdom, and the United States) since it was formed in November 2019. United States Central Command, "Lithuania Joins the International Maritime Security Construct," March 26, 2020, available at www.centcom.mil/MEDIA/NEWS-ARTICLES/News-Article-View/Article/2126090/lithuania-joins-the-international-maritime-security-construct/.
34 The Cheonghae unit consists of a 4,400-ton KDX-II destroyer, a Lynx anti-submarine helicopter and three speedboats, according to South Korea's 2019 Defense White Paper. Jeong-jin Lee, "Horeumujeu e sasilsang dokja pabyeong . . . guk-ik e mi-iran gwa gwan-gye ttajyeo jeolchung [De Facto Independent Troops Dispatch to Hormuz . . . Compromise Based on National Interest and Relations with the U.S. and Iran]," *Yonhap News*, January 21, 2020.
35 Ji-weon Roh and Ji-hyun Bae, "'Horeumujeu pabyeong' miguk iran sai jeolchung-an taek-haetta ['Hormuz' Troops Dispatch Was a Compromise Decision Between the U.S. and Iran]," *Hankyoreh*, January 22, 2020.
36 Yonhap News, "US Welcomes S. Korea's Troop Dispatch to Strait of Hormuz," *The Korea Herald*, January 22, 2020.
37 Ibid.; Hae Won Jeong, no. 24.
38 Seo-Hyun Park, no. 17.
39 Hae Won Jeong, no. 24. As Terry notes, "South Korea has contributed troops to every U.S. war since the Korean conflict; it sent more than 300,00 troops to fight in the Vietnam War and at one point had the second-largest foreign troop contingent in Iraq." Sue Mi Terry, "The Unraveling of the U.S.-South Korean Alliance," *Foreign Affairs*, July 3, 2020.
40 Newsis, "'Gyeoljeong jonjung vs 'gyeolsa bandae' . . . yeoya, horeumujeu pabyeong ondocha 'dduryeot' ['Respect Decision' vs. 'Total Opposition' . . . Clear Divide in Political Climate]," *Dong-A Ilbo*, January 21, 2020.
41 Ibid.
42 Hae Won Jeong, no. 24.
43 Pew Research Center, "Global Attitudes & Trends," available at www.pewresearch.org/global/database/indicator/24/ (Accessed October 30, 2019). In addition, a joint survey by EAI-ARI in October 2011 showed that over 59 per cent of South Koreans believe that China holds a negative attitude towards Korean unification. See Suk-hee Han, "South Korea Seeks to Balance Relations with China and the United States," *Council on Foreign Relations*, November 9, 2012.
44 Seo-Hyun Park, no. 4, pp. 10–11.
45 Choe Sang-Hun, no. 20.

Index

5G club 110
5G dilemma 37, 55, 109–10, 170, 185
5G technology 170
5G telecommunications 37
5G wireless networks 110
1984 Summer Olympics 194; Soviet decision to boycott 194
1988 Seoul Games 194
1997–1998 Asian Financial Crisis 134
2003 SARS epidemic 70
2005 WHO International Health Regulations 69
2008 global financial crisis 52
2015 Paris Climate Change conference 21
2019 Shangri-La Dialogue 2
2020 East Asia Summit 33

Aatmanirbhar Bharat (Self-reliant India) 105, 110, 113
Abe, Shinzo, Prime Minister 149–50; visit to Manila 149
abuse 17; governmental 17
accommodation 42
Acharya, Amitav 18
Acme-McCrary Corporation 85
Acquisition and Cross-Servicing Agreement (ACSA) 93–4, 109
Act East Forum 113
activism 42; sustained 42
adventurism 115
affairs 1, 6–8, 10, 17, 19, 21, 25, 44, 47, 51, 163, 178; African 44; domestic 1; foreign 163; internal 19, 25; regional 10
Afghanistan 21, 204; conflict in 21
Africa 32–3, 37, 44, 110, 113, 161, 188
aggression 39, 70; coastguard 70; naval 70; outright 39
agri-businesses 71
Ahn Gyu-baek 204

aid 8, 23, 82, 88–90, 92, 94–5, 114, 147, 186, 195–6; foreign 82, 88–9, 95; MCC-type grant 89
aircraft 22–3, 38, 147–8, 150, 152, 204; carriers 22, 38; fighter 23; manned 22; unmanned 22
Alagappa, Muthiah 18
Alibaba 169–70
alignment(s) 6, 8–10, 20, 24, 35, 43, 83, 84, 96, 103, 105, 112–3, 115, 117, 165, 189, 195, 197–8; formal 8; limited 9; structures 117
alliance-building 33
alliance-management 12, 194, 199, 202, 204, 206; issues 12, 194, 206
alliance(s) 8–9, 12, 20–1, 33, 35, 39, 43, 47–9, 54, 56–8, 67, 96, 104–6, 110–14, 116–17, 148–9, 152–3, 161, 164, 189, 193–4, 196–206; Atlantic 54; bilateral 21; commitments 49, 199, 204; contestation 194, 198; embryonic 39; formal 8, 35; mechanisms 43; military 8; partners 20, 48; quadrilateral 33; relations 9, 193–4, 197–9; South Korea and U.S. 193, 196–7, 200; strategic 43; structure 20, 106, 111, 116; tensions 194, 196, 203; ROK and US 47, 203
ally(ies) 1, 24, 36, 49, 53, 82, 114–16, 162, 167, 169, 193, 196, 202; Asian 24; formal 193; US 1
Anti-alliance mobilisations 200
Anti-Americanism 196–7
Anti-American mobilisations 193, 201
Anti-China exercises 137
Anti-China hue 112
Anti-China mood 1
Anti-China rhetoric 12, 103–5, 111, 161, 163–4
Anti-China sentiments 194

Index

Anti-Chinese containment strategy 5
Anti-Chinese riots 181
anti-communism 196
anti-fascist coalition 179
Anti-Fascist People's Freedom League (AFPFL) 179
anti-globalisation sentiment 28
anti-haze regime 69
anti-Japanese mobilisations 193
anti-Japanese sentiments 194
anti-piracy mission 203
anti-ship ballistic missiles 22
anti-ship cruise missiles 22
anti-US-rhetoric 1
Anwar Ibrahim 164
appeasement policy 12, 116, 142–3, 146–7, 152–3
Arakan Army (AA) 187
Arbitral Tribunal of the UNCLOS 144
armed: conflict 19, 43, 182, 187; control agreements 41; mistrust 39
Armed Forces of the Philippines (AFP) 143, 147–50; counter-terrorism operations 148; modernisation programme 148
artificial intelligence (AI) 37, 165, 170
artificial islands 39, 147
ASEAN and China 23, 137–8, 151–3, 168; CoC 151, 153; maritime exercises 137–8; trade 168
ASEAN Centrality 107, 130–1, 138
ASEAN-China Dialogue 152
ASEAN Defence Ministers Plus [ADMM+] 18, 20, 129
ASEAN Outlook on the Indo-Pacific 138
ASEAN Plus One 137
ASEAN Plus Three (APT) 129
ASEAN Regional Forum (ARF) 5, 18, 20, 129, 136
ASEAN-US Maritime Exercises 138
Asia 1–3, 5–12, 17–24, 27–8, 32–8, 41–2, 44, 47, 49–50, 52–4, 56–7, 59, 65–6, 68–70, 72–3, 76, 82–4, 87, 90–1, 95, 104, 110, 112–14, 116–17, 127–39, 144–6, 150, 152, 160–1, 166–7, 169, 171, 177–80, 186, 188–90, 195, 198, 202, 205; contemporary 134; geopolitical, conditions 132 (dominance in 72); global rise 82; great power, competition in 132 (conditions 11; politics 9); hedging in 9; international, order 53
(politics 8); middle powers in 47, 50, 53 (strategies in 56); multilateral cooperation in 11; post-Cold War 132; power structures in 133; regional security in 57, 59; resident power in 5; security order 11; shifting great power conditions 132; state transformation in 65; strategic dynamics of 32; China and US rivalry on 2 (impact of 2); US, dominance in 1 (military presence in 1; prowess in 9)
Asian: powers 36, 83, 138; security order 17, 71; small power 81; statecraft 44; strategic environment 24; values 165
"Asian Century", 103
Asian Development Bank 186
Asian Infrastructure Development Bank 103
Asian Investment and Infrastructure Bank (AIIB) 3, 21, 23, 92, 103, 135–6, 186
Asian partners and US 134
Asian security 17, 55, 58, 65–6, 68, 71–2, 76, 193; impact on 66; implications for 68, 72 (Belt and Road Initiative 72; transnational governance 68)
Asian states 6, 8–10, 18, 23, 50, 65, 68, 72, 127–30, 132–6, 138–9, 160, 189
Asia-Pacific Center for Security Studies, Honolulu 186
Asia-Pacific Economic Cooperation (APEC) 20
Asia Pacific Group 69
Asia-Pacific order 21
Asia-Pacific Region 2–3, 10, 17, 19, 23, 27, 47; challenges for 2; economies 17; erosion of confidence in 17; future of 47; notion of 33; peace in 17; post-Cold War 28; regional hegemony in 2; regionalism 20; regional order in 22, 50; socio-economic progress in 17; stability of 2; trade and services 134
Asia Pacific Strategy for Emerging Diseases 69
Asia-Pacific War 205
Asia security summit, Singapore 36
aspirations 2, 112, 171, 186
assertiveness 3, 33, 40, 65; Chinese 40, 65; foreign policy 3; pan-regional 33
assistance 11, 74, 76, 81, 88–92, 94–5, 110, 145, 149–50, 164, 170, 180, 182, 186; Chinese 76, 90; development 11, 81, 88–9, 91, 94–5; economic 145, 182; humanitarian 89, **106**; international 92; military 74, 180; technical 186
Associated Press 147
Association of Southeast Asian Nations (ASEAN) 5, 11–12, 18–19, 23, 27–8, 36, 52, 65, 69, **106–7**, 110, 127–39, 144–5, 148, 151–3, 164–5, 168, 177–8,

Index   213

184–6, 189, 201; consensus decision-making practices 130; developmental divide in 136; non-interference norms 130; positionality of 131; practice of consensus 131; role for 28, 127; soft-balancing approach 151; Treaty of Amity and Cooperation 19
atlantic alliance 54
Aung San Suu Kyi 12, 179, 182, 184
Australia 4–5, 33–40, 42–3, 49–52, 92–3, 104–5, **106–9**, 110–13, 115–17, 131, 138, 169, 177; 2017 foreign policy white paper 42; alliance-building 33
Australia and China 104; tariffs 104; ties 104
Australia and India 33, 39, 109, 112, 116; bilateral Strategic Partnership 109; defence cooperation 116; Mutual Logistics Support Agreement (MLSA) 109, 112
Australia and Japan 49, 105, 111–13
Australia and US 112, 115
Australia-India Comprehensive Economic Cooperation Agreement (CECA) 113
Australia-India-Indonesia 39
Australia-Japan-India Trilateral Meeting (AJI) 111–13
Australia's Department of Foreign Affairs & Trade (DFAT) **106–8**
authoritarianism 1, 206
autonomy 7, 9–10, 24, 48, 53–6, 58, 128–31, 133, 138, 160, 180, 197–8, 200; European 54; industrial 54; military 54; national 128–30, 133, 138; policy-making 24; political 54; strategic 48, 53–6, 58, 160 (European 48, 54, 58)
axis of evil 199
Azhar, Masood 112

Bago Yoma 181
balancing 9, 12, 52–3, 68, 76, 84, 96, 103, 112, 127, 142–3, 147, 149, 151–2, 160; institutional 52–3; power 68; soft 12, 142–3, 149, 152
Balikatan 148
balkanisation 132
ballistic missiles 22, 197
Bandung Conference 8, 180
band-wagoning 6, 9, 127, 160
Bangladesh-China-India-Myanmar Economic Corridor 178
bankruptcy 73
bargain 18–19, 195–6; political 196; security 196; social 196; state and society 19; state-society 18

Barisan Nasional 162
Baruenmirae Party 204
Baru, Sanjay 104
Battle of the Titans 12
Bay of Bengal 39, 111, 177, 184, 187
BCP 179, 181, 183
BDN and India 113
Beijing Xiangshan Forum 136
belligerence 105, 116
Belt and Road Initiative (BRI) 3–5, 11–12, 23, 33–4, 36, 38, 40, 42, 49, 55, 58, 66, 72–6, 82–3, 90–2, 105, 110, 113–14, 135–6, 144–6, 160–3, 166–8, 171, 178–9, 183–6; challenges and pitfalls of 4; investment 73, 92; Malaysia's policies towards 12, 162; mplications for Asian security 72; obstacles and challenges 4; strategic impacts of 38; transformative effects 3
Belt and Road initiative for Win-Winism 168
Benelux 51
Bersatu 164
Bhutan and China border disputes 105
Biden, Joe, US President 24, 27, 82, 103–4, 110–11; "renew" alliances 104
big power politics 164, 166
bilateral: agreements 5; alliances 20–1; cooperation 11, 116, 145; defence cooperation 109, 116 (constructive 142); dialogues 142; diplomacy 39; economic ties 20; FTA 85, 87; military exercises 93; relations 2, 28, 49, 138, 165, 182, 185, 193, 197; security cooperation 109; settings 130; ties 3, 23; trade 4, 85, 87, 162, 188 (agreements 4; deficit 87)
bilateralism 20
Bilateral Strategic Partnership 109
bipartisan consensus 26, 104
bipolarity 10, 117
Bisley 53
Blinken, Anthony, US Secretary of State 104, **109**
Blue Dot Network (BDN) 105, 113–4
Blue Economy 116
border/boundaries 9, 32–3, 35, 40, 42–4, 67, 92, 110; China's 71; clash 41; collapsed 43; disputes 105, 195; Europe-Asia 33; imagined 33; Indo-Pacific's 44; international 40; mental 35; social 67; territorial 67; Thai-Laotian 70
Brazil 110
Bretton Woods settlement 67
Brexit 54
Britain and Russia 37

214 Index

British Broadcasting Corporation (BBC) 6; global country poll 6
British Commonwealth 180
Britten-Norman Islanders 150
Burma 8, 179–81, 187; *see also* Myanmar
Burma Communist Party (BCP) **181**
Burma Independence Army 179
Bush, George W., US president 199
Business environment 87
Business regulations, digitisation of 87

C-130 Hercules transport aircraft 204
Cambodia 8, 19, 70, 134–5, 144, 178, 188; human rights sanctions on 135; Vietnamese withdrawal of troops from 19
Camp Humphreys 202
Canada 50–2, 110
Canberra 110–11, 115
capabilities 2, 6, 8, 51, 54, 56–7, 92–3, 95, 114; aerial assault 114; bridging 56; diplomatic 51; economic 51; material 56; military 2, 51; technological 2
capability 39, 48, 50, 56–7, 59, 81–2, 92, 148, 169; military 50, 81–2, 92; networking 56
capacity 9, 23, 26, 39, 51, 54–8, 69–71, 73, 75, 81, 92–6, 104, 116, 148, 150, 203; building 54, 92, 95, 116, 150; coastguard 70; entrepreneurial 53, 58; military 56; national security 81, 92; reasonable 57; small powers 96; surplus 73, 75; technical 53, 58
capital 67, 73, 75, 87, 89, 162, 179, 185, 187; accumulation 73
capitalism 66
capitalist crises 67
capitulation 10, 32, 40
Caporaso 52
Carr, Andrew 57
Cayetano, Alan Peter, Philippine Foreign Affairs Secretary 147
Centers for Disease Control and Prevention (CDC) 69
Central Asia 3, 146, 161, 167
Central Intelligence Agency (CIA) 180
Chico River Pump Irrigation Project 147
China, People's Republic of (PRC) 1–13, 18–29, 32–44, 47–50, 52–9, 65–6, 68–75, 81–5, 87–94, 103–5, 109–17, 128, 130–9, 142–53, 159–71, 177–90, 193–5, 197, 201, 204–5; adversaries 41; 'aggressive' behaviour 5, 17; ambitions 25; ascent 32; assertive 9; audacious encroachments 143; behaviour in South China Sea 147; bullying and unlawful behaviour 116; capacity and influence of 104; civil war in 180; claims, East China Sea 3, 23 (maritime 142; over South China Sea 3; South China Sea 23; sweeping, expansive, and illegal 10, 32, 142); coercive and revisionist behaviour 109–10, 112; debt trap diplomacy 91; defence budget 22, 34; dependency on 27, 104, 113; development, financing 74 (first agenda 19); domestic affairs 1; domestic economic reform 26; dominance 2; economic growth 104; economic prowess 2; economy 20; ethnic minorities issues 168; expansionism 115; FDI to Sri Lanka 88; foreign exchange reserve 104; foreign policy 1, 3, 21 (ambitions 21; assertive 1, 3; relations 7); geopolitical ambitions 5; India's policy 103, 105; influence 82, 150 (diplomatic 150; economic 82; political 82, 150); infrastructural initiative 110; infrastructure projects in Sri Lanka 87; interests 33, 38, 49; Japanese companies in 104; Japan's war against 179; liberalization in 1; maritime expansion 147 (in South China Sea 147); material power 19, 20; militarization of South China Sea 143; military, acquisitions 24 (adventurism 115; build-up 114); national restoration of 3; naval power in the South China Sea 143; naval reach 74; objectives 163 (economic 163; foreign 163; political 163); oil supply 12; over-dependence on 27; overseas assets 75; policies 1, 20, 37, 110 (confrontational 112; expansive 37; revisionist 110; Reform and Opening' 19–21, 27); politico-economic model 25; power 82 (economic 82; military 82); proximate waters 38; reassurance strategy 20; rise of 2–3, 5, 21, 26, 47, 49, 81, 132, 159; rising 10, 34, 82, 115, 128, 161–2, 171; sanctions on South Korea 195; sovereignty claim over 3, 23; US' policies 103–4; vision of regional order 19; "Westphalian" images of 69
China and India 41, 105, 117; economic and security approach 105; Galwan clash 105; relations 41; ties 117

Index   215

China and Japan 23, 41, 105, 131–2, 195; competitive dyads 132; relations 23, 41, 105; territorial conflicts 21
China and Malaysia 12, 115, 161–3, 165–6, 169, 171; bilateral, relations 165 (trade 162); conflicts 165; diplomacy 163; engagement 12, 161; investment 162; relations 12; ties 166; trade 165
China and North Korea relations 194
China and Philippines 142, 144–9, 153; bilateral cooperation 145; economic cooperation 145; economic partnership 149; infrastructure cooperation 146; maritime dispute 144; Memorandum of Understanding (MOU) on the BRI 146; rapprochement 148–50; relations 142, 144, 153 (diplomatic 153; economic 153); tension in 142
China and Southeast Asia 145, 161, 171; interactions 171; relations 161
China and South Korea 193–5; bilateral relations 193; diplomatic relations 195; economic tensions 195; garlic battle 195; imports 195; relations 194–5; trade 194; trading 194
China and Soviet Union operative dyads 132
China and Sri Lanka 11, 81, 87–8, 93; diplomatic support 92; engagement 11; FDI 87–8; foreign aid 88; foreign relations 81, 94; FTA 88; imports 87; infrastructure projects 87; security, cooperation **86** (relations 81, 93); ties **86**; trade deficit 87
China and US 1–3, 6, 9–13, 17–21, 24–8, 34, 36–7, 40–3, 47–50, 53–6, 58, 66, 81–2, 84, 88, 94, 103–4, 117, 128, 130, 132–9, 150, 159, 161–2, 166, 169–70, 177–9, 185, 189, 205; competition 47–50, 53–6, 58, 134, 136, 138–9, 189 (institutional 136; intensification of 48–9; maritime 134); competitive dyads 132; conflict 10, 23, 47, 50; confrontations 159; contentious issues 20; crises 41; decoupling 81; engagement 1; exports 20; industrial interdependence 37; operative dyads 132; relations 1–2, 18, 20, 22, 26, 48, 134 (bilateral 2, 49; competitive 48; cooperative 48; deterioration in 17, 24, 26; economic 20, 134; tensions in 28; uncertain 2); rivalry(ies) 1–3, 6, 9–10, 12, 24, 26, 28, 50, 55, 66, 81,
104, 128, 159, 161, 170, 177–8, 189, 193 (conceptual aspects of 10–11; impact of 24; negative impact of 178; strategic 10); tensions 18, 20–1, 24, 26–8, 43, 82, 104, 133–4 (intensification of 127; maritime 134); ties 20–1, 24, 103 (economic 20, 24; normalisation of 20–1; political 24); trade, deficit 20 (dispute 12, 47; tensions 169; war 12, 134, 137, 169, 205)
China-ASEAN foreign ministers' meeting 151
China card 163
China Communications Construction Company (CCCC) 166
China Connect policy 103
China Harbour Engineering Company (CHEC) 91
China-Indochina Economic Corridor 178
China Merchant Ports (CMP) 75
China Myanmar Economic Corridor (CMEC) 12, 178, 183–5
China's Export-Import Bank 75
Chinese: aggressive behaviour 12, 153 (in the South China Sea 12, 153); aspirations 112; assertiveness in South China Sea 65; claims, expansive 144 (on South China Sea 103); commercial loans to Sri Lanka 92; debt 90, 92, 146; domestic technical standards 4; dominance 9, 35; economic, assistance 145 (largesse 24); economy 34, 104, 134, 136, 165; energy needs 166; grand strategy 72; influence 12, 42, 83, 149, 193; initiatives 136–7 (regional 137); interests 44, 74; investments 4, 144, 146–7, 164 (public-sector 146–7); loans 75, 92, 146; military posturing 115; outbound investment 73; policy 34; security 70; socialism 3; state apparatuses 11; strategy 38; strength 40; system 37
Chinese Coast Guard 115, 147
Chinese Communist Party (CCP) 3, 40, 179, 190; 19th Party Congress 25
Chinese diaspora 179, 188
Chinese military 38, 93, 115; overseas base 38
Chinese patrol ships, incursion attempts 105
Ciorciari, John D. 8
citizenship 51; global 51; international 51
civil conflict 81, 83–4, 87, 89, 92; end of 83

216 *Index*

civilisation(s) 40, 165, 188; clash of 40
civil society 43, 182, 188, 190
civil war 180, 182–4
climate change 21, 39, 41, 47, 49–50, 55, 58, 85, 92; policy 55
coalition 8, 33, 35, 39, 52–3, 56–8, 67, 69, 83, 89–91, 103, 111, 117, 129, 160, 162, 164, 179, 189, 197, 199, 203–4; anti-fascist 179; competing 52; diplomacy for 35; flexible 39; Indo-Pacific 35, 111; national 179; of resistance 33; pre-electoral 162; security 117; three-sided 39
coalition-building 8, 53
coastguard 23, 70; capacity 70
Code of Conduct (CoC) of Parties 23, 142, 151–3; negotiations 151–2
coercion 36, 38, 40–1, 43–4, 115; Chinese 38; economic 43
coexistence 2, 20, 40–1
coherence 67–8
cohesion 22, 51, 58, 197, 202; internal 22
Cold War 2, 8–13, 18, 21, 28, 40–2, 48, 65, 68, 103, 116, 132–8, 177–8, 180, 186, 188–9, 194–8, 204–5; analogies 134; divisive dynamics of 138; second 11; strategic overlays 132; structure of international relations 68
Colombo Air Symposium 93
Colombo Port 83, 91
colonialism 38, 65, 167; new 38, 167
Commissions for Discipline Inspection 70
commitment(s) 18, 20, 25, 48–9, 84, 116, 129, 137, 148–9, 151, 193, 195, 203; alliance 49; national autonomy 129; normative 18, 129
commonwealth 96, 180
communication(s) 19, 23, 37, 41, 90, 142, 147, 167; channels 41; hot lines 23; networks 41
Communications Compatibility and Security Agreement (COMCASA) 109
Communist Party 3, 37–8, 40, 179
communist: rebellion 180
Community of Common Destiny 178
competition 1–2, 8–10, 21, 28, 32–3, 37–8, 40–1, 47–50, 53–6, 58, 65, 81, 88, 127, 132–9, 169, 177–8, 185–6, 188–9, 195–6, 198–9, 201, 205–6; China and US 47–50, 53–6, 58, 134, 136, 138–9, 189 (intensification of 48–9; maritime 134); comprehensive 37; geo-economic 38; geopolitical 54, 81, 136; great power 1, 8, 65, 127, 132–3, 138; ideological 196; Indo-Pacific power 40; institutional 136 (effects of 135); major powers 9, 127, 132–5, 137–8; political 199, 206; strategic 32, 40; Soviet Union and United States 48
competitive advantage 85
competitiveness 19, 67–8
Comprehensive and Progressive Agreement for Trans-Pacific Partnership (CPTPP) 28
Comprehensive Strategic Partnership (CSP) 109, 111
concealment 70
Conference on Interaction and Confidence-Building Measures in Asia (CICA) 136
confidence 6, 17–18, 39, 133, 137, 144, 151; erosion of 17
confidence-building 39, 151; measures 39
conflict(s) 1, 3, 8, 10–12, 19, 21, 23, 32, 38–41, 43, 47–8, 50–1, 55–6, 59, 66, 68, 81–5, 87–9, 92, 104–5, 131, 133–5, 151–2, 164–5, 180, 182–8; armed 19, 43, 182, 187; China and Malaysia 165; China and US 23, 47, 50; civil 81, 83–4, 87, 89, 92; ethnic 184; great power 1, 48; limited 41; major power 10; management 51, 56, 151; multiple 3, 104; nationalist 131; of interest 56; open 1; peaceful resolution of 8; resolution 41, 51; risks of 38–9, 41; socio-political 66; stabilisers 50; territorial 21
confrontation(s) 40–1, 44, 152, 159, 165, 169; China and US 159; risks of 41
Congo 85, 180
connectedness 18, 41, 56; economic 41
connectivity 5, 34, 37–8, 43, 44, 82, 88, **106**, 111, 113, 135, 144, 165, 184, 186–8; air 88; economic 44; infrastructure 5, 82, 135; interests 187; maritime 34; multifarious 188; overland 38; race of 37; self-centred 186
consolidation 18, 21–2, 197; state 22
constructivism 52, 161–2
Container Security Initiative 70
containment 5, 42, 88, 180, 185; strategy 5
contestation 40, 43, 50, 52–3, 132, 178, 194, 198–9; alliance 194, 198; great power 50; selective 132; sublimated form of 53
contested multilateralism 2.0 52
contested waters 142
contingency planning 42

Index   217

contract 19, 74, 179
Cook, Malcolm 189
Cooper, Andrew 50, 129, 193; four approaches 50–1
cooperation 8, 10–11, 21, 28, 33, 37, 39–41, 47, 51, 54–9, 65, 68, 72, 74, 82, 92–5, 105, **107**, 109, 113, 115–16, 130, 133, 135–7, 142–3, 145–6, 148–50, 152, 165, 171, 180, 186, 196–202, 204; agreements 93, 94; bilateral 11, 116, 145 (tracks of 11); economic 55; interstate 65; maritime **106**; multilateral 8, 11, 47, 58, 105; Philippine-US 148; rules-based 59; security 11, 82, **86**, 92, 94–5, 115–16, 137, 149–50; Sri Lanka and US 93
Cooperation Afloat Readiness and Training Exercise (CARAT) 93
Cooperative Mechanism in the Straits of Malacca and Singapore 70
Cormoront Strike 93
corruption 4, 74, 113, 184
counter-mobilisations 201
counter-terrorism 94, **106–7**, 148–9; operations 148; training 148
countries/nations/states: apparatuses 11, 66–7, 70; Asian 3–4, 8, 34, 87, 144–5, 178, 193; assets 67; behaviour 66; billiard-ball 72; capacities of 53, 58; conception of 66; consolidation 18, 21–2; developed 51; developmental 19; diverse 32; engagements 127; European 55, 58; foreign policy behaviour of 8; fragile 39; fragmentation 68; island 36–7, 40, 114; lightweight 34; like-minded 8, 49, 52, 55–8, 106, 109; littoral 70, 92; major 20–2; middle-income 89; middle power 48; middle-sized 51; national 67; neighbouring 20, 104; non-regional 145; non-Western 171; passive 34; pivotal 38; power 66; powerful 33, 69; reform 67; regional 10, 17, 20, 22–3, 26, 28, 135; rich and poor 50; secondary 7–8; small 7–8, 169; smaller 7–9, 129–30, 138, 204; Southeast Asian 9, 23, 36, 127–30, 132–6, 138–9, 160, 189; sovereignty 25; strategies 128–9, 132; strong 7; substantial 34; theory 66–7; trading 19, 22, 104 (European 48, 54, 58); transformation 65–7, 69, 70, 72, 75–6; transformation of 11; weaker 7, 25; Weberian-Westphalian 67–8; Western 83

COVID-19, 1, 22, 24–5, 27, 33–4, 38, 47, 70, 81–2, 88, 95, 103–4, **108**, 110, 114, 159, 177, 189; containment measures 88; economic shock of 34; impact of 22; investigation into the origins of 104; outbreak of 1, 47, 70
credibility 24–5, 27, 49; US 27, 49
crime 41, 69, 82, 95; transnational 41, 69
crisis-management 1, 41
cronyism 184
cruise missiles 22
Cuban missile crisis 41
Cultural Revolution 159, 180
currency manipulator 103
customs 69, 84
cyber-attacks 41
cyber intrusions 41
cyber security 49, 55, 58, **107**, 164; threats 49
cyber-theft 26

D10 club 110
debt 4, 73–6, 90–2, 94–5, 146, 184; Chinese 90, 92, 146; crisis 74–5; excessive 73; non-Chinese 75; sovereign 74; sustainability 76, 92; transparency 92
debt trap 4, 74–5, 90, 92, 94, 184; Chinese 90, 92; diplomacy 74, 91
decentralisation 67–8, 70–1
decision-making 7, 20, 130; consensus 20, 130
Declaration on a Code of Conduct (DoC) of Parties in the South China Sea 151
decolonisation 67
decouple/decoupling 5, 19, 26–7, 37, 81, 95, 134–5; disruptive 37; US and China 81
defence 2, 5, 22–3, 25, 28, 34–5, 37–8, 43, 54, 84, 90, 92–4, 105, 109, 112, 114–16, 129, 137–8, 143, 148–50, 152, 197, 199, 202, 204; agreements 90, 93; budget 22, 34; budgets 35; capacity 23, 94; cooperation agreements 93; exchanges 23; expenditure 34; pact 28; policies 105; policy 5, 54; shared 25; spending 34, 202; territorial 149
defence burden-sharing negotiations 202
defence exercises 109
Defence Seminar 93
defence technology transfer pacts 109
Delfin, Lorenza, Philippines Defence Minister 2, 116

218 *Index*

democracy 33, 35, 38, 43, 110, 180, 182, 184–6, 188, 196, 200; 'D-10' of 43; electoral 182; federalist 184; plural 184; quadrilateral alliance of 33; South Korean 200
democratic countries, foreign policy of 48
democratic order 48, 58; global 48; world order 106
Democratic Party 200–1, 204
democratisation 56, 196, 206
Deng Xiaoping, Chinese Priemer 19, 104, 194; policy of economic opening 194; reform process 104
Department of Foreign Affairs (DFA) 143
Department of National Defence (DND), Philippines 143
deprivation and resentment 71
destabilisation 17
destroyer(s) 22–3, 38
deterrence 24, 28, 42, 72; US's 24
developing countries 2, 25, 68
development: agencies 76; assistance 11, 81, **86**, 88, 91, 95; economic 3, 12, 18, 74, 89, 95, 135, 167, 171, 183, 186, 196, 205; domestic 169; financing 74, 83; infrastructure 5, 90, 144–5; institutional 17; integrated model 19; interests 25; negative 17, 28; networked production 21; networked trading 21; projects 68, 90, 196; service-sector-led 83; Southeast Asian 135; strategies 96, 145; strategy 75; sustainable **107**; technological 47; technologies 26; uneven 67
development assistance 88–9, 94; effectiveness of 81; great powers and Sri Lanka 81
development cooperation 33, 51, 56–7; international 56, 57; Dharma-Guardian exercise 109
dictatorship 180, 182
Diego Garcia 38
digital economy 164
Digital India 113
digital technologies 40
dignity 10
dilemmas 10, 12, 32, 159, 162, 169, 171; international 10, 32; implications of 12, 162
diplomacy 23–4, 27, 32–3, 35, 37–9, 42–4, 47–8, 51, 53, 56, 74–5, 84, 91, 104–5, 114, 135, 137, 143, 146, 159–61, 163, 166, 168, 171, 205; bilateral 39; changing nature of 105; China and Malaysia 163; Chinese 33; coercive 23; creative 48; debt-trap 74, 75, 91; for coalitions 35; middle power 53, 56; multilateral 39; niche 56; pandemic 84; regional 27; vaccine 38; wolf-warrior 104
diplomatic: achievements 200; activity 36; arrangements 40; balance 55; ballast 39; capabilities 51; domino effect 36; growth 116; impasse 41; institutions 38, 41; outcomes 53; priorities 35 (middle power 54); process 23, 115; reassurance strategy 22; relations 153, 159, 185, 195; strategies 19, 54, 58; summits 41; support 92; talks 200; ties 142
disaster(s) 19, 39, 41, 89, 111, 149, 164; natural 41; relief 39, 111, 149; unanticipated 19
disengagement 9, 161
dispute(s) 12, 19, 23, 25, 29, 41, 47, 50–1, 81, 105, 115, 136, 142, 144–8, 150–3, 164, 169–70, 188, 195; border 105, 195; freedom of expression 41; internal 12, 188; international 51; resolution of 115, 151; territorial 147, 164; trade 12, 47
diversity 9, 42, 131
divide and rule 132
Djibouti 38
Doi Moi 19
Doklam stand-off 103
domestic: affairs 1; agendas 166; development agenda 169; economic reform 26; ideational factors 7; insecurity 128; instabilities 2; institutions 68; legitimacy politics 201; liberalization 1; market 83, 87; policies 105; policing agency 70; political, competition 199, 206 (consequences 203; constraints 12, 193–4, 198; crises 200; economy 161, 166, 168; mobilisations 193; system 49; will 50); politics 3, 7, 9, 66–7, 83, 90, 160, 196; priorities 163, 165; relations 18; struggles 66; technical standards 4
domestic/international divide 69
Dominguez, Carlos, Finance Secretary 1–2, 3, 9, 29, 35, 72, 81, 103, 146, 198, 205; Chinese 9, 35; economic 81; military 81; US 72, 103; world 72
drug(s) 71, 92
duality(ies) 44
Duterte, Rodrigo, President of Philippine 12, 142–50, 152–3; confrontational policy on China 144; economic strategy

Index   219

145; policy, of appeasement 143 (on China 143); visit to, China 142, 145 (Japan 149)

East Asia 3, 12, 18–19, 33, 41–2, 56, 66, 73, 82, 117, 129–30, 135, 136, 152, 177, 180, 198; flashpoints in 41; inter-state tension in 19; middle powers in 135; post-colonial 19
East Asia Summit (EAS) 5, 18, 33, **106**, 129, 136; 2020 Summit 33
East China Sea (ECS) 3, 21, 23, 41, 105, 109, 114–5; China's claims over 3; sovereignty claims over 23
East Coast 12, 162, 166
East Coast Rail Link (ECRL) 12, 162, 166–9, 171
East-West maritime trade route 82
East-West trade and industrial corridors 82
Ebola crisis of 2014, 21
economic: activity 36; advancement 22; assistance 145, 182; benefits 89, 110, 112, 117, 160; capabilities 51; coercion 43; connectedness 41; connectivity 44; contraction 134; cooperation 55; development 3, 12, 18, 74, 89, 95, 135, 167, 171, 183, 186, 196, 205; differences 134; disparities 159; dominance 81; engagement 103, 112; exchange 17, 27; freedom 89; globalisation 27; goals 163; growth 17–18, 34, 57, 70, 72, 89, 104, 114, 135, 145, 166, 169, 198; inequality 17; influence 82; integration 73; interests and agendas 58, 75, 164, 170–1, 203; issues 68; largesse 24; liberalisation 83; outcomes 21; partnership 27, 149; policies 4–5, 83, 105; practices 10; prosperity 21; recovery 38; reform 26; regionalisation 27; relations 27, 116, 189; resources 162; risk 74; sabotage 41; shock 34, 95; statecraft 75; strategy 95, 145; strength 50; threats 104; ties 9, 20, 24, 32, 195; traffic 188
economic cooperation 95, 143, 145, 201–2; regional 95, 202
economic corridors 146, 178
economic crisis 82, 110; COVID-19-induced 82
economic flows 68–9; cross-border 68, 69
economic framework, US-styled 136
economic interdependence 20–1, 24, 26, 28, 37, 53, 135

economic issues 21, 26; securitisation of 26
economic order 20
economic prowess 2
economic relations 35, 95, 137; trans-Pacific 35
economic-security nexus 26
economy(ies) 1, 3, 10, 12, 17, 19–20, 22, 26–7, 32, 34–5, 37, 47, 49, 66–7, 69, 71, 73, 81–3, 87, 89, 95, 103–4, 113–14, 116, 128, 134–6, 159–66, 168–9, 205; Asia-Pacific 17; Chinese 20, 34, 104, 134, 136, 165; developed 73; developing 114, 128; export-led 27, 83; global 26; Indian Ocean 116; India's 113; market 1; middle-income 81, 89; national 67; open 27, 83; outward-oriented 82; post-COVID-19, 95; regional 19, 26, 82; small 82; Southeast Asian 134–5; state-led 19; statist 49; US 34 (illiberal 1; state-run 1); world 17, 82–3
eco-system 18
education 186, 188
Egypt 33
energy 37–9, 90, 111, 115, 146, 161, 166; demand for 37
engagement 1, 8–9, 11–12, 34, 42, 51, 81, 89, 95–6, 103, 106, 112, 114, 130, 136, 161, 164, 177, 182; China and Malaysia 12; China and Sri Lanka 11; China and US 1; conditional 42; economic 103, 112; expanded 136; great powers and Sri Lanka 11; multilateral 51; regional 34; Sri Lanka and US 11
engagements 9, 51, 53, 58, 127, 135–6, 138, 149, 161; contingent 9; flexible 9; institutional 135–6; multilateral 51, 53, 58; state 127
Enhanced Defence Cooperation Agreement (EDCA) 147–8
environment 2, 21, 24, 37, 47, 82, 87, 116, 151, 189, 198; international 2; natural 37; stable 21; strategic 24, 47; structural 198
environmental degradation 69
epidemic prevention and control 70
equality 112, 130; sovereign 130
espionage 40
ethnic: conflicts 184; groups 66; identity 159; minorities issues 168; nationalities 182; politics 163
EU and North Atlantic Treaty Organization (NATO) 54; relations 54

220   *Index*

Eurasia 33, 38
Europe 3, 6, 33, 36–7, 42, 48–50, 53–8, 67, 82, **109**, 146, 170, 186; global strategy 54; response strategy 58; strategic, autonomy 54–5, 58 (choice in 57)
European: autonomy 54 (strategic 48, 54, 58); countries 55, 58; middle power strategy 54 (implications for Asia 54); sovereignty 54
European Defence Union 54
European strategic autonomy 48, 54, 58
European Union (EU) 5, 43, 54–5, 58, 83–4, 114, 167; common security and defence policy 54; criticism of United States 54, 58
European Union (EU) and Sri Lanka relations 83
evacuations 39
exchange(s) 17, 19, 23, 27, 91, 104, 109, 116, 136, 146–8, 195; defence 23; economic 17, 27; military information 109
Exclusive Economic Zone (EEZ) 92, 115, 143, 145, 150
expansionism 115–16, 188; Chinese 188
exploitation 44
Export and Import 19–20, 27, 55, 71, 75, 83, 85, **86**, 87–8, 91, 95, 104, 135, 180, 195, 202–3; Chinese 88; dependence 55, 95; economy 83; markets 19; oil 203; services and goods 20; Sri Lanka and US 85; trade 19
Export-Import Bank of China 91, 167
External Affairs Minister (EAM) 117
extrapolation 35
extremism 148

fake news 40
fake olds 40
Far East 33, 188
fatalism 43
feminism 65
Filipino fishing vessels 147
Finance 67, 82–3, 89, 92, 94, 144, 146–7, 164
financial: crisis 21, 27, 52, 73, 82; governance 57; institutions 75, 95, 103; integration 144
Financial Action Task Force (FATF) 69
Financial Development Assistance **86**
financing 71, 73–4, 83, 91–2, 145, 167, 168; development 74, 83

fishing 39, 92, 115, 147; grounds 147; illegal 39, 92
Five Eyes 43
Food and Agriculture Organization (FAO) 69
foreign: affairs 163; exchange reserve 104; hostile forces 2; interference 40; investors 83; reserves 75; trade and investment 85, 113, 144
Foreign Affairs 187
foreign aid 82, 88–9, 95; China and Sri Lanka 88; Sri Lanka and US 88
foreign direct investment (FDI) 11, 83, 85, **86**, 87–8, 90–1, 94–5, 161–2; bilateral 85; China and Sri Lanka 87–8; cumulative 85, 88; export-oriented 91; infrastructure-related 90; Sri Lanka and US 85, 87–8
Foreign Policy Analysis 66
Foreign Policy Framework of the New Malaysia 164
foreign policy(ies) 1–4, 6–13, 21, 27, 36, 42, 48, 51–2, 54, 57, 59, 66–7, 75, 81, 83–4, 92, 96, 103, 105, 109, 112–3, 117, 127, 143, 149, 159–66, 168, 171, 177–8, 193, 194, 197–8, 200–1, 204; agendas 13, 164, 194; aggressive 103; ambitions 21; assertive 1; assertiveness, impact on 8; *bebas-aktif* (independent and active) 8; behaviour 7–9, 51; Chinese 3; choices 7, 159; complementarities 11; coordination 8; doctrines 8; formulation and implementation 171; framework 12; Indian 117; institutionalisation and implementation in 171; Mahathir's 166 (domestic-driven 164); Malaysian 159, 161; middle powers' 51; Myanmar's 177–8; non-aligned 81, 92; options 7, 12, 159, 171; outlooks 36; pattern 9; Philippines 149; post-war 198; 'public' 178; Southeast Asian 127; South Korean 10, 194, 204; strategic choice of 57; strategies 12; traditions 11–12
fragmegration 68
fragmentation 11, 17, 22, 67–8, 70, 71
France 5, 34, 39, 43, 52, 54, 58, 110
Fraud 70
Free and Open Indo-Pacific (FOIP) 3–5, 36, 42, 82, 92, 106, 115, 136, 138
freedom of expression 41
freedom of navigation and overflight 4, 106, 115, 149; rights 115

Freedom of Navigation Operations (FONOPs) **106**, 115
freedom of navigation rights 115
free-riding 24
Free Trade Agreement (FTA) 5, 83, 85, 87–8, 94–5, 114; bilateral 83, 85, 87; China and Sri Lanka 88; comprehensive 87; multilateral 5; negotiations 95; Sri Lanka and US 87
free trade and investment agreements 4
French Indochina 180
friction(s) 2, 35, 42, 87, 160, 180, 195; China 35
Fujitsu Ltd 110

G-20 Summit 111
Galle Dialogue 93
Galwan 41, 103, 105, 111, 113, 115–7; border clash at 41, 105; Chinese incursion in 111
garlic battle 195
garment 85
garment industry 85
garments 83, 85, 88
General Security of Military Information Agreement (GSOMIA) 201
geo-economic: competition 38; hotspot 116; powerplay 38
geo-economic motives 4
geo-economics 37–8, 42
geographic: boundaries 32, 42; location 82; proximity 47
geography 23, 33, 67; political 67; shared 33
geopolitical: agendas 32; ambitions 5; challenges 128, 134; circumstances 44; competition 54, 81, 136; conditions 131–2; dominance 72; entanglements 88, 94; gambit 66; hotspot 116; influence 84; interests 171, 186; motives 4; reality 132; restrictions 56; sentiment 28; shift 2
geopolitics 11, 34, 65, 184; multipolar 34
Germany 5, 34, 52, 54, 58, 110, 162, 180, 186
Gill, Bates 186
global: ambitions 25; capitalism 66; challenge 47; citizenship 51; competitiveness 19, 67–8; economic, contraction 134 (growth 17; order 20); economy 3, 19, 26, 35, 37, 82, 103, 169; governance 26, 52, 56, 67, 73, 189; investment 18; issues 50; multilateral

order 50; peace and prosperity 96; problems 47–8; production chains 17, 20, 27–8; prosperity 41; ramifications 41, 49; relations, power 32, 163; society 18; supply chains 18, 22, 24, 27; trade 18
global affairs 6
global backlash 103, 104
global economic development, impact on 3
global financial crisis of 2008, 21, 27, 52, 73, 82
global health pandemic 22, 24, 28
globalisation 17–18, 27–8, 37, 47, 66–7; economic 27; process of 17
global order 22, 41, 47–8, 51, 56, 72, 110; democratic 48; liberal 110; rules-based 48, 110
global power 2–3, 13, 32, 163, 206
global problem, seriousness of 48
global recession 27
global rules-based: cooperation 59; order 84
Global South 67
global supply chains 82, 111, 114, 165; post-pandemic 111
Global Times 114
governance 11, 18, 26, 52, 56–7, 65, 67–74, 76, 89, 189; domestic 69–70; effective 18; global 26, 52, 56, 67, 73, 189; outbound investment 74; port 70; regional 65; regulatory 67; security 68–71; structures 67, 76; transformation 69; transnational 11, 68
Governing Borderless Threats 69
Gramscian state theory 66
Grand National Party (GNP) 200
grand strategy 4, 38, 65, 72–3, 75–6; top-down 72
Great Game 2, 36, 37, 177, 179, 187–8; Britain and Russia 37
Great Game Redux 188
great power(s) 1, 6–12, 37, 42, 48, 50–1, 56, 65, 76, 81–5, 88, 92, 94–6, 127–8, 132–4, 138, 149, 161–2, 164, 169, 177, 186, 189, 193–4, 197–8, 204–5; challenges 128; changes 132; competition 1, 8, 65, 127, 132–3, 138; conflicts 1, 48; contestation 50 (practices of manoeuvring 9); foreign policies of 6; politics 7, 9, 10, 12, 161, 162; preponderance of 7; relations 11, 81, 94, 96, 193; responses of 81; rivalries 12, 84, 169 (manoeuvring 12)

Index

great powers and Sri Lanka 11; development assistance 81; engagement 11; foreign trade and investment 85; relations 81, 94 (foreign trade and investment 81, 85)
Greece 33
green growth 56–7
Gross Domestic Product (GDP) 18, 34–5, 89, 91, 160, 202; combined 34–5; growth 18
group/groupings 66, 111–12, 186; bureaucratic 66; ethnic 66; gendered 66; military 66; religious 66; trilateral 111
Group of Seven (G-7) 110–11
Group of Twenty (G-20) 111
GSPGeneralised System of Preferences Plus (+) 83–4
Guangxi Beibu Gulf International Port Group 166
Guangxi Zhuang autonomous region 69
Guanlei Port 70
Gulf of Aden 203
Gulf War 204

Haacke, Jürgen 9, 131
Haiti 85
Hambantota Port 74–5, 83–4, 90–1; agreement 91; control over 91; development of 91; lease 91
Hameiri, Shahar 67–9
Han 7, 188
health 22, 24, 26–8, 69–70, 116, 186, 188; crisis 27 (emergencies 69); infrastructure 27; pandemic 22, 24, 26–8; systems 69
hedge/hedging 6, 9, 28, 36, 159–62, 166, 170–1, 178, 185, 193; behaviour 9; inclinations 36; realpolitik 9; strategy 28, 160
hegemony 2, 4, 7, 42–3, 103; regional 2
Heginbotham, Eric 22
Heiduk, Felix 178
Higgott, Richard 129
highs-peed rail projects 170, 184, **187**; BRI-financed 146
Hindu, The 104
Hoang Thi Ha 189
Holbraad, Carsten 50
Honduras 85
Hong Kong 81, 105
hostility 21, 28, 180
Hotlines 41, 71; river-side 71

Huawei technologies 12, 49, 55, 109–10, 162, 166, 169–71; Mahathir's positions on 12, 162, 169, 171
Hub-and-spokes system 195, 205
human security 65
humanitarian assistance 89, **106**
Humanitarian Assistance and Disaster Relief (HADR) **106**, 149–50
human rights 49, 83, 92, 135, 164, 185, 196; issues 83, 92
Hungary 146
Hwang Gyo-an 201

identity 37, 65–6, 159, 161, 164–7, 171, 195–6, 205; ethnic 159; national 167, 195–6, 205; politics 196; regional 65
ideological: ambition 26; competition 196; differences 20–1
immigration 69, 92
inclusion 5, 109–10, 130, 133; political 130
inclusiveness 20, 24, 28, 43
incorporation 42
India 4–5, 8, 11, 32–9, 41–4, 82–4, 91–3, 95, 103–5, **106–8**, 109–17, 131, 138, 177–8, 182, 185–7; 5G dilemma 110; anti-China narrative 103 (post-Galwan nationalistic 103); "China Connect" policy 103; China policy 103, 105, 116; economy 113; foreign policy 112–3, 117 (post-COVID 113; post-Galwan 113; radical shift in 105; strategic imperative in 105); Indo-Pacific overtures 105; interests 111, 113 (diplomatic 111; economic 111, 113; security 111; strategic 113); Narendra Modi government 105; overtures in SCS 114; policies 105 (domestic 105; multi-alignment 117); strategic trade partners 113; technological advancement 110; trade 83
India and Japan 4, 11, 39, 109, 111–12, 115, 182; 2 + 2 Foreign and Defence Ministerial Meeting 109, 112
India and Philippines bilateral defence cooperation 116
India and US 11, 105; alignment framework 105; cooperation 116
India Economic Strategy 112
India Ideas Summit 117
India-Japan-Australia 39, 111; Supply Chain Resilience Initiative (SCRI) 111
Indian Ocean 4, 12, 32–3, 36–8, 41–3, 82–3, 92, 94–6, 114, 116, 177; Chinese

Index 223

presence in 33; economies 116; maritime security 82; power 38; sea lanes of 32, 37; trade-led growth in 82
Indian Ocean Region (IOR) 92, 95–6, 116; militarisation of 92
Indian Ocean Rim Association 96
India's Ministry of External Affairs (MEA) **106–8**
Indochina wars 186
Indonesia 8, 33–6, 38–9, 42–3, 69, 114, 117, 135, 138, 146, 150; foreign policy 8
Indo-Pacific 4–5, 10–11, 23, 32–44, 82, 103–5, **106–7**, 110–17, 136, 138, 148, 160, 177, 201; a multipolar system 36; boundaries 44; China's influence in 111; coalitions 111; conception of, "open and inclusive", 138; concept of 5, 32, **109**; conceptualization of 5; conflict in 41; cooperation in 11; definitions of 36; extension of 5; governments 41; partners 35, 105, 112, 115; partnerships in 114; power 34, 44 (competition 40; narrative 36); pragmatic blueprints 42; principles 43; restructuring of 4; Sino-centric reorganization 4; strategic competition in 40; strategic system 36; worldview 34
Indo-Pacific axis 39
Indo-Pacific coalitions 103, 111
Indo-Pacific Oceans Initiative (IPOI) 117
Indo-Pacific partner-states 105
Indo-Pacific Strategy 23, 82, 160, 201; American-backed 23
industrial: autonomy 54; corridors 82; development and services 91; interdependence 37; overcapacities 73; policy requirements 73; revolution 67, 169; zone 91
industrialisation 82
Industrial revolution, fourth 169
Industrial Revolution 4.0 164
industry 85, 87, 91, 183; capital goods 87
Industry 4.0 technology 170
inequality(ies) 17, 52, 145, 196, 206; economic 17; power 52; structural 206
information sharing 71, 203
information technology 82, 113
infrastructure 4–5, 12, 27, 32, 37–8, 41, 73–4, 82–4, 87–92, 94–5, 110–11, 113–4, 135, 137, 144–7, 150, 152, 162, 170, 178, 183–6, 188; commercial loans for 83, 89; connectivity 5, 82, 135; development 5, 90, 144–5; hard 4; health 27; interrelated projects 4; investment 4, 91; policy 5; regional connectivity 82; soft 4
infrastructure projects 4, 83–4, 87–9, 92, 144, 146, 150, 152, 162, 170, 178, 184–5, 188; Chinese-funded 84
insecurity 22, 128; domestic 128; political 128
instability(ies) 4, 22, 27–8, 47; domestic 2; political 4
institutional: arrangements 52–3, 136; balancing 52–3; competition 136; development 17; engagements 135–6; expression 129; frameworks 127, 130; initiatives 136; norms and practices 129; politics 135; strategies 11, 127–34, 137–9
institution-building 52; efforts 52; regional 52
institutions: ASEAN-centred 65; ASEAN-linked 129, 137; domestic 68; intergovernmental 68; regional 4, 11, 20, 65, 68, 127–31, 135–8, 178; supranational 68
insurgency 92, 148, 180; communist 180
integration 18, 68, 73, 132, 137, 144; economic 73; financial 144; transnational 68
integrity, territorial 1, 112
intellectual broadening 65
intellectual property (IP) 26; protection for 26; weak laws 26
intelligence 37, 43, 69, 71, 94, 148, 170, 201; partnership 43; sharing 43, 69, 94
interaction 18, 37, 136; China and Southeast Asia 171; rule-governed 18
interference 1, 19, 25, 40, 43, 65, 68, 92, 129–30, 142, 151, 204; activities 43; external 142; foreign 40; internal 40; outside 151; political 40; US 1
intergovernmental organisations 76
interlinkages 19–20
international: agreements 49; assistance 92; boundaries 40; citizenship 51; development cooperation 56–7; differences 44; dilemmas 10, 32; disputes 51; environment 2; financial governance 57; initiatives 70; issues 57, 96; law **106**; migration 50; multilateral order 57; negotiations 8; norms 56, 58, 104, 106; norms and standards 56; organisations 51–2, 69, 71, 76, 131, 164; policy 50; political economy

224 Index

12, 81, 159, 162; power 51, 58, 161 (politics 161); problems 51; tensions 43; trade 67, 164; trade and finance 67, 164; treaties and agreements 164; understanding 50
international affairs 7–8, 47, 51; great powers in 7
international benchmarking 87
international community 2, 50, 112; state-centric conception of 50
international cooperation, multilateral engagements in 51
international institutions 7, 33, 56, 129; dysfunctionality of 7
internationalisation 11, 67, 70
international law 39, 106, 115, 144, 151
international manufacturing chains 37
International Maritime Organisation's International Ship and Port Facility Security Code Programme 70
International Maritime Security Construct (IMSC) 203
International Monetary Fund (IMF) 84, 92, 95
International Monetary Fund (IMF) Extended Fund Facility 84
international order and system 2–7, 18, 48, 53–8, 68, 73, 82, 103; alternative 48; Asia's 53; China-led 48; contemporary 82; formation of 55; institutionalized 7; interdependent 7; liberal 56, 73; post-COVID-19, **108**; power relations in 54, 58; rules-based 4–7; state-based 18
international politics 7–8, 53, 161, 163
International Port Security Program (IPSP) 70
International Relations (IR) 2–3, 6–7, 52, 65–8, 160–1, 169, 171; Cold War structure of 68; constructivist approach in 160, 171; frameworks 66; mainstream 7, 68; new type of 3
International Ship and Port Facility Security Code programme (IMO-ISPFS) 70
international society, norms of 52
interrelatedness 19
interstate diplomacy, top-down 74
interventions 41, 68–9, 95, 137, 139
Intra-ASEAN fault lines 136
investment(s) 4, 11, 18, 23, 26–7, 73–4, 81, 83, 85, 87, 89, 91–2, 95, 111, 113, 115, 128, 134–6, 144–7, 150, 161–4, 167, 170, 182, 184, 186; BRI 73, 92;

Chinese 4; decisions 27; developmental 128; foreign 113, 144; global 18; high-risk 4; importance of 4; infrastructure 4, 87, 91; non-BRI 73; outbound 73–4; outward 73; partner 23; productive 73; public-sector 146; regional 18; shoddy practices 74; state controlled 4; two-way 26
Iran 21, 203–4
Iran and US 203; nuclear agreement 21; tensions 203
Iraq War 204
ISEAS 189
ISIS Praxis conference 168
Islamic State of Iraq and Syria (ISIS) 148, 168
Islamist extremists 150
island-building 145, 148
Israel 110

Jaishankar, Dr. S., External Affairs Minister (EAM) **107–9**, 117
Japan 3–5, 8, 11–12, 20–1, 23, 25, 32–43, 49, 52, 93, 104–5, **107–9**, 110–13, 115–16, 131–2, 145, 149–53, 177, 179, 182, 186–7, 194–7, 201, 205–6; 2013 Defence White Paper 36; defence white paper 115; interest in SCS 112; priorities 5; war against China 179
Japan-America-India (JAI) 39, 109; joint maritime exercise 109; trilateral meeting 11
Japan-America-India Trilateral Meeting (JAI) 11, 111–12
Japan and Philippines 116, 149, 150; economic and security ties with 150; maritime security cooperation 150; security partnership 149; trade and security engagements 149
Japan and South Korea 196
Japan and US 11
Japan-Australia Economic Partnership Agreement (JAEPA) 113
Japan-India Act East Forum 113
Japan International Cooperation Agency (JICA) **187**
Japan Self-Defence Forces (JSDF) 149
Japan's Maritime Self-Defence Force 115
Japan's Ministry of Foreign Affairs **107–8**
Japan's Ministry of Foreign Affairs (MOFA) **106–7**
Jessop, Bob 66
Jinghan Zeng 72

job creation 91, 146
Johnson, Lyndon B., US President 180
Joint Comprehensive Plan of Action (JCPOA) 199
joint maritime exercise 109
joint military exercises 23, 148, 202
joint naval exercises 115–16
joint patrols 71, 145
Jordaan 51

Kachin Independence Organization (KIO) 182
Kai 52
Kaladan Multimodal Waterway 187
Kamandag 148
Kang Kyung-wha, South Korean Foreign Minister 203
Karen (*Kayin*) rebel forces 180
Kashmir 112
Kayin militia 188
Kenya 74
Keohane 8, 52
Kim Dae-jung, South Korean President 197, 205; Sunshine Policy 197
Kim Jung-Un, North Korean leader 25
KMT forces 180
Konferensi Asia-Afrika 8
Korea, Democratic People's Republic of (DPRK) 197
Korean Institute for National Unification (KINU) 203
Korean Peninsula 8, 41, 47, 195, 200, 202; nuclear-weapons-free, commitment to 195; US troops on 200, 202
Koreans 47, 193, 197, 203–5
Korean unification 47
Korean War 194–5
Korea, Republic of (ROK) 25, 34, 47, 110, 203
Kuantan Port 166, 168
Kuik 160
Kuomintang/Guomindang (KMT) 180
Kuwait 204
Kyaukphyu deep sea port 184, 186, **107**

labour 67, 83, 202; cheap 83
Lampton, David M. 184
Lancang-Mekong Cooperation Mechanism 178
land: acquisition 146; features 143, 148; routes 146
Laos 8, 70–1, 144, 178, 184–5, 188
Laos' railway system 144

Lashio-Muse railway line 187
Latin America 88
leader/leadership 6, 12, 19, 21, 24, 27, 33, 35, 49–50, 53–5, 58, 67, 72, 74, 93, 112, 145, 148, 152, 166, 186, 193–4, 196–9, 204–6; Chinese 27, 74; functional 50; initiative-oriented sources of 53, 58; political 12, 67, 193–4, 196, 198–9, 205; regional 50, 112; US 49; Vietnamese 19
Lebanon 204
Lee 11, 28–9
Lee Hsien Loong, Prime Minister 28
legitimacy 18, 27, 37, 49, 138, 164, 167, 198–9, 201, 205; performance 18; political 37, 167, 198, 205; politics 201
leverage 33–4, 55, 178; political 178
liberalisation 1, 83, 88, 95; domestic 1; economic 83; tariff 88; trade 88, 95
liberalism 66
liberal order 49, 73, 111
Liberty Korea Party 200–1, 204
Libya 204
Li Keqiang, China's Premier 152, 167
Li Li 116
Lim Guan Eng, Finance Minister 170, 193
Line of Actual Control (LAC) 103
Liow, Joseph 169
Lippert 54
Liu Zhenmin, Chinese Vice Foreign Minister 151
live-and-let-live approach 73
livelihoods 71, 134
LM-Lancang-Mekong Integrated Law Enforcement and Security Cooperation Centre (LESC) 71
loan(s) 38, 74–5, 83–4, 89–92, 94, 145–7, 150, 166–7; Chinese 75, 92, 146; commercial 83–4, 89–90, 92; soft 166; unsustainable 74
lobbying 72
logistics 43, 82–3, 91, 93, 109, 112
Logistics Exchange Memorandum of Agreement (LEMOA) 109
Logistics Support Agreement (LSA) 112
long game 32, 35
long-range missiles 197, 203; restrictions on 203
Lorenzana, Delfin, Philippine Defence Minister 116

Maas, Heiko, Germany's Foreign Minister 186
Made in China 2025, 26

226　*Index*

Mahathir Doctrine 165
Mahathir Mohamad, Prime Minister of Malayasia 12, 159–71; anti-China election campaign 163–4; China policy 159–60, 162, 170; domestic development agenda 169; foreign policies 166; *Malay Dilemma, The* 159; policies towards China 170; policy towards China 165, 170; position on, China 163 (Huawei 12, 162, 169; South China Sea 168); visit to China 167
Major Defence Partner (MDP) 109
major player 42
major power(s) 9–11, 55, 84, 106, 127–35, 137–9, 145, 159, 163–4, 169, 177–8, 188; agendas 130; challenges 128–9, 132, 134; competition 9, 127, 132–5, 137–8 (effects of 135); conflict 10; engagements of 9; relations 133; strategies of 11
Make in India 113
Malabar naval exercise 39, 109, 112, 115, 116
Malacca Dilemma 166, 168
Malacca Strait 39
Malaysia 12, 38, 74, 87, 115, 135, 159–71; 14th General Election 162–3; attitudes to the trade war 169; Chinese FDI 162; dilemmas, implications of 12, 162; economic growth 169; economy of 159; ethnic politics 163; foreign policy 159, 161, 163 (options 12, 159); future diplomacy 160; gross domestic product (GDP) 160; implications of 12, 161–2; Najib administration 162; national identity 167; national interests 169; policies towards the BRI 12, 162; politics 159; resources 162; UMNO-led coalition 162
Malaysia-China Business Council (MCBC) 170
Malaysian Chinese Association (MCA) 163
Malaysian Islamic Party (PAS) 167
Maldives 74, 114
Mandala model 44
Mandalay 187–8
manoeuvrability 194, 199, 201
Marawi City siege 147–50
marines 38
maritime 12, 32, 34, 37–8, 43–4, 70–1, 82, 91–5, 105, **107**, 109–11, 113, 115–17, 131, 134, 136–8, 142, 144–52, 187; bullying 43; connectivity 34; cooperation **106**; incidents 105; issues 144; patrol 95, 150; reconnaissance 149; routes 146; security **106** (governance 70); services 91; tensions 134
Maritime Asia 32, 110
Maritime exercises 137–8; ASEAN-China 137–8; joint 109; warfare 93
Maritime Safety Administration (MSA) 70
Maritime Security Initiative (MAI) 70, 148
Maritime Self-Defence Force 115
Maritime Silk Road Initiative (MSRI) 3, 83, 114, 145
Maritime Southeast Asia 38, 44; sea lanes of 44
market(s) 1, 19, 26, 73, 83, 85, 87–9, 91, 95, 134, 169; Chinese 88; domestic 83, 87; economy 1; export 19; reforms 26
Marxism 65
MAS Holdings 85
material: capacity 23; advancement 20; power 8, 19–20, 160; wellbeing 10
media 1, 40, 90, 114, 185, 199, 205; organisations 40; reports 185; state-controlled 1; state-run 114
mediation 51
medium powers 128
Mekong 8, 69–71, 137, 178, 180, 186
Mekong Basin Disease Surveillance (MBDS) 69
Mekong River Commission 186
Memorandum of Understanding (MOU) 12, 23, 94, 146, 183; CMEC 185; Sri Lanka and US 94
mentality 38, 206; traditional 38
Metternich 33
Mexico 85
Middle East 19, 32–3, 161, 201, 203–4
Middle East and South Korea 203; strategic and economic interests in 203
middle-income trap 85, 95
middle players 34–6, 39, 42–3
Middle Power Diplomacy Initiative 56
middle-powermanship 51; countermeasure strategies 52; multilateralism 52; concepts of 48; multilateralism of 48; role of 47, 50, 53, 57
middle power(s) 10–11, 13, 34, 36, 40, 42–3, 47–59, 128, 131, 135, 162, 177–8, 206; behavioural approach 51; characteristics of 50; concept of 51–2; definitions of 50; diplomacy 53, 56; diplomatic strategies of 58; emergence of

Index 227

177; foreign policy 51; limitations of 54; multilateral, activities of 53 (approach of 56; engagement of 51; order 48, 57; strategy of 55); multilateralism of 51, 58; multiplicity of 135; new 48, 52–3, 58; non-Western 51; preferences 51; role played by 50; South Korea as a 56; states 48; strategies 51, 53–4, 56, 58 (diplomatic 54; European 54); structural position of 56; traditional 52
Migdal 66
migration 50
militancy 184
military 1–3, 6, 8, 19–21, 23–6, 33, 36–9, 43, 50–1, 54–7, 65–6, 74, 76, 81–2, 92–4, 104–5, 109–10, 112, 114–15, 134, 136–7, 147–9, 152, 178–80, 184–8, 194–7, 201–2, 205; access arrangements 43; acquisitions 24; activity 36; adventurism 115; alliances 8; assistance 74, 180; autonomy 1, 54; build-up 39, 115; capability 2, 50–1, 81–2, 92; capacity 56; Chinese 38, 93, 115; dominance 81; equipment 21, 92; groupings 66; information exchange 109; inter-operability 109; interstate dynamics 65; joint exercises 23, 148, 202; logistics 43, 109; logistics agreements 109; modernization 1, 6; posturing 104, 115; provocations 25; repressive dictatorship 180; starkly dimension 38; technology growth 110; ties 3
military exercises 23, 43, 93, 105, 109, 115, 148–9, 202; bilateral 93; China 105; multi-nation 43; trilateral 115
military power(s) 19, 50; weak 50
military relations, interstate 65
Millennium Challenge Corporation (MCC) 89–91, 94; agreement 91
Mindanao, counter-terrorism operations in 148
mines 22
minilateralism 11, 39
Ministry of Commerce (MOFCOM) 71, 73
Ministry of Public Security (MPS) 70–1
misinformation 43
missiles 22, 147, 197, 201, 203; ballistic 22, 197; surface-to-air 22, 147
mistrust 39–41, 95, 184; armed 39; strategic 41
modernisation 1, 6, 22, 56, 136, 148; military 1, 6; naval 22

Modi, Narendra, Indian Prime Minister 36, 103, 105, 110, 113–14, 116–17, 185; foreign policy 113; keynote speech at an Asia security summit 36
money laundering 69
monopoly 3
Moon Jae-in, South Korean president 194, 198–203; domestic policies 201; foreign policies 201; political manoeuvrability 201
moral power 50–1
Morse 52
multi-alignment 105, 113, 117
multiculturalism 73
Multi-Fibre Arrangement (MFA) 83
multilateral: activities 52–3; approaches 5, 57; cooperation 8, 11, 47, 58, 105; diplomacy 39; engagements 51, 53, 58; free trade agreements 5 (inclusive 21); groups 49; institutions 3, 20, 28, 50, 52–3, 189; moral powers 50; norms 135; organisations 21, 28; regional institutions 11; rules-based order 96; security cooperation 115; strategies 53, 58; strategy 55
multilateral institutions 53
multilateralisation 130–1
multilateralism 24, 47–54, 56, 58–9, 84, 128; aspects of 53; contested 50, 52; democratic 50; formal mechanism of 53; informal aspects of 53; international relations theory of 52; middle powers 48, 51, 58; notions of 51; proponents of 51; regional 53; rules-based 49–50; second wave of 52; significance and relevance of 47; strands of 52
Multilateralism 1.0, ASEAN-led 52
multilateralisms 11
multilateral order 10, 47–50, 57–8; international 57; liberal 49; middle power 48; rules-based 10, 47–8, 58; US-centred 58 (disruption of 58)
multinational corporations (MNCs) 83, 87
Multiple Actor Platforms 131
multipolar world order 104
multipolarity 32, 43–4, 56
multipolar order 72, 117
Multi-Role Response Vessels (MRRV) 150
mutual: adjustment 42; protection 44; respect 42, 44, 165; vulnerability 41
Mutual Defence Treaty (MDT) 25, 116, 147–8; Article 5, 25
Mutual Logistics Support Agreement (MLSA) 112

mutual obligation 35
Myanmar 8, 12, 18, 70–1, 74, 135, 144, 177–90; anti-Chinese riots 181; Chinese economic presence in 188; foreign policy 177–8; human rights sanctions on 135; junta rule 180–1; nationalist movement 179; political pluralism 188; quasi-federal constitution 180; repressive military dictatorship 180; security 12; *see also* Burma
Myanmar and US diplomatic relations 185
Myanmar military 184
Myanmar National Convention 181
Myitsone dam project 179, 182

naivety 43
national: aspirations 186; coalition 179; economies 67; formations 67; identity 159, 167, 195–6, 205; narratives 37; resources 35; societies 67; stability 18, 133; states 67; unification 57; welfare states 67
national autonomy 128–30, 133, 138; commitment to 129
National Development Bank (NDB) 103
national interests 9, 25, 53, 66, 96, 117, 164, 168–9, 204; categories of 164
nationalism 37, 182, 188, 195; Han Chinese 188; mono-ethnic 182
nationalist (*Kuomintang/Guomindang*) Party 179
nationality 182; ethnic 182
National League for Democracy (NLD) 178–9, 181–2, 185
national security 34, 55, 81, 92, 129–30, 196, 198, 205–6; capacity 81, 92
National Security Law (*Gukka Boan Beop*) 105, 196, 205
National Security Strategy (NSS) 1, 103; interests 40
National Unity Front (NUF) **181**
NATO and Russia relations 55
natural: disasters 41; environment 37
naval: aggression 70; bases 28; blockades 41; joint exercises 39, 93, 115–16; modernisation 22; tactics 25
naval port 187; facility 187
navy 22, 38–9, 75, 83, 91–3, 114, 116, 143, 145; frigate-based 22
Near East 33
NEC Corp 110
negotiations 5, 8, 21, 23, 49, 95, 114, 137, 152, 159, 167, 201–3; CoC 151, 152;

defence burden-sharing 202; FTA 95; international 8; process of 167; RCEP 5, 23, 137
neighbourhood 3, 103, 116; immediate 3, 116
neighbours 7–8, 19, 57, 113, 144–5, 177; China 19; immediate 113; regional 19; Southeast Asian 144; sub-regional 19
neoclassical Realism 66
neo-imperialism 72
neo-liberalism 160
neo-realism 160
Nepal 105
Netherlands, the 5, 34, 51–2, 144, 162
neutrality 96, 178
neutral non-alignment 84
New Development Bank 3
New Economic Policy (NEP) 159
Ne Win, General 180; visit to US 180
New Zealand 38, 110, 114, 138
NGOs 76
Nikkei Future of Asia Conference 169
nine-dash line 144
Non-Aligned Movement (NAM) 8, 84, 178, 180
non-alignment 83–4, 96, 105, 112, 117, 165
non-interference 19, 25, 65, 68, 129–30; norms of 19, 25, 130
non-military resistance 43
non-proliferation **106–7**
non-state actors 47
non-traditional Security (NTS) 65, 69, 71; issues 69, 71
Nordic countries 51, 54, 58
Nordpolitik 195
norms and practices 7, 18–20, 23–6, 28–9, 47–8, 52, 56–9, 72–3, 104, 106, 129–30, 135, 151–2, 161; diffuser 56; foundational 26; inclusiveness 20; institutional 129; international 56, 58, 104, 106 (society 52); multilateral 135; non-interference 19, 25, 130; non-use of force 23; regional 19; region-specific 130; rules and 18; state sovereignty 25
North Atlantic 33, 43, 54, 109
North Atlantic Treaty Organization (NATO) 43, 54–5, 109
North East Sri Lanka 83
North Korea 18, 21, 25, 50, 57, 194–9, 201–2, 205; military provocations 25; nuclear programme 21; US policy on 199

Index   229

North Korea and South Korea 57; gap in relative power 57
North Korea policy 195, 197, 201
Norway 51–2
Nossal, Kim 129
nuclear: agreement 21; non-proliferation 57; programme 21; proliferation 70; weapons 41

Obama, Barack, US President 20, 104, 136–7, 148; Pivot to Asia 20, 104
obligation 24, 35; mutual 35
Ocean 32, 35
Odgaard's claim 68
Official Development Assistance (ODA) 146–7, 150
oil: shipments 82; supply 12; trade 12
one belt, one road approach 72
Ong Kian Ming, Deputy International Trade and Industry Minister 168
open-seas protection 38
Opioid Substitution Programme (OSP) 71
opium 71
oppression 196
order(s): China-led 6–7, 10, 49, 58, 72, 132; democratic 48, 58; liberal trading 82; mutually exclusive 6; post-Cold War 189; post-COVID 111, 114; post-Galwan 117; rules-based 47, 50, 84, 96, 105, 111; transitions in 22; types of 6; US-led 6, 10, 48–9, 58
organisation(s): formal 52; intergovernmental 76; international 51, 69, 71, 76, 131, 164; minilateral 43; multilateral 21, 28 (inclusive 21); regional 18, 65, 69; sub-regional 18
overgeneralization 7
over-reliance 129, 166

Pacific Island Countries 113
Pacific Ocean 4, 32, 35, 117
Pakatan Harapan 164
Pakistan 8, 40, 112, 146, 184
pandemics 22–4, 26–8, 38, 47, 49, 69–70, 81, 84–5, 87–8, 104, 110–11, 114–15, 159, 177, 186, 189; avian flu 70; avian influenza 69; bird flu 69; dengue fever 70; diplomacy 84; management 38; preparedness 69; swine flu 70; typhoid 70
Panglong Peace conference 182
pan-regional awareness 42
Paracel and Spratly Islands 115

Paracels 115
para-diplomacy, quasi-autonomous 68
paramilitary coastguard vessels 23
Paris Agreement on Climate Change 85
Paris Climate Change Convention 21, 49
Park Geun-hye, South Korean President 200
Parti Keadilian Rakyat 164
Parti Pribumi Bersatu Malaysia 164
partisan divides 1
partner/partnership 12, 32, 38, 42–3, 56, 58, 92, 105, 111, 113–4, 116–7, 145, 149, 152; cooperative 116; creative 43; defensive 42; economic 149; extra-regional 128; intelligence 43; reciprocal 111; security 12, 149, 152; strategic 43
Pax Americana 3
Payne, Marise, Foreign Minister of Australia **107**, 108, **109**
peace 6, 10, 17, 22, 27–8, 35, 39–41, 48, 51, 56, 96, 106, 116, 145, 152, 165, 182, 184, 186, 188–9, 195, 204–5
peace and prosperity 6, 27–8, 96
peacekeeping 39, 51, 85, 180, 204; operations 51, 85
People's Liberation Army Navy Marine Corps (PLANMC) 114
People's Liberation Army Navy (PLAN) 38, **75**, 114, 143, 152
People's Liberation Army (PLA) 35, 38, 114, 143
people-to-people movement 88
perception 26–7, 40, 112, 137, 197
perceptions 40, 105, 161, 193, 197, 206
peripheral players 127
Permanent Court of Arbitration (PCA) 115, 142
Permanent Structured Cooperation (PESCO) 54
Pew Research Center 6, 204
Philippine Air Force (PAF) 147, 150
Philippine Coast Guard (PCG) 150
Philippine Navy (PN) 145, 150
Philippines, the 2, 8, 12, 25, 66, **106**, 114–16, 142–50, 152–3; balancing policy on China 147; China policy 12, 143–4; Chinese influence on 149; claims in the South China Sea 25; Duterte administration 12, 142–5, 147, 149–50, 152–3; foreign policy 143, 149 (confrontational 143); infrastructure-building programme 147; territorial rights in the West Philippine Sea 142; US Navy in 145

Philippine waters 143; Chinese warships in 143
Philippines and China maritime dispute 144
Philippines and US 145, 147–9; alliance 147, 148; cooperation 148; security partnership 149; tension 145
piracy 38–9, 41, 70, 92, 150, 203
Pivot to Asia 20
Pivot to China 145
PLA Daily 114
pluralism 73, 131, 188; political 188
pointed-alignment 113
polarisation 2, 13, 205; adversarial 2
policy(ies) 1–13, 19–21, 23–7, 34, 36–7, 42–3, 48, 50–2, 54–5, 57, 59, 66–8, 71–3, 75–6, 81, 83–4, 92, 95–6, 103–5, 109–10, 112–14, 116–17, 127, 133, 135, 142–4, 146–7, 149, 152–3, 159–66, 168, 170–1, 177–8, 180, 185, 187, 193–201, 204–6; appeasement 12, 116, 143, 146–7, 152–3; challenges 127; China Connect 103; Chinese 34; climate change 55; containment of China 185; coordination 8, 43, 144; defence 5, 54, 105; divides 43; domestic 105; economic 4–5, 83, 105 (opening 194); expansive 37; export-led 19; guidelines 72; implementation 71; industrial 26, 73; infrastructure 5; insurance 23; international 50; isolationist 116; joint security and defence 54; options 7, 12, 72, 159, 171; public 67; reassurance 25; responses 76 (multilateral approaches to 5); security 4–5, 54, 66; soft balancing 143, 152; soft-balancing 143, 149, 152; trade 5 (internal 40)
political: agendas 90, 164, 169; ambitions 184; autonomy 54; bargains 196; competition 199, 206; constraints 12, 193–4, 198; crises 200; differences 134; geography 67; goals 163; inclusion 130; influence 38, 82, 150; insecurity 128; instability 4; interests and agendas 166, 171, 197; interference 40; issues 55, 195; leaders 12, 67, 193–4, 196, 198–9, 205; legitimacy 37, 167, 198, 205; leverage 178; manoeuvrability 194, 201; mobilisations/movements 193, 195–6, 199; oppression 196; pluralism 188; practices 10 (clash of 40); regimes 7; relations 116; resources 162; risk 74; self-centred purpose 33; standing 130; struggles 67, 198; survival 198; systems 40, 186; ties 9, 24; warfare 40; will 50
political economy 12, 66, 69, 71, 73, 81, 159–63, 166, 168; international 12, 81, 159, 162
politics 3, 6–10, 12, 35, 37–8, 47, 52–3, 66–7, 75, 83, 90, 135, 159–64, 166, 182, 196, 200–1, 205–6; Asian power 35; big power 164, 166; Chinese 75 (practices of manoeuvring 9); complex 38; domestic 3, 7, 9, 66–7, 83, 90, 160, 196; electoral 182; ethnic 163; global 3; great power 7, 9–10, 12, 161–2; identity 196; institutional 135; international 7–8, 53, 161, 163; legitimacy 201; local 38; majoritarian 182; power 7, 9–10, 12, 35, 161–2, 164, 166; world 6, 52
Pompeo, Mike, former US Secretary of State 103, **107–8**, 110, 116, 148; visit to Manila 148
populism 28, 182
port access rights 38
Port Klang 166, 168
Port of Rangoon 179
port(s) 4, 37–8, 70, 74–5, 82–4, 90–1, 166, 168, 179, 184–7; deep sea 184–5; governance 70; transhipment 91
positionality 129–31, 139; advantaged 130
post-colonialism 65
post-structuralism 65
Poulantzas, Nicos 66
poverty 17, 27, 145, 167; absolute 17, 27
power-partner 105
power relations 11, 32, 54, 58, 81, 94, 96, 127, 133, 163, 193; rearrangement of 54, 58; advantages 38; Asian 36, 83, 138; balance of 3, 11, 34, 57, 76, 132, 184; balancing 68; benevolent 29; Chinese 35, 42–4, 65; constellations 8, 11; deficit 57; diffusion of 56; distribution of 23, 48; European 38, 132; external 38, 132, 151; global 2–3, 13, 32, 163, 206; Indian Ocean 38; Indo-Pacific 35, 44; inequalities 52; international 51, 58, 161; leading 34; medium 127–30, 138; military 19, 50; mix 11; monopoly on 3; moral 51; projection 39, 92; redistribution of 22, 27; regional 35, 92, 95, 129; revisionist 1, 103, 105, 112; rising 32, 68, 127; sharp 40; small 7, 36, 84, 89, 95–6, 127–31, 138, 161–2; smaller 7, 129–31, 160, 171; soft 40, 83, 183; transitions in 22

Index 231

power(s): balance of 66; distribution and use of 69; lobbying for 72; non-major 129, 133; opportunities 129; parity of 103; politics 7, 9–10, 12, 35, 161–2, 164, 166; regional versus global 13, 206; secondary versus middle 13, 206; small 11, 81–2, 94–6, 169; state 66; structural condition 129; struggle for 66; transition 132
preferential access 83, 85
priorities 5, 35, 54, 55–6, 58, 74, 81, 85, 88–9, 94–5, 131, 138, 163, 165; diplomatic 35; domestic 163, 165; Japan's 5
priorities and initiatives 5
pro-American mobilisations 201
pro-communism 205
production: networked 19, 21; rates 23
production chains 17, 19–20, 27–8; global 17, 20, 27–8; regional 17, 27
professional services 82
Proliferation Security Initiative (PSI) 70, 199
propaganda 40
prosperity 6, 17, 21–2, 27–8, 35, 37, 41, 47, 50, 57, 96, 106; economic 21
prosperity and order 41
protectionism 169
proxies 8
public communications 90
public health infrastructure 27
public-private partnerships 113
Pulwama terrorist attack 112
Purchasing Power Parity (PPP) 34–5

Qing China 204
Quad 2.0 105, 109, 115
Quad Plus 105, 110–11, 114–15; endorsement of 110
quadrilateral dialogue 38, 39
Quadrilateral Security Dialogue 178
Quadrilateral Strategic Dialogue 105
Quad (U.S.-Australia-India-Japan Quadrilateral Security Dialogue) 5, 39, 105, **106–7**, 109–11, 113–16; official consultations **106**
Quasi-allies 196

race 37, 40, 42, 200; 'soft power' 40
railway 37, 144, 146, 166, 184, **187**
Rainsy, Sam 187
Rajapaksa, Gotabaya, Sri Lankan President 84, 90–1

Rajapaksa, Mahinda, Sri Lankan President 74, 83–4, 89–91; pro-China policy 83
Rakhine state 185, **106**
ramifications 41, 49
rapprochement 133, 144, 148–50; China and Philippines 148–50
rationality 28, 160
Ravenhill, John 19
Razak, Najib, Prime Minister of Malaysia 160, 162–4, 166–7, 169
Realism 7, 52, 66, 160
reality(ies) 8, 26, 33–5, 37, 40, 66, 75, 117, 127, 132, 163, 197; complex 33, 34; empirical 66, 75, 197; geopolitical 132; shifting 35
reassurance 19, 20, 22, 24–5, 195; dual 195; policies 25; strategy 20, 22
rebalance 4, 21
recession 27
reciprocity 111
reconciliation 44, 195
reconnaissance aircraft 150
reconnaissance equipment 148
Red China 180
red tape 87, 95, 113
reform(s) 2, 7, 19, 26, 67, 104; economic 26; market 26; movement 19; processes 7; state 67
regional: affairs 10; agendas 131; ambitions 25; arrangements 127; balance of power 3, 184; constraints 57; cooperative architecture 28; dialogue 86, 93; diplomacy 27; distribution of power 23; economic, contraction 134 (cooperation 95, 202); economies 19, 26, 82; engagement 34; forums 5; frameworks 113, 130; governance 65; hegemons 8; hegemony 2; hub 83; identity 65; infrastructure connectivity 82; initiatives 130, 137; institutional strategies 134; institution-building 52; institutions 52, 139; investment 18; leaders 50; leadership 112; multilateralism 53; multilateral organisations 28; neighbours 19; norm of non-interference 19; organisations 18, 65, 69; power constellations 11; powers 35, 92, 95, 129 (power 32); production chains 17, 27; relations 18; resilience 18, 19; rules-based order 96; security architecture 11, 65; shocks 18; stability 2, 18, 133; states 10, 17, 20, 22–3, 26, 28, 135; supply chains 18, 22, 24, 27;

232 Index

trade 18; trading hub 83; transition 20; uncertainty 42
Regional Comprehensive Economic Partnership (RCEP) 5, 23, 137; negotiations 5, 23, 137
regional cooperation 130, 135; multi-actor 130
Regional Cooperation Agreement on Combating Piracy and Armed Robbery Against Ships in Asia 70
regional institutions 4, 11, 20, 65, 68, 127–31, 135–8, 178; multilateral 11; multilateral character of 130; process-driven 20
regional integration 137; China-inclusive 137
regionalisation 17–18, 27; economic 27; process of 17
regionalism 20, 33, 165; Asia-Pacific 20; East Asian 165; organic concept of 165
Regional Maritime Security Initiative 70
regional order 3, 5, 19–20, 22, 32, 36, 44, 50, 53, 72, 151–2; ideas and concepts of 3; power-based 151; transitions in 20
regional security 2, 11, 42, 50, 57, 59, 65, 68, 130, 193, 195; hub-and-spokes 195; non-traditional 11, 82, 92; US-led 193
regional versus global power 13, 206
Reiichiro Takahashi 113
relations 1–3, 6–8, 11–3, 17–24, 26–8, 32–3, 35–6, 40–1, 48–9, 52, 54–5, 57–9, 65, 68, 81, 83, 85, 87, 90, 93–6, 104–5, 113, 116, 127, 129–30, 133–5, 137–8, 142, 144–5, 147, 149–50, 153, 159–65, 169, 171, 178–85, 188, 193–9, 204–5; bilateral 2, 28, 49, 138, 165, 182, 185, 193, 197; China and India 41; China and Japan 23, 41, 105; China and Malaysia 165; China and Philippines 142, 144 (deterioration in 17, 24); China and South Korea 194–5; China and Southeast Asian 161; China and Sri Lanka 81, 94 (foreign trade and investment 85); China and US 1–2, 18, 22, 26, 48, 134 (economic 134; instabilities in 27; tensions in 28); domestic 18; economic 27, 116, 189; EU and North Atlantic Treaty Organization (NATO) 54; EU and Sri Lanka 83; grant-based 90; great power 11, 81, 94, 96, 193; great powers and Sri Lanka 81, 85, 94; international 2, 3, 52, 68, 169, 171 (assessments of 133; competitive 133; power 32); inter-state 27; NATO and Russia 55; normalisation of 19; political 116; power 11, 32, 54, 58, 81, 94, 96, 127, 133, 163, 193; reciprocal 18; regional 18; small power–great power 11, 81, 96; social 66; South Korea and US 195; Sri Lanka and US 81, 83, 94; state-to-state 27; strategic 178
religion 184, 190; politicization of 184
religious: groups 66; militancy 184
Republican Party 24
resilience 18–19, 43, 189; regional 18–19; sub-regional 18
resistance 33–4, 37, 43, 52, 65; coalitions of 33; collective 43; non-military 43; realist 65
resource(s) 33, 35, 37, 49, 51, 54, 66, 68–9, 72, 74–5, 90, 95, 116, 127–8, 151, 161–2, 178; allocation of 33, 95; control over 68; depletion 41; distribution and use of 69; economic 162; lobbying for 72; marine 116; material 51, 54, 128; national 35; natural 82; political 162; struggle for 66
response strategy 58
retaliation 110, 200
rights: freedom of navigation 115; human 49, 83, 92, 135, 164, 185, 196; legal 39; port access 38
Rim of the Pacific Exercise (RIMPAC) 93, 137
risk-reduction measures 41
rivalry(ies) 1–3, 6, 9–12, 18, 24, 26, 28, 41, 50, 55, 65–6, 69, 76, 81, 84, 104, 128, 132, 134, 159, 161, 169–70, 177–8, 185–6, 189, 193, 198, 201–2; China and US 1–3, 6, 9, 12, 24, 26, 28, 55, 66, 81, 104, 128, 159, 161, 170, 177–8, 189, 193 (conceptual aspects of 10, 11; impact of 24); great power 12, 84, 169 (manoeuvring 12); intense 18 (impact of 2); inter-state 12; strategic 10, 55; systemic 55
Road Forum 4
Roh Moo-hyun, South Korean president 194, 199–200
Roh Tae-woo, South Korean President 195; policy of Nordpolitik 195
ROK and US alliance 47, 203
Rosenau 68
Rule of law 115
rules-based order 47, 50, 84, 96, 105, **106**, 111; global 48, 110

Russia 33, 36–7, 39, 54–5, 58, 103, 150, 161, 177, 197
Russian Far East 188

Sadae 204
Saifuddin Abdullah, Foreign Minister 165, 170
Samuels, Richard J. 22
sanctions 135, 169, 171, 195; trade 169, 171
San Francisco Peace Treaty 195
Scarborough Shoal 147
scepticism 27, 49
Schriver, Randall, Assistant Secretary of Defence 148; visit to Manila 148
Sea lanes 32, 37, 39, 44; Indian Ocean 32, 37; maritime Southeast Asia 44
Sea Lanes of Communication (SLOCs) 115
Search and rescue 39, 95
Secondary versus middle power 13, 206
Second Indochina War 180
Security 1–2, 4–5, 11–12, 17–26, 28, 34, 36–8, 42–3, 47–50, 54–5, 57–9, 65–6, 68–72, 76, 81–2, 91–5, 103, 105, 109–11, 114–17, 129–30, 133–4, 137–9, 147–50, 152–3, 160, 164–6, 178, 181, 184, 186, 193, 195–6, 198–9, 201–3, 205–6; bargain 196; Chinese 70; choices 193; coalitions 117; concept of cooperative 18, 20, 23; consequences 19; cooperation 11, 82, **86**, 92, 94–5, 115–16, 137, 149–50; forms of 23; governance 68–71; guarantor 48; human 65; interests 25; maritime 106; Myanmar's 12; national 34, 55, 81, 92, 129–30, 196, 198, 205–6; non-traditional 11, 18, 57, 65, 82, 92, 137; order 11, 17, 65, 68, 71, 195; partnership 12, 149, 152; policy 4–5, 54, 66; problems 68; relations, approaches to 129; traditional 11, 18, 55, 57–8, 65, 82, 92, 137 (multilateral approaches to 5)
security architecture 11, 20–1, 65; formal 21; 'hub and spokes' 20; regional 11, 65
security governance 68–71; maritime 70; practical form and operation of 69; regimes 69; transnational 68–9, 71
security order 11, 17, 68, 71, 195; Asian 17, 71
self-defeating 40
self-determination 112
self-image 6, 34
self-interest 53, 178

Senkaku-Diaoyu Islands 21, 25, 105
sentiment 24, 27–8, 144; anti-globalisation 28; geopolitical 28
Severe Acute Respiratory Syndrome (SARS) 70
Shambaugh, David 2
Shangri-La Dialogue 2, 28
Shan state 180
SHINYUU Maitri-2019, 109
shipbuilding programme 38
shipments 39
shipping 70, 91; merchant 70; sailing 38
Shwe Kokko 188
Silk Road Economic Belt (SREB) 3, 146; old 146
Silk Road Fund 3, 4
Silk Route exercise 93
Singapore 2, 28, 36, 39, 70, 83–4, **106–7**, 152, 162, 166, 169
Singapore and US defence pact 28
Sirisena, Maithripala, Sri Lankan President 83, 91
Sittwe deep water port 185, 187
Small and Medium Enterprises (SMEs) 88
smaller players 36
smallest powers 127
small power–great power 11, 81, 95–6; relations 11, 81, 96
small powers 36, 128, 131, 162; capacity of 96
small-to medium-sized enterprises 165
smuggling 70, 92
social: contracts 196; bargain 196; boundary 67; classes 66; relations 66; stability 18
socialism 3, **181**
society(ies) 10, 17–9, 26, 43, 52, 66–9, 95, 170, 182, 184, 188, 190; civil 43, 182, 188, 190; global 18; national 67
socio-economic: power constellations 8; progress 17
socio-political, conflict 66–7
Soe San 12
soft balancing 12, 142–3, 149, 151–2; policy of 143, 149, 152
soft power 40, 83, 183; strategies 83
Sohn Yul 56
solidarity 32, 34, 36, 42–4; code for 43; strategic 43
Solingen, Etel 19
Somali piracy 38
South Asia 11, 33, 37, 83, 91, 95, 130; economic cooperation in 95

234　*Index*

South China Sea *imbroglio* 142, 144, 152
South China Sea (SCS) 1, 3, 12, 21, 23, 25, 29, 38–9, 41, 50, 65, 70, 103, 105, 109, 112, 114–16, 134, 136, 142–53, 164–5, 168, 177–8, 183; ASEAN consensus on 134; China's claims over 3; Chinese aggressive behaviour in the 12, 153; Chinese assertiveness in 65; Chinese claims 103; claims in 25; India's overtures in 114; Japan's interest in 112; militarization of 143; military equipment on 21; naval power in 143; negotiations on 23; patrols in 150; sovereignty claims over 23; tensions in 21; US warships in 1
South China Sea (SCS) dispute 50, 136, 142, 144, 146, 148, 150–3; conflict-management process for 151; resolution of 142, 152
Southeast Asia 8–9, 11–12, 33, 36–8, 42, 44, 69, 87, 114, 127–32, 134–9, 144–5, 150, 152, 160–1, 166, 171, 177–9, 186, 188–90, 202; challenges in 128; development 135; dominance in 9; economies 17, 134, 135; foreign policy 127 (pattern in 9); infrastructure needs 135; institutional, strategies 129 (strategies in 128–9); major power challenges 132; multilateral institutions 20; post-Cold War era 9, 18, 116, 133; powers 39, 41 (foreign trade and investment 85; networked 27; power 32, 163); redistribution of power in 22 (role for 23); regional institutions in 11, 128; small and medium powers 127–8, 130, 138; strategies 128; US in 23 (role in 43; security commitments 193)
Southeast Asian Nations 5, 9, 18, 23, 36, 65, 105, 110, 127–30, 132–6, 138–9, 144–5, 160, 177–8, 189, 193; challenges for 134, 136; conceptions of 129; institutional strategies 129; strategic response 127
South Korea 8, 10–13, 25, 36–8, 47–8, 52–3, 56–9, 110, 114, 116, 131, 138, 177–8, 193, 194–206; as a middle power 56; consequences for 48; defence spending 202; foreign policy 10, 194, 198, 204 (post-war 198); Great Power relations in 194; interests, economic 203 (strategic 203); membership to the United Nations 195; oil imports 203; policy choices 206; political mobilisations/movements in 193–4; post-Cold War 13, 197, 205; post-war 196; South Korean government 25, 195, 202–3; strategic options 57
South Korea and US 193–7, 200, 204; alliance 193, 196–7, 200 (cooperation 200); imports 202; relations 195, 204
South Pacific 33, 38, 41
South-South Cooperation 164–5
sovereignty 23, 25, 35–6, 43–4, 54, 65, 68–9, 93, 110, 112, 115, 129–30, 146; absolute 68; claims 23; disputes 23, 25; European 54; state 25; strategic 54
Sovereignty-Enhancing Platforms 131
Soviet Union 8, 48, 132–3, 195
Soviet Union and US 2, 48, 132; competition 48; operative dyads 132; rivalry, impact of 2
Special Economic Zone (SEZ) 184–5, **187**
Special Measures Agreement (SMA) 202, 203
Sri Lanka 8, 11, 38, 40, 74–5, 81–5, 87–96, 114, 184; 2019 presidential election cycle 90; British rule in 83; Chinese, commercial loans to 92 (debt 92); civil conflict in 2009, 81, 83; coalition government in 89; commercial loans for infrastructure projects 83; counter-terrorism support 94; defence capability 92; development, advantage 84 (projects in 90); Easter Sunday attacks in 2019, 87, 93–4; economic opportunity for 83; foreign direct investment (FDI) 83 (inflows from China 88); foreign policy 83, 92 (non-aligned 81, 83, 92); foreign relations 81, 94; gifts of naval vessels 92; human rights issues 83; land administration in 89; Mahinda Rajapaksa regime 74; maritime boundaries 92; maritime security needs 93; middle-income economy status 81; national security capacity 81; policies 83 (economic 83; implications for 81); post-conflict 81, 88 (China and US rivalries in 81); post-COVID-19 economy 95; priorities 81, 94 (economic 81, 94; security 81, 94); pro-China policy 84; regional trading hub 83; strategic importance in the Indian Ocean region 82; strategic location 83; tourist arrivals to 88 (Chinese 88; US 88); trade balance 85; US FDI inflows 88; US military base in 94

Sri Lanka Air Force 93
Sri Lanka and US 11, 85, 88, 93; assistance 89; cooperation 93 (security **86**); defence agreements 90, 93; engagement 11; export and import 85; FDI 85, 87–8; foreign aid 88; FTA 87; Memorandum of Understanding (MOU) 94; relations 81, 83, 85, 94 (manufacturing 85); ties **86**; trade surplus 85
Sri Lankan Navy 75, 83, 91–3
stability 2, 17–18, 20, 23, 41, 51, 58, 70, 87, 106, 116, 133, 135, 148, 152, 164, 196, 198; national 18, 133; regime 70, 135; regional 2, 18, 133; social 18
start-up India 113
state apparatuses 11, 66–7, 70; transformation of 67
state authority, fragmentation of 67
statecraft 33, 44, 48, 75; Asian 44; economic 75; elaborated 48
statehood 11, 67–8; form of 67
state-owned Enterprise (SOE) 26, 73–5, 83, 87, 91, 95, 161, 166; Chinese 91
state-society: bargain 18; blocs 68; compacts 67
Status of Forces Agreement (SOFA) 93, 94
Stiftung Wissenschaft und Politik (SWP) 54
Stilwell, Joseph, American General 179
Storey, Ian 9
Strait of Hormuz 203
Strait of Malacca 166
Straits Times 143
strategic: agency 127; alliances 43; behaviour 75; capital 112; challenges 32; change 11; choices 26, 48, 55, 57; competition 32, 40; consequences 44; dialogues 21; dissonance 54; effects 11, 128, 130; environment 24, 47; impacts 38; imperative and priority 132, 148; interests 11, 57, 106, 113, 185, 203; location 83, 85; manoeuvring 9, 105; mistrust 41; multilateral groups 49; narrative 10, 129; needs 105; options 9, 57, 131; partnership 43; planning 74; positioning 169; proactive roles 129; relations 116, 178; response 127–8; rivalry 10; rivals 55; role 35; shift 12; solidarity 43; sovereignty 54; trade partners 113; transition 10, 17; uncertainty 9, 23, 53, 133; vulnerabilities 12
strategic autonomy 48, 53–6, 58, 160; concept of 54, 56; European 48, 54, 58; Europe's 54–5, 58; implementation of 54; value of 54
Strategic hedging 159–62, 166, 170–1; concept of 160
strategy and approaches 1, 4–5, 9–12, 19–20, 22–3, 28, 33, 36–8, 42, 44, 48–9, 51–6, 58–9, 65, 69, 72–6, 82–3, 95–6, 103, 112, 114, 116, 127–34, 137–9, 145, 160, 168, 171, 178, 194, 201; Chinese 38; comprehensive 42, 116; conceptualisation of 130; containment 5; countermeasure 52; development 75, 96, 145; diplomatic 19, 54, 58; diversity of 9; economic 95, 145; foreign policy 12; games of 37; hedging 28, 160; Indo-Pacific 23, 82, 160, 201 (European 54); institutional 11, 127–34, 137–9; middle power 51, 54, 56 (diplomatic 54); multilateral 53, 55, 58; reassurance 20, 22; response 48, 58; soft power 83; Southeast Asian 11, 128, 131; state 128–9, 132; US 42
structural: change 7; external pressures 12, 194; factors 7; over-determinism 7; powers 6, 7
structuralism 65
submarines 22, 38, 83, 203
subsidies 71, 87–8, 104
sunshine Policy 197
superiority 44
superpowers 8, 189
Supply Chain Resilience Initiative (SCRI) 111–12
supply chains 18, 22, 24, 27, 37, 82, 113–14, 134, 165; global 18, 22, 24, 27; international 37; operations 110; post-Covid network 113; regional 18, 22, 24, 27
supply shocks 27
surveillance 94, 147–8, 150
sustainability 37, 76, 92; debt 76, 92
Sweden 51, 52

tactics 25, 142, 202; delaying 142; naval 25
Taiwan 1, 24, 37, 41, 105, 114
Taiwan Straits crisis 24
Tan Kok Wai 170
Tanzania 146
Taoguang yanghui 19
tariff(s) 88, 104, 135, 195; Australia and China 104; liberalisation of 88
TC-90 reconnaissance aircraft 149–50

236 Index

technical/technological: assistance 186; capabilities 2; development 47; innovation 26, 169–70
technology(ies) 1, 26, 37, 40–1, 47, 81–2, 93, 109–11, 113, 165, 169–70, 185; advanced 26; cutting-edge 1; development 26; digital 40; growth 110; transfer 109; warehousing 170
telecommunications 37, 90
Tencent Holdings 170
tension(s) 2, 18–21, 24, 26–8, 41, 43, 82, 95–6, 104, 133–4, 142, 145–6, 160, 169, 171, 180, 189, 193–7, 199, 202–4; alliance 194, 196, 203; China and Philippines 142; China and US 18, 20, 21, 24, 26–8, 43, 82, 104, 133–4 (maritime 134); economic 195; international 43; inter-state 19; intra-alliance 196, 203; maritime 134; Philippines and US 145
territorial: boundary 67; conflicts 21; defence 149; dispute 147, 164; integrity 1, 112
terrorism 39, 41, 69, 94, 148–9, 164; countering **106**
terrorist 21, 70, 112, 148, 150, 187; attack 112; violence 21
Thailand 8, 70, 83, 87, 105, 135, 137, 146, 185
Thakin Than Tun 181
Theater High Altitude Area Defense (THAAD) 197–201; deployment of 198
Thirty Comrades 179
threat(s) 1, 8, 11, 20, 25, 29, 41, 49, 65, 68–9, 81–2, 92, 96, 103–5, 115, 117, 132, 148–9, 171, 189, 193, 196–7, 204; common 41; Communist 8; cyber security 49; economic 104; security, non-traditional 11, 65, 82, 92
ties and interdependence 3, 9, 20–1, 23–4, 26–8, 32, 37, 44, 53, **86**, 92, 103–6, 109, 112–4, 116–7, 133–5, 139, 142, 150, 163, 166, 181, 195–6, 198, 200; antagonistic 116; Australia and China 104; bilateral 3, 23; China and India 117; China and Malaysia 166; China and Sri Lanka **86**; China and US **86**, 103; diplomatic 142; economic 9, 20, 24, 32, 150, 195; intra-Asian 139; military 3; political 9, 24 (bilateral 4); security 92, 150
Tiger Triumph 109
Tilly, Charles 198

Toshimitsu Motegi, Foreign Ministers of Japan **107–9**
tourism 88, 94, 144
tourist arrivals 88, 187
trade 1, 3–5, 11–12, 18–19, 23, 26, 32, 38, 47, 55, 67, 81–3, 85, 87–8, 94–5, 104, 110–11, 113, 115, 133–7, 144–5, 149, 159, 160, 162, 164–9, 171, 188, 193–5, 205; agreement 23; agreements 4, 5, 83, 85; balance 85; bilateral 4, 85, 87, 162, 188; China and ASEAN 168; China and Malaysia 165; China and South Korea 194; China and Sri Lanka 87; concessions 145; dispute 12, 47; East-West 82; export 19; fair 4; free 4, 5, 83, 167, 169; global 18; goods 104; international 67, 164; investigation and tariffs 135; liberalisation 88, 95; logistics 82; networked 19; oil 12; reciprocal 4; regional 18; restrictive practices 169; sanctions 169, 171; secrets 104; Sri Lanka and US 85; strategic partners 113; surplus 85, 94; transhipment 83; two-way 26; unions 67
Trade and Investment Framework Agreement (TIFA) 87
trade-offs 193
trade policies 1, 5, 135; aggressive 135; automatic resistance to 34
trade war 3, 12, 134–5, 137, 169; negative effects of 137; US-China 134, 137, 169, 205
trading 19–23, 82–3, 94, 104, 159, 162, 165, 169, 194; agreement 21; networked 21; partners 20, 159, 169
trading order 82, 104; liberal 82; US-led 104
trafficking 70
training exercises 93
tranquillity 27
transition(s) 7, 10, 17, 20, 22, 95, 105, 132, 143; impact of 7; order 22; power 22, 132; regional 20; strategic 10, 17
Trans-Pacific Partnership (TPP) 21, 28, 82, 136–7
Trans-Pacific Partnership trading agreement 21
transparency 18, 41, 90, 92; debt 92
transportation 19, 38, 146
Treason 205
treaties and agreements 4–5, 12, 23, 25, 41, 43, 49, 53, 83, 85, 90, 93–4, 109, 116, 148, 152, 164, 193, 195, 202; arms

Index   237

control 41; bilateral 4–5; cooperation 93–4; defence 90, 93; formal 43, 53; Hambantota 91; international 49, 164; lease 75; MCC 91; military logistics 109; multilateral 53; mutual defence 25, 148; nuclear 21; trade 4–5, 23, 83, 85 (bilateral 4); trading 21
Treaty of Amity and Cooperation 19
trilateral: cooperative frameworks 105; groupings 111; meeting 11; military exercises 115
Trilateral Coordination and Oversight Group (TCOG) 197
trilateralism 11, 111
Trincomalee Harbour 83
trouble spots 39
Trump, Donald, US President 4–5, 6, 24–6, 35, 44, 47, 49, 54, 58, 82, 104, 111, 113, 134–8, 148–9, 159–60, 169, 198–200, 202–3; "America First" policies 47, 49, 104; China approach 104; electoral losses 24; withdrawal from; Paris Climate Change Convention 49 (Trans-Pacific Partnership (TPP) 82)
Two-ocean region 32
Type 075 amphibious assault ships 114

Uighurs, plight of 1
uncertainty 4, 9, 17, 20, 22–3, 25, 37, 42, 47, 53, 133, 160; regional 42; strategic 9, 23, 53, 133
unemployment 91, 95
United Kingdom (UK) 38, 52, 110–11, 162, 169, 180
United Malays National Organisation (UMNO) 162, 164, 167
United Nations (UN) 24–5, 41, 84–5, 96, 112, 115, 142, 180–1, 195; India's resolution in 112
United Nations (UN) Convention on the Law of the Sea (UNCLOS) 25, 29, 84, 115, 142, 144, 151–2
United Nations (UN) General Assembly 24
United Nations (UN) Mission in the Democratic Republic of Congo 85
United Nations (UN) Peacekeeping operations 85
United States (US) Agency for International Development (USAID) 89, 91
United States (US) Army 181
United States (US) Department of Defence 6

United States (US) Department of State **106–8**
United States (US) Department of Treasury 103
United States (US) Forces Korea (USFK) 49
United States (US) Marine Corps 93
United States (US) National Defence Strategy 1
United States (US) of America (US) 1–6, 8–13, 18–29, 32–43, 47–50, 52–9, 66–7, 69–70, 72, 75, 81–5, 87–90, 92–4, 103–5, **106–7**, 109–13, 115–17, 128, 130–9, 145, 147–53, 159–62, 165–6, 169–71, 178–81, 184–6, 188–90, 193–206; ability to reassurance 24; alliance, partners 20 (system 21); alliance commitment 49 (in Asia 49; in Europe 49); Biden administration 24, 82; bid to thwart China 32; bipartisan consensus in 26; China policy 103–44; China strategy 49; credibility 49; decision to ban Huawei 169; defence spending 34; deterioration of the image 6; deterrence 24; domestic instabilities in 2; dominance 72, 103 (Asia 1); economies 34; EU's criticism of 54, 58; FDI inflows into Sri Lanka 85; FOIP strategy 138; foreign policy in Asia 112; hegemony, challenge to 4; Indo-Pacific, strategy 160 (vision 111); interests 1; investments 135 (infrastructure 135); leadership 49; military, base in Sri Lanka 94 (hardware 202; presence in Asia 1, 20); Obama administration 20, 104, 148; over-dependence on China 27; policy 4, 5 (defence 5; economic 4; foreign 4; on North Korea 199; policy towards China 4; security 4, 5); role of 4, 48, 185, 193, 196, 206 (as a hyper-superpower 48; infrastructure investment 4); security, assurances 24 (commitments 25, 193); strategic choices 26; strategy 42; terror attacks of 9/11, 204; trade policies, aggressive 135; trading partners 20; Trump administration 5, 24, 26, 82, 104, 137–8, 149, 159, 160, 169, 198, 200, 202 (withdrawal from the Trans-Pacific Partnership (TPP) 82); values 1; warships in the South China Sea 1; withdrawal from several international agreements 49

238 *Index*

United States (US) Special Operations Forces 145
Unity Party 200
US and Vietnam Visiting Forces Agreement 25
US, Australia and Japan 105, 113, 115
US-Australia-India-Japan quadrilateral security dialogue 4; revival of 4
US-China Business Council 20
US-DPRK Joint Communique 197
US-Japan-South Korea consultative mechanism 197
US-Sri Lanka bilateral Trade and Investment Framework Agreement (TIFA) 87
US, the Philippines and Japan 116; joint naval exercise 116

vaccine: deal 38; diplomacy 38
value chain 19
values 1, 37, 39, 47, 49, 51, 53, 73, 130; liberal 49; Western 51
Vasco da Gama 39
Venezuela 75
vessel(s) 23, 71, 92–3, 115, 143, 147–8, 150, 203; Chinese 115; coastguard 23; water police 71
Vietnam 8, 19, 24–5, 35, 38–9, 70, 105, 110, 114–5, 133–5, 143, 146, 148–9, 151, 178, 180, 186, 188; reform movement 19; withdrawal of troops from Cambodia 19
violence 17, 21, 185; sources of 17; terrorist 21
Visiting Forces Agreement (VFA) 25, 147

wage growth 67
Wall Street Journal 202
Wang Yi, Chinese Foreign Minister 2, 33, 151
warehousing 91, 170; technology 170
war(s) 2–3, 8, 10, 12, 17, 22, 27, 39, 41, 47, 71, 74, 81, 94, 134–5, 137, 169, 179–80, 182–4, 186, 196, 198, 201, 205; civil 180, 182–4; ethnic-oriented 183; Indochina 186; inter-state 10, 17, 27; state 17, 22, 27
warships 1, 22, 38–9, 143, 169; Chinese 143; Indian 39; Japanese 39; US 31, 9
water police vessels 71

waters 25, 38–9, 142–4, 151–2; defence 38; disputed 25, 142, 144, 151; distant 38; Indian Ocean 38; offshore 38; proximate 38; territorial 143
waterway 165–7, **187**, 203
weaponry production rates 23
Weberian state theory 67
Weberian-Westphalian states 67–8
welfare states 67
Western: countries 83; development programmes 68; values 51
Western Pacific 39, 150
West Germany 180
West Pacific Naval Symposium 70
'Westphalian' model 11
West Philippine Sea 142
wolf-warrior diplomacy 104
Wood, Bernard 50
World Bank 87, 90, 160
World Bank's 2020 Doing Business Study 87
World Health Organization (WHO) 69, 70
world order 1, 6, 25, 47–50, 52–3, 58, 104, 106, 136; democratic 53, 106; liberal 48, 49, 106; multipolar 104; new 49, 58; pluralist 25; post-war 47; rule-based 53; US-led, alternatives to 48, 49 (free 6; repressive 6); visions of 136
World War, Second 2, 48, 83, 130, 177–80, 195

Xi Jinping, Chinese President 1–3, 6, 21, 23–6, 35, 37–8, 72–3, 75, 104, 142, 145–7, 152, 161, 168, 183, 190; 2015 proclamation 38; foreign policy 2, 3; power grip 3; visit to Philippines 146–7

Yang Jiechi, State Councillor 25
Yangon Circular Line 187
Yangon-Mandalay line 187
Yasay Jr., Perfecto, Foreign Secretary of Philippines 144
Yemen 204
Yunnan 69–71, 183, 187

Zero-sum approaches 50
Zheng He, Admiral 38
Zone of Peace, Freedom and Neutrality (ZOPFAN) 165
Zürn 52

Printed in the United States
by Baker & Taylor Publisher Services